STUDIES IN THE FORMATION OF THE
NATION-STATE IN LATIN AMERICA

Studies in the Formation of the Nation-State in Latin America

Edited by
James Dunkerley

Institute of Latin American Studies
31 Tavistock Square, London WC1H 9HA
http://www.sas.ac.uk/ilas/publicat.htm

Institute of Latin American Studies
School of Advanced Study
University of London

British Library Cataloguing-in-Publication Data
A catalogue record for this book is available
from the British Library

ISBN   1900039 41 9

CONTENTS

NOTES ON CONTRIBUTORS

Miguel Angel Centeno studied at Yale University as an undergraduate and post-graduate. He is Professor of Sociology, Master of Wilson College, Director of the International Networks Archive and Founder of Princeton Prep. He has written widely on Mexico and Latin America as a whole. His publications include *Mexico in the 1990s* (La Jolla, CA, 1991), *Democracy within Reason: Technocratic Revolution in Mexico* (University Park, PA, 1997) and he co-edited with Fernando López-Alves, *The Other Mirror: Grand Theory and Latin America* (Princeton, 2000). His *Blood and Debt: War and Statemaking in Latin America* will be published in 2002.

Malcolm Deas is a Fellow of St Antony's College, Oxford, where he was one of the founders of the Latin American Centre. He is University Lecturer in the Politics and Government of Latin America, and his chief interest is in the politics and history of Colombia. His publications include essays on Colombian history, politics and literature collected in *Del poder y la gramática*, (Bogota, 1993), *Vida y opiniones de Mr William Wills*, 2 vols (Bogota, 1997), and, on Colombian violence, *Intercambios violentos* (Bogota, 1999).

James Dunkerley is Professor of Politics and Director of the Institute of Latin American Studies, University of London. He also holds a chair in politics at Queen Mary, University of London. He is an editor of the *Journal of Latin American Studies*. His most recent books are *Americana. The Americas in the World, around 1850* and *Warriors and Scribes: Essays in the History and Politics of Latin America* (both London, 2000).

Paul Gootenberg is Professor of History, Director of Latin American Studies, SUNY–Stony Brook (USA) He is the author of *Between Silver and Guano* (Princeton, 1989), *Imagining Development* (California, 1993) and editor of *Cocaine: Global Histories* (Routledge, UK, 1999). His interests include Andean history, social science and the history of drugs.

Alan Knight is Professor of the History of Latin America, Oxford University, and Director of the LAC, Oxford. He is the author of *The Mexican Revolution* (2 vols. Cambridge, 1986) and has published widely on Mexican history and politics. He is currently working on the history of Mexico in the 1930s, and is soon to publish the first two volumes of a three-volume general history of Mexico (Cambridge, 2002).

Colin M. Lewis is Senior Lecturer in Latin American Economic History at the London School of Economics and Political Science, and Associate Fellow of the Institute of Latin American Studies, University of London. He has written widely on patterns of industrial growth and industrialisation in Latin American. His writings on state-formation include (co-edited with Christopher Abel) *Latin America: Economic Imperialism and the State* (London, 1985), and chapters in D.A. Smith et al. (eds.), *States and Sovereignty in the Global Economy* (London, 1999) and J. Buxton and N. Phillips (eds.), *Case Studies in Latin American Political Economy* (Manchester, 1999).

Fernando López-Alves is Associate Professor of Political Science at the University of California, Santa Barbara. He is the author of *State Formation and Democracy in Latin America* (Durham, NC, 2000). His research utilises a comparative historical methodology to analyse the formations of democracies and other state formations in Latin America.

Florencia E. Mallon teaches modern Latin American history at the University of Wisconsin-Madison. She is the author of *The Defense of Community in Peru's Central Highlands: Peasant Struggle and Capitalist Transition, 1860–1940* (Princeton, 1983) and *Peasant and Nation: The Making of Postcolonial Mexico and Peru* (Berkeley, 1995) and many articles on social theory and on agrarian, political and social history. Since 1996 she has been researching the twentieth-century relationship between the Mapuche people and the Chilean state. She is the editor and translator of Rosa Isolde Reuque Paillalef, *When a Flower is Reborn: the Life and Times of a Mapuche Feminist*, forthcoming in 2002, and she is completing *Courage Tastes of Blood: The Mapuche Indigenous Community of Nicolás Ailmo and the Chilean State, 1906–2000*.

David McCreery is Professor of History and Director of Graduate Studies for the History Department of Georgia State University. His most recent publication is *The Sweat of Their Brow: A History of Work in Latin America* (Armonk, NY, 2000) and currently he is at work on a history of Brazil's centre-west frontier during the nineteenth century.

Seemin Qayum is currently researching projects on the cultural dynamics of nationalism in nineteenth- and twentieth-century Bolivia, and on domestic servitude in the twentieth century in Kolkata, La Paz and New York. The chapter in this volume is based on a chapter from her doctoral thesis, 'Creole Imaginings: Space, Race, and Gender in the Making of Republican Bolivia' (Goldsmiths College, University of London).

Guy Thomson is Reader in History at the University of Warwick. He is author of *Puebla de los Angeles. Industry and Society in a Mexican City* (Westview, CT, 1989), and (with David LaFrance) *Politics, Patriotism and Popular Liberalism in Mexico. Juan Francisco Lucas and the Puebla Sierra* (Wilmington, DE, 1999), and he has recently edited *The European Revolutions of 1848 and the Americas* (London, 2002). He is currently working on comparative aspects of nineteenth-century Mexican and Spanish liberalism.

Steven Topik is Professor of History at the University of California, Irvine. His books include *Trade and Gunboats. The United States and Brazil in the Age of Empire* (Stanford, 1996); with Allen Wells, *The Second Conquest of Latin America* (Austin, 1998); and with Ken Pomeranz, *The World that Trade Created. Society, Culture and the World Economy 1400–Present* (Armonk, NY, 1999). He is currently co-editing, with William Clarence-Smith, *The Global Coffee Economy in Africa, Asia and Latin America, 1500–1989*, forthcoming from Cambridge University Press

Preface

James Dunkerley

The deliberately varied chapters that comprise this volume consider the erratic evolution of the Latin American nation-state from a number of viewpoints. None of the essays seeks to provide an all-encompassing model, and none takes its subject at face value or on the terms of the state's symbolic account of its own history and nature. All the authors treat the nation-state as a phenomenon of continuing complexity and constant change. This was true before the end of the Cold War, and even if some of the claims about globalisation made today are exaggerated, it is a process that accelerated discernably during the 1990s. Indeed, there is a strong sense in which all the nation-states of the region are still 'in formation' at the start of the twenty-first century, when such nation-forming no longer dominates the spirit of the age.

The present book adopts an historical perspective, and its authors are here primarily concerned with the past, although some of them are social scientists or treat that study of the past with a dynamic application to contemporary life. Related issues of pressing relevance, such as regional integration and the challenge of multiculturalism, are the subjects of separate books derived from the programme of the Institute of Latin American Studies (ILAS).[1] At the same time, this volume extends beyond the parameters of the nineteenth century, even if that period (understood in both its 'long' and 'short' versions) provides the focus for most of the chapters. The authors were provided with no specific brief with respect to periodisation, and whilst many themes treated here overlap with those addressed in the books produced by the ILAS nineteenth century workshop series, our chronological scope is more open.[2]

---

[1] Victor Bulmer-Thomas (ed.), *Regional Integration in Latin America and the Caribbean: the Political Economy of Open Regionalism* (London, 2001); Rachel Sieder (ed.), *Multiculturalism in Latin America: Indigenous Rights, Diversity and Democracy* (Forthcoming, 2002).

[2] Eduardo Posada-Carbó (ed.), *Wars, Parties and Nationalism: Essays on the Politics and Society of Nineteenth-Century Latin America* (London, 1995); Eduardo Posada-Carbó (ed.), *In Search of a New Order: Essays on the Politics and Society of Nineteenth-Century Latin America* (London, 1998); Anthony McFarlane and Eduardo Posada-Carbó (eds.), *Independence and Revolution in Spanish America: Perspectives and Problems* (London, 1998); Eduardo Zimmermann (ed.), *Judicial Institutions in Nineteenth-Century Latin America* (London, 1999); Austen Ivereigh (ed.), *The Politics of Religion in an Age of Revival* (London, 2000); Rebecca Earle (ed.), *Rumours of Wars: Civil Conflict in Nineteenth-Century Latin America* (London, 2000); Guy Thomson (ed.), *The European Revolutions of 1848 and the Americas* (London, 2002); Iván Jaksic (ed.), *The Political Power of the Word: Press and Oratory in Nineteenth-Century Latin America* (Forthcoming, 2002); Nancy Priscilla Naro (ed.), *Blacks and Identity in Nineteenth-Century Latin America* (Forthcoming, 2002). All these titles are published by ILAS.

It is a matter of some note that whilst an important interpretative school on nations, nationhood and nationalism identifies them as stemming from an essentially 'modern' process, starting in the late eighteenth century, the experience of Latin America, which largely acquired independence in that period, is rarely considered by that school or, indeed, in much of the extensive comparative literature.[3]

The clear exception to this tendency is Benedict Anderson, whose brief book of 1982, *Imagined Communities. Reflections on the Origin and Spread of Nationalism,* considered Latin America prominently, albeit in the light of the experience of Asia. It is something of an irony that a text written when its author could not read Spanish should have exercised such influence in the fields of cultural studies and literary theory, and Tony Judt makes a reasonable point when he identifies it as 'a book whose metaphorical reach exceeds its historical grasp'.[4] Perhaps it was because Anderson's work opened up such a rich new field for students of culture that his relative lack of expertise in the region was passed over. In all events, a subsequent essay makes a fundamental point about the terms of nationhood to show why an understanding of material institutions and 'stateness' cannot be divorced from literary or other 'imagining' and 'inventing' of a collectivity:

> We are all only too aware of how incessantly people speak, not merely of 'seeking' 'roots' and alas, 'coming close to losing' their 'identities'. But these searches, which rhetorically move inwards towards the site that once housed the soul, in fact proceed outward towards real and imagined censuses, where, thanks to capitalism, state machineries and mathematics, integral bodies become identical and thus serially aggregable as phantom communities.[5]

The chapters that follow pay particular attention to this 'outer realm' because their authors are concerned precisely with the conjunction of nation and state as a compound, hyphenated noun. This has been approached less in the rather derogatory terms employed by Freud — 'the narcissism of minor differences' within and between nations — than as a scholarly reaction to Weber's famous but limited definition of a state: 'A compulsory political organisation with continuous operations will be called a "state" insofar as its administrative staff suc-

---

[3]   The leading authors upholding the 'modernist' thesis are Eric Hobsbawm, *Nations and Nationalism since 1780. Programme, myth, reality* (Cambridge, 1990), and John Breuilly, *Nationalism and the State* (Manchester, 1982). The latter is a Germanist and makes virtually no mention of Latin America whatsoever. The former is, of course, a scholar with a deep knowledge of the region and provides a wider treatment. But he is true to his thesis that 'states create nations' and, seeing the early Latin American states as weak, correspondingly presents its nations as partially — imperfectly? — formed.

[4]   *New York Review of Books,* 26 May 1994.

[5]   'Replica, Aura and Late Nationalist Imaginings', in Benedict Anderson, *Spectre of Comparisons. Nationalism, Southeast Asia and the World* (London, 1998), p. 44.

cessfully upholds the claim to the *monopoly* of the *legitimate* use of physical force in the enforcement of its order.'[6]

Weber's conviction that this was essentially a 'western' phenomenon has endured in the elaborations of his characterisation undertaken by social scientists and now established in the mainstream of social theory. What, however, twentieth-century experience and scholarship have perforce added is an extrapolation on Weber's 'legitimate' — emphasised but still merely adjectival. For Samuel Finer, 'the nation-state is not [just] the "national state": it goes much further because it asserts that this national state does not belong ... to anything else but to ... its people.'[7]

Finer expands the tight Weberian prospectus to six principles in order to depict not only a 'western' but also a 'modern' phenomenon:

> First comes the *nationality* principle as the basis for territorial organisation, as contrasted with the 'traditional' bases of dynasty, kinship or lineage, or religious community. The second is the principle of *popular sovereignty*, as the legitimizing principle of all political authority, as contrasted with the 'traditional' bases in theocracy, divine right, noble birth or caste. The third is the *secular principle*: the separation of all processes from religious distinctions, activities and values. The fourth is *social purposiveness*: 'the state as a work of art', as against the traditional unreflecting reverence for pre-existing authority whether cultural or religious or political. The fifth is *economic independence*, not in the sense of autarky but as a construction of an independent and nationally sovereign basis for health, wealth and power, implying extensive industrialisation as contrasted with the traditional rural economy. The sixth is the notion of *citizenship*, which goes further than the formal guarantees of civil and political rights, and stipulates economic and social rights such as the right to education, to work and to social welfare benefits.[8]

Even for the contemporary United States of America such criteria might only combine as ideals, and the notion that they cohered as some kind of unproblematic historical process puts one in mind of Renan's pithy observation that, 'L'oubli et je dirai même l'erreur historique, sont un facteur essentiel de la formation d'une nation et c'est ainsi que le progrès des études historiques est souvent pour la nationalité un danger'.[9]

For the case of Latin America the gap between enunciated theory and observable practice would seem to be unsustainably wide — one reason, per-

---

6   *Economy and Society*, (1922–23) (Berkeley, 1978), vol. I, p. 56.

7   *The History of Government. Empires, Monarchies and the Modern State* (Oxford, 1997), vol. III, p. 1478.

8   *Ibid.*, p. 1475.

9   *Qu'est que c'est une nation?* (Paris, 1882), p. 6.

haps, why some commentators simply deny the region membership of 'the west', even in the post-Cold War epoch.[10] However, it certainly matters that such ideals were often recognised and sometimes embraced through the Americas as a whole from the time of their emergence. One may encounter 'patriotic republicans' in some parts and 'money-making democrats' in others, capitalism only in very few, but imagination mattered throughout and sometimes it took the form not only of a consequential yearning but also social invention. Moreover, an understanding of practical experience that simply stops at its differentiation from espoused theory is pretty threadbare, even for narrow political purposes. Most of the scholars whose work follows were brought up in countries where contestation over the meaning of Weber's 'legitimate' has largely been in terms of Finer's six principles. Yet what Samuel Huntington sees as a finite margin of exclusion, they approach as a topic of fascinating malleability, harbouring all sorts of surprises and opportunities to review our presumptions.

The collection is opened by Florencia Mallon's comparative survey of Peru, Mexico and Chile over what she terms the post-colonial era, from 1780 onwards. In an engaged essay Mallon provides a commentary no less on the historiography than on the substantive history of these experiences. Employing a more expansive and flexible characterisation of the nation-state than that of Weber, she identifies two phases of modern historical interpretation: first, that of the 1960s and 1970s, when the emphasis was on 'national liberation', and, secondly, that of the 1980s and 1990s, 'marked instead by the unravelling of state-centred national projects; repression and authoritarianism followed by redemocratisation; and market reforms and globalisation' (p. 19).

Mallon is in little doubt about 'the universal failure of state directed models of national development' (p. 52), but her chapter concentrates much more on the alternatives generated by subaltern social actors, often in conditions of considerable adversity and on the very margins of traditional history-writing. Whilst tracing the different national trajectories of such endeavours in its prose, her essay also provides a precise and exhaustive bibliographical service in its apparatus. Drafted almost simultaneously with the publication of the special issue of the *Hispanic American Historical Review* on the controversy over Mexican cultural history in which she has played a leading part,[11] Mallon's pres-

---

[10] 'Latin America has a distinct identity which differentiates it from the West ... it has a corporatist, authoritarian culture'. Samuel Huntington, *The Clash of Civilizations and the Remaking of the New World Order* (New York, 1996), p. 46. For this statement Huntington relies entirely upon Claudio Véliz, who has famously allowed for a 'liberal pause' of some one hundred years (up to 1930) in Latin America's otherwise 'centralist' trajectory, *The Centralist Tradition* (Princeton, 1979).

[11] *HAHR*, vol. 79, no. 2 (May 1999). 'Mexico's New Cultural History: *Una Lucha Libre?*'. For an earlier statement, see, 'The Promise and Dilemma of Subaltern Studies: Perspectives from Latin American History', *American Historical Review*, vol. 99 (1994), pp. 491–515.

ent piece displays a similarly dynamic approach over a wider geographical field and is likely to be just as provocative of scholarly debate.

Miguel Angel Centeno's chapter addresses the complex and critical issue of (largely 'structured' or institutional) violence in the construction of national states. In the case of Latin America this topic has not found favour in academic interpretation, being far less popular than literary and cultural studies of the early promotion of national identity and consciousness. That should, of itself, not be a matter of surprise since the military dictatorships of the late twentieth century barbarously violated many positive convictions about state formation and nation-building shared between mainstream liberalism and the proponents of national liberation. Moreover, as Brian Downing has put it, 'War is not an agreeable thing to study; it does not fit with most academic research; we have in our day welcomed the decline of large-scale war.'[12]

Departing, like the next chapter by Malcolm Deas, from an allied interest in taxation, Centeno takes his margin of comparison from the Europe of the eighteenth and nineteenth centuries to ask why the new Latin American states were not positively constituted through the experience of warfare even though most of them initially emerged from it. He argues that it is the social context — rather than the narrow technological and physical conduct — of war that is of decisive consequence. Albeit focused primarily on 'state-building from above', the attention paid by his essay to issues of regionalism, ethnic conflict and elite division in Latin America means that it shares discernible interpretative territory with that of Florencia Mallon.

Miguel Centeno writes as much with a sociologist's predisposition for the general and strategic register of analysis as he does with recognition of the specificities of historical experience and knowledge.[13] In the case of Malcolm Deas's essay on conscription, this order might fairly be said to be reversed. Most of the contributors to this volume were trained in the profession of history, which, as an institution, has not overly cared for the public pretensions and expressive palate of social scientists even if it has promiscuously pilfered their objects of study and methodological insights. Such an embracing of this disciplinary tension is nowhere more marked than in Deas's welcome offer to match the inferential method of Cuvier in a chapter that reflects many years' study of the nineteenth century, particularly with regard to military affairs, and especially in Colombia, which here provides an optic for the region as a whole.

---

[12] 'War and the State in Early Modern Europe', in Theda Skocpol (ed.), *Democracy, Revolution and History* (Ithaca, NY, and London, 1998), p. 54.

[13] In many ways the 'companion volume' to the present book is Miguel Angel Centeno and Fernando López-Alves (eds.), *The Other Mirror. Grand Theory through the Lens of Latin America* (Princeton, 2001), in which are to be found as contributors not only the editor but also Paul Gootenberg, Alan Knight and Steven Topik.

It would be quite wrong to see the analysis of conscription as intrinsically dry and elitist history, not least because its very objects/subjects were (and remain) members of those social sectors which Mallon has highlighted as being simultaneously on the frontier and at the heart of often ephemeral, sometimes invented and generally imagined communities. Indeed, at the start of the twenty-first century there are some signs of a reemergence of a class of literary soldiers just as capable of reflecting on their own professional conduct and its wider social context as those schooled exclusively in the trenches of the academy.[14] From a very different tradition and in a quite distinctive tone to that of Mallon, but with a comparable sympathy and sensibility, Deas here traces the operational and material constraints on a practice pursued almost everywhere when, by the exact definitional margin prescribed by Weber, the nation-state existed nowhere at all in the sub-continent.

In a further declension of this concern with the practical means of securing stability through the state-based management of the military, Fernando López-Alves provides a precise case study of the Uruguayan experience. As with most of the chapters, López-Alves's survey both takes issue with some established lines of interpretation and engages in a substantive account based on primary research. In this instance, he questions the existence of any innate 'conservatism' of the Uruguayan oligarchy, and he makes a spirited case for a proactive, state-led and money-driven welfare reform, within which the role played by military pensions was arguably as decisive as any cooptation of the working classes. López-Alves's timeframe is 1890 to 1930 — years that epitomise transition between political regimes in most countries, but particularly so in Uruguay. Early in the twenty-first century one is struck by the thought that a not so dissimilar pact was struck in the 1980s, when the country returned to civilian administration without either governmental collapse or the open judicial settlement of accounts attempted almost everywhere else.

The experience of Brazil has never been readily accommodated into general theories of any Spanish American 'political tradition', which for much of the twentieth century was dominated by notions of 'centralism' that sit uneasily with much of the evidence presented in the current volume. Here two quite distinct but equally suggestive approaches have been adopted. Steven Topik compares the national experience with that of Mexico (in lieu of the usual slavery-based comparison with the southern states of the USA) within the context of international political economy, whilst David McCreery fixes his analytical eye on a sub-national level of analysis — the frontier state (with a 'small s') of Goiás.

---

[14] Juan R. Quintana Taborga, *Soldados y ciudadanos. Un estudio crítico sobre el servicio militar obligatorio en Bolivia* (La Paz, 1998). This text could be considered part of a lineage that opens with Gunnar Mendoza (ed.), *José Santos Vargas. Diario de un Comandante de la Independencia, 1814–1825* (Mexico, 1982), and that passes through Gary Prado Salmón, *La guerrilla inmolada. La campaña del Che en Bolivia* (Santa Cruz, 1987).

Topik questions the precise qualities of the Brazilian state — both imperial and republican — in the nineteenth century, taking us concisely through the different interpretative schools of recent decades. Recognising that, on the military plane at least, the Brazilian experience was of a piece with that of Spanish America, he opens the book's first sustained treatment of political economy, financial policy and, by direct implication, international relations. Topik is concerned to identify a growth of both state and nation prior to, rather than following, the erosion and collapse of slavery and empire, and he questions conventional interpretations of political form that overestimate the power of the monarchy and undervalue that of the First Republic. His notion of a 'hollow state' captures the sense in which these matters were not properly sequential and causative but dynamically intertwined.

David McCreery's essay provides an apt counterpoint because, although concerned exclusively with the imperial period, it disentangles many of the daily underpinnings of power and administration at the then territorial margins of the formal state (now, of course, Goiás is right next to the Distrito Federal). Here we find few names of national renown and minimal evidence of wider causes and parties, let alone ideology. And yet McCreery can discern a distinct sense of 'Brazilianness' amidst the patrimonialism, clan feuds, fiscal adversity and mercurial rule of law. As already suggested by Centeno, Deas and Topik, the local state forces are no more or less ill-treated, susceptible and unreliable than elsewhere, but if they are not Bismarckian, nor are they nothing. Equally, although the inhabitants of Goiás did not particularly wish to be on a frontier, they simply were, and however much they emulated the customs of Rio, it was the central state's very weakness which ensured that their extemporised existence constituted the cutting edge/backdoor of civilisation.

Colin Lewis breaks with the traditionally politicised depiction of Argentine state-making that promotes the figures of Rosas, Roca and Perón, the Constitution of 1853 and the Saenz Peña law, all beneath the apparently perennial dichotomy between civilisation and barbarism. Lewis's time-frame runs from the overthrow of Rosas to that of Perón, but his fundamental interpretative interest is at a deeper level of political economy, in particular with the role of railways, money and the market. Just as for the cases of the USA and Great Britain, where railway development occurred only a few decades earlier, there is a sophisticated and energetic scholarly debate over the detailed operation and wider consequences of the sector.

In showing so clearly how 'money mattered' in Argentina, Lewis's chapter also serves to highlight our relatively weak knowledge of the monetary history of Latin America as a whole, but the clear suggestion is that the currency regimes and fiscal mechanisms through which resources were captured and states precariously founded were as varied as they were shallow. Like Topik's essay, the chapter by Lewis looks outward to the wider world — one which, by the 1880s, is engaging with Latin America precisely in the form of capitalism. As such, both domestic and foreign interests were concerned about the provision of private goods under conditions of general equity, but these in turn depended upon what, in the language of economics, are termed public goods (macroeconomic stability and basic legal guarantees) and, indeed, such semi-public goods as health and welfare that were now understood by some to contribute to 'efficiency', even if they were only intermittently included in input-output calculations.

Liberalism, in short, positively needed a state — something understood by the late nineteenth-century liberals, who built railways, in a manner quite distinct to the neoliberals of the late twentieth century, who closed them down. Colin Lewis ends his chapter with reference to the first Baring crisis in the 1890s without needing to remind us that the same bank failed spectacularly one hundred years later or that at the start of the new millennium Argentina's public being was entirely in the thrall of its fragile, pseudo-magical currency arrangements.

One might be tempted to claim something similar for Mexico, salvaged thrice from bankruptcy in the closing years of the century. Yet while these states do share some key attributes, their historical experiences are, in fact, as contrasting as any of a region that is no better understood through its unity than its diversity. As we have seen, Steven Topik uses Mexico as a means through which better to understand Brazil. In a very different style, but with a similar objective, Guy Thomson uses Spain — the 'mother country' to New Spain — to throw light on nineteenth-century Mexico. In fact, his chapter is thoroughly equitable in its treatment of both national experiences, compared through a number of themes — *desamortización* (privatisation of corporate, principally ecclesiastical, property); liberal constitutionalism; relations between Church and state; and the educational-ideological construction of a patriotic identity.

Perhaps no other nineteenth-century international contrast was quite as illuminating as that between this former colony and its erstwhile imperial metropolis in that so many common qualities — not least the waging of civil wars, a deep sense of the local past and profound suspicion of foreign power and interest — evolved in such a disparate fashion over the same time-frame. The resulting parallax throws important light on the deeper qualities of 'nation' and 'colony', so that Thomson can persuasively close, not in 1861 or 1898, but in 1975, with Spain's transition to democratic rule. And, indeed, with the defeat of the Partido Revolucionario Institucional (PRI) in the presidential elections of 2000, one is likely to find as much illumination in the *longue durée* as in the *conjuncture*.

The liberalism discussed by Thomson is not really the same as that at the heart of Lewis's analysis of Argentina. Rather, it is a liberal patriotism — 'a powerful mythology that exalted the leaders of the struggles against Spain, the conservatives, the Catholic Church and foreign invaders. During the 1920s and 1930s, this secular religion was given additional cultural and social substance by revolutionary nationalists' (p. 210). That legacy, then, forms a part of Alan Knight's exhaustive consideration of the 'weight' of the state in modern Mexico. This treatment takes its cue from a challenge issued by Stephen Haber in the late 1990s that a much more rigorous appraisal be made of the presence and activity of the state as part of that wider historical debate into which Florencia Mallon and others have entered on rather different grounds. Knight begins with a careful discussion of what it might mean to 'measure' the state and civil society, moves on to consider the economy and infrastructure, takes up the significantly less quantifiable issues of society and legitimacy and then discusses four types of autonomy: that in the international arena ('Prussian'); that related to capitalist accumulation and growth ('economic'); that concerned with promoting the legitimacy of the prevailing social order ('political'); and that devoted to the particularist interests of the state incumbents and their dependents ('mafioso').

As with much of his work over recent years, Knight subjects the procedures and analytical ambitions of social science to a full and exacting test in twentieth-century Mexico.[15] His findings, though, are rather sober — 'careful calibration, however desirable, especially for comparative purposes, is always difficult and often impossible' (p. 251). Yet Knight is palpably unhappy at the prospect of historians forever standing fair on a hill of fastidious footnotes — 'to know more and more about less and less' — whilst social scientists remain comfortably camped out on a plain of capacious categories — 'to know less and less about more and more'. It is, rather, in the mutual stimulation and challenge between these distinct forms of inquiry and knowledge that one seeks — and sometimes finds — reward. 'Revisionism' is not just a form of intra-disciplinary cannibalism; it can harness a much wider intellectual energy and, whether driven by primary empirical information or abstract reflection, it has the capacity to overcome scholastic distemper and partisanship.

The two final chapters of the book are set in Peru and Bolivia, and both revolve about the imaginations of elites. Reflecting upon and developing his own past work, Paul Gootenberg identifies three stages in the formation of the early Peruvian state: breakdown, 1824–45; consolidation, 1845–50; and the liberal guano-age, 1850–1870s. Gootenberg is particularly interested in the manner by which economic ideas about development — not nearly so 'obvious' in the mid-nineteenth century as one hundred years later — interacted with the mental construction of a republic, and so of citizenship, in a state heavily pop-

[15] 'The Mexican Revolution: Bourgeois? Nationalist? Or just a "Great Rebellion"?', *Bulletin of Latin American Research (BLAR)*, vol. 4, no. 2 (1985), pp. 1–37; 'The Peculiarities of Latin American History: Mexico compared to Latin America, 1821–1992', *Journal of Latin American Studies (JLAS)*, vol. 24, Quincentenary supplement (1992), pp. 9–144; 'Habitus and Homicide: Political Culture in Revolutionary Mexico', in Wil G. Pansters (ed.), *Citizens of the Pyramid. Essays on Mexican Political Culture* (Amsterdam, 1997), pp. 107–29; 'Populism and Neo-Populism in Latin America, especially Mexico', *JLAS*, vol. 30, no. 2 (1998), pp 223-48; 'The Modern Mexican State: Theory and Practice', in Centeno and López-Alves (eds.), *The Other Mirror*, pp. 177–218; 'Democratic and Revolutionary Traditions in Latin America', *BLAR*, vol. 20, no. 2 (2001), pp. 147–86.

ulated by indigenous people who had lost their own 'republic' possessed under the Spanish colony and yet are effectively excluded from the new polity.

The Peruvian elite confronted not just a general logistical challenge of developing modern infrastructure in industry, commerce, railways, etc., nor simply an operational problem in projecting this as a legitimate enterprise to millions for whom it was, by contrast, a completely alien and often threatening endeavour. It was, beyond this, faced with the profound possibility that the plans at the heart of its continued existence were but a dream. Gootenberg's movement back and forth betwixt individual thinkers and expansive programmes captures both the power and the fragility of these prospectuses for the future of Peru, somehow hedged in between the shadow of the Andean sierra and the power of foreign purses and warships over the Pacific horizon. At the same time, though, his patchwork account shows that not all was crisis and that the state was even fortified through the autonomy of those elite forces operating around and through it in a much less predictable pattern than in Mexico and Brazil.

Seemin Qayum takes the rather more modest arena of the Geographical Society of La Paz to explore similar challenges at the end of the nineteenth century. This final essay echoes some of Florencia Mallon's concerns in the first, perceiving a reach of colonialism that goes well beyond that exercised internationally and at the level of formal institutions through to the 1820s (1898 in the cases of Cuba and Puerto Rico). In her study of Bolivia — the Alto Perú of the Spaniards now renamed after the Liberator — Qayum draws on the theses concerning the imperial appropriation of geographical and historical imagination in Edward Said's *Orientalism*, mapping out an *internal* form of colonialism, exercised by a small creole-mestizo elite over a population dominated even more than that of Peru by the indigenous communities.

The fact that this undertaking was proposed precisely as a scientific, liberal and republican endeavour sharpened its contradictions to a point quite the equal of that seen for Peru in earlier decades. Yet, as Qayum shows in her survey of the dominion imposed over indigenous property and society in the last decades of the nineteenth century, what might have started out as sheer flights of fancy soon acquired finite power through judicial execution and the building of infrastructure, even as externally Bolivia lost a string of wars and swathes of its territory. Again, the very railways so assiduously promoted by the gentlemen of the Sociedad Geográfica, capitalised by them as well as Chilean and British firms, and then nationalised after the 1952 Revolution, have in recent years been sold to international interests, and either closed down or cut right back.

By early 1880 the Bolivian state had lost — perhaps for ever — a seaboard of its own. The ruling class still had to contend with the threatening external forces, which were in so many respects the examples that they wished to emulate and that they thought represented the future. Yet — as with many other smaller or weaker states of the region — little progress was possible without those selfsame local elites mentally reorganising their own internal space. Eager to be part of the world, they could only anticipate membership on the grounds of a distinctiveness calibrated as much by imagination as by any quantum or 'scientific' method.

The chapters of this book were originally presented as papers to a conference at ILAS in June 1999. They were subsequently discussed in a study group held at St Antony's College, Oxford. Funding for these events was provided by the William and Flora Hewlett Foundation. The authors and editor are most grateful to the following for their comments and suggestions: David Brading; Victor Bulmer-Thomas; Paulo Drinot; Jeffrey Gould; Andrew Hurrell; David Lorey; Tony McFarlane; Eduardo Posada-Carbó; Rachel Sieder; Rosemary Thorp; and Laurence Whitehead.

CHAPTER 1

Decoding the Parchments of the Latin American Nation-State: Peru, Mexico and Chile in Comparative Perspective

Florencia E. Mallon

Throughout the twentieth century historical interpretations of Latin American nation-states evolved in symbiosis with the evolution of those nation-states themselves. With the crisis of the colonial system in the late eighteenth century, nationhood and citizenship were, for a time, potentially inclusive, egalitarian ideas that were debated broadly and differentially understood. By the second half of the nineteenth century, however, nation and citizen were concepts applied to a select group, usually property-owning, of European descent, literate, and male. It was only in the first decades of the twentieth century that debates emerged once again on the dynamics of inclusion and exclusion within Latin American nation-states, and this wave of debate continues to this day.[1] Major and critical processes — the Mexican Revolution; the Depression; the 'Guatemalan spring' of 1944–54 and its overthrow; the Cuban and Nicaraguan revolutions; authoritarianisms and dirty wars; the rise and fall of populisms and state-directed economic development — have served as touchstones for existing notions of if, how, when and under what conditions nations and states came to be. As more popular and inclusive visions of the national community have fallen victim to repression, isolation or marketisation, the very meaning of nation or national identity has been put into question. And as the value and viability of interventionist, protectionist or welfare states has everywhere come under suspicion, interpretations that gave the state a central role in making Latin American nations have also become the subject of scrutiny and scepticism.

In this chapter, I use the cases of Mexico, Peru and Chile in the postcolonial era — defined as the period from the colonial crisis of the 1780s through the marketisation of the 1980s and 1990s — to reflect on the double evolution of nation-states and their analysts. In part a semi-autobiographical commentary

---

[1]   By nation I mean two often interrelated things: a) a project for collective identity based on the premise of citizenship or individual membership, that is available to all individuals in a collectivity on the assumption of legal equality; and b) a moral project of unity or loyalty based on abstract notions of belonging, as defined by Benedict Anderson, *Imagined Communities: Reflections on the Origin and Spread of Nationalism* (London, 1983). By state, I also mean two interrelated things: a) a pact of domination or rule; and b) a series of physical, material sites and institutions where conflicts over power are constantly resolved and hierarchically reordered. For further reflections on these definitions, and what they might illuminate about 'really existing' nation-states, see Florencia E. Mallon, *Peasant and Nation: The Making of Postcolonial Mexico and Peru* (Berkeley, 1995), ch. 1.

on the state of the literature, it is also a modest attempt to suggest some future directions for research and conversation. After a brief overview of the historical trends shared by all three countries, as well as the distinct historiographical traditions that have attempted to make sense of them, I move to a more detailed look at debates on nation-state formation in each case. I then conclude with some general remarks on the similarities and differences between and among the literatures on the three countries, and a discussion of the empirical, methodological and theoretical implications for future work.

Though in very different ways, the nineteenth-century balances of power achieved in Mexico, Peru, and Chile experienced deep crises in the first three to four decades of the twentieth century. All three countries had in common the fact that rurally and oligarchically based sociopolitical orders were being challenged from below by a combination of newly emerging social groups, including urban workers, peasants, urban and/or provincial middle classes. In all three cases, these new social actors brought into focus the 'social question' — shorthand for the fact that nineteenth-century national projects had generally included only the property-owning and investing classes, while tying Latin American economies tightly to the economic ups and downs of the industrialising world. In Mexico, the reconstituted landowning and investing class that had served as the main buttress for the late years of the *Porfiriato* (1876–1910) rule fell prey to a combined set of agrarian, regionalist and popular challenges, and the resulting revolution generated a corporatist, interventionist state. In Peru, first the exclusionary Aristocratic Republic and then Augusto B. Leguía's *Oncenio* succumbed to pressure from *limeño* working class movements, anarchist and *indigenista* intellectuals, student mobilisations, and emerging provincial middle class and labour movements, initiating a long-term crisis of rule and direction not fully confronted until the 1968 military revolution. And in Chile, the model of selective political inclusion and intra-elite negotiation that had emerged with the post-1891 parliamentary regime reached its limits with the 1920s populism of Arturo Alessandri, initiating a decade-long crisis that ended with the election of Pedro Aguirre Cerda and the first Popular Front coalition government in 1938.[2]

---

[2]   The literatures on these processes are too broad to cite in their entirety. Initial guides can be found, for Mexico, in Héctor Aguilar Camín and Lorenzo Meyer, *In the Shadow of the Mexican Revolution: Contemporary Mexican History, 1910–1989*, trans. Luis Alberto Fierro (Austin, 1993); Alan Knight, *The Mexican Revolution*, 2 vols. (New York, 1986); and Jan Bazant, *A Concise History of Mexico: from Hidalgo to Cárdenas, 1805–1940* (New York, 1977). For Peru, Alberto Flores Galindo and Manuel Burga, *Apogeo y crisis de la república aristocrática: oligarquía, aprismo y comunismo en el Perú, 1895–1932* (Lima, 1980); Peter F. Klarén, *Modernization, Dislocation, and Aprismo: Origins of the Peruvian Aprista Party, 1870–1932* (Austin, 1973); and Frederick B. Pike, *The Modern History of Peru* (New York, 1967). For Chile, various 'takes' can be found in Brian Loveman, *Chile: the Legacy of Hispanic Capitalism*, 2nd. ed. (New York, 1988); Luis Vitale, *Interpretación marxista de la historia de Chile*, edición ampliada (Santiago, 1994); Simon Collier and

The nature of the crisis in each country, already dependent, of course, on previous nineteenth-century trends and events, helped mark the character of historical approaches to nation-state formation in each case. Mexico and Chile emerged, at the end of the 1930s, with relatively stable and interventionist states that directed processes of industrialisation and economic development behind tariff barriers, and formulated social welfare policies aimed at including broader sectors of the population within an expanded 'national community'. Not surprisingly, the historiographies in these two cases have tended to be more state-centric and, whether supporting or criticising the status quo, more ready to accept the existence of a successful national project directed by the state. In Peru, on the other hand, the failure of efforts at national consolidation across spatial and ethnic lines, as well as the maintenance of an 'open economy', resulted in an early bifurcation of historiography into a Lima-centred, elitist 'patriotic history' and a more critical, revisionist counter-tendency that attempted to take seriously the contributions of popular movements and of highland and indigenous society to Peruvian history more broadly. Among the issues that divided the two sides in Peru was precisely the question on which most Mexican and Chilean historians seemed to agree: the viability and success of a state-directed national project.[3]

After World War II a second crisis, initiated from countries unable successfully to confront the historical limitations of their own processes of nation-state formation, once again put on the table the same set of issues that had brought Mexico to revolution in 1910: agrarian and labour reform, political inclusion, and national economic development. In so doing, the Guatemalan, Bolivian, and Cuban revolutions (1944–54, 1952, 1959) ushered in what one might call the period of 'national liberation': in Cuba, Nicaragua, Guatemala, and El Salvador, a more inclusionary and state-directed national project was to be installed through people's war, with socialism bringing to fruition the kind of nation that capitalism proved too weak and dependent to create.[4] The currency of this vision was especially intense between 1959 and 1979, when revolutionary movements successfully took power in Cuba and Nicaragua and instituted reformist programmes

William F. Sater, *A History of Chile, 1808–1994* (New York, 1996); and Gonzalo Vial Correa, *Historia de Chile, 1891–1973* (Santiago, 1981).

[3]   Rosemary Thorp and Geoffrey Bertram, *Peru, 1890–1977: Growth and Policy in an Open Economy* (New York, 1978); and Pike, *The Modern History of Peru*. But see also Paul Gootenberg, *Imagining Development: Economic Ideas in Peru's 'Fictitious Prosperity' of Guano, 1840–1880* (Berkeley, 1993).

[4]   Of course, neither Guatemala nor Bolivia experienced 'national-liberation' or socialist-inspired revolutions, but hybrid attempts at socioeconomic and political reform that had more in common, perhaps, with the 1910 Mexican Revolution. Still, the failure of both helped set the context for the evolution, throughout the region, of a more socialist-oriented project for national autonomy based on the Cuban model.

of agrarian reform, labour organisation, education and social welfare for the population at large. While Mexico, Peru and Chile did not witness major revolutionary outbreaks over these years,[5] the influence of the Cuban revolution was especially strong, generating confrontations between social movements and state actors that resulted in major shifts in all three political systems. In Mexico, the student movement of 1968 pulled back the curtain on the nature of the postrevolutionary state, initiating a process of intellectual rethinking and political realignment that has yet to come to an end. In Peru, a military tired of repressing highland peasants and doing the oligarchy's bidding took power in a progressive 1968 coup with a reform agenda that aimed to broaden and deepen the national project in ways similar to earlier attempts in other parts of the region. And in Chile, the radicalisation of students, workers, and peasants in the late 1950s and early 1960s helped usher in the decade of agrarian reform, during which presidents Eduardo Frei Montalva and Salvador Allende expanded the state-directed national project to include the peasantry, and in so doing called into question the 'gentleman's agreement' that had earlier allowed for the inclusion of urban and industrial workers and leftist parties in the 'compromise state'.[6]

---

[5]   This does not mean that there was no violence in these three countries. Mexico and Peru both experienced shortlived guerrilla movements between the mid-1960s and 1970s, while in Chile the Movimiento de Izquierda Revolucionaria (MIR) espoused armed struggle, mainly in words rather than actions, during Salvador Allende's Popular Unity government (1970–73). In the 1980s the Chilean MIR's attempt at armed overthrow of the military dictatorship, followed by the Communist Party's creation of the Frente Patriótico Manuel Rodríguez, would prove costly failures.

[6]   For Mexico, see Judith Adler Hellman, *Mexico in Crisis*, 2nd. ed. (New York, 1983), Elena Poniatowska, *La noche de Tlatelolco* (Mexico City, 1971) and *Fuerte es el silencio* (Mexico City, 1980); Héctor Aguilar Camín, *Saldos de la revolución: cultura y política de México, 1910–1980* (Mexico City, 1982); Pablo González Casanova and Enrique Florescano (eds.), *México hoy* (Mexico City, 1979); Stanley R. Ross (ed.), *Is the Mexican Revolution Dead?* (New York, 1966). On Peru, François Bourricaud, *Power and Society in Contemporary Peru* (New York, 1970); Julio Cotler, *Crisis política y populismo militar en el Perú* (Lima, 1969), 'A Structural-Historical Approach to the Breakdown of Democratic Institutions: Peru', in Juan J. Linz and Alfred Stepan (eds.), *The Breakdown of Democratic Regimes: Latin America* (Baltimore, 1978), pp. 178–206, *Clases, estado y nación en el Perú* (Lima, 1978); José Matos Mar (ed.), *Hacienda, comunidad y campesinado en el Perú*, 2nd. ed. (Lima, 1976), *La reforma agraria en el Perú* (Lima, 1980); and Abraham F. Lowenthal (ed.), *The Peruvian Experiment: Continuity and Change under Military Rule* (Princeton, 1975). On Chile, Arturo Valenzuela, *The Breakdown of Democratic Regimes: Chile* (Baltimore, 1978); Pamela Constable and Arturo Valenzuela, *A Nation of Enemies: Chile under Pinochet* (New York, 1991); Loveman, *Chile*; Edward Boorstein, *Allende's Chile: An Inside View* (New York, 1977); Richard E. Feinberg, *The Triumph of Allende: Chile's Legal Revolution* (New York, 1972); and Kyle Steenland, *Agrarian Reform under Allende: Peasant Revolt in the South* (Albuquerque, 1977).

At the level of historiography, both in the various Latin American countries themselves and within a revisionist and politically active generation of young researchers in the United States, this period of radicalisation encouraged the development of a Marxist-influenced, 'bottom-up' history that emphasised the contributions of popular sectors and the dependent, *entreguista* nature of national bourgeoisies. In Mexico, much of the post-Tlatelolco literature focused on the corruption and authoritarianism of the postrevolutionary state, the reconstruction of a privileged elite, and the agrarian and social welfare promises left unaddressed in the 1940s and beyond.[7] In Peru the literature of the 1970s and 1980s had two main goals: recovering popular agency through a social history from below, focused on workers and indigenous peasants; and exploring the effects of economic dependence on the socioeconomic and political projects of Peruvian elites.[8] In Chile, a strong Marxist current challenged the images of stability, national autonomy, and elite unity that had been emphasised by the more traditional historiography, focusing instead on imperialism, dependency, and the evolution and repression of working class and peasant movements.[9]

---

[7] Roger D. Hansen, *The Politics of Mexican Development* (Baltimore,, 1971); Roger Bartra, *Caciquismo y poder político en el México Rural* (Mexico City, 1975), *La democracia ausente* (Mexico City, 1986); José Luis Reyna and Richard S. Weinert (eds.), *Authoritarianism in Mexico* (Philadelphia, 1977); Pablo González Casanova; *Democracy in Mexico*, trans. Danielle Salti, 2nd. ed. (New York, 1970); Ross, *Is the Mexican Revolution Dead?*. The revisionist school that dealt with the Mexican revolution also had its start in this critique and reflection. A useful introduction can be found in David Brading, *Caudillo and Peasant in the Mexican Revolution* (New York, 1980).

[8] See, for example, Alberto Flores Galindo, *Arequipa y el sur andino: ensayo de historia regional (siglos XVIII-XX)* (Lima, 1977), and *Los mineros de la Cerro de Pasco, 1900–1930: un intento de caracterización social* (Lima, 1974); Heraclio Bonilla, *La expansión comercial británica en el Perú* (Lima:, 1974), and *Guano y burguesía en el Perú* (Lima, 1974), *Un siglo a la deriva: ensayos sobre el Perú, Bolivia y la guerra* (Lima, 1980); Bonilla and Karen Spalding (eds.), *La independencia en el Perú* (Lima, 1972); Manuel Burga, *De la encomienda a la hacienda capitalista: el Valle del Jequetepeque del siglo XVI al XX* (Lima, 1976), with Wilson Reátegui, *Lanas y capital mercantil en el sur: la Casa Ricketts, 1895–1935* (Lima, 1981); Nelson Manrique, *Colonialismo y pobreza campesina: Caylloma y el valle del Colca, siglos XVI–XX* (Lima, 1985), and *Campesinado y nación: las guerrillas indígenas en la guerra con Chile:* (Lima, 1981), and *Mercado interno y región: la sierra central, 1820–1930* (Lima, 1987), *Yawar mayu: sociedades terratenientes serranas, 1879–1910* (Lima, 1988); Ernesto Yepes, *Perú 1820–1920: un siglo de desarrollo capitalista* (Lima, 1972); Florencia E. Mallon, *The Defense of Community in Peru's Central Highlands: Peasant Struggle and Capitalist Transition, 1860–1940* (Princeton, 1983); Steve J. Stern, *Peru's Indian Peoples and the Challenge of Conquest: Huamanga to 1620* (Madison, 1982); Karen Spalding, *Huarochirí: An Andean Society under Inca and Spanish Rule* (Stanford, 1984); and Paul Gootenberg, *Between Silver and Guano: Commercial Policy and the State in Postindependence Peru* (Princeton, 1989).

[9] Hernán Ramírez Necochea, *Balmaceda y la contrarrevolución de 1891*, 3rd ed. (Santiago, 1972), *Los Estados Unidos y América Latina, 1930–1965* (Santiago, 1965), and

In general, then, the revolutionary critique of nation-state formation formulated during the 1960s–80s period tended to focus on the limits of national inclusion and on the limitations of the traditional historian's gaze. In much 'bottom-up' social history the state was little more than a repressive agent; and even when authors took a more subtle, Gramscian perspective, potential lower-class participation in systems of domination was harder to accept at a time when a revolutionary option still seemed to exist. As a result most radical historians in this 'national liberation' period, when not attempting the archaeology of the popular classes, emphasised forms of *dependentista* economic and political history in which the state was mainly a mediator for foreign capital. For those historians engaged in the political debates and struggles of the time, demonstrating the impossibility of elite-led nations would open the way for a socialist-led national revolution that would finally create the kind of inclusive and egalitarian national community they perceived as the most important popular goal.[10]

Historia del movimiento obrero en Chile; antecedentes siglo XIX (Santiago, 1956); Peter DeShazo, *Urban Workers and Labor Unions in Chile, 1902–1927* (Madison, 1983); Michael Monteón, *Chile in the Nitrate Era: The Evolution of Economic Dependence, 1880–1930* (Madison, 1982); Gabriel Salazar, *Labradores, peones y proletarios: formación y crisis de la sociedad popular chilena del siglo XIX* (Santiago, 1985), and *Violencia política popular en 'las grandes alamedas': Santiago de Chile, 1917–1987* (Santiago, 1990); Peter Winn, *Weavers of Revolution: The Yarur Workers and Chile's Road to Socialism* (New York, 1986); Maurice Zeitlin, *The Civil Wars in Chile (or The Bourgeois Revolutions that Never Were* (Princeton, 1984); and Charles W. Bergquist, *Labor in Latin America: Comparative Essays on Chile, Argentina, Venezuela, and Colombia* (Stanford, 1986).

[10] In this period the Mexican literature was undergoing its own development in a post-Tlatelolco context, emphasising the authoritarianism of the state and the broken promises of the 1910 Revolution. Some examples of this trend in the 1970s and early 1980s are Armando Bartra, *Los herederos de Zapata: movimientos campesinos posrevolucionarios en México* (Mexico City, 1985); R. Bartra, *Caciquismo y poder político*; Brading, *Caudillo and Peasant*; González Casanova, *Democracy in Mexico*; Hansen, *The Politics of Mexican Development*; Gilbert Joseph, *Revolution from Without: Yucatán, Mexico, and the United States, 1880–1924* (New York, 1982); Jean Meyer, *Problemas campesinos y revueltas agrarias (1821–1910)* (Mexico City, 1973); Reyna and Weinert (eds.), *Authoritarianism in Mexico*; and Arturo Warman, *...y venimos a contradecir: los campesinos de Morelos y el estado nacional* (Mexico City, 1976). In Peru and Bolivia, a strong school of radical historians explored the nature of popular history and economic dependency, often combining an understanding of lower class agency with a perspective on imperialism and underdevelopment. See especially Bonilla, *Guano y burguesía*; Bonilla and Spalding (eds.), *La independencia en el Perú*; Flores Galindo, *Los mineros de la Cerro de Pasco*, and *Arequipa y el sur andino*; Brooke Larson, *Colonialism and Agrarian Transformation in Bolivia: Cochabamba, 1550–1900* (Princeton, 1988); Mallon, *The Defense of Community*; Nelson Manrique, *Campesinado y nación*; Silvia Rivera Cusicanqui, *Oprimidos pero no vencidos: luchas del campesinado aymara y qhechwa de Bolivia, 1900–1980* (La Paz, 1984), 'Apuntes para una historia de las luchas campesinas en Bolivia (1900–1978)', in Pablo

If the 1959–79 period was the generation of 'national liberation,' the 1980–2000 generation has been marked instead by the unravelling of state-centred national projects; repression and authoritarianism followed by redemocratisation; and market reforms and globalisation. Traditional political parties have been pressured by so-called 'new social movements', of which the revived indigenous movements of the 1970s and 1980s have arguably been among the most creative and politically successful. While some of the experiments with marketisation and political 'modernisation' have been deemed more successful than others, nowhere in the region has a new and inclusive national project emerged to take the place of the failed state-directed alternatives of the 1960s and 1970s. In Mexico the 1970s witnessed the end of the 'economic miracle', land distribution and the rise of new peasant movements, urban grassroots organisations, and indigenous activism, leading ultimately to the 1988 election crisis, the formation of the Partido de la Revolución Democrática (PRD), and the rise of the Ejército Zapatista de Liberación Nacional (EZLN).[11] In Peru the failure of the 1968 military revolution was followed in the 1980s by political redemocratisation and by a deep economic and political crisis that fostered the rise of Sendero Luminoso. The ensuing civil war affected all of national territory, facilitating the rise of Alberto Fujimori's populist authoritarianism; Sendero was ultimately defeated by a combination of Andean community resistance and

González Casanova (coord.), *Historia política de los campesinos latinoamericanos* (Mexico City, 1984–85), vol. 3, pp. 146–207; Yepes del Castillo, *Perú 1820–1920*. In Chile, the leading Marxist texts from the 1960s and early 1970s include: Arnold Bauer, *Chilean Rural Society from the Spanish Conquest to 1930* (New York, 1975); James Petras, *Politics and Social Forces in Chilean Development* (Berkeley, 1969); Ramírez Necochea, *Balmaceda y la contrarrevolución de 1891, Los Estados Unidos y América Latina, historia del movimiento obrero en Chile*; and Vitale, *Interpretación marxista de la historia de Chile*.

[11]   The literature on these processes is too extensive to cite in its entirety. Some important works include: Diane E. Davis, *Urban Leviathan: Mexico City in the Twentieth Century* (Philadelphia, 1994); Joe Foweraker and Ann Craig (eds.), *Popular Movements and Political Change in Mexico* (Boulder, CO, 1990); Carlos Fuentes, *Tiempo mexicano* (Mexico City, 1971); Judith Adler Hellman, *Mexico in Crisis*, 2nd ed. (New York, 1988); David Levy and Gabriel Székely, *Mexico, Paradoxes of Stability and Change*, 2nd ed. (Boulder, CO, 1987); Alejandra Massolo, *Por amor y coraje: mujeres en movimientos urbanos en la ciudad de México* (Mexico City, 1992); Carlos Monsiváis, *Entrada libre: crónicas de la sociedad que se organiza* (Mexico City, 1987); Elena Poniatowska, *Fuerte es el silencio* (Mexico City, 1980); *Nada, nadie: las voces del temblor* (Mexico City, 1988); *La noche de Tlatelolco* (Mexico City, 1971). On the rise of the EZLN, see George A. Collier and Elizabeth L. Quaratiello, *Basta! Land and the Zapatista Rebellion in Chiapas* (Oakland, 1994); Neil Harvey, *The Chiapas Rebellion: The Struggle for Land and Democracy* (Durham, NC, 1998); John Ross, *Rebellion from the Roots: Indian Uprising in Chiapas* (Monroe, 1995); John Womack, Jr., *Rebellion in Chiapas: An Historical Reader* (New York, 1999).

Lima policework.[12] In Chile, dramatic radicalisation during the Popular Unity government (1970–73) was cut short by a bloody military coup that fractured Chilean society and ushered in a seventeen-year dictatorship. Ultimately successful market reforms were accompanied by deepening socioeconomic inequality and repression, the redemocratising coalition governments in the 1990s have been both unable fully to deal with the social and human rights legacies of military rule, nor incorporate into resuscitated party structures the new social movements (including indigenous organisations) that arose in the 1980s.[13]

Thus, in all three countries, the deep crisis of earlier models has remained in stalemate, with little evidence that new models of inclusion will emerge in the near future. One potential source of optimism, until now restricted mainly to the drawing board, comes from the visions of diversity within national states that have emerged from indigenous movements. While clearly different in each case, given distinct national histories and disparate trajectories of native-state relations, recent demands placed on national states by indigenous groups have reopened debates on government policy in all three countries. In Mexico indigenous movements have, since the 1970s and early 1980s, raised the banner of diversity, decentralisation and ethnic self-determination in several regions of the country, the most dramatic example being the Zapotec Coalición de Obreros, Campesinos y Estudiantes del Istmo or COCEI, in Juchitán, Oaxaca. In the 1990s the most obvious and well-known example of a multi-ethnic and decentralised version of a national project was the Maya-influenced programme of the EZLN, though government repression and policies of low-intensity conflict kept Chiapas in stalemate despite several efforts at negotiation.[14] In Peru the *ronderos*,

---

[12] A recent collection that summarises many of these trends, and provides leads to important additional works, is Steve J. Stern (ed.), *Shining and Other Paths: War and Society in Peru, 1980–1995* (Durham, NC, 1998). Among the authors represented in the collection, Carlos Iván Degregori is perhaps the most prolific and well-known analyst of Shining Path and the 1980s civil war, while Orin Starn has worked extensively on the *rondas campesinas*, or peasant militias, that resisted the guerrillas in highland communities. See also Gustavo Gorriti, *Sendero: historia de la guerra milenaria en el Perú*, 2 vols. (Lima, 1990); and Deborah Poole and Gerardo Rénique, *Peru: Time of Fear* (London, 1992).

[13] Good places to begin exploring a very extensive literature are Pamela Constable and Arturo Valenzuela, *A Nation of Enemies: Chile under Pinochet* (New York, 1991); Paul Drake and Iván Jaksic (eds.), *The Struggle for Democracy in Chile*, rev. ed. (Lincoln, NE, 1995); Patricia Politzer, *Miedo en Chile* (Santiago, 1985); Teresa Valdés and Marisa Weinstein, *Mujeres que sueñan: las organizaciones de pobladoras en Chile, 1973–1989* (Santiago, 1993); Augusto Varas, *Los militares en el poder: régimen y gobierno militar en Chile, 1973–1986* (Santiago, 1987); and Patricia Verdugo, *Los zarpazos del puma* (Santiago, 1989).

[14] On the COCEI, see Jeffrey W. Rubin, *Decentering the Regime: Ethnicity, Radicalism, and Democracy in Juchitán, Mexico* (Durham, NC, 1997). On the EZLN see, in addition to the relevant sources in footnote 11, June Nash, 'The Fiesta of the Word: The Zapatista Uprising

essentially government- and military-sponsored community militias organised to resist Sendero Luminoso, became central participants in government-supported grassroots efforts to rebuild Andean communities destroyed by civil war. Given the broader erosion of civil society fostered in Peru by the 1980s civil war and in the 1990s by Fujimori's authoritarianism, however, the future political impact of reconstruction remained unclear at the turn of the century.[15] And in Chile the Mapuche indigenous movement of the late 1970s and 1980s (formed initially to resist a military government initiative that would have privatised all indigenous lands and abolished indigenous communities) was instrumental in the passage of a 1993 Indigenous Law that recognised the rights of Chilean indigenous groups and created the Corporación Nacional de Desarrollo Indígena (CONADI), the first decentralised government organisation to have a national office not in Santiago but in Temuco, in the middle of the most heavily indigenous part of the country. Yet the inability of Concertación governments further to decentralise power and democratise institutions seemed to have suppressed, at least for now, CONADI's potential for innovation.[16]

---

and Radical Democracy in Mexico', *American Anthropologist*, vol. 99, no. 2 (1997), pp. 261–74; Lynn Stephen and George A. Collier (eds.), *Reconfiguring Ethnicity, Identity and Citizenship in the Wake of the Zapatista Rebellion*, Special Issue of the *Journal of Latin American Anthropology*, vol. 3, no. 1 (1997); John Gledhill, 'Agrarian Social Movements and Forms of Consciousness', *Bulletin of Latin American Research*, vol. 7, no. 2 (1988), pp. 257–76; Fernando Alvarez, 'Peasant Movements in Chiapas', *Bulletin of Latin American Research*, vol. 7, no. 2 (1988), pp. 277–98; and Neil Harvey, 'Personal Networks and Strategic Choices in the Formation of an Independent Peasant Organisation: The OCEZ of Chiapas, Mexico', *Bulletin of Latin American Research*, vol. 7, no. 2 (1988), pp. 299–312.

[15] I do not mean to suggest here that Peru's *ronderos* have a project similar to the EZLN or can be considered in any way as radicals interested in revolutionary transformation. The connection is, rather, that they represent a form of grassroots initiative and struggle for local autonomy that seeks to rebuild local communities in coalition with a cooperative state. See Orin Starn, *Nightwatch: The Politics of Protest in the Andes* (Durham, NC, 1999); 'Villagers at Arms: War and Counterrevolution in the Central-South Andes', in Stern (ed.), *Shining and Other Paths*, pp. 224–57; *Reflexiones sobre rondas campesinas, protesta rural y nuevos movimientos sociales* (Lima, 1991); and Starn (ed.), *Hablan los ronderos: la búsqueda por la paz en los Andes* (Lima, 1993).

[16] Florencia E. Mallon, 'Cuando la amnesia se impone con sangre el abuso se hace costumbre: El pueblo Mapuche y el estado chileno, 1881–1998', in Paul Drake and Iván Jaksic, *El modelo chileno. Democracia y desarrollo en los noventa* (Santiago, 1999); Roberto Morales (ed.), *Ralco: modernidad o etnocidio en territorio Mapuche* (Temuco, 1998); Domingo Namuncura, *Ralco: ¿represa o pobreza?* (Santiago, 1999); José A. Marimán, 'Cuestión Mapuche, descentralización del estado y autonomía regional' (1990), URL: http://www.xs4all.nl/~rehue/art/jmar1.html, 'Movimiento Mapuche y Propuestas de Autonomía en la Década Post Dictadura' (1997), URL: http://www.xs4all.nl/~rehue/art/jmar4a.html, 'Transición democrática en Chile: nuevo ciclo reivindicativo mapuche?' (1994), URL: http://www.xs4all.nl/~rehue/art/jmar5a.html; Pedro Cayuqueo, 'La autodeterminación

Despite a common lack of resolution and many differences among the cases, however, the revitalisation of indigenous movements and politics has, in all three countries, opened new questions and perspectives in the historiography on nation-states. This is perhaps most easily seen in Mexico and Peru, where the demographic presence of indigenous peoples, the longstanding traditions of ethnohistory and engaged anthropology, and the existence of key historical conflicts and conflagrations in which peasants and indigenous communities actively participated, have all linked the history of the nation-state to the study of native peoples. Chile is, in this context, the limiting case. Its native population, mainly Mapuche, has been a minority throughout the postcolonial period and regionally concentrated in the south of the country; moreover, the Mapuche do not possess the kind of longstanding, settled community tradition of either Andean or Mesoamerican peoples. Nor does Chile possess, historiographically speaking, the rich tradition of regional histories that has begun to nurture, in the other two countries, anthropologically sensitive research into the local manifestations of nation-state formation. Politically, Chile's early development of a vital and competitive political party system with strong ties to popular sectors and leftist unions, in conjunction with an effective and precocious centralisation of state power, has meant the survival of precious little space for autonomous political projects. For a longer time than in Mexico, where after 1940 the Partido Revolucionario Institucional (PRI) also limited the effectiveness of independent political mobilisation, in Chile alternative national projects seem to have always developed in dialogue with, and to some extent dependent on, the hegemonic discourses of the state. Yet after 1973 repression and new forms of mobilisation changed the rules of the game, generating as well an intellectual rethinking of what Chilean society and politics have been, and what they could become.

It is in the context of this common crisis and intellectual opening, then, that it becomes most productive to reflect on recent historiographical developments. If our historical interpretations of nation-state formation have necessarily evolved in relation to the changing contemporary politics of nations and states, perhaps a historical debate informed by notions drawn from contemporary politics can also expand our consciousness about future perspectives. For some analysts, of course, the era of the nation-state is over; and this may well be the case for the particular practices and balances of power that have characterised national states in the past two hundred years. Yet, as any survey of the field of popular political history

---

mapuche en el marco de un Estado multinacional,' Ponencia presentada en el Foro: Estado y Pueblo Mapuche: Derecho Indígena, Territorio, Autonomía, Universidad Academia de Humanismo Cristiano, Santiago, Chile, junio 1999, URL: http://Linux.soc.uu.se/mapuche/mapuint/cayuqueo990623.html; Identidad Mapuche Lafkenche de la Provincia de Arauco, 'De la deuda histórica nacional al reconocimiento de nuestros derechos territoriales', Tirúa, VIII Región, Chile, mayo 1999, URL: http://Linux.soc.uu.se/mapuche/mapuint/lafken990600.html.

quickly demonstrates, the same cannot be said for the dreams and aspirations for community, solidarity and equality fostered by the revolutionary discourses of nation-state formation. Perhaps a deeper, historically informed discussion of this distinction — between exclusion and inclusion in the nation's imagined community, between the practice and the promise of a politics based on citizenship — can help us distinguish, in the twenty-first century, which pieces of political baggage it is still worthwhile to carry with us.

Was There Ever a Nation Worth Talking About? Debates on Peruvian Nation-State Formation in the Age of Shining Path and Beyond

More than anywhere else in Latin America, except Haiti, it was in the Andes that the painful contradiction between nationalism's inclusionary promise and exclusionary practice earliest became clear. Between the 1780s Andean Civil War and the Pumacahua rebellion in Cuzco (1813–15) indigenous peoples and their leaders in what is today southern Peru and Bolivia struggled to envisage and fashion a project for autonomy that began from Andean principles of social organisation. Sinclair Thomson and Charles Walker have recently demonstrated that this project, while not necessarily a republican one, was an internally varied and contentious attempt to fashion a multiethnic and autonomous polity that claimed an Inca (and broadly Andean) genealogy. Its repression by royalist forces brought to an end the only autonomous national project to have emerged in the Peruvian viceroyalty, ensuring that independence would ultimately be brought from outside and giving primacy, during the first postcolonial generation, to intense regional struggles between liberal and conservative creoles who nevertheless agreed to ignore the potential citizenship of the indigenous population.[17] A variety of regional identities nevertheless emerged during these conflicts, identities that were formed in struggle with each other over national power and over projects for political and economic consolidation.

---

[17]   Sinclair Thomson, 'Colonial Crisis, Community, and Andean Self-Rule: Aymara Politics in the Age of Insurgence', PhD. Dissertation, University of Wisconsin-Madison, 1996; *Colonial Latin American History Review*, vol. 8, no. 2 (1999), thematic section on 'Insurgent Peasant Politics and Colonial Crisis in the Bolivian Andes during the Late Eighteenth Century' (with articles by Sergio Serulnikov and Sinclair Thomson, introduction by Brooke Larson and comments by Christine Hunefeldt), pp. 241–306; Charles F. Walker, *Smoldering Ashes: Cuzco and the Creation of Republican Peru, 1780–1840* (Durham, NC, 1999). For an early treatment of the Túpac Amaru movement as an Andean 'bourgeois-nationalist' revolution, see René Zavaleta Mercado, *Lo nacional-popular en Bolivia* (Mexico City, 1986). For an introduction to an extremely rich Bolivian literature dealing with issues of indigenous nationalism, and a broader historiographical reflection on its evolution in the context of recent events, see Brooke Larson, 'Cochabamba: (Re)constructing a History', new chapter in *Cochabamba, 1550–1900: Colonialism and Agrarian Transformation in Bolivia*, expanded ed. (Durham, NC, 1998), pp. 322–90.

If in the first half of the nineteenth century the main confrontation was between an 'upstart' Lima elite with foreign connections and a free-trade, reformist agenda, and a Cuzco-based conservatism that hearkened back to colonial organisations of space and the privileging of trade routes with Upper Peru, by the second half of the century Lima seemed to become the colonial retrograde, conquered first by the 'white' republicanism of Arequipa, then by the bourgeoisie-in-formation from the northern coast.[18]

At the same time, as both Walker and Mark Thurner have shown, Peruvian indigenous peasants creatively engaged emerging postcolonial institutions, using the courts where possible to limit exactions, expropriations, and exploitation, and redefining republican discourse to fashion, in Thurner's analysis, 'a subaltern form of Indian citizenship wrapped up in the hybrid notion of *republicano*'.[19] Still, the military defeat of an earlier autonomous vision, when combined with the post-Pumacahua abolition of many Andean *kurakazgos*, led as well to a crisis of political leadership and mediation within the communities, which across the nineteenth century would be partially resolved only with the rise of a peasant leadership more dependent on the state, the *alcaldes de vara* or *alcaldes pedáneos*. At least for Cuzco, as Walker demonstrates, political repression and isolation was reproduced in the insignificant participation of indigenous peasants in the many *montoneras* that roamed the countryside, fighting in the endemic civil wars through which regional elites sought to establish their claims on, and help construct, national power. Only with the War of the Pacific and the crisis of the Chilean occupation (1881–84) would opportunities open up for indigenous and village *montoneras* to participate in defending and redefining the nation

The repression of those indigenous movements, both in the central highlands and in Huaraz — as well as their engagement with national leaders and expectations of rewards and equal treatment — have now been well documented. The long-term political and intellectual consequences of this repression, however, are only beginning to be understood. The military defeat, territorial fragmentation, financial collapse, and civil war associated with the War of the Pacific were, from the perspective of intellectuals and politicians, ample signs of

---

[18]   Sarah Chambers, *From Subjects to Citizens: Honor, Gender, and Politics in Arequipa, Peru, 1780–1854* (University Park, PE, 1999); Michael Gonzales, *Plantation Agriculture and Social Control in Northern Peru, 1875–1933* (Austin, 1985); Heraclio Bonilla, *Guano y burguesía*; Paul Gootenberg, 'North–South', in Joseph Love and Nils Jacobsen (eds.), *Guiding the Invisible Hand: Economic Liberalism and the State in Latin American History* (New York, 1988), pp. 63–97; and *Between Silver and Guano: Commercial Policy and the State in Postindependence Peru* (Princeton, 1989).

[19]   Mark Thurner, *From Two Republics to One Divided: Contradictions of Postcolonial Nationmaking in Andean Peru* (Durham, NC, 1997), p. 35. For Indian use of the courts, see also Walker, *Smoldering Ashes*, especially pp. 71–83.

the lack of a Peruvian nation.[20] But as Thurner has recently argued, '[c]reole intellectuals would increasingly blame the unresolved "Indian problem" for Peru's woes, arguing that the Andean masses were insufficiently integrated into the life of the nation'. By recasting a problem of race and class repression as a lack of indigenous modernity, Thurner concludes, creole elites essentially buried their own practices of racist exclusion in a lament about the 'prepolitical' or 'prehistorical' Indian. In so doing Peruvian intellectuals helped reconstruct a colonial dualism that would, across the twentieth century, indelibly mark intellectual and political debate. The starting point of this dualism, however, was false: Indians had never been prepolitical. Indeed, '[t]he uplifting of the previously "degraded race" was championed so that "the Indian" might assume his rightful place in a national pantheon where he had already stood — only to be thrown out'.[21]

The dualism between Indian and white, between highlands and coast, became the Peruvian palimpsest on which most twentieth-century Peruvian intellectuals, no matter what their political position or goal, were forced to write. Beginning with Manuel González Prada, the Lima anarchists in the Asociación Pro-Indígena and the regionalist Cuzco *indigenistas*, and flowing through the Andean and communal utopianism of Luis Valcárcel and Hildebrando Castro Pozo into the original Peruvian socialism of José Carlos Mariátegui, a strand of radical thought in the first half of the twentieth century looked for inspiration in the deep traditions of Andean peasants and their collectively organised communities.[22] These communities and their inhabitants were, for these intellectuals, '*el Perú profundo*' into which any attempt at effective nationbuilding must, of necessity, delve. Opposed to this broad tradition of

---

[20] On highland movements in the War of the Pacific, their repression, and some of the long-term consequences for Peruvian nation-building, see Heraclio Bonilla, 'The War of the Pacific and the National and Colonial Problems in Peru', *Past and Present*, Nov. 1978, pp. 92–118, and 'The Indian Peasantry and "Peru" during the War with Chile', in Steve J. Stern, *Resistance, Rebellion and Consciousness in the Andean Peasant World, 18th to 20th Centuries* (Madison, 1987), pp. 219–31; Manrique, *Campesinado y nación, passim.*, and *Yawar Mayu*, pp. 17–79; Mallon, *The Defense of Community*, pp. 80–122, and *Peasant and Nation*, pp. 176–275, 310–30.

[21] Thurner, *From Two Republics to One Divided*, pp. 54–136. The discussion of intellectual consequences, as well as the direct quotations, occur on pp. 151–2.

[22] Representative works from this tradition include Hildebrando Castro Pozo, *Nuestra comunidad indígena*, 2nd ed. (Lima, 1979), orig. ed. 1924; Manuel González Prada, *Horas de lucha*, 2nd ed. (Callao, 1924), *Pájinas libres*, 2 vols. (Lima, 1966); *Nuevas páginas libres* (Santiago, 1937); José Carlos Mariátegui, *Siete ensayos de interpretación de la realidad peruana* (Lima, 1952), *Polémica del indigenismo*, prólogo y notas de Luis Alberto Sánchez (Lima, 1976); Luis Valcárcel, *Tempestad en los Andes* (Lima, 1972). Works that give important context to the period and the debates involved are Alberto Flores Galindo, *La agonía de Mariátegui: La polémica con la Komintern* (Lima, 1980); and Valcárcel, *Memorias*, edited by José Matos Mar, José Deustua and José Luis Rénique (Lima, 1981).

indigenista radicalism was a militant *hispanismo* which found a positive legacy for Peru only in Spanish, Catholic and colonial traditions. Influenced by events in Europe in the 1930s some of these authors embraced fascism as the best way to establish order and unity in Peru.[23] Emerging from the *arequipeño* tradition of 'white' republicanism, on the other hand, Víctor Andrés Belaúnde attempted to chart a middle course between *indigenismo* and right-wing *hispanismo*.[24] Despite the deep differences among these perspectives, however, they all shared the basic assumption of a dualistic Peru organised spatially and racially, from which followed a need to deal with indigenous 'backwardness'; they differed on how deep the backwardness went (and thus on whether the Indian was redeemable at all), and on what was the best solution to the problem (education, integration, agrarian reform, revolution).

In the second half of the twentieth century, responding both to a wave of Peruvian highland peasant mobilisations and land occupations and to the continent-wide reaction to the Cuban revolution, intellectuals once again debated the problem of the Peruvian nation, adding an almost utopian faith in armed struggle resuscitated by the Cuban revolution to the tense contest between class and ethnic principles of national integration already in play. In combination with the Sino-Soviet split that pushed most of the Peruvian left into the Maoist camp, the *foquismo* of the 1960s made armed struggle into a kind of mantra for Peruvian leftists, many of whom seemed to believe in this period that transcendence through violence might be the only way to solve the inherited and constructed dualisms of the past. A final ingredient in this explosive mix was the rise of a new generation of Marxist intellectuals who took their cue from the emerging literatures on proletarianisation and class formation to argue that Peru was in a process of transition to capitalism, during which proletarianisation would ultimately become the panacea for the problem of ethnic division. This new kind of integrationism sought to fold indigenous peasants and their communities (now seen as vestiges of conservatism, backwardness, and colonialism) back into the national mix by transforming them into rural proletarians who could be part of a revolutionary Marxist class alliance.[25]

---

[23] For a discussion of these trends, see Pike, *The Modern History of Peru*, pp. 184–281.

[24] Víctor Andrés Belaúnde, *Meditaciones peruanas* (Lima, 1932), *Peruanidad*, 3rd ed. (Lima, 1965); see also Chambers, *Subjects to Citizens*. It is interesting, in this context, to consider Fernando Belaúnde Terry's presidential campaign, and the founding of Acción Popular in the 1960s. The first candidate to campaign assiduously in the highlands and to talk about 'the conquest of Peru by Peruvians', Belaúnde Terry proposed a by-our-own-bootstraps form of development which was, in many ways, heir to the concepts of 'white republicanism' that had given Arequipa its specific regional character in contradistinction to 'colonial' Lima.

[25] For an illuminating summary of these years, and some suggestions for further reading, see Iván Hinojosa, 'On Poor Relations and the Nouveau Riche: Shining Path and the

The new perspective, while clearly drawing on already existing socialist traditions of class-first politics, also arose in counterpoint with an emergent academic dualism/ integrationism that gained influence in the 1960s. Led by social scientists associated with the newly formed Instituto de Estudios Peruanos, such as José Matos Mar, Julio Cotler, Fernando Fuenzalida, and others, this school of thought worked within a conceptual model dominated by functionalist and modernisation paradigms. Emphasising the separation between highlands and coast, Indian communities and political society, these scholars argued that only modernisation and mobilisation could ultimately break the anomie and isolation of the indigenous peasantry. Once again, however, the main issue for debate between modernisation and proletarianisation scholars was not the nature of indigenous political culture and its potential contribution to Peruvian nationalism, but rather the principle and method through which backward indigenous peasants would be integrated into a modern nation.[26] In such a context it is not surprising that one of the most intense confrontations on issues of modernisation and national integration in Peru during the 1960s should have occurred at the Instituto de Estudios Peruanos, at a round table called to discuss *indigenista* novelist José María Arguedas's 1964 novel *Todas las sangres*. French anthropologist Henri Favre and Peruvian sociologist Aníbal Quijano led an attack on the work that basically deemed it to be outdated and potentially dangerous, since it did not take into account the expansion of modernity and of class relations in the Peruvian countryside.[27] This was indeed an ironic turn of events, since Arguedas's works had, since his first novel *Yawar fiesta* (1940), explored Andean contributions to Peruvian modernity and development, suggesting that communal forms of organisation and politics might have much to contribute to a specifically Peruvian path to development. In the novel under attack, in fact,

---

Radical Peruvian Left', in Stern (ed.), *Shining and Other Paths*, pp. 60–83. For an interesting suggestion that the Peruvian Left's 'blindness' to racial and ethnic questions had a long history among critical intellectuals throughout the 20th century, see Marisol de la Cadena, 'From Race to Class: Insurgent Intellectuals *de provincia* in Peru, 1910–1970', in *ibid.*, pp. 22–59.

[26] José Matos Mar (comp.), *Hacienda, comunidad y campesinado en el Perú*, 2nd ed.[1st ed. 1970] (Lima, 1976); Julio Cotler, *Haciendas y comunidades tradicionales en un contexto de movilización política*, Estudios del Valle del Urubamba, 1 (Lima, 1968); José Matos Mar et al., *Perú problema; 5 ensayos* (Lima, 1968); José Matos Mar et al., *Dominación y cambios en el Perú rural: la micro-región del valle de Chancay* (Lima, 1969); Fernando Fuenzalida et al., *Estructuras tradicionales y economía de mercado; la comunidad de indígenas de Huayopampa* (Lima, 1968); Henri Favre, Claude Collin-Delavaud and José Matos Mar, *La hacienda en el Perú* (Lima, 1967); Robert G. Keith et al., *La hacienda, la comunidad y el campesino en el Perú* (Lima, 1970); Fernando Fuenzalida et al., *El indio y el poder en el Perú* (Lima, 1970).

[27] José María Arguedas et al., *¿He vivido en vano? Mesa redonda sobre* Todas las sangres (Lima, 1985).

Arguedas had developed a narrative tying indigenous land recuperation movements to an egalitarian nation that began from indigenous and socialist principles. These various elements were articulated together in the figure of indigenous
leader Rendón Willka, who is ultimately executed by a military detachment after
having convinced the owner of the hacienda on which he is an administrator to
distribute the land among the residents. Having witnessed the execution of a
mother and her son, both labourers on the estate, and about to be shot himself,
Willka gives a speech in Quechua that emphasises the power of indigenous
mobilisation — based on the connection between the natural world and a new
consciousness of the nation — and predicts that, no matter what the soldiers do,
they will not be able to 'kill the *patria*'. The officer has him shot anyway, of
course; but the scene ends with a millenarian prophecy of what is to come: 'The
officer had him killed. But he was left alone. And he, like the other soldiers, heard
a massive shaking underground, as if the mountains were beginning to walk.'[28]

Perhaps it was the class collaborationist tinge to the novel, in which a 'good'
hacendado collaborates with 'his' Indians to create an egalitarian production
cooperative. Perhaps it was the idea that *indios* talking in Quechuanised Spanish
could lead a socialist revolution. Or perhaps it was the echoes of old *indigenismo*,
similar to the utopianism of Arguedas's mentor Luis Valcárcel — the telluric
movement that starts underground to finally bring justice to the postponed
indigenous masses — that put the young socialist intellectuals off that night at
the Instituto de Estudios Peruanos. But for whatever reason, Arguedas's critics
were continuing to write upon the same dualist, postcolonial palimpsest fash-
ioned by creole intellectuals in the aftermath of the War of the Pacific.

Another historiographical trend in Peru during the 1970s was the dependency school. It shared with most other academic currents a lament about the lack of
a viable Peruvian nation, but sought the explanation not in the 'backwardness' of
highland culture per se (though neither was this truism attacked directly), but
instead in the inability of the Peruvian bourgeoisie to do its job by becoming a
viable capitalist class, building an internal market, and thus creating the conditions for a viable nation-state. While some authors concentrated on Peruvian
investors' excessive focus on international markets and speculative investments,
others suggested that, even when there was local capital investment and innovation, firms from the much more powerful and advanced industrial nations won
out in any direct competition. In short, Peru was unable to become a viable nation
because, having attempted to enter the world market late and under difficult conditions, Peruvian investors could not form a feasible bourgeoisie.[29]

---

[28] José María Arguedas, *Todas las sangres* (Buenos Aires, 1970), vol. II, p. 259.
Translations mine. See also *Yawar fiesta*, 2nd ed. (Buenos Aires, 1974).

[29] See, among many other authors, Yepes, *Perú 1820–1920*; Bonilla, *Guano y burguesía*;
Mallon, *Defense of Community*. For a critique of this literature, see Gootenberg,
Imagining Development.

Yet a more decentralised sensibility also emerged in the 1970s and 1980s, as committed social scientists engaged in a variety of regional research projects that reformulated the history of the highlands. Partly due to the new documentation available in the *Archivo del Fuero Agrario* after the Agrarian Reform, and partly due to the development of departmental archives in Ayacucho, Arequipa, Cajamarca, Cuzco, Puno, and elsewhere, new research began to reach across the dualisms of the past and ask new questions about economic innovation and complexity, political engagement, and state formation. Especially in the 1980s, scholars debated various interpretations of popular politics in relation to the state, and began to address these issues in comparative Andean perspective. Yet even as these new discussions were proceeding, contemporary violence and civil war demanded scholarly attention, generating deep and widespread pessimism.[30]

Increasingly, the story of Peru's failure as a nation, laced through as it is with myriad forms of racism, dualism, and violence, seemed the 'chronicle of a path foretold'.[31] As the violence of civil war peeled back the veneer of nationhood to expose an empty shell, there seemed to be an eerie inevitability to it all: individuals seemed little more than the pawns of social forces beyond their control, locked in rigid two-steps whose choreography had been decided centuries before. When I made the final revisions and wrote the conclusions to *Peasant and Nation* in 1994, I was heavily influenced by this vision, by the failure at mediation between indigenous and non-indigenous political cultures, the continuously reconstructed ethnic and spatial dualities between highlands and coast and the enduring marginalisation of indigenous rural peoples from the construction of national society. My impression was further deepened by my comparison of events in Mexico and Peru in the late 1980s for, as I wrote elsewhere in 1994, '[f]or [Cuauhtémoc] Cárdenas, the conflict is over what the hegemonic legacy really means. For Sendero, it is about the total bankruptcy of

---

[30] Among the new work one finds the following: Jean-Pierre Deler and Yves Saint-Geours (comps.), *Estados y naciones en los Andes*, 2 vols. (Lima, 1986); Heraclio Bonilla (comp.), *Los Andes en la encrucijada: indios, comunidades y estado en el siglo XIX* (Quito, 1991); José Deustua and José Luis Rénique, *Intelectuales, indigenismo y descentralismo en el Perú, 1897–1931* (Cusco, 1984); José Luis Rénique, 'State and regional movements in the Peruvian highlands: the case of Cusco, 1895–1985,' PhD diss., Columbia University, 1988; Carlos Iván Degregori, Cecilia Blondet, and Nicolás Lynch, *Conquistadores de un nuevo mundo: de invasores a ciudadanos en San Martín de Porres* (Lima, 1986); and Luis Miguel Glave and María Isabel Remy, *Estructura agraria y vida rural en una región andina: Ollantaytambo entre los siglos XVI–XIX* (Cusco, 1983).

[31] The phrase is taken from the title of my article 'Chronicle of a Path Foretold? Velasco's Revolution, Vanguardia Revolucionaria, and "Shining Omens" in the Indigenous Communities of Andahuaylas,' in Stern, *Shining and Other Paths*, pp. 84–117; but is, of course, derived from Gabriel García Marquez's *Chronicle of a Death Foretold* (New York, 1983).

the Peruvian state'. And, I concluded, '[i]n Junín and Ayacucho, the struggles between Senderistas and the anti-Senderista village militias called *rondas* continue to reproduce the figure of the ever-vigilant guerrilla, eternally on the margins of a nonexistent nation.'[32] Yet as the dust began to clear in the second half of the 1990s, and even as the wounds of the civil war continued to bleed, a consciousness of small and incremental changes, many of them taking shape among the folds of terror, displacement, poverty, and civil war, began to encourage a renewal of alternative, more positive, perspectives.

For one thing, as Sendero and other parts of the Left battled with each other and with the military — in rural villages, urban neighbourhoods and provincial cities — for the hearts and minds of the Peruvian population, *senderista* practices of class-first integrationism, lack of understanding and respect for village culture and institutions, and the use of violence as a substitute for a realistic political programme, became a mirror in which other sectors of the Left began to recognise themselves. Events in the second half of the 1980s — the fall of the Berlin wall, the failure of the Sandinista revolution, and the 'Special Period' in Cuba — brought Sendero's astoundingly exaggerated Maoist discourse into clearer focus. Many non-*senderista* Peruvian leftists decided that the ends did not justify the means, and that a class-first project of egalitarian nationalism led neither to equality nor to greater national integration.[33] As deeper, more self-critical reflection became the order of the day, it became possible to reopen the lines of critical thinking that had begun to emerge in the 1980s, reemphasising the importance of ethnicity, and of Andean political culture and expression since the time of Túpac Amaru in the 1780s. Mirroring some of the most positive elements in earlier forms of *indigenismo*, especially in its utopian communitarianism and *mariateguista* strands, these intellectuals sought in Andean political culture the clues for how a Peruvian nation might be formed, governed not by European republicanism, but by indigenous visions of justice and autonomy.

The pioneer figure in this movement, who faced much controversy and misinterpretation before his premature death from brain cancer in 1990, was Alberto Flores Galindo. A historian who began his career studying workers and regional commercial circuits, Flores Galindo underwent a major shift in the 1980s. Political events in his homeland, as well as his experiences writing an intellectual biography of José Carlos Mariátegui, prompted a renewed interest in Andean politics and culture. His book *Buscando un inca*, which won the Casa

---

[32] Florencia E. Mallon, 'Reflections on the Ruins: Everyday Forms of State Formation in Nineteenth-Century Mexico', in Gilbert M. Joseph and Daniel Nugent, *Everyday Forms of State Formation: Revolution and the Negotiation of Rule in Modern Mexico* (Durham, NC, 1994), pp. 69–106; direct quotations on p. 106.

[33] Alberto Flores Galindo, *Tiempo de plagas* (Lima, 1988); Flores and Nelson Manrique, *Violencia y campesinado* (Lima, 1985).

de las Américas prize in 1986, was an exploration of the various forms of indige-
nously focused utopian aspirations that, across the Andes, had inspired people
of distinct ethnic backgrounds to imagine alternatives to existing systems of
rule. Beginning in the colonial period and following through to the present,
Flores traced the myriad forms taken by these dreams of a different order,
including even the dreams of idealistic, crazy creoles who at the beginning of
the nineteenthth century sought in Cuzco a descendent of the Incas they could
place on a new throne. In this context it is perhaps not surprising that, at the
time of his death, Flores was working on a biography of Arguedas.[34]

Where do things stand now? Single-factor or macro explanations (and solutions) for Peru's fragmentation — whether based on class, race, ethnicity or economics — have generally fallen into disrepute. Peruvian and foreign scholars
have rediscovered the agency and complexity of indigenous communities and
culture, and have begun to trace internal differences and historical changes.
Increasing focus has been placed on regional forms of politics and the differential relationships of regions to the Lima state. All of these developments are, to
my mind, extremely positive, for they help us move in the direction of proces-
sual and historicised explanations for the blocked Peruvian path to nationhood.
Yet there are also several ways in which recent trends have not moved us far
enough or might somehow double back into old conceptual cul-de-sacs.

One of the warning bells comes with the fact that, despite paying homage to
the importance, historical diversity, and dynamism of indigenous community
politics, few recent studies have really entered the world of the Andean communities in order to trace intra-community relations of power, social and economic
differentiation or gender hierarchy. Whether reading more familiar documents
against the grain — such as demographic and tributary evidence, government
correspondence or notarial records — or using more anthropologically based
methods such as ethnography or life histories, most recent studies of Andean
communities at best gained access to the level of local male elites.[35] Perhaps this
is inevitable, at least for research done in the 1980s when living in communities
for any length of time was dangerous, if not impossible. It may also be true in
periods of peace, simply because the nature of the documentary record makes it

---

[34] Alberto Flores Galindo, *Buscando un inca*, 3rd ed. (Lima, 1988). I hasten to add, however, that Arguedas's vision of Andean peasants participating in a socialist revolution also
found its way — in a deformed version — into *Sendero Luminoso*. Arguedas's Chilean-
born widow, Sybila Arrendondo, is today in the maximum security prison in Puno
accused of being a member of Shining Path. When I interviewed her about Arguedas in
1975, she emphasised to me that he had always insisted that the Andes were full of
Rendón Willkas.

[35] Examples of this would include: Thurner, *From Two Republics*; Walker, *Smoldering
Ashes*; Starn, *Nightwatch*; and David Nugent, *Modernity at the Edge of Empire: State,
Individual, and Nation in the Northern Peruvian Andes, 1885–1935* (Stanford, 1997).

difficult to get below the level of village elites, whether in court, notarial or government records. Even if we face an intractable problem in this regard, however — especially for time periods about which we can no longer get access to oral history — I think it is important to recognise the problem openly, because it has important conceptual implications.

Simply noting the importance and complexity of indigenous politics and resistance, or even getting beyond this to understand the relationship between communities and regional or national state actors, does not give us access to the full story. Moving beyond the dualistic Peruvian palimpsest also necessitates understanding internal communal debates about culture, ethnic identity, politics, justice, and national belonging, and somehow being able to discern how these changed over time in relation to other regions, social groups or state actors.[36] Unless we somehow gain access to this complexity, we are in danger of folding our rediscovery of indigenous political culture back into a new form of dualism, in which Andean society once again becomes undifferentiated and flat — even if now in a heroic sense — because its internal relations of ethnic and cultural power are not understood and traced historically. For now this remains mainly a programmatic statement, and we may even be in danger of losing access to twentieth-century oral history over the next generation; but it bears repeating that researching these forms of Peruvian cultural and political history should be a high priority for historians of nationalism.

Another important task that remains outstanding is a deeper exploration of the formation and transformation of the Peruvian state. Given the longstanding influence of both Marxist and dependency-based explanations of Peruvian history, the Peruvian state has often been seen as merely the enforcer of oligarchic rule. The fact that it took a military coup to usher in a reformist agenda also helps explain why most analysts have not made an internal analysis of state structures a priority, though at the same time the military revolution, by reorganising state institutions, did stimulate more research on the state itself.[37] Recent regional research has also helped fill in some of the blanks in our understanding of local power and state institutions, but we still need to do a great deal

---

[36] Recent debates on 'lo andino' have made clear that simply revindicating indigenous culture does not historicise it. Though superficial in its treatment of historiography, Orin Starn, 'Missing the Revolution: Anthropologists and the War in Peru', *Cultural Anthropology*, 6 (Feb. 1991), pp. 63–91, brings up many of these points.

[37] Cotler, *Clases, estado y nación*; Alfred C. Stepan, *The State and Society: Peru in Comparative Perspective* (Princeton, 1978); José María Caballero, *Agricultura, reforma agraria y pobreza campesina* (Lima, 1980), and the same author's 'From Belaunde to Belaunde: Peru's military experiment in third-roadism', Cambridge, Centre of Latin American Studies, University of Cambridge, Working Paper No. 36, 1981; and Cynthia McClintock and Abraham F. Lowenthal (eds.), *The Peruvian Experiment Reconsidered* (Princeton, 1983).

more work articulating regions to the Lima state.[38] I believe this is an important agenda for future, not because the Lima state has been successful at constructing the nation, but because the coalitions that have vied for state power have been formed, in capillary fashion, through interactions between Lima and other regions, among distinct regional elites, and between regional elites and sectors of the popular classes. Comprehending the failures (and occasional successes) of broader coalitions in constructing the nation must of necessity begin from an understanding of these capillary political negotiations.

Finally, the understanding of regionalism in the process of nation-state formation remains a crucial and unfinished task. The need to comprehend the specifics of Andean communities, cultures and politics should not blind us to the fact that nation-state formation is also and everywhere a battle for predominance among regions — and their socioeconomic formations, interests, and political cultures — and for the privilege of having their particular form of identity become the 'national' one. Seeing debates over national policy in regional terms can also help us understand what might otherwise seem inexplicable decisions. One example of this might be the puzzling inability of the development-oriented nineteenth-century intellectuals recently analysed by Paul Gootenberg to convince a politically significant faction that their projects were advisable or necessary. Beyond the economic circumstances of boom and bust that Gootenberg suggests made economic innovation difficult, there were also political costs to the 'guided diversification, Andean social integration, and import substitution' that served as this group's guiding principles. Indeed, it is more than likely that instituting such a policy agenda would have substantially transformed the balance of power between Lima and north coast elites — just in the process of establishing dominance over the state — and regional elites in Arequipa, Cuzco, and the northern and central highlands. Only further research will clarify the potential political dynamics that could have underlain the free-trade disasters associated in Peruvian history with the guano boom and War of the Pacific.[39]

An agenda for future research on Peruvian nation-state formation would include, I suggest: a historically nuanced and internal analysis of indigenous community politics and culture; a detailed, deconstructed and historically dynamic inquiry into the formation and transformation of state structures; and

---

[38] Nugent, *Modernity at the Edge of Empire*; Michael F. Brown and Eduardo Fernández, *War of the Shadows: The Struggle for Utopia in the Peruvian Amazon* (Berkeley, 1991).

[39] Gootenberg, *Imagining Development*. Direct quotation from p. 206; reflections on why there was such a difference between existing ideas and policy occur mainly on pp. 203–10. When discussing this same issue at the conference at the Institute of Latin American Studies, University of London, from which this volume has emerged, Gootenberg also suggested that the very lack of a clear and organic policy connection gave some Peruvian thinkers a greater freedom to imagine, a freedom to think utopically.

a careful consideration of regionalism and the construction of regional identities, in relation to the state and to the formation of regional elites. A tall order, indeed. Perhaps this means that we must look toward more collaborative projects, in which several scholars take on together the challenge of investigating the formation of a particular nation-state. It certainly means that we must bring the study of nation-states down to the regional level, though also never forget to tie it back up to the national level. It also means that, in post-*senderista* Peru, combining innovative academic research and analysis with contemporary political sensibilities and commitments will remain an enduring challenge.

Who Owns *El México Profundo*? The Reindianisation of Debates on the Mexican Nation-State

The established interpretation of Mexican Independence focuses on events in the Bajío and other parts of the central plateau, where multi-ethnic coalitions of villagers, urban plebeians, provincial merchants and other mediators, and more radically separatist creoles initially all followed the leadership of two parish priests, Miguel Hidalgo y Costilla and José María Morelos. After nearly a decade of civil war and royalist counterinsurgency, tired insurgents agreed to a pact with conservative creoles that brought the country to independence; but the truncated nature of the process ultimately assured a period of instability, economic depression, and civil war that would not end until the consolidation of liberalism between 1855 and 1867. In this interpretation, the project for Mexican national autonomy emerged in central Mexico from a coalition of Enlightenment-influenced intermediate elites and a multi-ethnic plebe. This project was essentially a form of radical republicanism that, even if it contained a variety of ethnic and racial elements, was governed by European principles and ideas. The peripheral regions of the country to the south, north, and west, coincidentally as well the areas of greatest indigenous population, were not protagonists in the process and would remain outside the confines of Mexican nationalism for much of the nineteenth century.[40]

Recent work has begun to revise this interpretation in a variety of ways. From David Brading's encyclopaedic analysis of creole nationalism, which has refocused attention on elite literary and intellectual contributions to national thought, to studies that have examined the complex political dynamics of Independence in peripheral regions previously pronounced unchanged, new research has begun to explore the multiple layers of conflict that existed in

---

[40] The classic synthesis of this position remains John Lynch, *The Spanish American Revolutions, 1808–1826* (New York, 1973), ch. 9. See also Hugh M. Hamill, Jr., *The Hidalgo Revolt: Prelude to Mexican Independence* (Gainesville, 1966); Wilbert H. Timmons, *Morelos: Priest, Soldier, Statesman of Mexico* (El Paso, 1963); Brian R. Hamnett, 'Royalist Counterinsurgency and the Continuity of Rebellion: Guanajuato and Michoacán, 1813–1820', *Hispanic American Historical Review*, vol. 62, no. 1 (February 1982), pp. 19–48.

Mexico over the project for, and meaning of, national autonomy. This has been true even for parts of central Mexico, such as Chalco, where John Tutino has recently uncovered a return to self-sufficient prosperity and a flattening out of gender hierarchy among hacienda peons in the post-Independence period, suggesting that the economic crisis and instability recorded in the national documentation might not have held true at the local level, within families and small communities that fell outside the gaze of macro-level statistics.[41]

Perhaps the richest revision of early nineteenth-century nation-state formation in Mexico has come from the regions that were not central protagonists in the established Independence narrative. In-depth research in the municipalities of Yucatán and Guerrero, by Terry Rugeley and Peter Guardino, has suggested that indigenous peasants engaged the political challenges of municipal reform with great creativity, searching for the best way to participate in broader political processes, limit state exactions, and advance their own projects of local autonomy and federalism. Though not focused on a specific subregion, the work of Antonio Annino, too, has suggested that the new municipal governments created by the 1812 Spanish Constitution, concentrated as they were in the indigenous areas of the country, presented local groups with 'new opportunities for social and political advancement'. In such a context, he goes on to suggest, the civil wars of the first half of the nineteenth century were not simply examples of instability, but had an internal logic and received legitimation from 'local practices of justice that were themselves articulated to the idea of popular sovereignty as embodied in the *ayuntamientos*'.[42] Guardino, for his part, has demonstrated how local village federalisms fed into and gave strength to Juan Alvarez's regional *cacicazgo*, ultimately flowing into the 1855 Liberal Revolution.[43] And Rugeley has argued that the Yucatecan Caste War can best be understood as a series of local political conflicts in which the ups and downs of newly created municipalities — most importantly of perceived promises of lower state and

---

[41] John Tutino, 'The Revolution in Mexican Independence: Insurgency and the Renegotiation of Property, Production, and Patriarchy in the Bajío, 1800–1855', *Hispanic American Historical Review*, vol. 78, no. 3 (August 1998), pp. 367–418. See also David A. Brading, *The First America: The Spanish Monarchy, Creole patriots, and the Liberal state, 1492–1867* (New York, 1991); Peter F. Guardino, *Peasants, Politics, and the Formation of Mexico's National State: Guerrero, 1800–1857* (Stanford, 1996); and Terry Rugeley, *Yucatán's Maya Peasantry and the Origins of the Caste War* (Austin, 1996).

[42] Antonio Annino, 'Soberanías en lucha', in Antonio Annino, Luis Castro Leiva, and François-Xavier Guerra, *De los imperios a las naciones: Iberoamérica* (Zaragoza, 1994), pp. 225–53, quotations on pp. 247 and 253, respectively; translation mine. See also Alicia Hernández Chávez, *La tradición republicana del buen gobierno* (Mexico City, 1993); and Marcello Carmagnani (coord.), *Federalismos latinoamericanos: México, Brasil, Argentina* (Mexico City, 1993).

[43] Guardino, *Peasants*.

Church exactions and greater egalitarianism — came into conflict with the ethnic politics of traditional Maya *batabs*.[44]

Perhaps the most revisionist vision of this period has been coming from the pen of Eric Van Young. Combining Brading's vision of creole patriotism with an Andean-influenced understanding of peasant localism laced with millenarianism, Van Young has radically challenged the traditional interpretation of Mexican Independence at the centre. Counter to existing interpretations that saw a multi-ethnic national movement governed by European republican principles, Van Young posits two parallel movements: one made up of creole patriots who envisioned a broader nation based on European principles; and the other a village revolt that was extremely radical at its base, at times even reaching the point of creating a form of village soviet, but that could only conceptualise something broader if it was of a millenarian character. Van Young argues that the two were connected only occasionally, and in a manipulative fashion, by provincial strongmen and bandits who could mediate with the villages but had almost no political agenda of their own.[45]

What we find for the Independence period more generally, then, is that as researchers have begun to deconstruct and open up the established version of events, interpretations have scattered in a variety of directions. All authors would agree only on the fact that, when researching the period closer to the ground, relationships look a great deal more complex than broader narratives could allow. That said, Tutino emphasises the post-Independence changes and victories for equality that occurred outside the gaze of official figures or historiography, while Annino traces the egalitarian opportunities offered by the Spanish Liberal Constitution. Rugeley and Guardino both downplay ethnic factors in their studies of local politics, while emphasising the capacity of indigenous peasants to participate in broader struggles that helped make the nation-state. Van Young does precisely the opposite, downplaying the capacity of indigenous peasants and villages to participate in broader national struggles except under the rubric of millenarian ideologies.

As the texts already cited make clear, debates about the nature of Independence have evolved, in Mexican historiography, parallel to a broader trend of rethinking that has also affected the later 1855–1940 period. For the period of the liberal revolution, Guy Thomson's and my work on the Sierra Norte de Puebla, as well as my work on Morelos, has explored local forms of communitarian liberalism through which Nahua peasants and villages sought to

---

[44]   Rugeley, *Yucatán's Maya Peasantry*, has taken on existing historiography on the caste war, but also Nancy Farriss's view of continuity within Maya culture: *Maya Society under Colonial Rule: The Collective Enterprise of Survival* (Princeton, 1984).

[45]   Eric Van Young, *The Other Rebellion: Popular Violence and Ideology in Mexico, 1810–1821* (Stanford, 2001).

understand and participate in the nationalist struggles of the time.[46] For the *Porfiriato*, Gilbert Joseph on the Yucatán, Ana María Alonso and Daniel Nugent on Chihuahua, and Patrick McNamara on Oaxaca, have all explored the myriad understandings of political community, national identity, and political legitimacy that emerged across the last several decades of the nineteenth century, and whose crises brought the country to revolution after 1910.[47] And for the first half of the twentieth century, the works of Marjorie Becker, Alan Knight, Gilbert Joseph and Daniel Nugent and Mary Kay Vaughan have all rethought the relationships among state actors and structures, political elites, and popular movements in the process and outcome of the Mexican Revolution.[48]

These rethinkings and emerging debates about the role of popular and indigenous cultures and politics in Mexican nation-state formation began with the first dramatic crisis of the Mexican postrevolutionary state, commonly thought to have occurred as a result of the 1968 student movement and the October massacre at Tlatelolco. Along with the slowing down of economic growth that would become deep crisis in the early 1980s, the political crisis beginning with Tlatelolco signalled the emptiness of the revolutionary promises or legacy upon which the postrevolutionary state rested its legitimacy. Across the 1970s and early 1980s urban squatter movements, independent peasant and worker unions, and revitalised indigenous movements, only brought the crisis into sharper relief, and it all entered free-fall after 1982 with the end of the oil boom. Add to this the Mexico City earthquake of 1985 and the 1988 election campaign of Cuauhtémoc Cárdenas, and the solid veneer of the postrevolutionary Mexican state seemed to peel away.

---

[46] Mallon, *Peasant and Nation*, chs. 1–5, 8–10; Guy P.C. Thomson, 'Agrarian Conflict in the Municipality of Cuetzalán (Sierra de Puebla): The Rise and Fall of 'Pala' Agustín Dieguillo, 1861–1894', *Hispanic American Historical Review*, 71 (1991), pp. 205–58; 'Popular Aspects of Liberalism in Mexico, 1848–1888', *Bulletin of Latin American Research*, 10 (1991), pp. 121–52; and with David G. LaFrance, *Patriotism, Politics, and Popular Liberalism in Nineteenth-Century Mexico: Juan Francisco Lucas and the Puebla Sierra* (Wilmington, DE, 1999).

[47] Allen Wells and Gilbert M. Joseph, *Summer of Discontent, Seasons of Upheaval: Elite Politics and Rural Insurgency in Yucatán* (Stanford, 1996); Ana María Alonso, *Thread of Blood: Colonialism, Revolution, and Gender on Mexico's Northern Frontier* (Tucson, 1995); Daniel Nugent and Ana María Alonso, 'Multiple Selective Traditions in Agrarian Reform and Agrarian Struggle: Popular Culture and State Formation in the *Ejido* of Namiquipa', in Gilbert M. Joseph and Daniel Nugent (eds.), *Everyday Forms of State Formation: Revolution and the Negotiation of Rule in Modern Mexico* (Durham, NC, 1994), pp. 209–46.

[48] Marjorie Becker, *Setting the Virgin on Fire: Lázaro Cárdenas, Michoacán Peasants, and the Redemption of the Mexican Revoluion* (Berkeley, 1995); Knight, *The Mexican Revolution*; Joseph and Nugent, *Everyday Forms of State Formation*; and Mary Kay Vaughan, *Cultural Politics in Revolution: Teachers, Peasants, and Schools in Mexico, 1930–1940* (Tucson, 1997).

Historians reacted to these events in two successive stages. Reactions to the crisis of Tlatelolco resulted in an emphasis on the authoritarianism of the Mexican state. Researchers sought explanations for this authoritarianism in the top-down *caciquismo* of the 1910 Revolution, the quick and thorough repression of the revolution's popular factions, and the rapid consolidation of a centralised and top-down postrevolutionary order. By the late 1970s and into the 1980s, however, the discovery of intellectual dead ends to *caciquismo* combined with the emergence of new grassroots movements to suggest the need for an alternative perspective, a way to 'bring the state back in without leaving the people out'.[49] The works of historians like Guardino, Joseph, Vaughan and myself, as well as by anthropologists Alonso and Nugent, have been at the centre of these efforts.

As in Peru, recent trends in Mexicanist historiography have been marked by efforts to write political history from the bottom and from the margins, but without leaving out the top or the centre. What this has meant in Mexico, however, given the distinct national histories and historiographies with which we are working, has been quite different. Whereas in Peru mainstream historians and their critics shared a dualistic view of Peruvian society and a common narrative of the failure of the Peruvian nation to integrate indigenous peoples, in Mexico the 1910 Revolution and postrevolutionary state had generated a mainstream history that emphasised popular contributions to nation-state formation and the integration of all into a common project that privileged *mestizaje* and national development. Indigenous peoples, in this narrative, were peripheral and backward groups who needed education and *indigenista* development to bring them into modern society. In Mexico, mainstream historians and their critics shared a common narrative of the essential success of the Mexican nation and of its postrevolutionary state, as well as the importance of popular contributions to this project. The alternative story, then, became an exploration of the authoritarian underpinnings of the postrevolutionary project, and in some cases a revindication of conservative and anti-state peasant movements, even a heroic rendition of indigenous or peasant isolationisms.[50]

The more that historians emphasised state authoritarianism and peasant resistance to state projects, the harder it became to make peace with the original interpretations of the revolution as a popular and agrarian struggle. Some historians emphasised manipulations at the top, pronouncing the conflict a bourgeois revolution. Others denied the existence of a revolution altogether, seeing it instead as a series of local conflicts that broke out at the same time or, in the words of one historian, as a 'great rebellion'. Most revisionists looked to the treachery of revo-

---

[49] Gilbert M. Joseph and Daniel Nugent, 'Popular Culture and State Formation in Revolutionary Mexico', in Joseph and Nugent, *Everyday Forms*, pp. 3–23, direct citation on p. 12.

[50] The pioneering work in this regard was Meyer, *Problemas campesinos y revueltas agrarias*, and *La Cristiada*, 3 vols. (Mexico City, 1974).

lutionary elites and to the selling out of the popular agenda, to the point that John Womack, the eminent historian of the most important of all popular leaders, was prompted to write in 1986 that the issues of 1910 were 'therefore no longer so much social revolution as political management,' because what really mattered was the 'defeat and subordination' of popular movements. Despite some neopopulist rethinking, agrarian struggles and their relationship to state formation increasingly became narrated as stories of defeat and isolation, rather than contribution to state formation. The popular revolutionary agenda, manipulated by emerging power elites to buttress their domination, was bent almost beyond recognition. Under these conditions, what could possibly be gained excavating the layers of popular participation or agrarian aspirations? Defeat meant defeat.[51]

With the tarnishing of the popular agrarian revolution, the crisis of the 1980s and emerging indigenous revivalism prompted an attempt to 'reindianise' Mexican politics, in the sense of remaking a pluralistic Mexican nation that did not relegate indigenous peoples to the periphery. In the hands of anthropologist Guillermo Bonfil Batalla, this attempt took on the quality of an alternative national project that went against the grain of the dominant liberal vision. Especially as the project of state-directed development entered crisis, Bonfil argued, and decisions were made ever more clearly at the international and global levels, the cultural diversity and pluralism of indigenous peoples emerged as 'a real alternative for the design of the new national projects our countries are demanding. Perhaps [they are] the only possible alternative.' The problem, however, according to Bonfil, was that previous history weighed Latin Americans down. Dominant approaches were both colonising — in the sense that they considered ethnic and racial difference to be a 'stigma' equal to underdevelopment — and colonised, in the sense that they attempted to install imaginary, imported models of nationalism that did not connect to reality. The result had been, he insisted, 'a senseless attempt to eliminate the "other" as a precondition for becoming ourselves, without understanding that this "other" was, in the end, an irrevocable part of that "us" that defined who we were.'[52]

But who, in fact, is this 'other'? Does it include the mestizo peasants who followed Emiliano Zapata as well as indigenous groups along Mexico's geographical periphery? If so, how are these different 'others' connected to each other historically? This question has yet to be explored in a satisfactory fashion. In part

---

[51] For the bourgeois revolution interpretation, see especially Héctor Aguilar Camín, *La frontera nómada: Sonora y la Revolución mexicana* (Mexico City, 1977) and John Womack, Jr., 'The Mexican Economy during the Revolution, 1910–1920: Historiography and Analysis', *Marxist Perspectives*, vol. 1, no. 4 (1978). The 'great rebellion' phrase comes from Ramón Eduardo Ruiz, *The Great Rebellion: Mexico, 1905–1924* (New York, 1980). The direct quotations come from Womack, 'The Mexican Revolution, 1910–1920', in Leslie Bethell (ed.), *The Cambridge History of Latin America*, vol. 5 (New York, 1986), p. 82.

[52] Guillermo Bonfil Batalla, *Identidad y pluralismo cultural en América Latina* (Buenos Aires and San Juan, PR, 1992), quotations on p. 20; translation mine.

inspired by Bonfil, a group of historians met in Mexico City in December 1993 to discuss comparatively the relationship of indigenous peoples to nation-states in different parts of Latin America. Their focus was dramatically vindicated only a few weeks later by the beginning of the Chiapas uprising, and by the time the conference volume was published its editors were able to justify the historian's gaze on the survival of indigenous forms of culture and community, and on the ways in which indigenous people had colonised or used liberal institutions in order to promote their own distinct interests by quoting the EZLN's pronouncement, 'never again a Mexico that excludes us'. What the volume did not address, however, was the fact that historians and the present-day EZLN coexisted uneasily with the more 'official' versions of the Zapatista legacy.[53]

The very success of Mexican nation-state formation has, I believe, deeply conditioned the terms of the historical debate, generating some unique strengths as well as blind spots or potential pitfalls that stand out in greater relief when compared with other parts of Latin America. An important strength has been a sophisticated literature on the nature of the Mexican state, and its evolution over time. This has included important work on the nature of local and regional mediation, as well as consistent dialogues with state theory. Particularly in the literature on the Mexican Revolution, Mexicanist historians have shown a deep understanding of regionalism, and of how distinct regional factions have battled to control and reconstruct national power.[54] At the same time, however, moving beyond the shadow of the 'official history' can be hard, and this is most evident in the recent literature on indigenous and popular contributions to nineteenth-century national politics.

---

[53] The results of that meeting were published in Leticia Reina (coord.), *La reindianización de América, siglo XIX* (Mexico City, 1997). For a discussion of the various discourses of *zapatismo* and their internal contradictions, see Florencia E. Mallon, 'Local Intellectuals, Regional Mythologies, and the Mexican State, 1850–1994: The Many Faces of Zapatismo', *Polygraph 10* (1998), pp. 39–78.

[54] On local and regional mediation see, among many works, Gilbert M. Joseph, *Revolution From Without: Yucatán, Mexico and the United States, 1880–1924*, 2nd ed. (Durham, NC, 1988); Thomas Benjamin and Mark Wasserman (eds.), *Provinces of the Revolution: Essays on Regional Mexican History, 1910–1929* (Albuquerque, 1990); Friedrich Katz (ed.), *Riot, Rebellion, and Revolution: Rural Social Conflict in Mexico* (Princeton, 1988); Wil Pansters and Arij Ouweneel (eds.), *Region, State and Capitalism in Mexico: Nineteenth and Twentieth Centuries* (Amsterdam, 1989); Eric Van Young (ed.), *Mexico's Regions: Comparative History and Development* (San Diego, 1992); John Womack, Jr., *Zapata and the Mexican Revolution* (New York, 1968); and Friedrich Katz, *Biography of Pancho Villa* (Stanford, 1998). For dialogues with state theory, see especially Nora Hamilton, *The Limits of State Autonomy: Post-Revolutionary Mexico* (Princeton, 1982); Davis, *Urban Leviathan*; Peter H. Smith, *Labyrinths of Power: Political Recruitment in Twentieth-Century Mexico* (Princeton, 1979); Arnaldo Córdova, *La política de masas del cardenismo* (Mexico City, 1974), *La revolución y el estado en México* (Mexico City, 1989); Ilene V. O'Malley, *The Myth of the Revolution: Hero Cults and the Institutionalization of the Mexican State, 1920–1940* (Westport, CT, 1986); and Joseph and Nugent, *Everyday Forms*.

On the one hand, the success of Mexican nation-state formation encourages reconstructions of Eurocentric liberal narratives of the nation, where the presence of popular or indigenous actors is either ignored or not problematised. Among the best examples of this reconstruction can be found François-Xavier Guerra's recent essays on Independence, where he tends to use '*pueblo*' as a legal-constitutional category while ignoring the potential participation of popular groups. Viewing the process from Europe and from above, he also distinguishes between a 'modern' or 'French' concept of nation as a diverse, democratic community formed through the free will of citizens and a more 'traditional' or 'Romantic' concept based on an original community that shares a common language, history, and culture. In contrast to Europe, Guerra suggests, where the problem of the nineteenth century was how to form many diverse nationalities into only a few nation-states, 'the problem in Hispanic America was how to build, starting from the same 'nationality', different states first, and then distinct nation-states'.[55] Thus are hundreds of indigenous groups erased with one stroke of the pen. Is it any wonder that the reaction would be, as in the case of Eric Van Young, to reindianise militantly, from the centre, and to the very roots?

The potential pitfall of such a debate, however, is that the lines get drawn too neatly and too hard, between an autonomous indigenous space that has not interacted with state power, and a centralised, 'European' or 'modern' state that has evolved in isolation from what Bonfil would call 'el México profundo'. As in the case of Peru, an inability or unwillingness to trace the relationships between an internally diverse, contradictory, and power-laden indigenous world, and an equally diverse, power-laden, and internally contradictory national state, can lead us down the path of continuously reconstructed dualisms. As a result, we end up with a village peasantry that cannot see beyond its belltower, a Maya peasantry that plays the municipal political game of the *ayuntamientos* but loses all ethnic particularity and complexity, other indigenous groups whose interest is simply to be left alone, and an elite that inhabits a generic and well-articulated modernity.[56]

So where does that leave us in the case of Mexico? A crucial question still unanswered, even as historians and anthropologists build on the legacy of Guillermo Bonfil Batalla, is who owns 'el México profundo'. Is it, as Bonfil has argued, the property of an internally diverse and creative amalgam of popular groups, indigenous and mestizo, rural and urban, who have reconstructed a Mesoamerican culture different from 'imaginary Mexico'? Does 'el México pro-

---

55 The foregoing is a summary of essays found in François-Xavier Guerra, *Revoluciones hispánicas: independencias americanas y liberalismo español* (Madrid, 1995), especially 'Identidad y soberanía: una relación compleja', pp. 207–39; and *Modernidad e independencias: ensayos sobre las revoluciones hispánicas* (Madrid, 1992). Quotation is in the latter, p. 320, translation mine.

56 Van Young, *The Other Rebellion*; Rugeley, *Yucatán's Maya Peasantry*; Guerra, 'Identidad y soberanía', and *Modernidad e independencias*.

fundo' lie instead, as both Carlos Salinas de Gortari and the EZLN seemed to have agreed, in the popular agrarian aspirations of the Mexican Revolution best symbolised by Emiliano Zapata? Or has 'el México profundo' been constructed, village by village, piece by piece, region by region, in the daily struggles of centre and margins, Indian and creole, peasant and *jefe político*, to create and reproduce political culture and national belonging? If the latter, we have barely begun to excavate the first layer of the embedded struggles that, over the past two centuries, have made, remade, and unmade the Mexican nation-state.

Was There Ever a '*Chile Profundo*' Worth Talking About? Order, Stability and Amnesia in the History of the Chilean Nation-State

We have seen that in Peru the nation-state remained a series of preliminary sketches on an artist's drawing board, while in Mexico the 1910 Revolution generated an official history that celebrated and flattened out popular struggle as midwife for the birth of a modern nation-state. In Chile, by contrast, it seemed that the nation-state was born, full-grown, from the head of Diego Portales. In the late eighteenth and early nineteenth centuries, Chilean-born creoles interested in Independence sought an older identity and warrior tradition in the Mapuche indigenous people, or Araucanos, celebrated as the first Chileans to successfully resist Spanish colonialism.[57] But eight years of royalist resistance in the South (1818–26), and especially the three-year guerrilla war known as *la guerra a muerte* (1819–22) that was led by Vicente Benavides and involved a motley coalition of small merchants, muledrivers, peasants, and Mapuche people, transformed *La Araucanía* from the fountain of nationhood into a source of barbarism and instability.[58] There followed nearly a decade of federalist experiments, initiated by Intendant of Concepción Ramón Freire, who had been responsible for the repression of the *guerra a muerte*; but in April 1830 Freire's liberal-federalist army was decisively defeated at the Battle of Lircay, near Talca, and a conservative government took power with Portales as its *éminence grise*. In 1830 and beyond, then, especially with the promulgation of the 1833 Constitution, Chile embarked on a road of seemingly uninterrupted stability, centralisation, and economic growth that would, in nineteenth-century Latin America and in the judgement of many historians until the present day, stand out as the 'exceptional' case.

An influential line of interpretation, best summarised most recently in Simon Collier and William Sater's general history of Chile, narrated this 'excep-

---

[57] Stephen E. Lewis, 'Myth and the History of Chile's Araucanians', *Radical History Review*, 58 (1994), pp. 112–41.

[58] Among the works developing this perspective was Benjamín Vicuña Mackenna, *La guerra a muerte*, 1st ed. 1868, 3rd ed. (Buenos Aires, 1972), which, even though revindicating the importance of the popular sectors in history, saw them mainly as barbaric cannon fodder.

tionalism' as a lack of conflict. At the time of the conservative victory, according to Collier and Sater, 'Chile was a compact land', if measured from the Norte Chico (Copiapó) to the Bío-Bío River. Valdivia and points south, until only four years before still considered royalist strongholds, 'were unimportant appendages of the new republic'.[59] If measured within these boundaries, Chile's population was ethnically homogeneous. 'The small creole upper class coexisted with the great mass of the labouring poor, mostly mestizo and mostly rural. The rural poor remained a largely passive factor in society and politics until well into the twentieth century.' And neither was regional conflict or diversity important because, even if the southern city of Concepción was a crucial source of military power throughout the 1820s, by 1851 the next regional revolution was successfully defeated.[60] Within this broader picture of social stability, the intense political centralisation of the Portalian regime — with all regional officials appointed by the president, the liberal use of imprisonment and exile (*relegación*) against opponents, and the expansion of the national guard as a counterweight to the military and a tool in the regular manipulation of elections — assured the maintenance of political equilibrium. To this would be added, by mid-century, the Chilean military victory against the Peru-Bolivian Confederation (1837–39) and an agricultural boom prompted by the California Gold Rush. From such a perspective, and particularly if one also remembers the impressive integration, through marriage, of commercial, mining, and agricultural wealth within a compact Chilean elite, it is hardly surprising that the main theme in Chilean national historiography should have been the unfolding of a stable, almost pre-ordained, national order, an order that continued, with some important modifications, well into the twentieth century.[61]

For many the wake-up call came in September 1973. Alfredo Jocelyn-Holt has recently written that, if he learned anything from the Chilean revolutionary period of the 1960s that ended on 11 September, it was that '[u]nderneath or parallel

---

[59] Collier and Sater, *A History of Chile*, quotations on p. 51.

[60] *Ibid.*, p. 52.

[61] *Ibid.*, pp. 55–89. Other books that take a similar perspective, for both the nineteenth and twentieth centuries, include Leslie Bethell (ed.), *Chile since Independence* (Cambridge and New York, 1993); Pamela Constable and Arturo Valenzuela, *A Nation of Enemies: Chile under Pinochet* (New York, 1991), which sees the 1988 plebiscite and subsequent 1990 political transition as a return to the civility and order of the past. For influential studies of the economic integration of Chilean elites, see Bauer, *Chilean Rural Society*; and Maurice Zeitlin and Richard Earl Ratcliff, *Landlords and Capitalists: The Dominant Class of Chile* (Princeton, 1988). What is interesting about this perspective is that it has been shared by conservative and liberal historians, Marxists and non-Marxists. While different historians disagree on what the moments of crisis have been and what has caused them, the broad line of narrative about the construction and persistence of an orderly nation, governed by the evolving rules of democratic competition, has been shared.

to order, there has always coexisted a history of disorder that threatens to overflow the banks of what had been previously established'. For Jocelyn-Holt and many others, the rupture of 1973 forced a deep rethinking, a historiographical sea-change, precisely because it could not be understood without a dramatically revised understanding of what had gone before.[62] Thus the need to focus on what had previously been considered, to cite Thomas Kuhn, 'anomalies': the civil wars of the 1850s and 1891; the war against the Mapuche and the colonisation of the south; and the evolution of a parallel, subaltern culture across the nineteenth and twentieth centuries that, even when occasionally touching or interacting with the established system, remained different and relatively autonomous.[63]

The upshot of all this, according to Jocelyn-Holt, is a series of new questions that have yet to be answered. 'Can we talk,' he asks, 'of a history founded upon order as such, when antagonistic visions of freedom coexist but hardly ever reconcile with each other? Does order exist when deep and mutual suspicions crisscross the very heart of society?' Anyone who can contribute to an answer, Jocelyn-Holt asserts, will 'help unravel the tangle of yarn our recent history has become, thus allowing us to find the exit to the labyrinth in which we are still caught'.[64] A

---

[62] Alfredo Jocelyn-Holt Letelier, *El peso de la noche: nuestra frágil fortaleza histórica* (Santiago, 1997), especially pp. 189–92; quotation on p. 189; translation mine.

[63] Thomas Kuhn, *The Structure of Scientific Revolutions* (Chicago, 1962). The key works that began a process of discussion in all three of these subjects were, in order listed, Maurice Zeitlin, *The Civil Wars in Chile, or the bourgeois revolutions that never were*; José Bengoa, *Historia del pueblo mapuche (Siglo XIX y XX)* (Santiago, 1985); and Gabriel Salazar, *Labradores, peones y proletarios*. Other important works dealing with these topics include, for the civil wars and the Mapuche, Arturo Leiva, *El primer avance a la Araucanía: Angol, 1862* (Temuco, 1984); on the Mapuche in the second half of the 19th century, Jorge Pinto R. (ed), *Araucanía y Pampas: un mundo fronterizo en América del Sur* (Temuco, 1996), *Del discurso colonial al proindigenismo: ensayos de historia latinoamericana* (Temuco, 1996), *Modernización, inmigración y mundo indígena: Chile y la Araucanía en el siglo XIX* (Temuco, 1998); and for the complexity and dynamism of Chilean subaltern culture, Julio Pinto, 'La caldera del desierto. Los trabajadores del guano y los inicios de la cuestión social', *Proposiciones* 19 (1990), pp. 123–41, *Trabajos y rebeldías en la pampa salitrera* (Santiago, 1998); María Angélica Illanes, 'Entre-Muros: Una expresión de cultura autoritaria en Chile post-colonial', paper presented at the IV Encuentro de Historiadores, Santiago, Chile, April 1986; Contribuciones, Programa FLACSCO-Chile, no. 39, August 1986, 'Azote, salario y ley. Disciplinamiento de la mano de obra en la minería de Atacama (1817–1850)', *Proposiciones* 19 (1990), pp. 90–122; Salazar, *Labradores, peones y proletarios*, 'Ser niño "huacho" en la historia de Chile (Siglo XIX)', *Proposiciones* 19 (1990), pp. 55–83, and *Violencia política popular en 'las grandes alamedas': Santiago de Chile, 1917–1987* (Santiago, 1990). A recent work that takes this rethinking into the area of the history of memory and repression is Elizabeth Lira and Brian Loveman, *Las suaves cenizas del olvido: vía chilena de reconciliación política, 1814–1932* (Santiago, 1999).

[64] Jocelyn-Holt, *El peso de la noche*, p. 193.

variety of paths to the exit have been suggested by recent Chilean historiography, many of them internally contradictory; weighing them in relation to and in dialogue with each other can help us comprehend the limits of Chilean stability and order, while uncovering some of the forms of amnesia or selective remembering that have plagued interpretations of Chilean political life.

One area of recent and intense debate has been the importance of the state in the construction of the Chilean nation. Jocelyn-Holt has called into question the preponderance of the state in constructing national stability, arguing instead that the source of nineteenth-century stability in Chile was social continuity and the lack of social change. His metaphor here is a phrase attributed to Portales that also gives his book its title, '*el peso de la noche*', the weight of the night, which he takes to mean the weight of things as they are, 'the social submissiveness of the popular classes, the hierarchical and seigneurial order that truly presided over and governed the country'. By switching the arrow of causality so that society, and especially a well-established traditional oligarchy, calls the political shots, Jocelyn-Holt negates the state and its bureaucracy as autonomous historical actors, in the process calling into question not only an august literature on Chile but also recent studies that have traced the importance of Chilean state institutions in fashioning civil society. In this latter case his main target is Sol Serrano, Chilean historian of education and of the Church in the nineteenth century.[65] The problem with this line of argument, however, seems to be that the state itself as an institution gets flattened out, reduced to bureacratic officialdom or to a (non-Marxist) instrument of class domination. Recent work on the complex and multi-layered nature of state institutions and state power is ignored, and agency is once again granted only to a seemingly all-powerful aristocratic elite. The reproduction of this power, however, is explained only by the submissiveness of the lower classes and the lack of conflict within the elite. But what if neither group acted the way it was supposed to?

Another difference of opinion about the centrality of the state in nineteenth-century Chile involves two historians of la Araucanía who have studied the final military campaigns that, between 1860 and 1880, brought the Mapuche under state control. Arturo Leiva has argued that national security was the key motivating factor behind the original decision to retake Angol, founding the first military fort to the south of the Bío-Bío river. In 1859, he writes, after the last federalist, regionalist uprising in Concepción was repressed, some of the leaders of that

---

[65] *Ibid.*, especially pp. 23–9; quotation on p. 27. For the attack on Serrano, see pp. 59–60, note 24. Among the august historians he criticises as statist are Francisco Encina, Mario Góngora, Alberto Edwards and Gonzalo Vial. It is interesting to note that, while Sol Serrano seems to have networked more successfully with a school of French-based historians of Latin America who generally view the state as constructing the nation (see her chapter in Annino, Castro, and Guerra, *De los imperios a las naciones*), Jocelyn-Holt, trained in the USA and the UK, favours a perspective where society constructs the state.

rebellion escaped south across the Bío-Bío and hid out among friendly Mapuche allies. Several of the federalist leaders, including General José María de la Cruz and the Pradel brothers, made proposals to the president on the peaceful incorporation of Mapuche territory under mechanisms of regional autonomy and self-government. In the light of recent regionalist uprisings, Leiva suggests, and when faced with projects for regional autonomy connected to frontier territories not yet under national control, the viability of a centralised nation-state depended on bringing those territories under military control. Jorge Pinto, on the other hand, has advanced a more structural, economic explanation, seeing the political debates of the time as reflections of deeper forces. If, in the colonial period, the state was interested in people as labour, and found the Mapuche too recalcitrant to be a viable labour force in the context of limited mineral wealth, under the republic the interest changed to the lands rather than the people, because these could now be brought under national control, sold on the market, and incorporated into export production. It was this deeper economic transformation, and the reorganisation of Chilean productive forces in relation to the new capitalist world market, that defined the need to conquer the Mapuche.[66] Here we get caught in a familiar debate about the primacy of economic versus political causes. Certainly the changing nature of economic production made the fertile southern lands increasingly attractive; but did their economic attractiveness, in and of itself, define the form taken by conquest and its ultimate success or failure?

Existing analyses of Chilean stability, as well as discussions over what caused the conquest of the Mapuche, miss an important issue that needs rethinking in nineteenth-century Chilean history. Though most historians have dismissed regionalism, and the federalist agenda promoted by some regional groups through 1859, as either over-intellectualised liberal utopianism or an ill-fated attempt to emulate the United States that went against deep-seated Hispanic centralist traditions, it seems to me that a key story of state formation is buried in the layers of failed federalism between 1820 and 1860.[67] Simply the recurrence of rebellions in the south — from the royalist *guerra a muerte* in the early 1820s to the two federalist uprisings and civil wars of the 1850s — all of which built coalitions with the Mapuche, suggests a potentially very different project for national consolidation and state power. The fact that the project failed has been the reason for dismissing its importance. But what would have happened if Concepción's military, commercial and landowning elite had brokered a pacification agreement with the Mapuche that included a form of regional autonomy? How would the state have looked, by 1900, if it had been based on federalist power negotiations

---

[66]   Leiva, *El primer avance en la Araucanía*; Jorge Pinto R., 'Crisis económica y expansión territorial: la ocupación de la Araucanía en la segunda mitad del siglo XIX', *Revista de Estudios Sociales*, no. 72, Corporación de Promoción Universitaria (CPU) (Santiago, 1992), pp. 85–126. .

[67]   The first author to suggest this was Zeitlin, *The Civil Wars in Chile*.

with distinct mining, landowning and commercial power groups in the different regions? How would these regional elites have interpolated the popular classes in their bid to transform themselves into players at the national level? Addressing these questions would deepen our understanding, not only of the roads not taken by Chilean nation-state formation, but also of the roads that were.[68]

Perhaps the discussion that best frames present debates on the state in Chile occurred during the presentation of Gabriel Salazar's 1990 book on popular politics and violence in twentieth-century Santiago. According to Salazar, the root or primary source of change in modern Chilean history was not (as Pinto suggests) economic structures, nor (as many mainstream historians have assumed) the actions of the state, but the politics, actions, and culture of the lower classes. Sociologist Tomás Moulián, while celebrating Salazar's investigation of the ignored or invisible processes in Chilean society, criticised him for assuming that 'one has to study the lower classes because Chilean history resides in and is made by them, and only them'.[69] When Salazar substituted what he saw as an ahistorical state-centred approach to Chilean society with a historicised vision of popular knowledge and agency, Moulián argued, 'Salazar falls into a populist distortion based on a disputable thesis, to say the least, about the formation of social subjects: the people, the poor, are seen as a transcendental, preconstituted historical subject' whose effective presence in history has been blocked by a conspiracy of the dominant intellectual class. 'It is true,' Moulián admitted,

> that in this [Chilean] society, we overemphasise governability, stablity, and legality; in short, there is an obsession about social order as the product of the political. But this is not the result of an ideological conspiracy carried out by elites and their spokesmen, the official intellectuals, but instead the result of Chile's own historical development, with all its specificities and particularities. When we speak of the State and politics, we are taking stock of a crucial node [in how Chilean society has been constituted]; not the only one, but yes a very important one.[70]

Moulián's criticism here applies as well to other recent approaches that have opposed a state-centred explanation of historical change. By seeking the pivotal explanation for Chilean continuity and change outside the state, by privileging social or economic structures to the exclusion of political structures, authors have tended to reconstruct an instrumental vision of the state. To quote Moulián once again,

---

[68] A recent experiment in this direction is Esteban Valenzuela, *Alegato histórico regionalista* (Santiago, 1999).

[69] 'Debate en torno a *Violencia política popular en las "grandes alamedas"*, de Gabriel Salazar', *Proposiciones* 20 (1991), pp. 287–99, quotation on p. 289.

[70] *Ibid.*, p. 288.

At bottom, [such an approach] adopts the belief that the State is nothing more than a set of apparatuses and tools of power that exist only as instruments at the disposal of a single class. It cannot perceive the State as capable of producing symbols that can be internalised by a population. When a strong and stable State exists, it penetrates national culture and, of course, popular culture, so that to speak of culture means to speak of the State inasfar as it is a constitutitive force. [...] In Chile not only has the State existed, but also stateness, in the sense of the State's capacity to produce culture.

It is for this reason, Moulián concludes, that popular culture has been interlaced with and embedded in the state, resulting in a system of political negotiation that has mixed conflict with compromise.[71] And this can be extended outward to suggest that all social classes and groups have had a history of negotiation and conflict with the state, so that an approach that dismisses the importance of state power in Chilean history will tend to recreate false dualisms — between state and civil society, between economics and politics. This kind of approach will also miss clues about regional constructions of power, and the conflictual mingling of class, culture and region in evolving systems of rule. The challenge that Moulián leaves open is how to advance, theoretically and empirically, toward a historical vision of the state that can take these complex and changing articulations into account.

Beyond the role of the state, the other major challenge in understanding Chilean nation-formation is unpacking the role of the popular classes and of popular culture. In addition to Salazar's groundbreaking work in highlighting the lives, experiences and struggles of those the official historiography had dismissed as quiescent and unimportant, recent research on the northern nitrate region, the mining centres, Santiago workers and the Mapuche has begun to suggest that subaltern people have played a much more important political and cultural role in Chilean history than previously recognised. There is an understandable compensatory tendency in some of this literature that sees the subaltern world as autonomous and non-hierarchical, whether in the evolving nineteenth-century world of small rural entrepreneurs and village markets that provide solidarity and sociability in *ramadas* and *chinganas* or in the burgeoning mining centres where popular urban celebrations are increasingly repressed and regulated after 1850. Indeed, the tendency is to see interactions between popular groups and the state as repression only, rather than as an articulation in which each participates in the construction of the other, each ends up embedded in the other.[72]

---

[71] *Ibid.*, p. 289.

[72] Julio Pinto, 'La caldera del desierto'; María Angélica Illanes, 'Entre-Muros' and 'Azote, salario y ley'; Salazar, *Labradores, peones y proletarios*, and *Violencia política popular en 'las grandes alamedas'*. Some of Julio Pinto's most recent work, especially his article 'El balmacedismo como mito popular: los trabajadores de Tarapacá y la Guerra Civil de 1891', in Luis Ortega (ed.), *La Guerra Civil de 1891: cien años hoy* (Santiago, 1991), pp. 109–26, has moved away from this tendency by beginning to consider the contradictory relationship between state actors and the memory of the popular classes.

The final piece of this particular puzzle is the role of the Mapuche. On the one hand, the Mapuche constitute a part of subaltern Chile, of the popular classes about whose role in Chilean society there has been so much recent debate. But on the other hand, the Mapuche are also a colonised group, a subordinated and conquered people who have continued to resist extermination and, after 1978, reconstituted an ethnic movement that wrested the first legal recognition of indigenous peoples from the first post-dictatorship government. Perhaps not surprisingly, given that the general tendency to minimise the importance of the marginal in Chilean historiography only increases in the case of a colonised 'other', a common way to think about the Mapuche in Chile is to deny that they presently exist. There has also been a literature more recently that has understood the frontier as a society of relatively peaceful exchange and commerce punctuated by occasional raids and uprisings, which benefited both Mapuche and non-Mapuche. Across the nineteenth century, this interpretation goes, this frontier was brought under military and political control without dramatic violence and with little loss of life.[73]

Politically and socially committed historians and anthropologists, however, both Mapuche and non-Mapuche, have narrated a different story, one of expropriation, hunger, and loss of life in the last military campaigns that gave way to poverty, expropriation, and resistance after 1883, but a story that ended in survival, ethnic resurgence, and the recovery of Mapuche cultural values that are important to Chile as a whole. José Bengoa, arguably the most influential historian of Mapuche society, took advantage of the opportunity presented by the Quincentenary to build on Bonfil Batalla's concept of *México profundo* for the Chilean case. Chile, he argued, in the midst of a frighteningly culture- and value-free process of modernisation and globalisation, was ending up with an 'empty identity'. This was due to the longstanding attempt to kill *lo indio*, to pretend it did not exist. But precisely due to this historical amnesia, this 'huge lack of self-acceptance', Chile was at the point of losing all sense of being. 'Recognising Chile's indigenous reality,' he wrote, 'is necessary, among other reasons, in order to recuperate our character as Latin Americans and be able to establish a grounded historical sense.' In addition, he concluded, homogeneity is not a virtue, because it prevents an understanding of diversity, difference, and pluralism.[74]

That brings us back to the same question with which we started out: is there, for the purposes of understanding nation-state formation, a *Chile profundo* worth talking about? If so, who composes it and how has it evolved historically? What role has it played in the formation and transformation of the Chilean

---

[73] Sergio Villalobos, *Vida fronteriza en la Araucanía: el mito de la Guerra de Arauco* (Santiago, 1995).

[74] José Bengoa, 'Un asunto de identidad', *Proposiciones* 20 (1991), pp. 277–86, first direct quotation on p. 278, and the rest on p. 283. Translations mine.

nation? We do not presently possess clear answers to these questions, but I believe there are several important issues around which answers might begin to be found.

I agree with Moulián that the story of the Chilean state cannot be told simply by denying its importance, nor by recourse to a single social class, group or region of the country. I have argued elsewhere that, 'because conflict is at the very core of the state, subaltern struggles are woven throughout the fabric of state institutions'. But understanding how these struggles are embedded in the state also means understanding the diversity and internal hierarchy of popular struggles — their divisions along regional, ethnic, class, cultural, and gender lines — and how state actors and institutions used, deepened, and reorganised these divisions through alliance or coalition.[75] Even among industrial workers the histories of confrontation and compromise with the state varied immensely between northern nitrate workers and Santiago artisans, mineworkers in El Teniente or textile workers in Santiago or Magallanes.[76] As is well known, moreover, the capacity of unionised workers and their leftist party allies to begin a partial colonisation of the Chilean political system after 1938 was not matched in the countryside; and this is true despite recent evidence that dispels the myth of rural quiescence before 1964.[77] We have only begun to consider, moreover, the potential differences between women's and men's experiences within any one of these groups; what we know so far suggests that political mobilisation, participation, and economic change were experienced and understood very differently along gender lines.[78]

The Mapuche must also be added to this mix, though how they fit is something that I am just beginning to comprehend in my current research. On the one hand, the conquest of *la Araucanía* facilitated the incorporation of a fertile region and its resources into a developing capitalist economy, providing landowners, merchants, and foreign colonists with decades of prosperity and

---

[75] Mallon, *Peasant and Nation*, pp. 9–10; quotation on p. 10.

[76] Julio Pinto, 'El balmacedismo como mito popular'; Charles W. Bergquist, *Labor in Latin America: Comparative Essays on Chile, Argentina, Venezuela, and Colombia* (Stanford, 1986); Peter DeShazo, *Urban Workers and Labor Unions in Chile, 1902–1927* (Madison, 1983); Thomas Klubock, *Contested Communities: Class, Gender, and Politics in Chile's El Teniente Copper Mine, 1904–1951* (Durham, NC, 1998); and Peter Winn, *Weavers of Revolution: The Yarur Workers and Chile's Road to Socialism* (New York, 1986).

[77] Brian Loveman, *Struggle in the Countryside: Politics and Rural Labor in Chile, 1919–1973* (Bloomington, 1976); 'Property, Politics and Rural Labor: Agrarian Reform in Chile, 1919–1972', PhD diss., Indiana University, 1973; and *El campesino chileno le escribe a Su Excelencia* (Santiago, 1971).

[78] Heidi Tinsman, 'Unequal Uplift: The Sexual Politics of Gender, Work and Community in the Chilean Agrarian Reform, 1950–1973', PhD diss., Yale University, 1996; Karin A. Rosenblatt, *Gendered Compromises: Political Cultures and the State in Chile, 1920–1950* (Chapel Hill, 2000).

high profits even as patterns of land privatisation still blocked the creation of an autonomous and viable non-Mapuche peasant smallholder class. Potentially, at least, this created conditions for a multi-class regional alliance of non-Mapuches, whose unifying discourse was built around a racist concept of Mapuche backwardness, in combination with a lament about the 'iron ring' of Mapuche community lands that, by preventing the true modernisation of the region's commerce and agriculture, was also responsible for rural poverty and the scarcity of land. Despite the sharing of many cultural traits between Mapuche and non-Mapuche peasants, and significant rates of migration and intermarriage from early on in the twentieth century, the state's interpelation of Mapuche and non-Mapuche subaltern populations was based on a policy of divide-and-rule. Until 1972 petitions from and transactions with Mapuche communities were still handled by the Ministry of Land and Colonisation, a 'colonial' holdover created from a subsection of the Foreign Relations Ministry when the Mapuche were finally conquered. Non-Mapuche peasants, on the other hand, were dealt with by the Ministry of Agriculture, denoting their inclusion in the class-based categories of the post-1938 welfare state.[79]

For Mapuche land-grant communities, whose very sense of identity and legitimacy had been reorganised at the time the state issued the *títulos de merced*, struggles for justice and the restitution of lands taken by landowners necessarily passed through a strategy of ethnic resistance that began from that original title. Given the failure of the Ministry of Colonisation in promoting justice restitution for the Mapuche, however, many Mapuche urban intellectuals and political leaders began to advance an agenda of cultural integration and class politics that would abolish the communities and Mapuche culture as signs of colonial domination and segregation. This initiated a conflict within Mapuche society that would culminate during the decade of Agrarian Reform, when the province of Cautín, the centre of Mapuche population and struggle, became a hotbed of mobilisation and one of the most important centres of land expropriation and distribution in the country.[80]

---

[79] The 'iron ring' discourse is well represented in León Elgueta, 'Situación jurídica y social de los indios mapuches', Informe del Fiscal de la Corte de Apelaciones de Temuco, dirigida al Fiscal de la Excma. Corte Suprema, Temuco, 3 Sept. 1955. The change in status for Mapuche peasants and communities brought about by Law 17,729 passed by the Allende government can be seen in the documentation of the Ministerio de Tierras y Colonización found at the Archivo Siglo XX in Santiago. See, for example, *Providencias*, 1973, vol. 9029–9044, Prov. 9036, 'Consultas acerca de la transformación de la Dirección de Asuntos Indígenas en Instituto de Desarrollo Indígena', Daniel Colompil Quilaqueo, Director, Santiago, 29 Sept. 1972.

[80] An early eyewitness account of those mobilisations is Kyle Steenland, *Agrarian Reform under Allende: Peasant Revolt in the South* (Albuquerque, 1977). My current research has also yielded a case study of a coastal Mapuche community, Nicolás Ailío, which is emblematic in this regard, and which forms the basis of my book manuscript, 'Courage Tastes of Blood': The Mapuche Community of Nicolás Ailío and the Chilean State, 1906–2000', in progress.

Despite their supposed disappearance, then, the Mapuche emerge again and again, across modern Chilean history, as a crucible of national conflict. Their very minority status — calculated, according to the 1990 Census, as ten per cent of the country's population — has been used to explain the dismissal and amnesia to which they have been subject, and yet at every major historical juncture in the nineteenth and twentieth centuries there they are, once again, symbolising what has been hidden and repressed in Chilean society.[81] In comparison to Peru and Mexico, of course, indigenous contributions to Chilean popular culture and politics are proportionately smaller, if only for demographic reasons. But the very process of racist othering, pretended disappearance, and dismissal to which the Mapuche and other indigenous groups have been subject has also facilitated, I believe, a deeper disrespect for minority rights, equality within diversity, and cultural difference in Chilean society as a whole. Thus, if in Peru and Mexico the embedded traces of indigenous and subaltern agency within the state can sometimes take the form of an alternative conception of nation, in Chile the traces are more often marks of erasure and amnesia, directly related to a denial of wrongdoing and of historical responsibility. This tendency toward denial, erasure and amnesia, which extends far beyond the specific case of the Mapuche, continues to mark Chilean politics — and historical analyses of politics — to this very day.

Conclusions: The Future of Nation-State Formation in Peru, Mexico and Chile

The universal failure of state-directed models of national development would seem to suggest that Latin American nation-states, as developed across the previous two centuries, are indeed a dying breed in the age of globalisation. At the same time, however, intellectuals like Guillermo Bonfil Batalla, José Bengoa and indigenous leaders in Guatemala, Colombia, Bolivia, Chile and other countries, have all attempted, in a variety of ways, to view the crisis of old models as an opportunity to rethink and rebuild national communities, starting not from exclusion, segregation or amnesia, but instead from a deepened democracy based on political and economic decentralisation, ethnic and cultural diversity and sustainable economic development. How such communities might be built is still a project in formation. Powerful counter-forces — established and centralised elites, investors and multinationals profiting from their domination of free-market production and members of traditional political parties — all have self-interested reasons to oppose such an experiment. Among those attempting to build these new com-

---

[81] For the best current demographic analyses of the Mapuche population, see the collaborative analysis of the 1992 National Census produced by Instituto de Estudios Indígenas (UFRO), Instituto Nacional de Estadísticas, Corporación Nacional de Desarrollo Indígena, Comisión Económica para América Latina y el Caribe, and the Centro Latinoamericano de Demografía, *Población Mapuche: Tabulaciones Especiales* (Temuco, 1998).

munities, moreover, there is much disagreement and lack of clarity about how to do it. Perhaps, then, the time of the nation-state has passed.

As a historian of popular politics, however, I have found that in all three countries I have been analysing, there is a hidden story of alternative projects of the nation, specific to each case, that provides us with clues as to what that a more democratic and diverse nation could contain. We are just beginning to decode the complexity of this hidden story, embedded in the diversity of local cultures, ethnic identities and regional politics of each country, and in the relationship of these to individual processes of state formation. If we can continue to resist the temptation to reconstruct dualisms, if we can learn to read the traces of state power embedded in popular and indigenous cultures, as well as the traces of subaltern cultures embedded in state power, we may yet contribute to a clearer understanding of how past practices and dreams of equality may still contribute to future projects for democracy and diversity within national communities.

If in there, somewhere, there is a nation worth saving, I believe it is highly relevant to the same subaltern populations that, throughout the continent, have long struggled for a polity that would include them with justice. I hasten to add that this is not meant as grandstanding or romanticisation. Subalterns are often divided among themselves. They inform on their neighbours and ally with the powerful for their own interests. Some are too enamoured of personal influence or gender privilege to opt for broader solidarity or democratic practices. Most inhabit several contradictory subjectivities or identities at the same time, choosing among them in changing and often unpredictable ways. But the key to understanding the possibility for future nation-state formation remains in uncovering, without romanticising or segregating, popular and subaltern contributions to what has gone before.

CHAPTER 2

The Centre Did Not Hold:
War in Latin America and the Monopolisation of Violence

Miguel Angel Centeno

The destructive capacity of war is obvious. Less so is the manner in which war or, more accurately, the process of going to war, can build. War may be rejuvenating. The demands of war create opportunities for innovation and adaptation. Wars help build the institutional basis of modern states by requiring a degree of organisation and efficiency which only new political structures can provide; they are the great stimulus for state-building.[1] Charles Tilly has best summarised this process whereby 'states make wars and wars make states'.[2] States, in a sense, are by-products of rulers' efforts to acquire the means of war; war is inherently an organising phenomenon from which the state derives its administrative machinery. According to Hintze, all state organisation is principally military in nature. The shape and size of the state may even be seen as deriving from the managerial potential and limits of military technology.[3] So, for example, the advance of bureaucratic forms may be partly explained by increasing demands for administrative efficiency generated by the demands of growing armed forces and the escalating costs of waging war.[4]

This at least, is the scholarly consensus on the European experience. On that continent, wars served as a crucial causal mechanism behind the growth of the state. The rise of the modern European state may be traced to the military revolution of the sixteenth and seventeenth centuries.[5] During this period, three critical organisational developments changed the nature of military struggle: control over the means of violence shifted from private to public control; the size of armies increased dramatically; and the composition became less varied and more based on a specific national identity.

---

[1] See Samuel P. Huntington, *Political Order in Changing Societies* (New Haven, 1968).

[2] See Charles Tilly (ed.), *The Formation of National States in Western Europe* (Princeton, 1975), p. 73.

[3] Richard Bean, 'War and the Birth of the Nation State', *Journal of Economic History*, no. 33, 1973, pp. 203–21.

[4] M. S. Anderson, *War and Society in Europe of the Old Regime, 1618–789* (New York, 1988).

[5] Outside Europe, the American Civil War both provided the major impetus for state expansion *and* allowed the industrial North to reshape the antebellum agenda (Bensel). Peter Karsten describes the links between the rationalisation of the armed services in the USA and similar organised efforts in other government sectors (1989). Bendix (1978)

War made the territorial consolidation of a state more feasible and more imperative. Only those states that could both wield great armies and guarantee control over their own territories could play the great game. Only those states able to impose that central control could survive the military revolution. Countries unable to do so, such as Poland, disappeared. The decline in the number of European states after the fifteenth century (from 1500 to just 25 by 1900) is an obvious indicator of the centralisation of power wrought by military conflict. Wars pushed power towards the centre.[6] War provided both the incentive and the means with which the central power was able to dominate. 'Military force performed the essential task of defeating particularistic rivals to the crown, lending authority to the expanding process of government.'[7] War served to consolidate the early Prussian state and to impose a discipline on its aristocracy.[8] Whether in the France of Louis XIII, seventeenth-century Prussia and Restoration England, violence was used to impose the rule of the centre. The means for this violence were provided by war.

This chapter analyses the contribution of war to the process of centralisation and empowerment of the nineteenth-century Latin American state. While generalisations are always dangerous, we may classify most of the Latin American states, even well into the twentieth century, as highly despotic yet infrastructurally weak. The first implies the ability of state elites to undertake decisions without routine negotiation with civil society. The second refers to the institutional capacity of the state or its ability to actually implement decisions. Despite its reputation for autocracy and repression, the Latin American state has been less able to impose itself on the relevant societies than European counterparts. The Latin American state has rarely been a leviathan, much less the oppressive equaliser of neoliberal myth or the overwhelming centraliser claimed by Véliz. What has characterised the Latin American state is not the concentration of power, but precisely the opposite. Gurr et al. note '… the pervasive failure of most Latin American societies to establish coherent, institutionalised political systems of either democratic or autocratic type … When coherent autocracies have been established in Latin America, their institutions usually were too weak to outlast the founding elite'.[9]

The present chapter will identify the critical elements which transform (or fail to transform) the anarchy of war into the imposition of order through monopolised violence. This will not only help us perceive the origins of the particular Latin

---

suggests that the effective rule of early Japanese shogunates may originate in the aristocracy's military experience.

[6] Michael Howard, *The Causes of War* (Cambridge, MA, 1984).

[7] Peter Paret, *Understanding War: Essays on Clausewitz and the History of Military Power* (Princeton, 1992).

[8] Reinhard Bendix, *Kings of People* (Berkeley, 1978).

[9] Michael Mann, *The Sources of Social Power*, vol. II (New York, 1992), p. 94.

American states, but also better understand the process behind the European experience. I will argue that war in Latin America was never able to break the disastrous equilibrium between a variety of powers and social interests. Successful state developments were attributable not to war in itself, but to the presence of a united elite, willing (or forced to) accept the loss of individual prerogatives for a collective good, and leading a society not already torn asunder by ethnic or racial divisions. Europe has been exceptional not only in terms of the sheer amount of organised violence in continental geopolitics, but also in the preconditions that allowed it to transform the bloodshed into modern political institutions.

This is not to imply that war is the only possible catalyst for state development or that the Prussian model is the only one available from the European experience. Nor does my analysis imply that Latin America did not suffer from warfare. The point of this essay is to analyse the Latin American experience through the prism of war. The empirical question of whether war assisted the development of the state in Latin America allows us to isolate theoretically critical aspects of the continent's experience and better to highlight the critical differences between the historical development of particular regions.

War and the Latin American State

Did wars help consolidate state power in Latin America? Did these explosions of brutality lead to the establishment of political authority? Do we note any obvious correlations between military activity and the ability to establish a monopoly over violence as defined above? The historical evidence indicates that the answer is generally negative.

In order to answer these questions we first need to estimate the effect of war. Measuring state strength, particularly without reliable data, is a risky enterprise. In another work, I analysed the contribution of war to the taxation capacity of the state.[10] Here I concentrate more on the state's ability to enforce a Weberian monopoly over legitimate use of violence.[11]

One of the most critical aspects of a modern state is its ability to create and enforce what Charles Tilly has called a 'protection racket'.[12] From this vantage point, the state is often little more than the typical Hollywood goon warning storeowners of the potential disasters awaiting them should they fail to purchase his particular brand of insurance. For all its flags, anthems and other sym-

---

[10]   Miguel Centeno, 'Blood and Debt: War and Taxation in Latin America', *American Journal of Sociology, vol.* 102, no. 6 (1997), pp. 1565–605.

[11]   '[The state] is thus a cumpolsory organisation with a territorial basis ... the use of force is regarded as legitimate only so far as it is either permitted by the state or prescribed by it.' Max Weber, *Economy and Society,* p. 56.

[12]   See Charles Tilly, 'War Making and State Making as Organised Crime', in Peter Evans, Dietrich Rueschemeyer and Theda Skocpol (eds.), *Bringing the State Back In* (Cambridge, 1985).

bolic paraphernalia, the state offers its citizens a simple proposal: in exchange for obedience to a set of laws, state institutions offer protection from both internal and external violence.

In order to assure its racket, the state has to be able to defend pre-set frontiers and to assure obedience to its laws within those frontiers. It has to defend its right to exist and to demand internal recognition of its domination. The internal element involves two aspects (they may be related, but it is important to keep them separate): a) Only state officials may have access to means of violence; and b) the central state institutions (claiming national coverage) have priority over any other regional or local competitors. The first is about controlling lawless violence. The second is about the number of governments inside the territory who are claiming the right (or duty) to stamp out the violence. I will refer to the first as a process of *pacification* and to the second as *centralisation*.

Table 1

Country	Centralisation*	Pacification*	Date of first national census**	RR km. in 1900 ***	Relevant war
Argentina	1880	1881	1869	16767	Triple Alliance
Bolivia	1900	1952	1900 (1831?)	972	Confederation and Pacific
Brazil	1850	1890s	1872	15316	Triple Alliance
Chile	1833	1881	1831/1835	4354	Confederation and Pacific
Colombia	1880s	1950s	1912 (1825?)	568	Thousand Days
Ecuador	1916	1950s	1950	92	?
Mexico	1880s	1920s	1895	13585	French Invasion
Paraguay	1820s	1820	1899 (1847?)	240	Triple Alliance
Peru	1895	1940s	1876 (1836?)	1800	Confederation and Pacific
Uruguay	1903	1900s	1908 (1852?)	1730	Guerra Grande
Venezuela	1870s	1930s	1873	858	?
United States	1865	1800s	1790	311160	Civil War

* Estimates based on federalisation of capital, end of major regional revolt or effective end of banditry and Indian attacks of major centres.

** First date is for recognised national census fulfilling basic criteria.
Second date is for possible earlier effort with significant limitations. Source: Goyer and Domschke.

*** Source: R.B. Mitchell, International Historical Statistics: The Americas

There is no precise measure to establish absolutely the date when centralisation or pacification were achieved in Latin America. For the first, we may use the last date of significant regional revolts. For the second we might consider the effective end of banditry. We are left obviously with some judgements that can be debated. Table 1 also includes two possible proxies for state capacity. One is the date of the first national census, which not only required that government representatives had authority to ask sometimes difficult questions, but also that they could be protected from random violence while performing their jobs. An alternative measure is the development of a communications and transportation infrastructure. If we use either measure as an indicator of infrastructural development we note the gap that existed between even the most developed Latin American countries and the United States. Extensive railroad development did not begin on the continent until the 1880s, while few countries were able to accurately count their populations before the end of the century. It is also around this time that we note the disappearance of regional or local currencies and the establishment of a monopoly over legal tender by the central government.

Such a time-line would make it difficult to argue for the causal significance of war as the most important conflicts had occurred at least a decade earlier. Even if we accept a historical lag in order to account for the possible influence of the Pacific and Triple Alliance Wars, their immediate effect was limited. The relationship between international wars and state-building is largely spurious as these wars did not play an important role in the centralisation and pacification of these countries.

However, the Paraguayan War did provide Mitre and later Sarmiento with a much stronger instrument with which to crush continued regional revolts in Argentina.[13] The 1860s did witness the last of the *montoneras*. The army that returned from Paraguay was much better equipped to suppress internal revolts. Both of these presidents also used the army and local garrisons as a means with which to impose their authority on the provinces. Yet, one could argue that it was not the war itself but the development of national institutions (of which the army was but one) under Sarmiento and his successors that consolidated rule from Buenos Aires. Those developments were not born from military victories, but from a series of political contracts and defeats within elite circles. The war had arguably even less effect in Brazil. The army shrunk and suffered from the very same political divisions and conflicts as the state; it certainly did not impose a solution until much later.

Paraguay's experience is perhaps closest to a typical 'unifying' war, but the relevant struggle was not in the 1860s (which left the country destroyed), but many decades earlier. By 1811, not only had the Paraguayans already defeated the army from Buenos Aires that attempted to maintain the capital's control over the province, but even more importantly, the *porteño* threat and the possibility of a Brazilian intervention forced the local elite to unite behind a single programme and junta. Having established a unitary government with all powered centred on Asunción, Dr José Gaspar de Francia was able to dominate the

---

[13] Although Argentina's central authority really consolidated in 1880 when Roca defeated the Buenos Aires Guardia Nacional led by Carlos Tejedor.

ruling junta and finally make himself supreme dictator in 1816. It is interesting to note that Francia was able to use hatred of a white elite to unite an Indian and mestizo population in support of the central state.

It has often been said that war made Chile, and it is true that the war against the Peruvian-Bolivian Confederation was accompanied by efforts to create a more solid and effective central authority. The first Peruvian war 'provided a basis for solidarity and legitimacy, as well as the leadership that spared Chile the political disorder and caudillismo'.[14] But one could argue that by the time Chile went to war in the 1830s, the Portalian Constitution had already established the mechanisms required to maintain central control. Moreover, it was the assassination of Portales that served to consolidate support for the war and the regime. If by 1859 Manuel Montt could declare 'political parties have disappeared in Chile', this had more to do with geography and elite interaction than with military developments.[15] The 'second' war of the Pacific increased government legitimacy and encouraged economic development. The large army created to defeat Peru was subsequently available for the last conquest of the Indians to the south. Nevertheless, it would be difficult to argue that the 1879–83 war made the Chilean state that much more centralised or pacified.

Overall, infrastructural and political development in the late nineteenth century appears more closely related to the expansion of the primary export economy than to the logistical needs of war. Argentina's railroads, for example, were not designed by a general staff seeking to accelerate mobilisation, but for and by the agricultural export interests. Almost simultaneously and across the entire continent, a variety of foreign missions led efforts to discipline national militaries and create more professional forces. These arguably produced more efficient and much less internationally active militaries. The link between these two trends is weak at best. Neither one was an expression of nascent states born out of war, but independent responses to Latin America's emerging role within a global economy and polity.

Even such a cursory overview indicates that precisely in the period when Latin America was most bellicose, the state was at its most undeveloped condition. During an extremely bloody century we can only speak of stable regimes in Brazil after 1840, Chile between 1830–91, and Venezuela, Colombia and Ecuador until the 1840s. Until the last decade of the nineteenth century, violence was endemic, power was fractured and authority was fragile in much of the continent, this despite a great deal of military conflict.

The relevant model is much more that of Austria–Hungary than Prussia.[16] Wars seemed to only highlight the intrinsic weakness of the regime and the

---

[14] Brian Loveman, *Chile: The Legacy of Hispanic Capitalism*, 2nd ed. (New York, 1988), p. 141.

[15] Simon Collier and William F. Sater, *A History of Chile, 1808–1994* (Cambridge and New York, 1996), pp. 66, 118.

[16] With thanks to Steve Topik.

fragility of any sense of nationhood. Only with the beginning of the 'long peace' do we observe the development of the forms of state capacity supposedly associated with military conflict. The apparent paradox is even more puzzling when we recognise that the forms of Latin American state with the characteristics most associated with 'modern' political institutions (extensive bureaucracies, closer interaction with larger parts of the population) did not appear until the 1930s and 1940s under corporate and populist guises and hardly influenced by the kind of geopolitical competition supposedly responsible for European development. If stability does require acts of force, authoritarian impositions and exercises in power justified by internal and external danger, why did the Latin American violence of the nineteenth century not produce a coherent state?

Why Wasn't War a State Builder?

What explains the limited significance of war on state development in Latin America? Certainly, the eighteenth and nineteenth centuries saw enough organised violence as to expect a concomitant evolution in state capacity. If the relationship between organised violence and institutional development is automatic, we might expect Latin America to follow the European pattern.

Wrong Kind of Wars?

We should first distinguish between the different kinds of wars and their respective state-building effects. Latin America, for example, has not experienced one of the most significant forms of warfare producing centralised authority. In many of the European cases, war contributed to state formation not as an unintended by-product, but as a direct result of conquest.[17] The two most obvious examples here are the Italian and German cases. These unifications involved not a central authority systematically expanding control over provinces, but a regional contender for supremacy defeating all other claimants. Prussia and Piedmont essentially conquered Germany and Italy. The same could also be said for England, Île de France, Castille or Muscovy.[18] One could say the same of the Northern victory in the US Civil War.

Civil wars in Latin America were at times defined territorially, but more commonly involved competing claims to central power. These conflicts were rarely about delimiting internal or external frontiers, but about deciding who controlled

---

[17] The sixteenth-century Conquest did produce an elaborate political institution and fostered separate identities, both between it and other imperial claimants and within it between ruling whites and dominated Indians and blacks.

[18] This is not to deny how non-Conquest wars may have contributed to the capacity of a region to establish itself as first among equals. Again, Prussia, Piedmont and England were made the powerful regions they were partly through the experience of war. It is this process rather than explicit conquest that we need to analyse.

the already defined national territory. Unlike in Europe, we have few cases (for example, the creation of Uruguay, the War of the Peruvian-Bolivian Confederation) where international war combined with the process of regional conquest. The principle of *uti possidetis* (right of possession) consecrated colonial boundaries. This prohibited the kind of Darwinian geopolitics that arguably fuelled state development in Europe. There are no Latin American equivalents to Sadowa or Sedan. The closest equivalent to the unification through conquest model would be Buenos Aires and the half-century long struggle for mastery over the Confederation. But, even here one could argue that the provinces conquered the capital as much as vice-versa, and it is arguable to what extent the final union was a product of war. Urquiza was not vanquished at Pavón, and the union of 1861–62 was really the result of elite pacts arrived at politically, not militarily.

It is interesting, given the relatively low level of technical capacity available to the combatants, that the Latin American wars were also extremely destructive — arguably more so than most European wars between Westphalia (1648) and Sarajevo (1914). The ruinous consequences of war were often not limited or far removed from population centres, but involved the destruction of one side. Losing a war was often disastrous for political order. Unlike the European case, where the military victor's rule would succeed the loser, the pattern in Latin America was closer to the creation of a vacuum. In the late 1880s, for example, the Peruvian countryside was not accessible to the state.[19] The Paraguayan case is even more extreme.

The historical record certainly supports emphasis on war type. The two wars of the Pacific, the War of the Triple Alliance and the Mexican-French War of 1862 (in part an internal conflict which was transformed into a nationalist one) all appear to have played at least a *limited* role in the subsequent consolidation of the *winning* nation-states (but still smaller than might be expected). The much more common conservative-liberal conflicts of Mexico and Colombia, the regionalist rebellions of Brazil and Argentina and the caudillo wars of Peru did little but destroy. Losing a war was universally a disaster.

Looking back at the critical contributions made by wars to state-making in Europe, we find Latin American conflicts did not generally embody the three critical characteristics of wars associated with the 'military revolution'. First, they often did not accompany a shift from private to public control of violence. In many cases, the chaos which followed them meant that powerful private actors remained the de facto laws of their respective lands. Moreover, as wars often were about establishing claims to power, they were perceived as private battles over public goods. Second, armies remained generally small and logistics severely constrained. None of the Latin American conflicts (with the exception

---

[19] Florencia E. Mallon, *The Defense of Community in Peru's Central Highlands: Peasant Struggle and Capitalist Transition, 1860–1940* (Princeton, 1983), pp. 102–3.

of the Paraguayan experience in the 1860s) were 'total wars' requiring the militarisation of every aspect of social and economic life. Third, the vast majority of the wars did not emphasise or support the development of a national identity (fighting yet another), but consisted of struggles where either such questions were irrelevant or where the very definition of that identity was at stake.

Wrong Societies?

It was not only the number or type of wars that distinguished Latin America, but the social context in which these were fought.[20] To understand the impact of war on the continent, we should not only analyse the conflicts themselves, but the societies that fought them. One place to start is prior to Independence when Latin America did undergo an attempt at centralisation of authority partly fuelled by military concerns: the Bourbon Reforms.

The Seven Years' War which ended in 1763, and the Spanish involvement in the campaigns against France beginning in 1793, challenged the status quo relationship which had developed between Iberia and America.[21] The reforms initiated by Charles III with their endeavours to re-centralise authority and increase revenue could be interpreted as an attempt to transform the unwieldy Bourbon Empire into something resembling a trans-Atlantic state. The Bourbon army was essentially created to deal with these external challenges.[22] The reforms were considerably successful even if they were met with opposition including violent protest.[23] Could these reforms have produced a state closer to

---

[20] It should also be clear that I am addressing questions of state-building from above. That war may have contributed to a nationalism from below or that it fostered different types of communities is now fairly accepted, see Florencia Mallon, 'Reflections on the Ruins: Everyday Forms of State Formation in Nineteenth-Century Mexico', in Gilbert M. Joseph and Daniel Nugent, *Everyday Forms of State Formation. Revolution and the Negotiation of Rule in Modern Mexico* (Durham, NC, 1994), pp. 69-106. The question still stands of why it did not seem to effect the construction of authoritative and inclusive political institutions at the level of the nation state.

[21] See John Lynch, *Spanish Colonial Administration, 1782–1810; The Indendant System in the Viceroyalty of the Rio de la Plata* (London, 1958) and his *Bourbon Spain, 1700–1808* (Oxford and New York, 1989); also John Fisher, *Government and Society in Colonial Peru; The Intendant System 1784–1814* (London, 1970); David. A. Brading, *Miners and Merchants in Bourbon Mexico, 1763–1810* (Cambridge, 1971) and the same author's *Haciendas and Ranchos in the Mexican Bajío, León, 1700–1860* (Cambridge and New York, 1978).

[22] See Linda Rodríguez (ed.), *Rank and Privilege: The Military and Society in Latin America* (Wilmington, 1994).

[23] See John Leddy Phelan, *The People and the King: The Comunero Revolution in Colombia, 1781* (Madison, 1978); also Steve Stern (ed.), *Resistance, Rebellion, and Consciousness in the Andean Peasant World, 18th to 20th centuries* (Madison, 1987).

the European model? Following Jaime Rodríguez (1998) one could imagine the development of such a political entity, and, more likely, the consolidation producing three or four larger states than arose out of the Independence Wars.[24] In any case, the Bourbon reforms do indicate that the role of war as a stimulus or incentive for institutional development and political consolidation was relevant to the continent prior to the nineteenth century.

This experience provides a hint of what would be the role of war in state-building.[25] Thanks to the increased need for the armed forces, the military was granted greater institutional autonomy through the *fueros*. The result was that while the military played a more important role in the region, it remained outside society and above the state, establishing a pattern that would continue for years to come. Most importantly, while the greater military and administrative capacity may have developed as a response to international threats, armed force was increasingly oriented inward. The colonial state came to be dedicated less to protecting the society from an external menace than to repressing internal threats.[26]

It is these real and perceived threats that best help explain the particular relationship between state and war making on the continent. While the Bourbon reforms did produce a more efficient political apparatus, they also brought to a head the internal divisions that would haunt Latin America over the next 100 years. Military tensions and concerns did create administrative and fiscal crises that encouraged the state to impose its authority, but the last quarter of the eighteenth century already saw the conflicts that would plague attempts to create more solid political structures. The society on which the state rested was not united enough to provide for an adequate arena for institutional consolidation. Institutional developments fuelled by military conflict were frustrated by the strength of geographical, social and racial divisions. These appeared in slightly different forms across the continent, but the result was generally the same. War did not lead to increased order and unity, but chaos and division. The next sections discuss each of these division in turn.

Regionalism

Despite the efforts of Charles III, Latin America entered the nineteenth century arguably more divided than ever. The Americas as a whole resented the imposition of an order dictated in Madrid. The various sub-units of the Bourbon domains wished to protect and expand their autonomy vis-à-vis the central

---

24 Jaime E. Rodríguez O., *The Independence in Spanish America* (New York, 1998).

25 See Christon I. Archer, *The Army in Bourbon Mexico: 1760–1810* (Albuquerque, 1977); also Leon G. Campbell, ' The Army of Peru and the Túpac Amaru Revolt: 1780–1783', *HAHR*, vol. 56, no. 1 (1976); and Lyle N. McAlister, *The 'fuero militar' in New Spain 1764–1800* (Gainesville, 1957).

26 It was also largely unsuccessful when it had to do so. For example, the British were thrown out of Buenos Aires in 1806 by forces organised and led by non-official actors.

power. The vice-regal seats in turn resisted efforts to create small more autonomous governments from their individual parts (for example, the captaincy-generals and *intendencias*). Granting greater local autonomy to one group as in the creation of the Viceroyalty of Río de Plata often meant diminishing that of others (for example, Paraguay) or forcing others to shift their administrative allegiances (for example, Charcas). Thus, efforts to create a greater whole (whatever the benefits to be derived from this) were met with resistance from those who felt that their individual part would suffer. Autonomist rebellions consistently brought to a head salient social divisions within the various regions.

Sovereignty had long been fragmented on the continent. The colonial regime had already recognised considerable regional diversity and autonomy and even had floated a plan of dividing the continent into three kingdoms — Mexico, Peru and Nueva Granada.[27] The conflicts over sovereignty were not simply between province and capital, but within the provinces themselves between regional and municipal governments.[28] In any case, the colonial state barely controlled large parts of the empire. Most of the north of Mexico was beyond its control as was the south of the continent. In part because of geographical and logistical challenges, and in part because of Spain's fears of trans-Atlantic autonomy, the Bourbon reforms established at least a semi-centralised state, but not a unitary one.[29] Each part of the empire was connected to the centre, but the separate regions were not linked to each other. The resulting political entity that faced the challenge of the Napoleonic invasion in 1808 lacked a solid territorial cohesion. The crown was the real source of sovereignty. Thus, when the political order came under strain and the crown lost much of its inherent legitimacy, there were weak links keeping the various parts together.

The early experiences with the Wars of Independence exacerbated these conflicts of sovereignty. In large part because of both sides' need to acquire resources, rebel and loyal administrations both sought to centralise power over areas under their control. Such efforts continued after the 1820s because of fear of post-war chaos. Since the royal governments and their successors were generally too weak to enforce their constitutional claims, attempts formally to increase their authority merely exacerbated local fears without resolving the conflict in their favour. Instead of a true federalism with enough assurances to ensure provincial loyalty or an autocratic centralism resolving regional differences, efforts at centralisation merely produced resentment and rebellion.

---

[27] Jaime Jaramillo Uribe, 'Nación y región en los origenes del estado nacional de Colombia', in Buisson et al. (eds.), *Problemas de la formación del estado y de la nación en hispanoamérica*. Special issue of *Lateinamerikanische Forschung*, vol. 131984, 1984.

[28] See Antonio Annino, 'Soberanías en lucha', in Antonio Annino, Luis Castro Leiva and François-Xavier Guerra (eds.), *De los imperios a las naciones: Iberoameéica* (Zaragoza, 1994), p. 250.

[29] Manfred Kossok, 'Revolución, estado y nación en la independencia', in Buisson et al., *Problemas de la formación del estado.*

The Wars of Independence witnessed the dispersion and dissipation of political authority. In New Granada the authority of the autonomist government in Bogotá did not extend much past that city as Cundinamarca and Santa Marta, among others, claimed different allegiances, and *patrias bobas* survived repeated attempts to centralise authority. In Ecuador, the long standing rivalry between coastal Guayaquil and highland Quito took on new levels as the latter became politically dominated by Venezuelans from the invading liberators. In Bolivia, Sucre provided the Charcas elite with the military protection it needed to separate from Peru and establish an independent nation. The very same logic that would allow La Plata to break from the rest of the empire seemed to permit each of the sub-provinces to divorce itself from Buenos Aires. Each new sub-unit produced further claims to autonomy. The state of Tucumán faced secession from Santiago de Estero, and la Rioja broke off from Cordoba. It was the failure of Buenos Aires to stop this process which is most critical to understanding the next 50 years. Forces in both Bolivia and Paraguay defeated *porteño* attempts to keep them in the old vice-royalty. These failures served as an inspiration to other regions. Moreover, the military and political effort that the various expeditions expended made it difficult to gather the resources needed to keep other provinces in line.

The pattern continued after Independence. During the nineteenth century the central Mexican state could not even eliminate inter-state barriers to national commerce. The Texas War, which began in 1835 and effectively continued until 1846, did not aid the institutional development of the Mexican state. The many civil wars impeded efforts to impose central authority as individual provinces could usually find a pretender to challenge any dictates from Mexico City or attempt to change the government. Ironically, Mexico City was accused of attempting to establish a new Tenochtitlán as it could not even control the road to Veracruz. Political regionalism arguably survived the Díaz era and was only stamped out after 1910.[30]

Even countries that were spared ruinous independence wars found regionalism an almost insurmountable obstacle. The first 30 years of the Brazilian Empire witnessed yearly efforts to bring a recalcitrant region or social group under the control of Rio. While the army did serve as a unifier during much of this period (particularly during the 1830s and 1840s), it also suffered from regional divisions. Military camps and barracks would often be divided according to the geographical origins of the troops.[31] The empire never established a strong central authority. Instead, it could be interpreted as a patrimonial state operating a network of favours, guaranteeing some legitimacy and serving as the policeman of last resort for elite squabbles.[32]

---

[30] Guy Thomson, 'Federalism and Nationalism in Mexico, 1824–1892: Sovereignty and Territoriality', in Eduardo Posada-Carbó (ed.), *Wars, Parties and Nationalism: Essays on the Politics and Society of Nineteenth-Century Latin America* (London, 1995).

[31] Frederick M. Nunn, *Yesterday's Soldiers* (Lincoln, NE, 1983), pp. 58–9.

[32] Richard Graham, *Patronage and Politics in Nineteenth-Century Brazil* (Stanford, 1990).

The independence project also suffered from a critical contradiction at its core. On the one hand, the independence of each region was always subordinated to the independence of the continent. No province was allowed to concentrate on its purely proto-national interests. The struggle was to free America. At the same time, however, the sovereignty of each region was never sacrificed to a central entity. Conquest was not allowed. San Martín could not conquer Chile for La Plata. But Chile did not completely control the armies within its borders. This resulted in a disastrous combination of a supra-national military with regional political authority. In turn, this produced a disjunction between military might and territorial limits that fatally weakened the centralising effect of war.

As Halperín-Donghi has often noted, the independence wars also established a particularly vicious connection between regional identities and divisions and military force. Thanks to the prolonged savagery of the independence struggle, the continent had literally dozens of armed groups contending for power by the 1820s. Perhaps more importantly, military power was autonomous. With few exceptions, armies did not evolve past a provincial militia mode with a few professionals leading local masses.[33] The military was not the armed representative of the state, but fought for either its individual leader or some vague notion of 'liberty'. Partly because of the relatively low technical requirements, partly because of the absence of competition, leaders of irregular armed forces could easily become independent of the governments that organised them. Armies were not under the domain of any central authority, but often under the control of precisely those who wished to be left alone by such powers. Armies, in this case, were not a way of establishing political authority, but keeping it at bay. Military mobilisation was not accompanied, much less proceeded, by political mobilisation.

Rather than mitigating regionalism, war often made geographical divisions even more detrimental to centralised authority. In order to survive in often difficult logistical situations or to obtain needed resources, armies (whether claimants to power or representatives of official authority) often had to negotiate deals with local powers. As recruitment was geographically concentrated, significant parts of armies also reflected their provincial origins and replicated their loyalties to their towns through their chiefs.[34]

The combination of colonial heritage and the particular military experience of the continent produced a very different variant of state-making to that seen in Europe, where states were built from the 'inside-out', and a region or province would carve its dominance over others. The state was built at the same time as the territory was acquired. In Latin America, by contrast, the fight was about assuming control over what was left of a patrimonial state, even if it did not exercise meaningful authority over large parts of the formally defined nation. Wars, there-

---

[33] Antonio Annino, 'Soberanías en lucha', in Antonio Annino et al. (eds.), *De los imperios a las naciones.*

[34] *Ibid.*, p. 252.

fore, were counter-productive for state-building. They were either internal squabbles that left domestic territory pillaged or fights between political pigmies that did not produce the necessary stimulus for organisational and institutional evolution. Unlike the case of Europe, the military did not conquer territory in order to make a state, but had to impose an order over a fractious set of local interests each irrevocably married to each other. Wars tended to remain within the family with the particular destruction and divisiveness that civil struggles tend to leave behind.

Racism and Ethnic Conflict

One could argue that some early military conflicts helped create a nascent Latin American identity. The militias and even formal armies established by the Bourbon reforms were largely staffed by colonials.[35] The military was arguably the first truly American institution and one that helped develop and consolidate a separate identity of *criolloism*. Yet a more salient response to the Bourbon reforms, and again one that would haunt Latin America to contemporary times, was increasing conflict between races, classes and castes. The Túpac Amaru and Quito revolts obviously had roots much deeper and much more complex than the Bourbon reforms. In the case of the Peruvian rebellion, we should take into account the frustrations of the old Inca aristocracy, the heavy weight of the *mita* forced labour, regionalist pressures to create a separate intendancy for Cuzco and, most importantly, racial strife. What is most relevant for our purposes, however, is that the spectre of race war hampered the progress of the rebellion and helped shape attitudes toward the loyalist victory in 1783.

Much more than in Europe and or even the USA, Latin American elites lived in constant fear of the enemy below. More than any competing elite across a border, the perceived threat to maintaining one's social status quo were the non-white subalterns. Such fears need to be understood in light of the demographics facing the white elite at the beginning to middle of the century. In Brazil, for example, slaves made up one-third of the population.[36] New Spain at Independence consisted of 20 per cent whites, 20 per cent mestizos, 40 per cent Indians and 20 per cent *castas*.[37] New Granada at Independence was 33 per cent white, 43 per cent mestizo, 17 per cent Indian and 6.5 per cent slaves while Venezuela had 60,000 slaves.[38] Quito was 90 per cent Indian.[39]

---

[35] Brian Loveman, *For la Patria: Politics and the Armed Forces in Latin America* (Wilmington, 1999), p. 15.

[36] See David Bushnell and Neill Macaulay, *The Emergence of Latin America in the Nineteenth Century* (New York, 1988), p. 150.

[37] Ernesto de la Torre Villar, 'El origen del estado mexicano', in Buisson et al., *Problemas de la formación del estado*, p. 128.

[38] Jaramillo Uribe, 'Nación y región', pp. 342–7.

[39] Javier Ocampo López, 'La separación de la Gran Colombia en el proceso de la desintegración del imperio colonial hispanoamericano', in Buisson et al., *Problemas de la formación del estado*, p. 370.

Racial conflicts were particularly critical to the historical impact of the War of Independence in Mexico. The Hidalgo and Morelos revolts of the first year of the century convinced a significant part of even autonomist *criollo* opinion that the dissolution of the political status quo would produce a race war in which they would suffer the fate of their equivalents in Guanajuato or — the true spectre — Haiti. The *criollo* elite united in supporting the authorities, and by 1814, loyalist control was assured. Rather than an assertion of liberal sentiment, the eventual independence of Mexico came as a reaction to the Cadiz Mutiny of 1820 and the threat it represented to vested interests and ideologies. The almost bloodless Iturbide revolt that produced an independent Mexico in 1821 was classic rebellion from above meant to slow social change through political restructuring.[40]

Racism and fear of armed non-whites also hampered Bolívar's early campaigns. The royal government successfully exploited these tensions. By 1812, a royalist army allied with blacks, Indians and *pardos* was able to impose its authority over Venezuela. Bolívar's next attempt did include an alliance with the *pardos* and, more importantly, with the *llanero* cowboys under José Antonio Páez. Later campaigns in Peru, in turn, appeared to have been hampered by perceptions of the independence army as Indian-dominated.

Throughout the next century the prospect of armed Indians alarmed white elites (much like the prospect armed ex-slaves and freedmen alarmed both northern and southern whites in the American Civil War). This was not only because of the immediate access to violence that guns provided, but also because of the perhaps more dangerous notion that participation in battle bestowed equality on Indians. Peasants who fought did indeed begin to believe in their own equality as soldiers and claimed to be treated accordingly.[41] Thus, the very fact that the military was at least perceived as serving as a ladder for social and ethnic mobility made its role as a national unifier problematic. The 'tool' was tainted by the very problems it was meant to solve.

This contradiction was complicated by the army's central mission in most of Latin America: the protection of 'civilisation' from either revolts by internal subalterns or defence of frontiers from 'savages'. Yet, large numbers of troops were ethnically (as well as socioeconomically and geographically) related to the 'enemy'. The military was composed of the very same threat from which it was to protect the nation.

Racism also often limited the potential authority of promising leaders, even when faced by war. Andrés Santa Cruz attempted to unite Peru and Bolivia, and faced war with Chile. Yet he received little support from the Lima elite who

---

[40] Sometimes, however, racial fears could actually assist central authority. Creole *yucatecos*' willingness to obey Mexico City certainly improved when they realised that they needed the central government's help to put down local Indian revolts in the 1840s.

[41] Mallon, *The Defense of Community*, p. 88.

despised him because of his race and class origins. Members of the Peruvian elite (along with future presidents Gamarra and Castilla) fought on the side of the Chileans against Santa Cruz.[42] Rather than consolidating a sense of nation and Lima's sovereignty, the war maintained the isolated fiefdoms defined by geographical regions. Gamarra and Castilla subsequently faced the same discrimination against their mixed origins when they assumed power.

Racial divisions determined some institutional sanctions. Well into the nineteenth century, for example, there existed *repúblicas indias* where the national government did not rule. There also existed pockets of territorial loyalties or *patrias chicas* often associated with indigenous groups. Liberal critiques of these separate nations were not completely off the mark in suggesting that no nation could arise as long as these communities existed. Obviously, this is not to deny the disastrous consequences for the Indian populations when liberals later in the century dismantled these protections. Yet, while they did serve to protect parts of the population against the commercial onslaught that was often to leave them landless, their existence made the consolidation of a single nation very difficult. The idea of two (if not more) nations haunted the nineteenth century.

While the major European nations created their nationalities as they were developing their territories, they were not as internally divided as Latin America. If making Italians, Frenchmen, Germans and Britons involved the forceful imposition of the culture of a single region or creation of a compromise national language, it did not require the mending of centuries-long racial gulfs closely correlated with the distribution of political and economic power. The very composition of 'the nation' was fraught with conflict. Under these circumstances wars were not occasions for institutional unity, but represented opportunities for groups to opt out of the national project. In the end, the *official* military was not organised to protect or even co-opt the people, but as a means to coerce them.[43]

Elite Divisions

Despite, or perhaps because of, their extremely privileged position, elites in most Latin American countries have been internally divided. This took a variety of forms during the Bourbon period. One was the struggle between state and Church. The Bourbon reforms sought to increase the power of the former at the cost of the latter. In some places, most prominently in the case of the Jesuits of Paraguay, this involved removing Church influence altogether. In others it simply meant a shift in control of resources. A second form of intra-elite struggle exacerbated by the Bourbon reforms was that between *criollos* and *peninsulares*. The

---

[42] Henry F. Dobyns and Paul L. Doughty, *Peru: A Cultural History* (New York, 1976), p. 158.

[43] I emphasise the form of military since we need to distinguish it from more popular armed organisations such as resisted the Chileans or fought against the French, see Mallon, 'Reflections on the Ruins'.

latter had the most to benefit from attempts to de-localise administration and associated efforts to increase immigration from Spain. While often dressed in the Enlightenment guise of liberty and rights, American opposition to the reforms often had more to do with the protection of sinecures and social positions. The imposition of mercantilist policies (which might have benefited the Iberian-American Empire as a whole) met with a similar response.

There were also divisions within the elite regarding the benefits of remaining within the imperial system. The Spanish crown did offer some American elites a series of important advantages: protection from external threats and internal security being perhaps the most important. While large portions of the American population might chafe under the control of Madrid (such as it was), significant groups saw it as preferable to a situation in which they would not be able to maintain their social, political and economic control. It is not surprising that some elites were loyal to the crown and that the independence struggle took nearly two decades to complete.

Elite divisions made it difficult to unify coercive capacity and use it constructively. Argentina and Chile should have enjoyed the best of all possible worlds in their experience with the Wars of Independence. While both (but especially Argentina) provided important logistical support for the liberation of other regions, neither suffered significant destruction. Yet, in both cases, the Wars of Independence did not produce the consolidated state one might have predicted and in one, such an institution would not arise until 50 years later. How do we explain this pattern?

In the case of Argentina, the first decade following May 1810 was characterised by elite divisions not simply along *peninsular/criollo* lines, but also between groups wishing different levels of separation from the government in Spain. By the Congress of Tucumán, Argentina had seen 'two juntas, two triumvirates, one assembly, one directorate with four office holders and a constituent congress'.[44] In part this may be explained by the very absence of a believable threat to Buenos Aires, but it also reflected real divisions in the Argentine elite both along instrumental and ideological lines. A fateful decision in this regard was to allow Buenos Aires' best general and considerable numbers of troops and resources to be devoted to the defeat of Loyalist forces in Chile and Peru. A San Martín in Entre Ríos or Santa Fe might have given a Buenos Aires dominated union a better chance. In this case, it would appear that external war sucked strength out of the nascent state. Had San Martín been needed to fight a believable Spanish threat in Montevideo after 1814, he might have been able to impose a unitary order on the other provinces.

The initial Argentine involvement in Uruguay, and fears of Brazilian reaction in the late 1820s, did produce greater support for a stronger president. Rivadavia certainly benefited from some of the victories against the Brazilians. He even envisioned using the army that had fought Brazil in Uruguay for local

---

[44] Buisson et al. (eds.), *Problemas de la formación del estado*, p. 156.

consolidation: '*haremos la unidad a palos*'.[45] But, his inability to exploit the peace created tension and actually led to the subsequent political dissolution.

On the other side of the River, the Cisplatine war was a disaster for Pedro I. The defeat (and Uruguayan Independence was perceived as such) weakened his authority and complicated the political balance between centrists and federalists. In both cases, divisions inside the ruling elites lead to the waste of the opportunity presented by international conflict.[46]

Elite divisions also helped to shape the independence struggle on the northern coast of the continent. In the early stages of the struggle, part of the elite feared that the collapse of the royal government in Spain would provide an opportunity for the non-white majority to threaten the social status quo, but a more radical segment wished to move towards full independence. The resulting power struggle allowed both hopes to be quashed. *Criollo* killed *criollo* under a variety of flags. Not even Bolívar's considerable military successes in 1813 could stop the infighting. By 1819, Bolívar once again controlled most of what would become Colombia and Venezuela. But the wars had left a devastated region, various groups (most importantly Páez's army) remained beyond the control of the central government and regional antagonisms remained. When Bolívar moved his army south, his representative Santander was not able to hold the various parts together.

Post-Independence Peru continued to suffer from elite divisions (often correlated with regions). The Lima elite was divided in its attitudes to Bolívar and San Martín and their successors. In turn, Lima was split from the merchants and miners of the highlands who also did not see eye to eye with sugar planters on the coast.[47] With the possible exception of Ramón Castilla, no single political entrepreneur could establish a monopoly over national power. From 1826 to 1865, 34 different men served as Peru's chief executive.[48] These divisions played a major role in the eventual defeat of Peru in the War of the Pacific. In the words of Florencia Mallon, 'no measure of heroic exploits or symbols could compensate for the lack of unity and national purpose of the Peruvian elite'.[49] In Bolivia, the independence army was soon torn apart between those who sought union with southern or western neighbours and those who wanted full independence.[50]

---

[45] David Rock, *Argentina, 1516–1982: From Spanish Colonization to the Falklands War* (Berkeley, 1985), p. 102.

[46] Wars in the Platine region did provide resources for central authorities to purchase political loyalty. Rosas' campaign against the Indians in the early 1830s gave him a great deal more land with which to reward allies. Similarly, Brazilian success in Uruguay following Rosas' defeat improved relations between the emperor and the elites of the southern states.

[47] See Tulio Halperín Donghi, *The Contemporary History of Latin America* (Durham, NC, 1993), p. 99.

[48] Dobyns and Doughty, *Peru*, p. 158.

[49] Mallon, *The Defense of Community*, p. 82.

[50] Inge Buisson, 'El ejército libertador y la formación del estado boliviano, 1825–1828', in Buisson et al. (eds.), *Problemas de la formación del estado*, p. 502.

The Mexican War of Independence also failed to provide the opportunity to consolidate authority in a post-colonial setting. On the one hand, elites were united enough to resist a popular insurrection that might have created a more socially revolutionary national government. On the other hand, once the threat of race war was removed, no individual segment was strong enough to impose its will on the others. Even more than in the case of Argentina and Chile, Independence destroyed what political authority had existed without leaving the framework for domination by a central government. Santa Anna's disastrous rebellions began in 1822 — merely a year after helping Iturbide come to power. Perhaps worse than Santa Anna's meddling was his failure for decades to establish a permanent domination over the Mexican state. Neither domineering autocrat nor obedient subject, Santa Anna made Mexican political stability impossible.

Latin America was also torn in a half-century struggle between what would be called (despite localised differences) liberal and conservative views of the role of the state.[51] The former — arguing for greater political inclusion and intellectual and commercial freedom — had dominated the independence struggles. But in the immediate aftermath of victory they faced a dilemma: how to protect individual rights while also constructing a new political order.[52] In opposition, the conservatives sought to protect what they saw as worthwhile inheritances from the colonial period: protection of the Church, property and some economic sectors. The two strands were also associated (in varying ways) with federalist and centralist projects. For much of the nineteenth century, Latin America was stuck between a liberalism that did not guarantee order and a form of nationalism that would inherently exclude a large part of the population.

The nature or outcome of the disputes was not as important as the fact that for many years neither tendency was able to completely dominate political life. The 'German' road to nationhood was not open given the ethnic divisions, but the state was not strong enough to enforce a 'French' road.[53] Nor could the two camps construct systems acceptable to each other. Without either consensus or hegemony, many Latin American states could not consolidate their rule. One war

---

[51] There were also cases where the struggles were more openly between elite factions not encumbered with so much ideological baggage as was the case with the Blancos and Colorados in Uruguay. In this instance elite divisions appeared to have been at least partly the product of international squabbles and subsequent conflicts. In this sense, wars were very much responsible for the underdevelopment of the Uruguayan state, see F. López-Alves, 'Wars and the Formation of Political Parties in Uruguay, 1810–1851', in Eduardo Posada-Carbó (ed.), *Wars, Parties and Nationalism*.

[52] Jeremy Adelman and Miguel Centeno, 'Law and the Failure of Liberalism in Latin America', in Bryant Garth and Yves Dezalay (eds.), *Internationalization and the Transformation of the Rule of Law* (Ann Arbor, 2000); see also Natalio R. Botana, *La tradición republicana: Alberdi, Sarmiento y las ideas políticas de su tiempo* (Buenos Aires, 1984).

[53] See Roger Brubaker, *Citizenship and Nationhood in France and Germany* (Cambridge, MA, 1992).

did help resolve these struggles and arguably played a role similar to conflicts in Europe. The Mexican War against the French (in many ways a continuation of the *Reforma*) destroyed the classic conservative elite. It also necessitated the creation of a truly national army garrisoned throughout the country. This army and the elimination of *some* elite divisions provided the basis for the *Porfiriato*.

The absence of an institutional consensus and the difficulties facing the establishment of order often forced the most successful rulers to ignore constitutional principles. That is, order often came purchased by the disregard of law that made the long-term consolidation of a political system and the creation of an elite consensus still more difficult. Vincente Rocafuerte best expressed this contradiction when he declared himself 'a true lover of enlightenment and civilisation, I consent to pass for a tyrant'.[54]

But it was not tyranny as such that represented a problem for the growth of the state, but on what forms of authority that tyranny rested. Here it is important to analyse the role of political entrepreneurs in Latin America. For much of the first 75 years of Independence, Latin America's critical political actor was not the institutionalised authority of the state, but the much more personalised rule of the caudillo. Arising from the destruction of colonial institutions, the emergence of local power centres and the need for some form of order, the caudillos sought to alternatively appropriate the power of the central state (as in the case of Paéz or Santa Anna) or challenge it (as in the classic Argentine regional caudillos such as Estanislao López or Facundo Quiroga),[55] If the 'worst' were full of passionate intensity and political prowess, the 'best' were unable to defend their authority. Santa Anna's antagonist, Lucas Alámán, for example, never served a government strong enough to impose a permanent centralised republic.

The more interesting cases are the caudillos who could have become much more. Páez did give Venezuela two decades of peace by successfully constructing an alliance between the military and pre-Independence elites, and Rosas temporarily managed an equilibrium of various regional leaders' interests. Such gifted caudillos were able to sometimes construct the semblance of states, but these were hardly institutional orders and rarely survived their founders. Perhaps the most mysterious of cases is Rosas. There is no question that he pacified the province of Buenos Aires or that he was at least first among equals in the Confederation. Once he had established his position, however, he seemed uninterested in expanding the region under his direct control. Rosas' nearly constant warfare, especially his conflicts with Britain and France, did help to consolidate his popular legitimacy, but he never used this to do anything but re-enforce his control over Buenos Aires province. The 40 years of civil war following Independence brought little more than superficial change to an Argentina still dominated by caudillos.

---

[54] Leslie Bethell (ed.), *The Cambridge History of Latin America* (Cambridge, 1984), vol. III, p. 369.

[55] See John Lynch, *Caudillos in Spanish America, 1800–1850* (Oxford, 1992).

Neither Argentina nor any of the other nations produced by Independence experienced a post-bellum order which institutionalised the changes brought about through political revolution and recreated the state in a new bureaucratic form. This produced the disastrous combination of local autocracy with little or weak central domination. The result was a continent of repressive enclaves with few links between them.

Towards the end of the century, several key figures who in previous times might have remained personalistic caudillos did begin to build the institutional basis for a state (Díaz in Mexico, Guzmán Blanco in Venezuela or even Roca in Argentina). I would argue that this was the result of a different institutional context of caudilloism. If during the first part of the century caudillos had secured their material and political base by controlling regions in conflict with central authority, towards the end of the century the road to power and wealth lay in expanding the capital's domain. The causes of this shift lay not in war or military competition, but in the requirements of capital and export production. As long as a hacienda economy writ large dominated the continent it made political sense for the state to be weaker than its most powerful subjects. When that changed, so did the goal of the armed political actors.

Wars provide opportunities for institutional development, but they do require an already elaborated political logic for centralisation. This can come from an already united elite that sees the growth of the state as in their interest. Alternatively it may come from a nascent class seeking to augment the territory under which it may function. Whether nationalist aristocracy or expanding bourgeoisie, these groups use war to defeat rivals or competing claimants. Latin America did not possess either group during its century of wars. There were many divisions and claims to power. Unlike the European case, wars did not provide opportunities for a single elite faction or family to impose its will on the others, but rather to perpetually maintain the possibility of rebellion.

Conclusions: Why the Latin American Difference?

I have argued that Latin America fought different wars and that it suffered from social, racial and geographical barriers that precluded state development. The question then becomes why these were particularly acute on the continent. Europe also had divided elites, regional identities and ethnic and class divisions. Why did these represent a more daunting obstacle in Latin America?

As discussed above, the forms of warfare were drastically different in the two regions. I would add, however, that differences in societal contexts were more important, and that the analysis of these can make a more important contribution to our understanding of state-making on the continent than any adjustment to the bellicist theory of political development.

First, regionalism in Latin America had an important natural ally. The physical geography of the country presented logistical and administrative obstacles only replicated in select parts of the European and North American continents.[56] Communications with the capital were uncertain and military support was irregular. Because of these problems, efforts to impose central authority in much of Latin America might be better compared to those of empires rather than nation-states. The apparent (if illusory) cultural homogeneity of the continent also supported regionalism in a perverse fashion. Given the absence of obvious and strong distinctions across regions, the natural centrifugal attraction of the nation-state appeared less obvious. Thus, Latin American countries faced more significant natural obstacles while not enjoying the attractive pull of differentiated pockets of cultural cohesion.

Ethnic divisions were also much more significant in Latin America as they were accompanied not only by obvious racial characteristics, but also supported by a legal and social system that institutionalised the minutest differences. Paris had to absorb Bretons and Provençal speakers, but it was much less successful with Basques. One can only imagine Spain's history with a sizable *morisco* population. Once again, the relevant European model is Austria–Hungary, where internal ethnic/national divisions overpowered most notions of a shared legacy or destiny. The presence of a significant ethnic divisions (and their legal recognition) is perhaps the characteristic which most distinguishes the experience of Latin America from that of Europe.[57] Once again, we might best understand the birth pains of independent states in Latin America by imagining them not as nations, but empires.

Finally, few elites could be as unruly as the European aristocracy that constructed states after the sixteenth century. Could the Argentine or Peruvian elites really claim to be more fractious than their French or English counterparts? One major difference was the long European association of elite status and military prowess (broken in Latin America soon after the Conquest). This relationship established a close link between martial competition and the viability of any elite group that never existed in Latin America. The control of violence was an intrinsic part of elite functions in Europe; considering the state irrelevant was never an option. In Latin America, on the other hand, political power was often secondary to economic control and this made the necessity to construct a state less urgent. European proto-states were also helped by the institution of monarchy which gave at least one family and political network a very strong stake in the development of political capacity. Not even the Brazilian monarchy developed that congruence between individual and collective interests that may be so crucial at early stages of political growth.

---

[56] One could even find a rough correlation between the success of statemaking in those regions and suitability of terrain. Certainly the plains of France made it easier to impose central authority than the mountains of south-eastern Europe.

[57] Obviously, the experience of the United States is relevant here. The counterfactual comparison might be an independent confederacy having to construct a democratic state in the aftermath of slavery.

Violence pervaded Latin American and European life during the development of their respective states. There was violence between elites, between classes, between races and between regions. Yet this did not generate the institutional development one might have expected from the European experience. The various regions of Europe competed with each other for supremacy and sovereignty, but they did so while recreating a political map and not attempting to conform to a colonial geography. Ethnic groups clashed, but they were not so hard to disentangle through territorial division. Elites might fight, but political entrepreneurs with monarchical legitimacy could impose institutional orders. With limited exceptions, Latin America did not possess the institutional or social kernel from which nation-states might have arisen and wars did little to encourage their development. Where local conditions more closely approximated the European cases, war did provide the necessary institutional cement to secure the development of more powerful and stable states. In general, however, the military road to political development was not available on the continent.

CHAPTER 3

The Man on Foot:
Conscription and the Nation-State in Nineteenth-Century Latin America

Malcolm Deas

This chapter explores conscription and the formation of armies, a neglected theme in nineteenth-century Latin American history, but one that is in many ways central to the formation and consolidation of nations and states.[1] Years

---

[1]   The literature on the theme is hardly so abundant elsewhere, and on first review seems often heavily preoccupied with injustices, abuses, resistance and desertion. An introduction is V.G. Kiernan's chapter, 'Conscription and Society in Europe before the War of 1914–18', in M.R.D. Foot (ed.), *War and Society* (London, 1973). There is a short chapter on military service in Eugene Weber, *Peasants into Frenchmen* (London, 1977), but in supporting its argument of latecoming Frenchness it passes over the experiences of several million Frenchmen in the revolutionary and Napoleonic wars in a couple of sentences; for a more recent example in support of a similar thesis see Alan Forrest, *Conscripts and Deserters. The Army and French Society during the Revolution and Empire* (New York and Oxford, 1989). Others are interested in what may be extracted from conscription records for different purposes; for example, the studies of Emmanuel Le Roy Ladurie, *Anthropologie des conscrits francais* (Paris, 1972). The treatment in Geoffrey Parker, *The Military Revolution* (Cambridge, 1988) is cursory. Much more attention is paid to the theme in M.S. Anderson, *War and Society in Europe of the Old Regime, 1618–1789*, 2nd ed. (Stroud, 1998), and in Geoffrey Best, *War and Society in Revolutionary Europe, 1770–1870*, 2nd ed. (Stroud, 1978). The articles 'Army' and 'Conscription' in the eleventh, 1910–11, edition of the *Encyclopaedia Britannica* are still valuable for their resumés of nineteenth-0century European and United States theory and practice, though no Latin American army earns even a mention. For all the differences in context, I have also found some stimulus in Richard D. Challener's classic *The French Theory of the Nation in Arms* (New York, 1952), in three relevant chapters of Peter Paret, *Understanding War. Essays on Clausewitz and the History of Military Power* (Princeton, 1992) and in two pages of John Keegan, *A History of Warfare* (London, 1993), pp. 233–4. In the recent Hispanic literature, the pioneer is Núria Sales de Bohigas, whose articles are collected in *Sobre esclavos, reclutas y mercederes de quintas* (Barcelona, 1974). On Mexico, see Guy Thomson, 'Los indios y el servicio militar en el México decimonónico. ¿Leva o ciudadanía?', in Antonio Escobar (ed.), *Indio, nación y comunidad en el México del siglo XIX* (Mexico City, 1993); on Argentina, Ricardo D. Salvatore, 'Reclutamiento militar, disciplinamiento y proletarización en la era de Rosas', in *Boletín del Instituto de Historia Argentina y Americana 'Dr E. Ravignani'*, tercera serie, no. 5, 1 semestre de 1992. The contemporary vocabulary makes many now forgotten distinctions in different countries between *reclutamiento, conscripción, quinta, leva, enganche*, etc; in the Colombian case, to which I frequently refer, *reclutamiento* usually means the forcible emergency seizure of men, as opposed to a more orderly *conscripción*. For her assistance in gathering Colombian data the author is much in debt to Patricia Pinzón de Lewin.

ago I had an interest in taxation, and also speculated on the presence of the state and of national political life in the provinces, small towns and countryside of nineteenth century Colombia. I also had an unavoidable interest in civil wars.[2] An interest in conscription is a natural consequence. Like taxation, it is a theme that encourages monomania: the palaeontologist Cuvier claimed, it is said, to be able to reconstruct the whole animal from one fossil bone, and various students of taxation have made the same claims for their subject: 'show me the fiscal system, and I will show you the society'. Here, the claim would be 'show me the system of military organisation, and I will show you nation, state and society'; more modestly, 'show me the way a country fills the ranks of its armed forces, and I will tell you quite a lot about that nation, if nation it be'.

The analogy with taxation is indeed a close one, for conscription in its various forms is in many senses a tax, and is often referred to a such, as in the commonly used Spanish term *contribución de sangre*, which also appears from time to time in English, 'blood tax'.[3] As tax collector and recruiting officer, the early appearances of the state are not commonly the most ingratiating.

The *contribución de sangre* is not an ordinary tax, and it is more than a tax. In most of Europe it is the focus of prolonged political debate. The questions of who has to perform military service and how the obligation is to be enforced are seen to be bound up with the larger themes of democracy, equality, the nature of a true liberal state. How can it be tolerated that, in a nation which aspires to be a republic of equal citizens, such a tax falls so unevenly, is so regressive, that the humble always suffer, that the rich escape?[4]

The spectacle of *reclutamiento*, of the forcible seizure of the defenceless poor, the irony of the chained-up *voluntarios*, these are a frequent theme of self-denigration in nineteenth century Spanish American writing and oratory. Something

---

[2] The relevant essays are 'Los problemas fiscales de Colombia durante el siglo XIX', 'La presencia de la política nacional en la vida provinciana, pueblerina y rural de Colombia en el primer siglo de la república'. and 'Poverty, Civil War and Politics: Ricardo Gaitán Obeso and his Magdalena River Campaign in Colombia, 1885.' A version of the first appeared in *Journal of Latin American Studies*, vol. 14, part 2, November 1982, of the second in Marco Palacios (ed.), *La unidad nacional en América Latina. Del regionalismo a la nacionalidad* (Mexico City, 1983) and of the third in *Nova Americana*, no. 2, Turin, 1978. All are reprinted in my *Del poder y la gramática* (Bogotá, 1993).

[3] Recruiting was for long naturally considered a part of political economy — see for example the very full treatment in Coquelin and Guillaumin, *Dictionnaire d'economie politique* (Paris, 1854), 'Recrutement', vol. 2, pp. 498–503.

[4] The Spanish debates were certainly followed in the Americas. For a sample of the rhetoric, see the two 1869 and 1870 speeches against the *quintas* in *Discursos parlamentarios de Emilio Castelar*, 3rd. ed., 2 vols (Madrid, 1877). Castelar, who had a large Spanish American following, argues for a citizen army and the abolition of the *quintas*, invoking the glorious traditions of the Spanish War of Independence — an argument with obvious Americas appeal.

is obviously rotten in the newly independent state, if its government has to have recourse to such brutal and crude means of filling the ranks. Not all of this sort of denunciation should be taken at face value: it clearly soon becomes a standard exercise in the display of sensibility, but it is still part of the picture.[5]

It also seems to me to be particularly American, and not so typically a product of the old Europe. I am inclined to think that it is a hemispheric trait: the Americas, South and North, do not love standing armies. They have a distinct military tradition, and it is not militaristic.[6]

Nonetheless, the raising and maintaining of armies was often the main state activity of the new republics. In this context one notes a surprising definition of its subject at the beginning of Nicholas Rodger's book on the eighteenth-century Royal Navy: 'the largest industrial unit of its day in the western world, and by far the most expensive and demanding of all the administrative responsibilities of the State'.[7] One is not accustomed to thinking of the navy of Vernon or Rodney or Nelson as an 'industrial unit'. One is not much accustomed either to thinking of nineteenth-century Spanish American armies as organisations or as the largest and most demanding organisations in their respective countries, but they were commonly both. In numbers their *pie de fuerza* commonly exceeded that of the only other organisation that might be thought to rival them in size and discipline, the Church.[8]

---

5   The recruit and his sufferings is a standard Spanish American *costumbrista* subject. The greatest Colombian poet, José Asunción Silva could not resist it, though the result was not one of his better efforts. The European literary archetype was perhaps Emile Erckmann and Louis Chatrain's *Histoire d'un Conscrit de 1813* of 1864; the authors' talent for writing melodrama is better known for Sir Henry Irving's favourite vehicle, *The Bells*.

6   For the United States, see Marcus Cunliffe, *Soldiers and Civilians: The Martial Spirit in America, 1775–1865* (Boston, 1968). Before the Civil War, the US army was small, little regarded and for its scant rank and file heavily dependent on poor immigrants; after the vast expansion of the Civil War it rapidly shrank again in numbers and prestige. See John Shy, *A People Numerous and Armed, Reflections on the Military Struggle for American Independence* (New York, 1976), pp. 240 and *passim.*, for nineteenth-century Americans' belief in 'free security' — the belief that the United States was well enough defended by nature, by geography and size not to need much of a military establishment — and their 'unthinking optimism about the natural American aptitude for warfare and ... ambivalent attitude toward those Americans who specialised in the use of force'; President Theodore Roosevelt, *Seventh Annual Message*, 3 December 1907: 'Declamation against militarism has no more serious place in an earnest and intelligent movement for righteousness in this country than declamation against the worship of Baal or Astaroth.' There is an interesting contrast between the 'sad' military spirit of Spain and the 'happy' one of the United States in 1898, in Guglielmo Ferrero's *El militarismo*, n.p., n.d. (The book is based on lectures given in Turin in 1897.) The nineteenth-century Latin American pattern has at least as many similarities with the US tradition as with the continental European.

7   Nicholas Rodger, *The Wooden World. An Anatomy of the Georgian Navy* (London, 1986), p. 11.

8   In the case of the nineteenth-century Colombian army the *pie de fuerza* was in some years smaller than the numbers of clergy, though that was not usually the case. Naturally, the military turn-over was greater.

The numbers involved can clearly at certain times be large. A reader of, say, José Manuel Restrepo's history of the Wars of Independence in the northern republics soon loses count of the armies repeatedly raised in more than a decade of fairly intensive fighting, armies which may have been individually small, which were not always composed of fresh levies, but which throughout the wars incorporate, discipline, move around and to some extent indoctrinate many tens of thousands.[9] Though Latin America is not a conspicuous field for international conflicts — particularly inconspicuous when subjected from outside to the usual rapid and incurious inspection of its past — certain wars did imply substantial and sustained mobilisations: the most obvious is the War of the Triple Alliance.[10] Even less visible affairs, like a casual Palmerstonian blockade, had local consequences that involved exceptional military effort and increased recruiting.[11]

---

[9] José Manuel Restrepo, *Historia de la Revolución de la República de Colombia*, 4 vols. (Besanzon, 1858) In the historiography of Spanish America the Wars of Independence suffer a sort of double exclusion: the old histories of Independence, many of them of high quality, tend to be either dismissed unread as *historia patriotera* or subjected to various forms of deconstruction, and few historians of the subsequent republican era show much interest in the earlier period anyway. Though one hesitates to make such a banal observation, the result is perhaps to obscure its obvious importance in the formation of nations and national consciousnesses. Military experience, military glory were essential elements in this. Veterans lived on. Some published their memoirs, with considerable success. For example, José Maria Espinosa, *Memorias de un abanderado* (Bogotá, 1876); and Joaquín Posada Gutiérrez, *Memorias histórico-políticas*, 2 vols. (Bogotá, 1865, 1881).

[10] Apart from their artistic quality, the paintings of Candido López of the war against Paraguay convey something of the scale, numbers, logistical effort and spirit involved on both sides. The pictures are the best immediate antidote I know to thinking that somehow Latin American wars were not real wars in the authentic European sense and did not contain the full range of *grandeurs et servitudes*. See Marcelo Pacheco, *Candido López* (Buenos Aires, 1998). The Paraguayan War certainly had major repercussions in Argentina and Brazil, many bound up with the experiences of recruiting for the war and the formation of national armies on a new pattern. The briefest list of international conflicts, far from complete, would also include the US–Mexican War of 1846 and the French Intervention, the war between Chile and the Peru–Bolivian Confederation and the War of the Pacific.

[11] The starting point for the diplomatic history of international conflicts in South America remains Robert N. Burr, *By Reason or Force. Chile and the Balancing of Power in South America, 1830–1905* (Berkeley, 1965). The military aspects of these wars have not attracted much recent attention, and the older historiography is little read. For some evidence of the national reaction in the New Granada of 1836 to Palmerston's actions in the trivial affair of Consul Russell in Panama, see Malcolm Deas and Efraín Sánchez, *Santander y los ingleses, 1832–1840*, 2 vols. (Bogotá, 1991), vol. 2, pp. 65 *passim*. For the later consequences of South American conflicts for military establishments see Frederick M. Nunn, *Yesterday's Soldiers. European Military Professionalism in South America, 1890–1940* (Lincoln, NE, 1983), which among other things has a good deal to say on the theory of obligatory military service, though not so much on the practice.

Though there is great variety in intensity, in methods of fighting and in the degree in which different regions and elements in the population are involved, formally or informally, by government or by rebellion, certain civil wars again involved high proportions of a country's inhabitants. Small permanent armies are expanded rapidly in times of civil strife.[12] When in 1930 the Colombian government legislated so that pensions might be paid to veterans of both sides of the republic's last formal civil war, which had ended 27 years earlier in 1903, 18,000 took the trouble to apply.[13]

Were the armies of Latin America '... by far the most expensive and demanding of the state's responsibilities'? Certainly the most expensive. Even small standing armies consumed high proportions of budgets. A random example, Rafael Carrera's Guatemala, in 1841–42, projected a military expenditure of $140,000 out of a budget of $263,000.[14] Carrera at times maintained proportionately large forces, a garrison of 6,000 in Guatemala City easily outnumbering New Granada's entire normal peacetime army, but my impression is that the high share of military expenditure is a common feature of early republican Spanish America. It is a principal preoccupation of those who attempt to govern, and hence for them the organisation of armies is a principal preoccupation too.

Both contemporaries and historians have been generally unsympathetic towards the recruiting officer, and some attempt ought to be made to rescue the organisers of armies from the hostility of the first and the immense condescension of the last.[15] What follows are a series of propositions which I hope will widen interest in the subject.

The colonial past offers only uncertain clues to subsequent developments.[16] The Spanish Empire was on the whole lightly garrisoned, and did not recruit

---

[12] The most spectacular example of such rapid expansion is that provided by the US Civil War. See the admiring comments in the 1911 *Encyclopaedia Britannica*. Such rapid expansions were also common in Spanish American civil wars.

[13] The *expedientes* are now in the Archivo General de la Nación, Bogotá.

[14] Figures from Ralph Lee Woodward, *Rafael Carrera and the Emergence of the Republic of Guatemala, 1821–1871* (Athens, GA, 1993), p. 409.

[15] E.P. Thompson's phrase, of course, but historians condescend in all sorts of directions. Thompson shows almost as little interest in the Napoleonic Wars in themselves as did Jane Austen. Nicholas Rodger in *The Wooden Walls* complains that far to much respect is shown to the version of naval life, all press-gangs and corruption, given in *Roderick Random*, by the veteran of Admiral Vernon's siege of Cartagena, Tobias Smollett. Perhaps Rodger overdoes the complaint. After all, Smollett was there, and Rodger was not — but few historians resist the temptations of literary sources when it comes to descriptions of recruiting and life in the ranks.

[16] This is not to deny altogether the importance of the Spanish and imperial institutional and legal antecedents. For the *sorteo*, the *leva* and a general resumé of ancien régime Spanish practices and regulations, Charles J. Esdaile, *The Spanish Army in the*

large numbers of men in the Americas. The most prominent regular imperial forces were in Mexico and in Peru. They certainly influenced the course of Independence in those viceroyalties, an influence which persisted with their problematic survival into the early decades of republican life. Militias, and the successor national guards, should not be confused with armies: they offer different gratifications and incentives and they make different demands. They are essentially local, and the prospect that they may turn into something else does not enthuse the rank and file: 'join a militia and you may find yourself in an army' is not a notion that will swell their numbers.

Militias are a subject for study in themselves. A preliminary examination discloses variety: in nineteenth-century Argentina provincial militias are not always militias in the usual sense, sometimes more like regular provincial armies; in Chile a disciplined national guard is an important feature of central government control; in Colombia and Venezuela it is often hard to discern, despite legislation, whether such forces had any real existence at all; in Mexico, though recent work has speculated about their political significance, their place in national military organisation is still far from clear.[17]

Some military problems of Spanish America are common to colonial and republican times — the example that springs to mind are the threats posed by a limited number of Indian frontiers in Chile, Argentina, the Goajira peninsula and in Northern Mexico. Though they have their importance, they do not seem to me to determine subsequent institutional developments. One small boon of colonial existence for the humble was that there was less likelihood that one would be recruited.[18]

Peninsular War (Manchester, 1988), ch. 1. For New Granada, Alan Kuethe, *Military Reform and Society in New Granada, 1773–1808* (Gainesville, 1978), which also discusses the work of Lyle McAllister, Criston Archer and Leon Campbell on late colonial Mexico and Peru, and Juan Marchena Fernández, *La Institución Militar en Cartagena de Indias, 1700–1810* (Seville, 1982). In the Colombian *Memoria de Guerra* of 1869 General Sergio Camargo complained that the bulk of the country's military *ordenanzas* were still those of Carlos III: 'Es singular el hecho i sinembargo es cierto que el Ejército de la República ha vivido moralmente fuera de la República.'

[17]   For Argentina, see Miguel Angel Scenna, *Los militares* (Buenos Aires, 1980), particularly ch. 3; for Chile, Simon Collier and William F. Sater, *A History of Chile, 1808–1994* (Cambridge, 1996), pp. 56–8; for Mexico, the relevant passages of Florencia Mallon, *Peasant and Nation* (Berkeley, 1995), and Guy Thomson, 'Bulwarks of Patriotic Liberalism: The National Guard, Philarmonic Corps and Patriotic Juntas in Mexico, 1847–88', *Journal of Latin American Studies*, vol. 22, no. 1, 1990. Robert Gilmore's *Caudillism and Militarism in Venezuela, 1810–1910* (Athens, OH, 1964) is more informative about legislation concerning militias than about reality, in a matter where legislation provides a particularly uncertain guide.

[18]   See the works of Kuethe, McAllister, Jara and Marchena cited above.

The Wars of Independence are the first severe school of recruiting. I have already referred to Nuria Sales's study on the recruiting of black slaves in the Independence Wars, which has been amplified for the River Plate region by George Reid Andrews's work.[19] A great deal more information on the subject is contained in the classic histories and memoirs of the period and in the monumental documentary collections that cover the era, and much of it ought to be appreciated even by those who prefer their history from below. Some of it is even written by persons at least fairly low down — Alexander Alexander, José Santos Vargas, José María Espinosa — and commanders and officers in those wars were frequently not much insulated from their troops; foreign arrivals often had difficulty in telling them apart.[20]

A vast amount of military skill and local military knowledge was obviously acquired in the course of these wars. Command was a school, political, administrative and military. The military knowledge acquired included the familiarity with society, geography and economy necessary for gathering forces, keeping them together and moving them. That familiarity was necessarily preserved after Independence, and was developed further in subsequent civil wars.[21] Much of it now appears to be forgotten. Even the recent historiography of caudillismo to my mind over-emphasises irregular, 'telluric', forces to the neglect of the usually small — Mexico and Peru began as exceptions — regular military establishments that all post-Independence governments maintained, one of whose essential functions was to recruit larger forces when required.[22] One might even argue that that was their principal function.

---

[19] George Reid Andrews, *The Afro-Argentines of Buenos Aires, 1800–1900* (Madison, 1980).

[20] Alexander Alexander, *My Life*, 2 vols. (Edinburgh, 1830), (Spanish version of the South American experiences, *La vida de Alexander Alexander escrita por él mismo*, edited by Jaime Tello (Caracas, 1978), is an extraordinary account of life in the ranks by a scotsman who joined Bolívar's forces in Guayana. Alexander had no interest in the cause he was fighting for, and an extraordinary memory and descriptive gift. José Santos Vargas was the author of *Diario de un comandante de la Independencia Americana, 1814–1825*, edited by Gunnar Mendoza (Mexico City, 1982); Santos Vargas rose to be an officer but began as a drummer, a *tambor*; his diary of Bolivian independence attracted some interest from readers not otherwise interested in Independence on the bogus grounds that it provided an antecedent to such recent guerrilla episodes as that of Che Guevara. Espinosa's *Memorias* have already been referred to above, note 9.

[21] In most republics Ministers of War were for decades drawn from the ranks of the veterans of Independence. Any other choice would have been unnatural and impolitic.

[22] Raising soldiers also seems to me to have little connection with landownership. Though a few *hacendados* or owners of *estancias* can occasionally be found leading peons or tenants into war, such behaviour generally ran counter to their economic and even to their political interest. There are more examples of landowners seeking to protect their labour force in various ways, including by paying for exemptions. For one such landowner, and for further

I shall attempt a broad picture. The governments of all the emerging republics maintained small standing forces. Rosas had his essential garrison at Santos Lugares, Páez and subsequent Venezuelan presidents had their *sagradas* near the seat of government, Carrera had his Guatemala City garrison, in Ecuador President Urbina had his favoured regiment of *tauras*, etc. These small forces, besides their praetorian function and their securing of a minimum of key points, often performed a number of other functions. They guarded the symbols of nationhood, flew the flag, performed the national rituals and parades that had some effect on the populace. They guarded prisons and customs houses and public offices, they enforced the salt monopoly, they escorted the mail, they sometimes, as *zapadores*, built or repaired roads, they guarded the arsenals, maintained a certain reserve level of technical military knowledge — artillery, cavalry, drill, discipline — and they recruited and trained.[23]

How was recruiting to these forces done? Like so much else, it is not as simple as one at first thinks. Most constitutions lay the obligation to serve in the nation's defence on all citizens, the chief fount of inspiration being the French revolutionary and Napoleonic legislation.[24] But recruiting was necessarily unfair and uneven. No government had either the resources or the inclination — the two go together — or the need to recruit an entire annual cohort: the recruits would be too many and the whole operation much too expensive. Service was usually for a longish time — six years appears to be common — so the annual contingent required was proportionately reduced. Most governments liked to keep a number of veterans in the ranks, as they had the necessary military skills and seasoning, and this further reduced the turnover; many were moreover wholly disadapted to civilian life.[25] So from the beginning of the process an element of discrimination and selection is necessarily present.

---

details of the local experience of recruiting, see my 'Santa Bárbara: A Cundinamarca Coffee Hacienda, 1870–1912', in K. Duncan and I. Rutledge (eds.), *Land and Labour in Latin America* (Cambridge, 1977).

[23] The varieties of activity mentioned here can all be found in the Colombian *Memoria de guerra* of 1892. In contrast with the politics of their officers, how Latin American armies spent and spend their time has attracted hardly any scholarly interest at all.

[24] For convenient summaries see Challener, op. cit., ch. 1; Forrest, op. cit., the article 'Conscription' in the eleventh edition, 1910–11, of the *Encyclopaedia Britannica* or the article 'Recrutement' in the *Dictionnaire de l'Economie Politique* already referred to.

[25] 'Por otra parte no debe olvidarse que los soldados viejos, ya no pueden ser agricultores, ni artesanos; ellos no estan habituados a otro servicio que el de las armas, ni a otra dependencia que la de sus jefes militares. Así, estos veteranos, cuyo moral perjudica muchas veces a los pueblos, miran con desdén a las autoridades civiles y menosprecian todo instrumento que no sea el de muerte que empuñaron en los peligros de la Patria.' Colombian *Memoria* of 1843.

The military-political arithmetic available suggests that the numbers required should be drawn from the different provinces in proportion to their population, and *Memorias de Guerra* begin to contain neat charts which set out the allocation of the burden. They are more neat than convincing, and this is frequently admitted: the censuses available were primitive, and to translate their information into practical recruiting a province had to be broken down into cantons and municipalities and districts of municipalities, which was a fraught and uncertain business.

How, indeed, did the government keep the score from year to year? If a region over-contributed at one point, should it not benefit at some later date from its generosity? Should not debtor regions be chased up?[26]

Conscription, as it is meant to be conducted according to national legislation, always requires the collaboration of a competent civil administration, particularly of mayors and judges — that was frequently not present. These officials were often weak, powerless, indifferent, partial and inclined towards a quiet life. Central government could threaten them and their districts with fines and other punishments for non-compliance, but in normal times had few sanctions to force them to perform their functions at all, let alone to the letter of the law.[27] Moreover, the constitutional procedures, with their emphasis on equity, were often simply not practical.[28]

Recruiting itself had costs. Once recruits had been chosen, they had to be brought to where they were to serve, and this meant expenses that might well include the cost of escorts. Poor governments were very cost-conscious about all this. They preferred to recruit where recruiting was cheap, where the population was apt for service, where they got more soldiers for the government peso.[29]

---

[26] See the Colombian *Memoria* of 1842, which records that up to 1841 each province ran some sort of recruiting 'account' with the central government.

[27] 'La ley no tiene parte penal para el que mal cumple con el reclutamiento.' Colombian *Memoria* of 1839.

[28] Colombian *Memoria* of 1840: 'El congreso en su sesión de 1840 expidió un proyecto de ley sobre reclutamiento y conscripción, pero el poder ejecutivo se vió en la necesidad de objetarlo por impracticable ... pues en las circunstancias aflictivas de 1840 si se hubiera practicado habría triunfado las facciones, por que el reclutamiento era impracticable y sin los remplazos oportunos el ejecutivo hubiera desaparecido.' The *Memoria* of 1842 makes the valid point that any law of conscription ought to be simple: the last thing suitable for emergencies is 'una ley complicada y minuciosa ... En tan angustiosos momentos, las autoridades no podrían proceder con la prontitud y eficacia que las circunstancias demandasen, su accion sería entorpecida.' Governments could only contemplate improving the law in quiet times, and in quiet times there was no sense of urgency to make them do so.

[29] The *Memoria* of 1839 complains of the expenses incurred in escorting from distant provinces infirm recruits and 'otros de talla muy pequeña'.

Recruiting also had political costs. Like taxation, it was rarely popular. Public order being often precarious, governments were reluctant to spread alarm and perturbation.[30] Resistance to recruiting and conscription through riot, *bochinche*, was commonplace.[31] It is too easily equated with a lack of a sense of national consciousness — it is perfectly possible to have at the same time some 'sense of national identity' and a keener desire not to be recruited; indeed, in many times and places that would seem to me to be the normal state of mind of the majority of people. It is not a 'lack of a sense of nation' or even a lack of patriotism, that typically produces resistance, but many more commonplace considerations: desire to stay at home or in the region of one's birth — no mean consideration in countries where brusque changes of climate could often be fatal — bad conditions of service, the risk of getting killed.[32] Many governments were aware that the first effects of their recruiting in times of incipient civil war would be an increase in the numbers of rebels, as people took to the local hills to avoid being seized.[33] Against this background, the fairly common practice of recruiting captured rebels into the government ranks is analogous to the fining of tax evaders.[34]

Some people were more recruitable than others. First, there were the *vagos y malentretenidos*, who figure particularly clearly in the Argentine literature. Recruiting undesirables, exacting military service as an alternative to other punishments, was common in Europe and was widely practised in nineteenth-cen-

---

[30] The Colombian *Memoria* of 1843 expresses official timidity eloquently, even at what might seem the not so daunting prospect of recruiting 1,000 men. Adoption of the *sorteo* would 'poner en peligro en un momento crítico la independencia nacional o la tranquilidad interior del país.' However, the system of *enganche voluntario* would not work. To get 500 men into the ranks the author calculates that desertion and unsuitabilty make it necessary to recruit double the number.

[31] By no means just a nineteenth-century phenomenon. I can recall a riot caused by arbitrary recruiting in the Tequendama district near Bogotá in the mid-1960s.

[32] '... llevad a las mas humildes aldeas de la República la noticia de que ha sido hollado el patrio territorio, decidles que los yankees, los venezolanos o los peruanos afrentan la República, y verás que al punto mismo se levantan todos para acudir a la defensa nacional, y que aun las mujeres y los niños y los viejos corren gustosos a ofrendar su sangre al pie de la bandera'. Adolfo León Gómez, 'Reclutamiento', speech in Congress reprinted in *La Patria*, Medellín, 15 September 1909. An exaggeration, no doubt, but it makes the distinction well. Colombians of all classes showed their capacity for patriotic reaction in the dispute with Peru over Leticia in 1932 — the photographic evidence for this is particularly eloquent.

[33] For an example of this see my essay on Ricardo Gaitán Obeso and the civil war of 1885, cited above.

[34] Complications resulted, inevitably. The Colombian *Memoria* of 1843, a post-civil war year, debates whether it is just and fair to demobilise such men before demobilising the regular government troops.

tury Latin America, combining economy with presumed gains in social hygiene. Like every other solution or nostrum in this field, it was however not without its own problems. There were not enough *vagos*, they might not be in suitable military condition, too high a proportion of such people might give even forces whose prestige was not usually high an intolerably bad name, making military service repugnant to any honest citizen, even to the poor. The definition of *vago* was obviously open to abuse, and also to legal complication: there was one Colombian complainer who argued that the legislation determining the recruitment of *vagos* had the effect of making the burden of filling the contingent fall excessively on the honest poor, as the *vagos* commonly had recourse to legal appeal and frequently got off.[35]

The unfairness of conscription and recruiting is, as we have said, the theme of much oratory and political writing. Another Colombian, the already quoted Adolfo León Gómez, made it a speciality, even writing a play on the subject. His speech as a deputy in Congress in 1909 is a good example of what was for long and in many places the standard line:

> una indignidad ... una esclavitud ... como los negreros de la Africa Central ... infame caceria de humildes labriegos ... muertes a balazos ... sus humildes chozas asaltadas ... esposas y hijas a merced de la soldadesca desenfrenada o de los gamonales del pueblo ... hipócritas ...[36]

No doubt recruiting, especially in emergencies, was brutal, and subject to all kinds of distortions and abuses by military and by local authorities; for the latter, deciding who should go and who should stay could be both a burden and an opportunity.[37] It was always unfair, as becomes clearer when one pon-

---

[35] The Law of 1836 '... estableció el modo de proceder contra los vagos para destinarlos al ejército. Este procedimiento, que entonces se creyó muy sencillo, vino a convertirse en una verdadera excepción en favor de estos hombres, por las dilaciones que necesariamente ocasiona su juicio, cuando, para reclutar a los demas granadinos, no se necesitaba sino de un simple orden de la autoridad civil.' Colombian *Memoria* of 1842. Previously, in the *Memoria* of 1839, the future president General T.C. De Mosquera had complained that the civil authorities lacked effective legal powers to seize recruits: '... faltan a las autoridades políticas encargadas facultades para estraer los reclutas de sus casas, porque la Ley de 3 de agosto de 1824 sobre allanamiento no lo autoriza'. One often encounters speculations on the need to recruit a better class of *vago*: *Memoria* of 1853: 'sería conveniente y aun justo que continuen siendo destinados al servicio de las armas antes que, acabandose de depravar, pasen de la clase de simples vagos a la de malhechores. Para ellos [the not terminally depraved] el ejército es una escuela de moralidad i frecuentemente se ve que cuando regresan a sus casas, despues de haber servido el tiempo que la lei les señala, vuelven laboriosos, obedientes a la autoridad i sobre todo, con ideas i prácticas de honradez i providad que tan comunes son en los militares'.

[36] See 'Reclutamiento', already cited above.

[37] One of many typical passages, this one from the *Memoria* of 1850: 'A pesar de que el Gobierno tiene recomendado a los Gobernadores que se destinen de preferencia a los

ders León Gómez's proposed remedies, which rather expose the hollowness of his rhetoric:

> Pues entonces, si es preciso reclutar brutalmente por razones de orden público, órdense por ley a los alcaldes que empiecen la sangrienta carnicería por los politiqueros, por los grandes, por los ricos, por nosotros los legisladores, que no encontramos medio de proveer a la formación del ejército de una manera racional y justa.
>
> ... que se dé a los que son atropellados en la totalidad de sus derechos, el de castigar matando a los reclutadores si fuera necesario; que se declare acción noble y distinguida de valor la del que por la fuerza liberte a los reclutas que sean cogidos de la manera atroz que aquí acostumbran ...

As in much of the European legislation, the common exemptions were made, excusing the married, the only sons of widows, priests and at times extending the immunities to government employees, the employees of mining companies, students and other specified occupations.[38] Apart from the obvious sociological unfeasibility of recruiting the better off and its lack of military practicality — one

---

vagos i perniciosos al ejército, la providencia no ha podido llenarse hasta ahora con puntualidad, ya por falta de energía en los jefes políticos, i alcldes, i ya por indebidas consideraciones de familia, pues, aunque sea desagradable, suelen encontrarse entre algunas bien respetables miembros que las deshonran i que son un escándalo para el resto de la sociedad. Entre tanto la contribución de sangre pesa casi esclusivamente sobre la parte mas infeliz del pueblo, falseando hasta cierto punto las dogmas constitucionales que hacen a todos los granadinos iguales delante de la lei i que obliga a todos con el deber de servir i defender a la República. I no es esto solo, sino que la época de reclutamiento es la época de las venganzas i las persecuciones, ejecutándose los actos mas vejatorios por los agentes subalternos del ramo administrativo, sin que las autoridades superiores puedan impedirlos, pues las mas (?) no llegan a su conocimiento porque los ofendidos o son hombres que ignoran las fórmulas para reclamar sus derechos o carecen de medios para hacerlo.'

[38] The Englishman William Wills, a frequent and outspoken commentator on the affairs of Colombia, his adopted country, protested publicly and privately against the detestable and unrepublican methods of recruiting. In a private letter to General Mosquera he also asked that men employed in the *aguardiente* monopoly, his business, should be exempted. See my *Vida y opiniones de Mr William Wills*, 2 vols. (Bogotá, 1996). In contrast to the enthusiasm for recruiting slaves shown in the Wars of Independence, a Colombian draft law of 1851 expressly excludes them: '... los esclavos a menos que lo pidan sus amos, pero en este caso quedarán libres, i su dueño no tendrá derecho a indemnización alguna'.

Exemptions were sometimes extraordinarily generous, to avoid spreading alarm and confusion. For example, *Memoria* of 1894: 'El contingente de los distritos no debe exceder en ningún caso del dos por mil de la población. Los conscriptos hábiles para el servicio tienen que reunir estas condiciones: ser mozos solteros; sanos de cuerpo y robustos, no ser hijos únicos, ni individuos que con su trabajo sostengan una familia; no deben ser propietarios, ni hallarse comprometidos en una empresa de carácter industrial que sufra con su retiro, ni en calidad de mayordomo en una agrícola, ni deben escogerse entre los que ejercen un oficio que les produzca un salario mayor que la ración del soldado.'

doubts that Leon Gómez's squad of legislators would have been of much military use, even in the impossible event of it having been recruited — the immunity of the more accommodated was frequently secured by the system of finding and paying substitutes or of payments direct to the state in lieu of service. This sometimes received a formal liberal justification, as a matter of contract between free citizens. Occasionally one finds interested but common-sense arguments: it was neither practical nor desirable, neither in the interests of raising and maintaining an economical army nor in those of the society and economy as a whole, to recruit the higher classes, the educated or even artisans and other usefully employed and not easily replaceable persons. As in France and Spain, the result was wide exemption and avoidance, with the burden falling on the rural poor.

But even there the incidence was uneven. Commanders and recruiters very soon learnt the significance of geography, of sociological and ethnic variation. It is no accident that much of the early 'classic' geography — the work of Colonel Agustín Codazzi, for example, in Venezuela and Colombia — is of military inspiration, and that the numbers and distribution of recruitable persons is one of its conspicuous concerns.[39]

The populations of most republics presented a complicated pattern of recruitabilty, hard to summarise adequately in generalisations about sturdy upland peasants, wild *llaneros* or indifferent Indians. In the case of Colombia, some sturdy upland peasants, the Pastusos for example, were in the wrong place, too far away from the seat of government; the *llaneros* may have been fine wild cavalry but they were unrecruitable — the Colombian *llanos* were at times officially exempted from providing any contingent at all — and too few in number.[40] Indians were certainly not all indifferent. From early days in some countries certain well-placed Indian groups were carefully cultivated: Antonio Nariño was criticised in 1813, in the era of the *patria boba*, for parading around Bogotá in his carriage with 'un indio llamado Astudillo', an influential figure in the Tierradentro region, the strategic support of whose people he was anxious to secure. The Indian peasantry of that area figure in most civil wars, usually on the central government side.[41]

[39] On the life and work of Codazzi and its significance see the definitive study by Efraín Sánchez, *Geografía y gobierno* (Bogotá, 1999).

[40] The *Memoria* of 1835 exempts Casanare from providing a contingent; that of 1844 exempts Cartagena and Riohacha.

[41] José María Espinosa, *Memorias*, p. 33. The liability of Indians to recruitment, and their involvement in civil and international wars, seems to me also to resist generalisation. For example, the Indians of Ecuador figure only marginally in civil wars, and it was apparently neither government nor revolutionary practice to arm them; nineteenth century Bolivia presents at least occasional contrasts. In Colombia, the Indians of Tierradentro in the south and of the Goajira peninsula in the north were by no means negligible elements in civil war. On the lesser-known *coaiqueres* of Túquerres, the government agent Rufino Gutiérrez reported in 1893: 'Don Salvador Moriano ha alcanzado

The nature and state of the local economy has a clear influence on recruitability. Where wages are high and labour is scarce recruiting is correspondingly difficult and desertion frequent:

> ... Hai provincias en la República en que los jornales son tan elevados, en que el trabajo es tan bien recompensado i en que los habitudes del pueblo le han inspirado tanta aversión a la carrera de las armas, que ni aun por medio de la conscripción forzoza se obtienen soldados de aquellas provincias; pues aun enrolados en los cuerpos por mui bien tratados que sean por sus jefes i oficiales i por mui distantes que se hallan del lugar de su nacimiento, aprovechan la primera oportunidad que se les presenta para abandonar las banderas. En aquellas provincias no es posible que haya voluntarios que se alistan en las filas del ejercito, pero hai otras en que siendo los jornales mui bajos, la vida dificil i menor la aversion al servicio militar, no sería imposible que hubiese quienes voluntariamente solicitara colocación en las filas, si se mejorase la suerte de la tropa.[42]

The same source reports that the current outdated soldier's pay of 56 reales a month is clearly insufficient to bring about this desirable state of affairs, the sum being way below the usual wages in many provinces, which have doubled since the 56 real level was fixed.

> No es mil veces mas feliz la suerte del último jornalero? El reune por un trabajo de pocas horas que no es igual al del soldado, un salario mui superior al prest de este.[43]

Increasing this pay to 80 reales and improving barrack conditions, this *Memoria* argues, would save money spent on escorts and lost through desertion; the deserter usually going off with his musket and uniform.

Wage levels were, of course, not the only significant consideration. The settlement pattern mattered. A government would naturally prefer a degree of density and accessibility. In the case of Colombia, a number of *Memorias* show clearly that the upland peasant lands of Boyacá and Cundinamarca supplied the largest contingents, above their proportional liability, and that more distant parts and distinct local economies got off lightly. Antioquia, with its scattered mining population, open frontiers, high income per capita, was never a good source of troops. In the riverine Atlantic Coast provinces it was almost impossible to recruit. It was too easy to avoid capture.[44]

---

tanto ascendiente sobre estos indios, cuyo idioma hablan él y su esposa, que en las épocas de revuelta ha logrado formar con ellos un batallón para defender los principios conservadores.' Rufino Gutiérrez, *Monografías*, 2 vols. (Bogotá, 1920–1), vol. 1, p. 155.

[42] Colombia, *Memoria de guerra*, 1853.

[43] *Ibid.*

[44] The *Memoria* of 1868, analysing the provenance of recruits to the Guardia Colombiana, the national army of the time, shows the two states of the central uplands, Boyacá and Cundinamarca, in strong 'surplus', supplying more than their share and the rest of the country in varying degrees of deficit.

José María Vergara y Vergara, in his *Olivos y aceitunos todos son unos* of 1868, gives a sketch of all the diverse national types present in the army that overthrew the Melo government in 1854:

> ... Habiendo venido gente de todos los extremos de la República (menos de Pasto), era curioso ver la variedad de tipos y vestidos en los soldados de la gran revista ... El indio timbiano, con su rústico vestido y su fusil limpio como la cacerola de una cocina de cuáqueros, se veía al lado del soldado de la Costa, que tiene sucio el fusil. El soldado de Boyacá sigue tras la animada fisonomía del mulato costeño, con su cara impasible en que nunca revela gozo, miedo, entusiasmo, ni dolor.[45]

They may all have been there, except from Pasto, but it was unlikely that they were all there in equal numbers.[46]

Nor, as a close reading of Vergara y Vergara hints, did they have the same military qualities or capacity. General Sicard Briceño wrote a *Geografía militar de Colombia* in 1922 in which under the heading *Razas* he summarised the received professional wisdom on this score, 'consultadas varias opiniones autorizadas y ayudados por la propia observación durante nuestra vida militar en todas las regiones del país': *pastusos* — good and courageous soldiers *on their own ground*; inclined to drink and do not like barracks life; *caucanos* — intelligent, bellicose and aggressive but lazy, undisciplined; the *costeño* — usually black, talkative, boastful, adapted to the local climate, clean, courageous in some places, but '*enemigo del cuartel en todo tiempo*'; *santandereanos* — tall, well-built, intelligent, clean, magnificent, etc.[47] (The *briceños* had Santander connections.)

The 'indio de Boyacá y Cundinamarca' — *indio* in the sense of *campesino* — who made up the major part of the ranks, does not come out all that well: '... aun puro en algunos puntos, es de pequeña estatura, de carácter taciturno, escaso de inteligencia en lo general, pero astuto y de valor que raya en estoicismo; es fuerte y sobrio en la comida'. But these men are above all available. The recruiting ground is near at hand, the wages are low, the churches and market places gather men together making for easy capture, the population is relatively submissive. Some villages of Boyacá and Cundinamarca even develop a local military tradition, for producing both officers and soldiers.[48] They are resistant,

---

[45] José María Vergara y Vergara, *Olivos y aceitunos todos son unos* (Bogotá, 1972) (1st ed., 1868), p. 56.

[46] Note to *cuadro* in *Memoria* of 1868: 'Según dicho cuadro, el Estado de Boyacá ha contribuido en cantidad de mas de 457 hombres, i el de Cundinamarca con 282. Al Estado de Antioquia le faltan 218, al de Bolívar 162, al del Cauca 179, al del Magdalena 66, al de Panama 166, al de Santander 19 i al del Tolima 84.' Uncollectable debts.

[47] General Pedro Sicard Briceño, *Geografía militar de Colombia* (Bogotá, 1922), pp. 68–70.

[48] There are signs of similar phenomena elsewhere, for example in Guatemala. Under Estrada Cabrera some villages supplied regular army contingents and their alcaldes customarily wore uniforms.

they are loyal, they were many of them of the right political colour, conservative, for most of the time. The *soldado boyacense* becomes a national type, for
most officers the preferred ranker. [49]

A concern for soldiers' conditions was never entirely absent, and it came to
include more than just physical conditions. Regulations were passed for the education of the soldier.[50] Surveys were even carried out — the Colombian *Memoria*
of 1882 reported that out of 3,264 'individuos de tropa' 1,004 could read and 938
could also write; what was more, 'la mayor parte de los individuos que saben leer
y escribir poseen nociones de aritmética, gramática, geografía, historia, y algunos
de inglés y de francés.' An argument for recruiting the rural poor was that by
doing so the army was reaching out and making citizens, was accompanying the
work of the schoolmaster and the priest, and was making more homogeneous a
nation divided by conquest and by race.[51]

But perhaps the locus clasicus in the hemisphere for arguments about the role
of the army as maker of citizens was Argentina. Argentina of all the republics is the

---

[49]   He appears, leaning on his rifle in his new Germano-Chilean uniform, on a Bogotá
postcard of 1914, with the following poem:

Humilde, silencioso y denodado
empuñe el Mauser y va a la guerra
a luchar por su Dios y por su tierra
con la fe legendaria del cruzado

Nadie le oirá decir ¡Estoy cansado!
ningún peligro táctico le aterra
lo mismo esta en la costa que en la sierra
con sed, con hambre o en sudor bañado.

No esquiva sus servicios ni se ofrece,
ama a su capitán, por sobre todo
y sin vacilaciones le obedece

Presta servicio siempre con buen modo,
vigila mucho, porque le parece
que llega el *liberal* y mata al *godo*.

In Colombia the political allegiances, sometimes pronounced, of different rural populations was a further complicating factor in recruiting.

[50]   The *Memoria de 1873* records that primary schools were established in the Guardia
by a decree of August 1872.

[51]   These arguments are prominent in the article by Major F. Charpin, one of the two
officers who headed the Chilean military mission to Colombia contracted after the War
of the Thousand Days by President Rafael Reyes. See 'El Ejército: Su Razon de Ser', *El
Nuevo Tiempo*, Bogotá, 16 August 1909. They had earlier reached lyrical heights in
Germany, their chief country of origin, heights never attained anywhere in the Americas;
see the article 'Conscription' in the *Encyclopaedia Britannica* cited above.

one that has some of the harshest memories and, in Hernández and Mansilla, the most eloquent literature of recruiting.[52] Indeed, there is a heavy proportion of military literature in the Argentine nineteenth century, reflecting the weight of the army and the military frontier in national affairs. Argentina is also the only Latin American republic that effectively established universal obligatory military service, conscription on the full continental European model.

The determining argument were aired in the debate concerning Ley no. 4031 of 1901, the proposal of Julio A. Roca's minister of war, the then Colonel Pablo Ricchieri.[53] Ricchieri won the vote with Roca's backing, and a rich and ambitious Argentina embarked on a cycle of military service that was to last for 80 years, until it was ended by the Falklands War. Part of Ricchieri's case was the need to make citizens. Though, as has been said, he won the vote, he did not win all of the arguments against those who defended the rationality and appropriateness of more modest and less militarist proposals, and who felt that citizens were best made by other institutions. However, nobody who reads the debate can fail to recognise the importance of the question. How the ranks were to be filled was a problem that had to be solved, and how it was solved impinged on national life and national consciousness in all sorts of ways.

---

[52] José Hernández in *Martín Fierro*, and Lucio V. Mansilla in *Una excursión a los indios Ranqueles*. Lucio V. Mansilla also has a story of a conscript in *Entre Nos*. See R. Rodríguez Molas, introduction to *El Servicio Militar Obligatorio*, series 'Debate nacional' (Buenos Aires, 1983), and also his *Historia social del gaucho* (Buenos Aires, 1982). (He records also that the gauchesco poet Hilario Ascsubi, the author of *Paulino Lucero* and *Santos Vega, o los mellizos de La Flor*, at the outbreak of the Paraguayan War was sent by Mitre to recruit soldiers in Europe.)

[53] For its antecedents and extracts from the debates, see Rodríguez Molas, *El servicio militar obligatorio*.

CHAPTER 4

State Reform and Welfare in Uruguay, 1890–1930

Fernando López-Alves

Until the 1900s the Uruguayan state had grown without a central army. The small nation-state had developed as a by-product of party competition, both at the ballot box and on the battlefield. Power was divided between the two guerrilla-like organisations, the Colorados and the Blancos, in terms of quotas of participation for the party in opposition, usually the Blanco, or National, Party. In the early 1900s, when a central government finally consolidated itself in power, a liberal state founded on the basis of a party system emerged. A two-party system imbued by liberalism differentiated this state from many others in Latin America, especially its powerful neighbours Argentina and Brazil. Welfare reform started early. By the 1910s, the Uruguayan government had began to transform the pension and social security provisions of the late nineteenth century into a bureaucracy that shortly afterward started servicing the unemployed and elderly citizens.

For good reasons the 1890–1930 period has occupied a central place in the literature as the most controversial and influential era of state reform in Uruguayan history. Indeed, it qualifies as one of the most singular developments in the New World. During the two presidencies of the liberal reformer José Batlle y Ordóñez (1903–07 and 1911–15), it could be argued that a pioneer welfare state emerged.[1] Albeit erratically, the process of reform continued after Batlle, and not only the *batllistas* but also distinguished members of the opposition in the Blanco Party supported welfare measures. It might even be said that the spirit of welfare reform preceded Batlle's first presidency. What is perplexing is not only the nature of these reforms, but their early timing in a country with a weak state and rather modest economic development; in the United States, it should be remembered, nationwide social insurance was not established until 1935. It is also intriguing that a country with a violent background of plotting, assassination of public figures and continuous armed struggles during the nineteenth century, could, a few years later, become an example of democracy and welfare

---

[1]   There is an abundant literature on José Batlle y Ordóñez, his reform policies and the social and economic context of the period. See, among others, Francisco E. Panizza, *Uruguay: batllismo y después* (Montevideo, 1990); the nine-volume collection by José Pedro Barrán and Benjamín Nahum, and by Barrán alone, *Batlle, los estancieros, y el imperio británico* (Montevideo, 1982–88). For the *batllista* 'model', see Milton Vanger, *José Batlle y Ordóñez of Uruguay, the Creator of his Times, 1902–1907* (Cambridge, MA, 1963) and *The Model Country: José Batlle y Ordóñez of Uruguay: 1907–1915* (Hanover, NH, 1980). See also Raúl Jacob, *Modelo batllista, variación sobre un viejo tema?* (Montevideo, 1988).

to be emulated elsewhere. This chapter addresses two puzzles. First, how can a democratic state be crafted after a chaotic period of warfare and violence? Second, why was welfare chosen? For all practical purposes of party competition, elite control and coalition formation in Uruguay, as in other parts of Latin America, a liberal state alone would have sufficed.

One possible explanation, as I have argued elsewhere, lies in the weakness of the conservative establishment.[2] For the most part the liberal state emerged triumphant because the conservative opposition had been weakened by the nineteenth century wars that pitted the two major political forces of Uruguay — the Colorado and Blanco parties — against each other.[3] The Church was weak, and no major conservative coalition able to unite urban and rural interests emerged.

There is also the question of cleavages. The historical record shows that it was conflicts among liberals, rather than the liberal-conservative divide, that shaped the Uruguayan state. State-making, therefore, reflected what we can call the contradictions of liberalism. Political and economic interests — rather than mere ideology — moved the major forces behind institution-building. Equally, conflict resolution among liberals lay at the heart of state-making, and strongly shaped the path that led to democracy and welfare. Yet while the predominance of liberalism helps to explain why a liberal democratic, rather than an authoritarian or liberal authoritarian, state emerged, it still does not fully explain why a welfare state had to be created. In other words, why were welfare policies enacted during the culmination of the process of power centralisation?

Customary explanations of democracy are not convincing explanations for the evolution of this state. Neither industrial development nor agricultural bonanza can be argued to have provided the engines of state-making and democracy. Working class pressure, a favourite variable of Marxists and pseudo-Marxian analysis, does not seem to suffice either. This chapter argues that one additional claim, at least, needs to be made in order to explain the puzzle of the *simultaneous* consolidation of the nation-state and the welfare state. We need to look more carefully at how the state spent its money and at the impact of that expenditure on civil-military relations. In Uruguay, the state imposed democracy from above,

---

[2]   See chapter 3 in Fernando López-Alves, *State Formation and Democracy in Latin America 1810–1900* (Durham, NC, 2000). See also my *Between the Economy and the Polity in the River Plate: Uruguay 1810–1890* (London, 1994), pp. 65–70.

[3]   The Colorado and Blanco parties emerged in connection with the conflict for independence. The military efforts of Argentina and Brazil to control Uruguay crafted the two political groupings. The Blancos usually supported Argentine influence in the Banda Oriental and the Colorados traditionally allied with Brazil. For a detailed account of party formation and evolution during the period of Independence and its aftermath, see Juan A. Pivel Devoto, *Historia de los partidos políticos en el Uruguay*, 2 vols. (Montevideo, 1942); and Pivel Devoto, *Historia de los partidos y de las ideas políticas en el Uruguay. La definición de los bandos: 1829–1838*, vol. 2 (Montevideo, 1956).

and it did so at a high cost. The system run by civilians during the nineteenth century established a delicate balance between the military and state-makers in the context of a fragile national budget. The addition of welfare expenses in the early twentieth century could have provoked the collapse of the system altogether. In order to explain why it did not, we must add to the weakness of the conservative establishment and problems of collective action within the landed elite, the history of a social security system that, starting with the military, provided the basis for civilian predominance and opened the door for welfare.

From the presidency of founder Manuel Oribe in 1835 the state devoted an unusually large portion of the national budget to military pensions for war heroes and their descendants. In this way, during the process of state-making, civilian governments were able to buy the support of most military officers.[4] Likewise, during the early twentieth century, the state devoted a considerable part of its budget to paying for a social security system that gained wide popular support for the government and an international reputation as the most advanced democracy of Latin America.

Welfare, as structured in Uruguay, allowed the government to control social benefits not only for public bureaucrats but also for workers in the private sector. The state, rather than organised labour or private capital, became the guarantor and controller of fringe benefits and pensions. The state, therefore, indirectly intervened in collective bargaining by defining the limits of union action and employers' power regarding benefits.

Welfare compensation benefited workers, but not necessarily unions, which lost control over the allocation of fringe benefits.[5] Welfare benefits alleviated pressure on employers because the state contributed to the cost, although employers still had to commit part of their budgets to benefits. In addition to its humanitarian value this welfare system secured the position of the Colorado Party in power and resolved the issue of how to integrate the lower classes within the newly-created state. The *batllista* group, in control of most of the Colorado Party and with the support of some important sectors of the opposition, conceived of the incorporation of the poor and working sectors of the population in terms of a popular doctrine called *organicismo*. According to Batlle,

> The concept that class struggle is a necessary component of modern society, and that all societies are divided into two antagonist and irreconcilable class-

---

[4]   I have suggested part of this argument, although without fully developing it, in 'La guerra, la formación del ejército, y el estado de bienestar: Uruguay 1850–1910', in *Violencia social y conflicto civil: América Latina siglo XVIII–XIX*, Cuadernos de Historia Latinoamericana, *AHILA*, no. 6 (1998).

[5]   Argentina, despite sharing important economic and cultural features with Uruguay, differed widely in this and other aspects of the political system. In Uruguay the control of fringe benefits remained essential to union survival and growth, and state and unions were partners in the control of organised labour.

es is false ... I do not believe that the interests of workers and capital are antagonistic. On the contrary, I believe in a superior social harmony.[6]

The state by-passed unions and welfare benefits strongly contributed to tie the popular sectors directly to the Colorado state. I suggest that welfare policy mirrored the system of pensions awarded in the nineteenth century to war heroes and their descendants.

The State of the Nineteenth Century: Liberals versus Liberals

Much of the literature on state formation in Latin America has stressed the conflict between conservative oligarchies and challenging liberals as the main reasons for violence and state formation. It has also pointed to the fall of colonial institutions and the emergence of new ones as the foundations for war and the emergence of new states. In Uruguay, the situation was quite distinct. Both the Colorado and Blanco parties generally adhered to liberal ideology. Both held similar views on free trade and the rights of men, both adopted liberal discourse and both rejected official ties between government and Church — despite mild support on the part of some Blanco caudillos for the Catholic faith. While, to my knowledge, no author has fully explored the implications of the similarities between the contending parties for the process of state-building, the notion that no strong conservative bloc emerged in Uruguay and that most political leaders adhered to liberalism, has, for the most part, been accepted.[7] Some have constructed theories assuming the cohesiveness and conservatism of the 'oligarchy'; but this has been more postulated than demonstrated.[8]

The Blanco party, traditionally considered the more conservative of the two parties, possessed a broad rural base and pursued a strategy of armed insurrection against Colorado governments based in Montevideo. The insurrectionary party's rural roots, however, have been mistaken for conservatism. Its distaste for centralisation, its anarchist leanings, its loose or non-existing connections with the Church and, all in all, its antipathy for authority, differentiated the Blancos from conservative parties elsewhere. Indeed, in the early 1900s the Blancos supported some laws promoting welfare; and, for some authors the Blancos played a pioneer role in the creation of welfare laws that benefited the poor and the working classes.[9]

---

[6]   Federico Fernández Prando, *Acercamiento a las raíces doctrinarias y filosóficas del batllismo* (Montevideo, 1991), pp. 99–100.

[7]   José P. Barrán and Benjamín Nahum, for instance, in *Historia rural del Uruguay moderno*, 7 vols. (Montevideo, 1967–78), implicitly accept that Uruguay had no strong right-wing conservative establishment. My own work on the nineteenth century concurs with this view.

[8]   Lucia Sala de Tourón et al., *La oligarquía oriental en la Cisplatina* (Montevideo, 1970). See as well Lucia Sala de Tourón and Rosa Alonso Eloy (with the collaboration of Julio C. Rodríguez), *El Uruguay comercial, pastoril y caudillesco*, vols. 1–2 (Montevideo, 1986–91).

[9]   On the libertarian and progressive leanings of the Blanco party, see especially Ricardo Rocha Imaz, *Los blancos* (Montevideo, 1978). See also Washington Reyes Abadie, *Breve historia del Partido Nacional* (Montevideo, 1989).

More than over deep ideological controversies about the nature of politics, the rights of citizens, private property or the role of the Church, Blancos and Colorados fought for a place in the decision-making process. The appointment of *jefes políticos*, the equivalent of provincial governors, and the fairness of elections remained at the centre of controversy from the 1850s all the way to *batllismo*. The state emerged out of these confrontations.

Both parties used a combination of electoral competition and guerrilla warfare to reach agreements. When these were violated the cycle of electoral competition and war started again.[10] Blanco caudillos, usually in opposition, constantly accused the victorious Colorados of electoral corruption and manipulation. As late as 1897, in the midst of a protracted war, the Blanco caudillo Aparicio Saravia wrote to his brother, a sergeant in the Colorado army, that his party had revolted again for the same reasons that it had resorted to war since its creation. He listed electoral fraud, corruption and the decimation of the country's wealth in the hands of Colorado governments.[11] There was not a word about the party's differences with the Colorados regarding Church-state relations, the rights of citizens or economic policy.

In 1903, still at war, Saravia reminded his party of its central objectives: to secure quotas of participation in government and to have a voice in the appointment of *jefes políticos*. Before the rank-and-file of the last Blanco insurrection, Saravia proclaimed, as many before him, that the party adhered to liberalism and democracy, but could not trust governments under Colorado auspices. If the Blancos did not take up arms, the party '... would lose the positions of power conquered with so much sacrifice and ... it would be at the mercy of its adversary in the next year's electoral contest'.[12]

Both parties, therefore, appealed in different ways to their constituencies in the name of *patria*, honour, virtue or their war heroes. But one can safely conclude that the parties belonged to similar versions of nineteenth-century liberalism. Party differentiation emerged from shared collective action and the particularities of the geographical areas the parties came to dominate. Since the end of the Great War in 1850 the Colorados traditionally had controlled Montevideo, the Blancos the rural areas. This made for a more cosmopolitan Colorado party and a more 'indigenous' or 'nationalistic' Blanco party. Up to

---

[10]   The cycle was broken in 1904, when the Colorado government of Batlle y Ordóñez defeated the Blanco guerrilla forces under the command of Aparicio Saravia.

[11]   From a letter to Basilicio Saravia, 6 May 1897. República Oriental del Uruguay, Comisión Honoraria pro Museo El Cordobés, 'General Aparicio Saravia' (Montevideo: Archivo de las Fuerzas Armadas).

[12]   'Correspondencia de Aparicio Saravia', República Oriental del Uruguay, Comisión Honoraria pro Museo Histórico El Cordobés (Montevideo: Archivo de las Fuerzas Armadas, 1978), pp. 85–86.

the 1870s the Colorados recruited more intellectuals and professionals, while the Blancos remained more a party of caudillos. But even this contrast in recruitment changed rapidly thereafter, and both parties started to resemble one another ideologically and organisationally.

This, then, was a state forged by caudillos and intellectuals who adhered to the liberal creed. Convergent ideology, of course, did not make violence the less threatening or intense. *El Día* reported that, of the 27 presidents up to 1913, two had been assassinated, nine had been ousted by force, 12 had confronted serious insurrections and only three had enjoyed peaceful terms of office.[13] Violent crimes and lawlessness constituted part of everyday life, not only in the countryside but also in the city of Montevideo. In addition to Barrán and Nahum's copious historical account of nineteenth-century violence,[14] sources not consulted by these two historians confirm such an image.[15] Bloodshed was common in daylight in the streets of Montevideo, and the police force still 'fired blindly over the citizenry at large'.[16]

Conflict among liberals contributed to low population growth and posed a threat to immigration. As late as 1900 the country's population was only 915,000, of whom some 268,000 lived in Montevideo. Immigrants preferred the relative peace of Buenos Aires, which owed some of its prosperity to the fact that most of Argentina's intense wars had been fought outside the city's boundaries. Equally, for most of the nineteenth-century Blanco insurrections contributed much to slow down rural development in Uruguay. The welfare state that emerged in the early 1900s struggled to control a national territory with deficient roads, no reliable railroad tracks and almost non-existent lines of communication between Montevideo and the rest of the territory, not to mention among the regions. Despite the modest recovery of the 1880s and 1890s, compared to Argentina, the rural economy never boomed.

Wars among liberals were disruptive enough to slow down the process of power centralisation considerably. Blanco caudillo Luis Alberto de Herrera correctly suggested that the fundamental feature of this state was that it emerged from agreements among contenders that could not defeat each other.[17] The Colorados ran Montevideo during most of the nineteenth century, but since the Blancos could not be completely defeated, the parties agreed on *cuotas políticas* or number of governorships, that gave them control of a particular region.

---

[13] *El Día*, March 7 1913 (Montevideo: Biblioteca Nacional, periodicals).

[14] Barrán and Nahum, *Historia rural del Uruguay moderno*.

[15] For an analysis of political violence during the nineteenth century using additional sources, see ch. 3 in my *State Formation and Democracy*.

[16] 'Mensaje del presidente de la república Pedro Varela al abrirse el tercer período de la undécima legislatura', February 1875 (Montevideo: Imprenta El Uruguay: Pasaje del Mercado Viejo. Biblioteca Nacional, Sala Uruguay).

[17] Luis Alberto de Herrera, *La paz de 1828* (Montevideo, repr. 1989).

These pacts provided the foundations of the nation-state. The 'social contract' of the early 1900s, however, represented a different type of agreement because it ended armed insurgency. It was, in a sense, a new state because both parties agreed that elections constituted the only vehicle by which to decide who controlled the state and what would be the share of the opposition. The Blancos, having been totally defeated, were now prepared to resort exclusively to elections. The Colorados perceived elections as the only available means to avoid further war and to increase the capacity of the state. Democracy or, better, the 'democratic method', in Shumpeter's sense, was thereby adopted.

State Reform, Popular Support and Welfare

In the emerging new social contract, the reformist *batllista* sector of the Colorados gained control and immediately made alliances with populist factions belonging to the Blanco party.[18] These state-makers created a larger bureaucracy, intervened in the economy and incorporated the defeated Blanco guerrillas into the national army. At the same time, the government banned the military from decision-making and secured widespread popular support without resorting to state corporatism. All these were to have an enduring legacy.[19] Indeed, Batlle's reforms influenced state development for a long time after his death in 1929.[20] During his first and, especially, his second presidency, the state opposed foreign (meaning British) investment, engaged aggressively in the service sector and controlled trade, industry and finance. It also started a remarkable process of state reform that resulted in the radical restructuring of the executive into the 'colegiado' system.

One can argue that institutional and social changes that characterised other Latin American states in the 1950s and 1960s took place in Uruguay starting in the 1910s. As early as 1908, 26.3 per cent of the active population of the country was engaged in activities related to services.[21] Immigration and services augmented both the urban working and middle classes. By 1914, 40.79 per cent of the residents of Montevideo were considered middle class and received 55.33 per cent of the total city income.[22] This new state, of course, cultivated many friends but also foes,

---

[18] For details on these agreements see Aldo Solari, *El desarrrollo del Uruguay en la postguerra* (Montevideo, 1967).

[19] Although one could treat the 1830s constitution as the founding contract upon which the state rested, the institutional design that prevailed through the twentieth century mostly resulted from the pact that emerged in the early 1900s.

[20] As M.H.J. Finch has put it, 'Batllism refers to a national style or ideology of development within which Uruguayan public life was conducted from early this century to the end of the 1960s', in *A Political Economy of Uruguay since 1870* (London, 1981) p. 2.

[21] Of this 26.3% only 8.5% were domestic servants, which leaves a good 16–20% still engaged in other services. Aldo Solari, *El desarrollo social del Uruguay en la postguerra* (Montevideo, 1967), p. 9.

[22] Barrán and Nahum, *Batlle, los estancieros*, vol. 1, p. 197.

leading to the 'halt to reform' that began in 1916 under President Feliciano Viera and gained momentum in 1919.[23] Overall, however, the state initiated a cycle of reform that shaped state development up to the present day.

Geography provides a good clue to understanding the emphasis on services. In the 1890s state-makers had perceived the long beaches of the coast as potential sources of revenue.[24] State expansion went hand in hand with state's support of private capital investment in the *balnearios*. During the first Batlle presidency the state became an investor itself and pursued coastal development as an official growth strategy. The government created coastal swimming pools and hotels to attract Argentines, Brazilians and European tourists. A considerable share of the state's budget went into the construction of the first four kilometres of a *rambla* (boardwalk). Construction of other *ramblas* and improvements in seaside resorts also become a top priority on the agenda of Batlle's successors.[25] In 1930, a local newspaper claimed that the coast had become 'the hub … and heart of social activity …' in the city of Montevideo.[26] The policy was one of the strongest legacies of the period and continued unabated during the rest of the century. The present government is pursuing a very similar strategy in the framework of Mercosur.

In a system where the option of war was now closed and popular support became the means to access political power, the parties intensified party patronage through the staffing of the public bureaucracy. The Colorados, and later the Blancos, created regional party cells, which, as Bruschera forcefully argued, differed from elite clubs and were soon transformed into neighbours' clubs.[27] They distributed favours and captured votes. In 1931 Congress issued a law requiring party patronage and job distribution within the public bureaucracy to mirror a party's electoral support. The parties, then, divided patronage according to electoral success; they became directly dependent upon their clienteles.

---

[23] On the opposition to reform, see the solid analysis of Gerardo Caetano, *La república conservadora*, 2 vols. (Montevideo, 1992).

[24] Already in the 1890s, many conceived the city of Montevideo as a resort, and a few years after, the whole country was perceived as such. Uruguay became a 'país balneario'. In that decade many private entrepreneurs invested in coastal areas, and in 1897 they promoted an aggressive policy of forestation on most of the eastern coast. See Raúl Jacob, *Modelo batllista*, p. 97.

[25] President Claudio William (1907–11) enthusiastically followed suit, and this continued under the second Batlle y Ordóñez presidency (1911–15). Despite disagreements between *batllista* reformers and President Feliciano Viera (1915–19) the state kept improving the coastal areas and services.

[26] *Diario del Plata*, Suplemento del Centenario, 1930, p. 171. For a good analysis of the importance of coastal development in Uruguay, and especially for the city of Montevideo, see Raúl Jacob, *Modelo batllista*.

[27] Oscar Bruschera, *Los partidos tradicionales y la evolución institucional del Uruguay* (Montevideo, 1962), p. 15.

The state's strategy to secure and control popular support was two-fold. First, the government discouraged the formation of interest groups and lobbying organisations. The goal was to establish a one-to-one relationship between government and the private citizen, rather than between the state and organised groups. Second, the state created the welfare system to reinforce urban lower class backing. Since the 1830 Constitution interest groups in Uruguay were looked upon as disrupting factions that — if allowed to grow stronger — could seriously undermine democratic competition. The resulting system, therefore, was pluralist because political parties could compete for office, but at the same time interest groups remained organisationally weak. Some of them, like the Rural Association, naturally possessed a very strong voice.[28] Nevertheless, groups were not encouraged to organise or to establish links with the state.

The relationship between the state and the 'popular sectors', as the *batllistas* called them, remained far from corporatist. Indeed, this arrangement set a strong precedent for the rejection of state corporatism in the mid-twentieth century.[29] No formal incorporation of the working classes into the state apparatus was attempted, nor did there ever emerge a hierarchically-arranged order of associations and interest groups under the state's tutelage. The scholarly literature has it that labour was not incorporated in Uruguay in a corporatist fashion because, unlike Argentina or Brazil, the small republic developed a pluralist system dominated by two competitive political parties. Yet countries such as Colombia, with a similar two party system, did incorporate labour organisations into their parties.[30] Part of the reason why the Uruguayan Colorados and Blancos did not is simple: welfare and populism did not need to operate through grass-roots organisations to secure popular support.[31] In addition, regular party staffing of the public bureaucracy contributed to effective linkages with the private citizen. Thus, party patronage and welfare sufficed. Lower class

---

[28]   See Caetano, *La república conservadora* vol. 1, pp. 23–9. See also Barrán and Nahum, *Batlle, los estancieros*, vols. 5 and 8.

[29]   For an analysis of why Uruguay did not adopt state corporatism in the early 1940s while Argentina did, see Fernando López-Alves, 'Why not Corporatism? Collective Bargaining and Political Intermediation in the Uruguay of the 1940s', in David Rock (ed.), *Latin America in the 1940s* (Berkeley, 1993). For a different position see Jorge Lanzaro, *Sindicatos y sistema político: relaciones corporativas en el Uruguay, 1940–1985* (Montevideo, 1986).

[30]   An in-depth comparison of Uruguay and Colombia in terms of their labour policy can be found in Fernando López-Alves, 'Why do Unions Coalesce? Labor Solidarity in Colombia and Urugua,' (unpubl. PhD diss., University of California, Los Angeles, 1989).

[31]   The Colorado Party's popularity under *batllismo*, the weakness of the opposition and friendly relations with emerging anarchist and, later, communist unions, made a corporatist solution unappealing to those in power, because corporatism appeared to be uncertain, expensive and troublesome.

incorporation in Uruguay took place through the individual citizen, rather than through organised groups. Governments of the nineteenth century had used a similar strategy to secure civilian control; they did not make agreements with the military institution per se, but with individual officers.

The state cultivated friendly relations with the working poor, and socialist overtones were frequent in *batllista* discourse. It also took several remarkable steps forward in terms of women's rights.[32] In agreement with anarchists, communists and anarchosyndicalists, the state allowed unions to organise rather autonomously and freely. Indeed, some anarchists even adopted the term *anarcobatllismo* to express their gratitude to the Batlle regime and to conceptualise their friendly relations with a government that took union autonomy as seriously as they did.

The leadership of the left could not but have noticed *batllista* radical discourse. At the 1925 convention of the Colorado Party, and while discussing tax policy, the leader astounded some Colorado party members when arguing that: '... property is a great injustice. The world, one can say without fear of error, belongs to us all ... Property, in reality, should have no ties to particular individuals.'[33] Years before, some *batllistas* had expressed even more radical views in their appreciation of private property in this country of ranchers. In 1910 Domingo Arena, one of Batlle's closest allies, wrote that 'After all, land in itself does not belong to anyone in particular, it belongs to all.'[34] While private property under *batllismo* was far from abolished, tax policy did reflect the socialist overtones of reform.[35] The unions also owed the 1906 Labour Law to the *batllistas*, which reduced the working day to eight hours and prohibited child labour; the same piece of legislation abolished the death penalty. And yet neither the left nor unions developed a close relationship with government. Organised labour did not become a partner in the ruling coalition, and the Colorados, for their part, kept unions and grass-roots organisations comfortably away from decision making. Government and labour remained friendly but distant.

---

[32] In May 1912, parallel to the creation of high schools in most of the departamentos, the state established the 'Universidad de Mujeres', and Congress approved a woman's right to divorce under her own initiative. From his first presidency, Batlle himself wrote a column in the newspaper *El Día* under the pseudonym 'Gloria' in which he advocated equal rights for women.

[33] June 1925 address to the Colorado Party Convention, Montevideo (Montevideo: Biblioteca Nacional, Sala Uruguay), p. 2.

[34] *El Día*, 4 April 1910, p. 4.

[35] For a good analysis of *batllista* tax policy in regard to land ownership, see José Rilla, 'La política impositiva: asedio y bloqueo del batllismo,' in Jorge Balbis et al., *El primer batllismo: cinco enfoques polémicos* (Montevideo, 1985).

Why Welfare?

Would party and state patronage, without welfare measures, have sufficed to secure popular support? Perhaps. But welfare laws provided an extra assurance that the lower class vote in the urban environment went to the party in power. Secondly, welfare offered the party in government a unique opportunity to bypass unions and remain the only source of social benefits. Electoral results reflected the success of the combination of patronage, clubs and welfare.

Table 1: Elections for the House of Diputados and the Constitutional Assembly 1905-20

Year	Total Votes to Congress		Total *Batllista* Votes	% *Batllista* Votes
1905	46,238	DIPUT.	26,705	57.7
1907	44,693		28,710	64.2
1910	31,262		24,982	79.9
1913	54,728		32,849	60
1916	146,632		60,420	45.2
1917	129,008		63,617	49.3
1919	188,352		55,623	29.5
1920	178,777	C. A.	93,292	52.2

Source: Carlos Zubillaga, 'El batllismo: una experiencia populista,' in Jorge Balbis et al., *El primer batllismo* (Montevideo, 1985), p. 37.

Unions agitated, but their members apparently voted for the *batllistas*. In Table 1 I have shown the popular vote to the Chamber of Representatives and the Constitutional Assembly, because I do not have figures showing votes for *batllismo* alone — while, under the electoral system of the time, the Colorado electoral ticket included other factions as well as the *batllista* group. Table 1 is mostly based on the growing urban vote and shows the popularity of *batllismo* from the defeat of Saravia in 1904.[36] The effect of welfare reform on the workers' vote is hard to gauge exactly, given the large numbers of immigrants who did not vote, but the table unequivocally reflects the rise of *batllismo*. Support for wel-

---

[36] By the 1925 election the electoral system had changed and support for the *batllistas* fell to 39.9%; it rose again in the 1926 election, reaching 48.9%. These ups and downs relate to the strong conservative reaction the *batllistas* confronted from the opposition, as we shall see immediately below.

fare measures also boosted the popularity of other political leaders belonging to different fractions, including the Blancos.[37]

Unions and capital negotiated over wages, but the state intervened in negotiations to secure industrial peace. In 1923, a distinguished *batllista* congressmen, Julio María Sosa, introduced a bill creating a *Consejo Consultivo*, which functioned as part of the National Labour Office. The *Consejo*, which included labour leaders, employers and state representatives, was charged with settling disputes and deciding on the terms of collective bargaining. This and other measures provided the groundwork for the so-called 'Co-Co' alliance of the 1940s and 1950s.[38] It can be argued that, until the late 1980s, despite solid working-class membership of anarchist, socialist and communist unions, urban workers generally supported the Colorado party in power.

When, in the 1910s, the state implemented welfare policies that granted benefits and pensions to individuals and their families, unions remained unable to control the fringe-benefits system. By the time the Great War started in Europe the Uruguayan state was offering, through the National Insurance Bank, welfare relief and pensions to all those who were unemployed due to work-related injuries. Congress also approved old age pensions. These came into effect in 1915. Each pension was a law, and each pension directly established a compromise between the state and the individual citizen. Pensions were issued as laws benefiting just one individual and his descendants and were tailored to meet individual needs.

This is not surprising, given that the social security system was not yet fully established. But this was also in line with the general *batllista* policy of dealing with the individual citizen rather than with organised groups. Pensions and provisions for the unemployed also mirrored the military retirement system of the nineteenth century. Democracy, to a great extent, rested on the welfare state; in turn, the welfare system mirrored the military pension system of the nineteenth century.

Officers, Liberals and Welfare

Welfare had its enemies: regional political bosses, for instance, who did not wish to lose control of the rural population and sought to retain exclusive control

---

[37] For an account of welfare reforms attributed to Blanco Party leaders, see Fernando Oliu, Hector Lorenzo Rios and Ricardo Rocha Imaz, *Los nacionalistas y la cuestión social* (Montevideo, 1988).

[38] During the late 1940s and 1950s 'Co-Co' stood for Colorado–Communist alliance. No formal linkage between communist unions and the Colorado party developed, however, and the idea of an 'alliance' may be an exaggeration. Yet communist labour leaders and state representatives usually saw eye-to-eye on issues of labour law and collective bargaining. The composition of the Consejo was as follows: one senator and two congressmen, one representative from the Chamber of Industry, one from the Chamber of Commerce, four workers' representatives, one representative from the banking sector and the Director of the National Labour Office. For details, see F. López-Alves, 'Why Do Unions Coalesce?', p. 154, and Federico Fernández Prando, *Acercamiento a las raíces*, pp. 82–3.

over benefits to their clientele. In many rural areas of the country their influence was unaffected by welfare. There also were urban sectors that opposed welfare measures, particularly small industrialists and traders who balked at the bill for social security. But the main opposition came from large landholders, who did not want to pay for benefits that for the most part favoured urban workers. Moreover, from the early 1910s, landholders grew concerned about *batllista* tax policy. As we have seen, *batllista* rhetoric even questioned the existence of large landholdings, '... which in our country is a shame we have not, so far, been able to eliminate'.[39] 'Elimination' was not a possibility; but an increase in the land tax certainly was. The landlords' strenuous reaction in 1916 against the imposition of Batlle's pet project, the *colegiado* system, expressed their general abhorrence of his reform, and so required negotiation.[40]

The other important actor in the new state, the military, was opposed to welfare on principle or by vested interest. Yet the officer corps had to be controlled if the state was to remain in civilian hands and the *batllistas* were to remain in charge. The government sought to secure loyalties using two interrelated strategies. One was intense recruitment of officers into the two major parties; the Colorados excelled at this. The other was to follow the nineteenth-century policy of granting pensions and benefits. Both strategies succeeded. Since the mid-nineteenth century consecutive governments had also used the military budget to restrain the officer corps, which had lacked the most basic resources, with troops having 'even to pay for their own shoes or swords'.[41]

Occasionally the army did gain in institutional strength, but it never proved able to retain this over time. In 1904, for instance, after the defeat of Saravia the army gained some power.[42] Batlle, who had fought against military regimes, thought of the army as incapable of conducting state affairs, but he still needed to create loyal infantry battalions in most *departamentos* to secure control of the national territory. In Montevideo three new battalions came under the control of the urban officer corps. The rank-and-file were trained in the use of more modern weaponry, and something close to modern military discipline was imposed on fresh recruits. Cavalry regiments experienced a most remarkable growth. Before

---

39　Quoted in José Rilla, , 'La política impositiva', p. 80.

40　For details, see José Rilla, 'La política impositiva', and Gerardo Caetano, *La república conservadora*.

41　*El soldado, revista quincenal*, Montevideo, 5 November 1887 (Montevideo: Archivo de las Fuerzas Armadas), pp. 161–2.

42　To a great extent this national army resulted from the unification of two armies, part of the defeated Blanco army that fought under Saravia and the Colorado-dominated army that followed Batlle. For details, see Fernando López-Alves, 'La formación del ejercito'.

43　The seventh cavalry regiment, along with the eighth, was created in 1904 to secure the Colorado victory over Saravia. In 1910 the same battalions were used to repress the frustrated 1910 revolution of the Partido Nacional. The ninth regiment was created in

1904 only five existed. By 1905 there were ten, all supporting the Colorados.[43] This newly modernised force became the government's most efficient weapon against further Blanco insurrections. Despite its growth and its increased influence, however, the army remained peripheral to decision-making. In fact, the state was able to reduce its influence considerably in the next two decades, and, in the 1924 national budget, the military was at the bottom of state expenditure.

Tellingly, no coup or even insurrection was staged in response to the progressive exclusion of the army as a political actor. Much has been made of the 1933 military takeover, yet its outcome was to place a Colorado, Gabriel Terra, in power. The 'military regime', backed by civilians and only a fraction of the army, lasted only for one year. In 1934, when a constitutional reform was approved by both houses of the legislature, power was turned back over to civilians, Terra was duly elected as president (1934–38). The most serious and lasting military takeover took place in 1973, when a group of officers staged a coup and dissolved the lower and upper houses.[44] And even in that case no military leader emerged, the coup being partly orchestrated with the support of Colorado factions. Until 1982 the country was governed by an anonymous military junta which included a puppet civilian president.

A second important reason why army officers respected civilian supremacy is to be found in the generous fringe benefits and pensions granted by the state to senior officers and their descendants. From the 1860s, army officers had obtained substantial benefits in terms of pensions and security of employment for themselves and their families, especially their unmarried daughters. They were given land property and local influence and some important tax exceptions as well. In 1899, congressman Eduardo Acevedo complained bitterly that, from a state budget of 15.8 million pesos, eight million was assigned to the public debt, especially for pensions to military retirees. According to Acevedo, by 1863 the public debt was already two million pesos, 400,000 of which were going to military pensions, 'Today, the passive classes take 1,400,000 from the public debt, which exceeds 127,000,000.'[45] Rather than borrowing further to balance the budget, Acevedo proposed taxing the 'clases pasivas' as the best possible solution to the deficit. However, he warned that this new law

> would be risky … because the next day the military would return asking for their jobs back and threatening government. Moreover, their widows and

---

1905 to repress the 'revolutionary works of Nationalist Caudillo Mariano Saravia'. In 'Historia del sexto, séptimo, y octavo de caballería', vol. 4, Blandengues de Artigas (Montevideo, 1984) p. 3.

[44] In addition to a paranoia related to the threat of communism, the coup was motivated by officers' dissatisfaction with salaries, promotions and their poor participation in decision-making, as well as the uncertain future of the military institution.

[45] Eduardo Acevedo, 'Clases pasivas. Bases para una ley de reforma' (Montevideo, 1899).

minors could even ask for more (money) and overburden even more the budget of the Executive.[46]

The breakdown of the budget in terms of beneficiaries is indicative of the importance of military pensions by the end of the nineteenth century. From a total budget of 1,934,878 pesos devoted to pay the public debt, retired officers, widows of officers and handicapped military men obtained 74,000. The organisation 'Citizens of Independence' and retired generals, obtained 427,000. Their widows and children obtained 338,101. Civilian retirees obtained 148,943 and minors and pension holders obtained 226,684 pesos.[47]

This system of military pensions was improved and augmented in the new *batllista* state. In the aftermath of Saravia's defeat, following a nineteenth-century tradition, the Colorados secured dissident officers' loyalties by either incorporating them into the national army or granting pensions. Each pension required approval by the executive, the lower house and the senate, so that the political elites had a very good sense of who was granted what, and under what circumstances.

Table 2 relates the number of yearly military pensions granted to officers — especially generals and colonels, for 'heroic deeds' and the 'defence of the national patrimony' — to the total number of laws and decrees passed by the senate in each particular year.[48] Despite some gaps in the information it shows that pensions and social security represented an important part of legislative activity.

The novelty of social reform under Batlle lay in its all-embracing character, expressed in the multiplication of *cajas* serving different sectors of the labour force, including workers in the private sector. The extension of benefits granted in the past to the military and some sectors of the public administration, therefore, constituted the core of the *batllista* reform. Land grants to military heroes were already a rare occurrence during the last decades of the nineteenth century; by the 1890s, retirement benefits and pensions for female descendants came to constitute the main offer of the package of benefits. What *batllismo* offered to the 'popular sectors' bears a very close resemblance to these packages, although the system was not as generous regarding female descendants. The political elite also benefited from the retirement system. After only ten years of active duty politicians could gain access to benefits similar to those of the military. Moreover, retirements were adjusted automatically to the level of salaries of those still on active duty.[49]

---

[46] *Ibid.*, p. 3.

[47] *Ibid.*, p. 4.

[48] Data for this table were obtained from the *Compilación de leyes y decretos de la república oriental del Uruguay*, vols. 12–35 (Montevideo, 1880–1930).

[49] See Aldo Solari, 'El sistema político', pp. 25–6.

Table 2: Military Pensions and Laws, 1880–1925

Year	Number of Military Pensions Approved as Laws	Total Number of Approved Laws in the Period	% Pensions as Total Number of Laws	Source
1880	6	36	16%	v. 12
1881	14	55	25%	v. 13
1882	4	38	11%	v. 13
1883	26	69	38%	v. 14 & 15
1884	46	111	41%	v. 15
1885	33	86	38%	v. 15 & 16
1886	7	40	17%	v. 16
1887	17	65	26%	v. 17
1888	20	72	27%	v. 17
1889	7	43	16%	v. 18
1890	13	46	28%	v. 18
1891	7	43	16%	v. 19
1892	4	43	9%	v. 19
1893	2	46	4%	v. 20
1894	19	60	32%	v. 20
1895	52	99	52%	v. 21
1896	32	78	41%	v. 21
1897	2	27	7%	v. 22
1898	2	58	3%	v. 22
1899	1	39	2%	v. 23
1900	3	59	5%	v. 23
1901	5	49	10%	v. 24
1902	8	58	14%	v. 24
1903	30	82	37%	v. 25
1904	9	50	18%	v. 25
1905	33	88	38%	v. 25
1906	56	126	44%	v. 26
1907	35	125	28%	v. 27
1908	82	161	51%	v. 28
1909	50	160	31%	v. 29
1910	70	146	48%	v. 30
1911	80	370	22%	v. 31
1912	216	354	61%	v. 32 & 33
1913	431	507	85%	v. 34 & 35
1914	273	364	75%	v. 36
1915	98	179	55%	v. 37*
1916	54	180	30%	v. 39
1917	388	518	75%	v. 40 & 41
1918	719	786	91%	v. 42 & 43
1919	23	371	6%	v. 44 & 45
1920	157	291	54%	v. 46
1921	16	110	15%	v. 46 & 47
1922	4	96	4%	v. 49
1923	10	140	7%	v. 50
1924	9	121	7%	v. 51
1925	7	105	6%	v. 52

* Volume 38 consisted entirely of decrees

Conclusion

Our interpretation of welfare in Uruguay as a strategy to obtain popular support without linking government and the parties to grass-roots organisations challenges some explanations of the emergence of welfare states. Did industrialisation have anything to do with the adoption of welfare, as a large body of literature claims? All nation-states respond to the growth of cities and industries by creating public measures to help citizens cope with economic dislocation.[50] Our study of the Uruguayan case, however, marks the limits of this literature.[51] The European experience does not apply here, nor does it fit the other pioneer experience of state welfare social policy in the Americas, the United States.[52]

Another well-known explanation of welfare stresses economic prosperity, which some have associated with the 'golden' era of Batllism.[53] I suggest, though, that while the country had made progress since the 1890s, it remained far from prosperous. Rather, stagnation prevailed through most of the nineteenth century, and very modest industrial development was evident in twentieth-century Uruguay. From 1913 to 1917 the country suffered a serious crisis that negatively affected commerce, industry and the already scant state revenue. In the early 1920s manufacturing and trade plunged, to modestly recover again to the level of 1919 only in 1923.[54] Growth was steady only in the very brief periods from 1923–24 and from 1929–30.

Another major strand in the literature on the welfare state emphasises the higher level of education among the political elite and the urban sectors. High levels of education among members of the political elite would have promoted support for welfare. This thesis is, at best, ambiguous. First, other educated elites in Latin America did not create welfare states. Second, while the prevailing level of education in Uruguay was good, it was not that high. Third, how literacy in the urban population and the political elite promoted welfare policy is

---

[50] See, for instance, Harold Wilenski, *The Welfare State and Equality* (Berkeley, 1975).

[51] These limits are stressed as well by Flora Peter and James Albert, 'Modernization, Democratization, and the Development of Welfare States in Western Europe', in Flora and Arnold Heidenheimer, *The Development of Welfare States in Europe and America* (New Brunswick, NJ, 1981), pp. 37–80.

[52] On the United States see, for instance, Theda Skocpol, *Social Policy in the United States* (Princeton, 1995); or Stephen Skowronek, *Building a New American State: The Expansion of National Administrative Capacities* (Cambridge, 1982).

[53] See the interpretation of Batllism advanced in José de Torres Wilson, *Diez ensayos sobre historia uruguaya* (Montevideo, 1973). In many ways this is also suggested by contemporaries. See the pioneering work of Alberto Zum Felde, *Evolución histórica del Uruguay: esquema de su sociología, comprende la evolución social y política del país desde los orígenes hasta el presente* (Montevideo, 1920).

[54] Raúl Jacob, *Modelo batllista: variación sobre un viejo tema?* (Montevideo, 1988) p. 11.

hard to discern. In addition, educational reform was not completed by the time of welfare; indeed, important measures aiming at reforming the educational system formed part of the welfare bill.

Educational reform evidently had illustrious precedents in the nineteenth century.[55] According to the national census of 1908, 52 per cent of the population in the national territory was literate, and only 27.3 per cent of those in Montevideo were illiterate — not a bad record. But the evolution of college instruction does not show such an enviable record. Despite its self-promoted image as a highly intellectualised, European-style society, at the end of the nineteenth century Uruguay was a country with sparse intellectual activity and poor formal education. In 1873, the rector of the only university in the country, José Ellauri, saw no need to establish chairs in medicine or pharmacology. He believed they would attract no clients and that the university was far from ready to afford such programmes. Only law was taught professionally. In 1900 the national university had only 400 registered students, including all schools and *cátedras*. It was state reform that changed this situation and 30 years later there were 2,600 students enrolled in a state-funded university that exuded self-confidence and possessed fairly decent resources. One might ask, then, whether democracy and welfare were just a show of civil progress, performed for the international community in an effort to gain admission as a member of the increasingly powerful coalition of liberal states. But if that had been the case, Uruguay would simply have qualified as a liberal state, without ever becoming a welfare state.

---

[55] José Pedro Varela's reform of the school system stands as one of the most important landmarks of instructional reform in Latin America. Varela was minister of education during the dictatorship of Lorenzo Latorre (1876–80).

CHAPTER 5

The Hollow State:
The Effect of the World Market on State-Building in
Brazil in the Nineteenth Century

Steven Topik*

In the nineteenth century European colonies in the Americas were not like ripen-
ing fruits, with the most mature, fecund ones developing most quickly into the best
formed nation-states.[1] Counter-intuitively, the colonies with the most integrated
and articulated state/church machinery and with the most prosperous market
societies were not the first to consolidate post-colonial state power. Indeed, one
could almost argue the inverse: the colonies where colonial capacity and penetration were the greatest, such as Mexico and Peru, had the more perilous and drawn-
out journeys to statehood in the nineteenth century. The haphazard contingencies
of history guided the formation of states as much as did institutional structures.
But the relationship to the world economy was also fundamental. In some cases, at
least, sovereignty and state capacity were built from without, slowly reaching into
the interior, helping to build a nation as well as a polity.

One of the least likely candidates for a relatively smooth transition to statehood
was continental-size, under-populated and weakly governed Brazil.[2] Yet many contemporaries and later scholars have held that Brazil did in fact experience a strong,
centralised post-colonial state in the nineteenth century. Unlike Spanish America,
Portuguese America did not break up into many independent states but remained
united. Indeed, Brazil greatly expanded its territory and the state extended its
reach. Moreover, Brazil's sovereignty received early international recognition.

*   The research for this chapter was funded in part by fellowships from the National
Endowment for the Humanities, the University of California's President's Fellowship in
the Humanities, UC Mexus and the UCI Humanities Center. I would like to thank Carlos
Marichal with whom I discussed some of these ideas, Rosemary Thorp for her insightful comments and stimulating discussions with the participants of the conference and
workshop on The Formation of the Nation-State in Latin America, particularly James
Dunkerley and Alan Knight.
1   Caio Prado Junior believed that with independence 'elements of Brazilian nationhood ... finally came to flower and reached maturity', see *The Colonial Background of
Brazil*, trans. by Suzette Macedo (Berkeley, 1971), p. 2. See also, José Honorio Rodriguez,
Independencia: revolução e contra-revolução (Rio de Janeiro, 1975) vol. 1, p. 301.
2   For a discussion of the recent literature on states, sovereignty and the world economy, see the introduction to David Smith, Dorothy Solinger and Steven Topik (eds.),
States and Sovereignty in the Global Economy (London, 1999).

A good case could be made that the state preceded, and indeed created, the nation, as was the case in Europe. Despite having the same ingredients as Spanish America to create 'creole nationalism' — a homogeneous European or Europeanised elite; a single mutually-comprehensible language for the free population;[3] the monopoly of the Catholic religion — Brazil was conspicuously late to develop nationalism or a sense of nationness.[4] The proto-independence movements prior to 1822, such as the Inconfidencia in Minas Gerais or the Taylor's Revolt in Bahia, which are often taken as evidence of precocious nationalism were either race wars or elite efforts to protect and increase local power.

This chapter will explore whether the new state derived its form, sovereignty, legitimacy and power as a natural outgrowth of its patrimonial colonial heritage, including the only successful New World post-colonial monarchy, or if it was more a product of the world economy and European liberalism. If foreign states, capital and trade helped to strengthen, and in some ways create, the incipient Brazilian state, did the foreign underpinnings of the new state also diminish its domestic capacity? Does the Brazilian experience demonstrate that the opening to the world economy was beneficial to state-building in Latin American colonies or that it created distorted, hollow states?

Brazil's monarchy in the nineteenth century was a hybrid state form that was unique not only to Latin America but in the world. It was the only successful new world monarchy with the trappings of European liberal constitutional parliamentary government yet based on the divine right of the emperor. Inheritor of a Portuguese tradition of a patrimonial state and a self-sufficient economy, Brazil also enjoyed a thriving export economy based on private initiative and African slave labour. As a result, the Brazilian state has served as a laboratory for students of state-building. To venture into this extremely involved question, I will sketch some comparisons with a very different colony and post-colonial state, Mexico.

---

[3] Despite the continental reach of Brazil, the Portuguese spoken in the Amazon by the elite was understandable by the elite two to three thousand miles away in Rio Grande do Sul. Yes, there were local expressions and slang and African languages had greater influence in say Bahia where there may have been a clandestine African pidgin dialect than in the Amazon where a creole 'lingua franca' with Tupi elements developed. But these affected the plebeians, who often could speak more Portuguese than the elite.

[4] Benedict Anderson, *Imagined Communities. Reflections on the Origins and Spread of Nationalism*, rev. ed. (London, 1991), pp. xiii, 46, 192. On Spanish American nationalism see: Jaime Rodríguez, *Spanish American Independence* (Cambridge, 1998) and Florencia E. Mallon, *Peasant and Nation* (Berkeley, 1995). On Brazil see José Murilo de Carvalho, *Pontos e bordados* (Belo Horizonte, 1998), pp. 101 and passim. There are respected historians such as Jobson Arruda who argue the reverse, that the nation (if not nationalism) preceded the state; see: 'Estados e sociedades ibéricas, realizacões e conflitos (Séculos XVIII–XX)', *Actos dos 3eiro Cursos Internacionais de Verão de Cascais, 1996*, p. 204.

Brazil's Patrimonial State

That the Brazilian independent state was admired and trusted by Europeans is beyond question. It was seen as a civilised, Europeanised regime. Yet the nature of the Brazilian imperial state and its secrets for success have been heatedly debated by Brazilians. Joaquim Nabuco, one of Brazil's leading statesmen, captured the paradoxical nature of the Brazilian imperial state. On the one hand, complained Nabuco, 'everything is expected to come from the state which, being the only active organisation, seeks and absorbs — through taxes and loans — all the available capital to distribute it among its clients by public employment ... As a consequence, then, government employment has become the "noble profession" and the vocation of all.' On the other hand, Nabuco denounced 'the feudal division of land' into 'a certain number of huge properties' that served as 'small ashantis in which only one will rules'.[5] So he saw a state that both dominated everything and a state that had no influence at all, at least in the countryside. It was a combination of a European realm and feudal fiefs and African ashantis. Modern students of the empire have emphasised different aspects of this heterodox state, seeing it as patrimonial, seignorial or liberal, centralised or fragmented, beholden to foreigners — either Portuguese or British — or exercising independent sovereignty.

Much of the analytical confusion derives from attempts to pigeon-hole the Brazilian experience into categories derived from simplistic notions of European history and to emphasise only one facet of the state and society rather than understanding how they fit together. In fact, Brazil combined elements of what appeared to be different historical epochs because until 1889 it had what appeared to be a centralised monarchy and yet had a slave-based export orientation. As a result, the state looked very different from the capital cities and from the countryside. That the nineteenth-century state could take different forms would not surprise a student of Mexico, which passed from colony to monarchy to federalist and centralised republic (several times) to monarchy again, back to oligarchic republic. Those changes are not viewed so much as signs of analytical confusion as evidence of political unrest.

Brazil, however, seemed to pass from colony to independent nation without the bloodbath and chaos that reigned in Mexico.[6] Unlike the mestizo caudillo regimes that Europeans scorned in Spanish America, Brazil was seen as a refined

---

[5]   Joaquim Nabuco, *Abolitionism: the Brazilian Antislavery Struggle*, ed. and trans. by Robert Conrad (Urbana, 1977), p. 106.

[6]   One should not exaggerate the peacefulness of the Brazilian independence process by focusing just on the final outcome. As José Murilo de Carvalho shows in *A construção da ordem, a elite política imperial* (Rio de Janeiro, 1980) and *Teatro de sombras* (Rio de Janeiro, 1996), p. 231, there were 18 revolts between 1831 and 1848 in 11 provinces. Some of them, such as the Cabanagem in Pará were very bloody and others, such as the Farroupilha in Rio Grande do Sul lasted a decade.

European-type monarchy, ruled by kings with royal European blood, with functioning parliamentary governments. (The millions of African slaves somehow did
not impugn the nation's perceived civility.) If the state's legitimacy was not much
contested and the emperor ruled with limited violence, why has there been this disagreement about how to characterise the nineteenth-century Brazilian state?

Part of the problem is in the definition of the state. To emphasise the
Europeanness of the system, the countryside generally has been seen as beyond
the pale, a separate, private world of the family and the plantation. Similarly,
Mexico is depicted as chaotic because the Mexico City regime is emphasised
rather than political forms on the periphery. Part of the key to understanding
both states is the symbiotic relationship between the countryside and the city,
the municipalities and the capitals. The relative power of the central government in Brazil and Mexico also differed because of the varying relationship
between the national economies and the world system.

Contradictory Views of the Brazilian Imperial State

Many contemporaries shared Nabuco's view that the imperial state was overweening. To them the state created the nation. There was little sense that nationhood had preceded the Portuguese or had arisen organically from shared experiences of the colonial populations, and certainly not from the pre-colonial peoples.
The Portuguese king imposed an absolutist state when he crossed the Atlantic in
1808. The Bragança family grafted its regal legitimacy onto the New World colony.
This Lusitanian import was seen as an absolutist regime. The liberal essayist
Aureliano Candido Tavares Bastos complained at mid-century of an 'extremely
powerful state' in which the excessive number of bureaucrats 'concern themselves
with everything and do nothing'.[7] The entrepreneur Visconde de Maua frequently attacked 'undue government intervention', while the German observer Carl von
Kosteriz concluded that 'there are few princes in the world whose will intervenes
so much in the destiny of their nations as does Dom Pedro's who, in the true
meaning of the expression, "reigns, governs and administers"'.[8]

Some scholars have subsequently endorsed this view. Political scientists and
historians such as Raimundo Faoro, José Murilo de Carvalho, Roderick
Barman, John R. Hall, Fernando Uricochea, Eul-Soo Pang and Ron Seckinger
posit a 'bureaucratic estate' or 'mandarins' with considerable autonomy from
the planter elite.[9] These authors see the empire as a patrimonial state that want-

---

[7] A.C. Tavares Bastos, *Cartas do solitario* (1863, São Paulo, 1975), p. 29.

[8] Irineo Evangelista de Sousa (Visconde de Maua), *Autobiografia* (1889, Rio de Janeiro,
1942), p. 235 and Von Kosteritz quoted in Anyda Marchant, *Viscount Maua and the
Empire of Brazil: A Biography of Irineu Evangelista de Sousa* (Berkeley, 1965) p. 267.

[9] In discussing the founding of the Brazilian Empire Raimundo Faoro says 'The most
important interests concentrate in Rio de Janeiro ... The State returns to its patrimonial origins and foundations, nourished by commerce, collecting along its long path new

ed to control the production and circulation of goods and capital. This was an urban-controlled regime of monopoly and privilege.

Others have argued that although the state was important in directing economic activity, it was far from autonomous. On the contrary, according to traditional Marxist historians such as Caio Prado Júnior, Nelson Werneck Sodré, Florestan Fernandes and Jacobo Gorender, it was an instrument of the landed ruling class and acted to insure their interests.[10] Here the state represented the interests of a specific class — export-oriented slaveholders. Because slavery was a precapitalist labour form, the ruling class was supposedly suspicious — not of *private* enterprise — but of capitalist enterprise, both national and foreign. Here we find a rather 'feudal' export-oriented regime, not the cosmopolitan mercantilist state of the patrimonial state school. The model is more Prussia than Portugal.[11]

Dependentistas such as Andre Gunder Frank and Theotonio dos Santos, on the other hand, disdained the 'corrupt state of a non-country'.[12] To them the state was not a strong actor, not even a night watchman, but a servant. They assert that the empire represented a marriage of a 'comprador' ruling class and foreign colonialists and imperialists whom the 'lumpen' state defended. Foreign investors and merchants, according to this view, were the privileged recipients of state largess. The *dependentista* state was a neo-colonial state. Many histori-

---

renovating colours without weakening its central trajectory, that ... leads to the mercantilist style ... Money and politics return to their embrace, subjugating the propertied class.' Raimundo Faoro in *Os donos do poder*, 2nd ed., vol. 1 (São Paulo, 1975), p. 329. Also see: Eul-Soo Pang and Ron Seckinger, 'The Mandarins of Imperial Brazil', in *Comparative Studies in Society and History*, vol. 9 (1972), pp. 215–44; Roderick Barman and Jean Barman, 'The Role of the Law Graduate in the Political Elite of Imperial Brazil', *Journal of Interamerican Studies and World Affairs*, vol. 18 (1976), pp. 423–94; Murilo de Carvalho, *Construção da ordem*, pp. 51–8; John Hall, 'The Patrimonial Dynamic in Colonial Brazil', in Richard Graham (ed.), *Brazil and the World System* (Austin, 1991), pp. 57–88; and Fernando Uricoechea, *The Patrimonial Foundations of the Brazilian Bureaucratic State* (Berkeley, 1980).

[10] Florestan Fernandes, *A revolução burguesa no Brasil: ensaio de interpretação sociológica* (Rio de Janeiro, 1974), pp. 54–60; Caio Prado Junior, *Historia económica do Brasil*, 15th ed. (São Paulo, 1972), pp. 192–209; Nelson Werneck Sodre, *Historia da burguesia brasileira* 3rd ed. (Rio de Janeiro, 1976).

[11] Some scholars have likened Brazilian development to the Prussian road that modernised while always maintaining the power of landlords. See Luís Carlos Soares, 'From Slavery to Dependence: A Historiographical Perspective', in Graham (ed.), *Brazil and the World System*, pp. 89–108. See also comparable studies of the USA such as Eugene Genovese's *The Political Economy of Slavery* (New York, 1965) and Jonathan Wiener's *Social Origins of the New South, Alabama 1860–1885* (Baton Rouge, 1978).

[12] Andre Gunder Frank, *Lumpenbourgeoisie, Lumpendevelopment* (New York, 1974), p. 70 and Theotonio dos Santos, 'Brazil, the Origins of a Crisis,' in Ronald Chilcote and Joel Edelstein (eds.), *Latin America: The Struggle with Dependency and Beyond* (New York, 1974), pp. 409–90.

ans such as Jacob Gorender refer to the 'colonial pact', which they argue went on until the end of the empire.[13]

A fourth perspective on the Brazilian imperial state returns to the feudal analogy, but this time rather than being an instrument for the feudal lords, the state disappears. According to Nestor Duarte, the 'Estado senhorial' had little effect.[14] The country was run by landed clans largely independent of state interference, and the emphasis now is not on the export orientation but rather on social control in the countryside.

One area in which there has been agreement is that slavery permanently marked Brazil's development and shaped the state's relationship to civil society, since Brazil was the last independent country in Latin America to retain slavery, abolishing it only in 1888. The consequences were contradictory. On the one hand human bondage limited state capacity and penetration, since in the most prosperous areas most labourers were not subjects but rather chattel over whom the state had little authority. Indeed, the Portuguese state could not intervene between the plantation owner and his workers as the Spanish state often did. Slaves had no traditional or political rights, and they did not pay taxes. There was no significant equivalent of Indian courts, parish priests or *corregidores*, who had a vested interest in protecting the working population to some degree as in New Spain. The Portuguese crown was much less interested in restraining the political power of planters over their dependents than in encouraging maximum productivity. The countryside was, then, effectively under the private control of clans. On the other hand, the threat of slave revolts and a Haitian-style revolution convinced the many large and small-scale slaveowners that they needed formally to recognise the authority of a state that was effectively a hollow state, seeming strong to foreign outsiders but with little reach into the interior.

This pattern continued into the national period. Although slavery was usually abolished in Spanish America within a decade or two of Independence, in Brazil it continued for almost 70 years, and the number of imported slaves swelled for three decades. Between 1831, when Brazil signed a treaty with Great Britain agreeing to abolish the slave trade, and 1851, when the British enforced the end of the Atlantic traffic, close to 700,000 African slaves entered Brazil.

Richard Graham, focusing on the politics of patronage that undergirded this relationship between the state and the latifundia has shown in a perceptive study that since

---

[13] Jacob Gorender, *O escravismo colonial* (São Paulo, 1978). See also Luiz Carlos Soares, 'From Slavery to Dependence: A Historiographical Perspective,' in Graham (ed.), *Brazil and the World System*, and Fernando Novais, *Estrutura e dinâmica do antigo sistema colonial* (São Paulo, 1974).

[14] Nestor Duarte, *A ordem privada e organização política nacional* (São Paulo, 1939). Francisco Jose Oliveira Vianna took a similar position in *Instituiçãoes políticas brasileiras*, 2 vols. 3rd ed. (Rio de Janeiro, 1974).

> Men of property dominated the Brazilian state in the nineteenth century ...
> Cabinets exercised their authority not against local leaders but through them,
> and these landed bosses, in turn, sought not to oppose the government but to
> participate in it. Thus emerges a crucial point in understanding politics in nine-
> teenth-century Brazil that greatly lessens the significance of any hypothetical
> opposition between private and public power.[15]

The objectives of both the state and society, according to Graham, were to
maintain the principles of authority, hierarchy and deference. Diverging from
Nabuco, Graham holds that slavery contributed to — but was not essential to
— this social formation. He emphasises local and national political manoeu-
vring within Brazil to maintain social peace and authority. David McCreery
brilliantly depicts that relationship in the interior province of Goiás in the present volume. This essay attempts to expand upon these insights by emphasising
the importance of Brazil's place in the world economy in constructing its pub-
lic-private relationships. Economics were, of course, a central part of the construction of the state. The state depended upon planters to generate wealth
while planters needed the state both to enforce authority and deference, and
also to put a civilised face on a system based on brute force and arbitrary power
so that Europeans would trade with, invest in and lend to Brazil.

The slave system was mostly run outside of state supervision by owners and
overseers — there were no slave codes. But the state did serve as the repressor of
the last instance of slave rebellions and regulated the transmission of slaves as
property. Fear of slave rebellions guided a rather peaceful independence process
and then united the elite in the late 1830s. The bloody revolts from Rio Grande
do Sul in the south to Pará in the north in the wake of Dom Pedro I's departure
in 1831 convinced the elite in 1840 to recognise the premature majority of Dom
Pedro II and centralised authority. A divinely appointed sovereign of European
royal blood united the troubled elite who worried that the urban popular classes would join with slaves. Nonetheless, the imperial state's legitimacy and
authority derived as much from its role as intermediary between Brazil and foreign powers as from state domestic control and the symbolic importance of the
emperor. Prosperous international trade and European loans sustained the
treasury and the state. The national state's sovereignty was recognised by overseas powers before most of its own subjects recognised it. Foreign states and
merchants were more responsible for supporting Brazil's post-colonial state
through the revenue they provided than for undermining it. Such foreign support allowed Portuguese America to consolidate its territory while Spanish
America fragmented. Indeed, Brazil more than inherited Portuguese America; it
grew in the nineteenth century, consolidating the nineteen captaincies under

---

[15] Richard Graham, *Patronage and Politics in Nineteenth-Century Brazil* (Stanford,
1990), pp. 1, 3.

Rio's rule and adding parts of Paraguay, Bolivia, Peru, Venezuela and Colombia. Obtaining external recognition and expanding national borders was easier than extending authority over the interior of this hollow state.

However, the external prop to Brazil's monarchy was a mixed blessing. It meant that the state did not much penetrate the interior. The empire negotiated between the interests of foreign merchants, investors and diplomats, and the landed exporting class. While this diversified dependence meant that imperial statesmen could play off foreign and domestic interests, the state's space to manoeuvre was sharply circumscribed. Local disputes tended to be resolved locally without becoming politicised at the national level, unlike Mexico, where a number of local revolts led to the overthrow of the president in Mexico City and a strengthened sense of national identity.

Although the Brazilian imperial state was extremely politically centralised, it was, in José Murilo de Carvalho's felicitous term, 'macrocephalic', centred in Rio and the port cities. Even there the state offered few basic services, such as health and education, and neither did it bolster the Church.

Brazil's peculiar history and its position in the world economy explain its unique state form. The Brazilian colony, named after a traded commodity (*pau brasil*), was, more than any other Iberian colony, the creation of the world economy. Its historical epochs can be summarised by listing commercial produce: Brazilwood, sugar, gold, coffee, rubber. Its most important trade goods were transplants, its labourers and capital were imports, and its commercial and ruling classes foreign. Mircea Buescu has estimated that over half of all commercial production in the colonial period was exported.[16] Brazil was more market-oriented than almost any other place on earth. The world's largest importer of African slaves and one of its greatest commodity exporters, Brazil was a typical circum-Caribbean export enclave ruled by rural latifundiarios with few government officials outside the ports and the gold fields.

Brazil underwent a remarkable and abrupt process of state-building in the aftermath of Napoleon's invasion of Portugal. Transferring the court to the New World in 1808, transporting the entire apparatus of state and much of the imperial ruling class across the Atlantic while converting the export colony into the centre of the Portuguese empire suddenly thrust together two different social formations. Lusitanian mercantilist institutions were transplanted in the tropics, but only in the urban civil society. Brazil had already occupied a central place in the Portuguese empire. Indeed, some argued that because of Brazil's thriving economy Portugal was a colony of Brazil even before the two became co-kingdoms in 1815.[17] But the institutions of government had to await the arrival of the

---

[16] Mircea Buescu, *Brasil: disparidades de renda no passado* (Rio de Janeiro, 1979), p. 17.

[17] Jobson Arruda, 'Mita e símbolo na história de Portugal e do Brasil', *Actas dos IV Cursos Internacionais de Verao de Cascais* (1998), vol. 3, pp. 213–28.

Portuguese prince regent, Dom João. For the first time a sizeable bureaucracy was created in Brazil, and attempts were made to subdue the countryside.

The arrival of the future king was neither purely an accident of history nor was it entirely imposed by the Portuguese invasion of Napoleon's troops. The British, who were running a trade deficit with Portugal largely because of Brazilian reexports, had begun planning the transfer of the monarchy to Brazil as early as 1801. London merchants sought to trade directly with their Rio counterparts rather than through the Portuguese. In other words, the success of Brazil's export economy convinced the British to make the fateful decision of first assisting in the movement of the court to America and then helping Brazil declare and sustain its independence from Britain's long-time Portuguese allies.[18]

Brazilians had the good fortune of throwing off a much weakened Portuguese master who was in no position to reimpose colonial rule. Their glory days more than two centuries behind them, the Portuguese had become dependent upon the British and the Brazilian colony. The ties were strengthened when the British navy escorted Dom João across the Atlantic, then protected him in Brazil while helping wage war in Portugal to return his throne. In fact, after the French were expelled from Portugal and while Dom João remained in Brazil, an Englishman effectively ruled Portugal by presiding over the Council of Regency. He later became commander in chief of the Portuguese army.[19] As Lord Strangford wrote: 'I have entitled England to establish with the Brazils the relation of sovereign and subject and require obedience to be paid as the price of protection.'[20] The British aim was for Rio de Janeiro to become 'an emporium for British manufactures destined for the consumption of the whole of South America.'[21] The treaty signed between the two countries in 1810 demonstrated the degree of Portuguese obedience. Not only did it enforce the royal decree of 1808 opening Brazil's trade to all countries, it set the maximum duty on the importation of British goods at only 15 per cent, allowed British merchants to set up shop in Brazil and awarded them extra-territorial judicial privilege. Brazil received no trade concessions in return. Renewed in 1827, this treaty opened the Brazilian economy to foreign merchants and foreign trade. It is ironic that Dom João VI, who, advised by his councillor José Bonefácio to seek a strong state developmentalist role to push industrialisation, instead wound up opening the path to free trade.[22] The crown did not lack a statist philosophy or statesmen well-versed in mercantilist thinking. Yet it now found itself in an export

---

18   *Ibid.*

19   Leslie Bethell, 'The Independence of Brazil', in L. Bethell (ed.), *Brazil. Empire and Republic, 1822–1930* (Cambridge, 1989), p. 25.

20   Quoted in Alan K. Manchester, *British Preeminence in Brazil, its Rise and Decline* (Durham, NC, 1933), p. 67.

21   Quoted in Bethell, 'The Independence of Brazil', p. 18.

22   Jean Batou in *Cent ans de résistance au sous-développement* (Geneva, 1990), pp. 218–21.

economy with little industrial infrastructure and a small market. The Portuguese had to adapt to the export climate of their host which British traders and ships facilitated. The situation was irreversible once the treaty lapsed in 1843.

Brazilians were not completely subservient to the British. They manifested sufficient sovereignty to avoid signing another trade treaty for almost half a century, to forestall for two decades the end of the Atlantic slave trade much sought after by the British and to evade the abolition of slavery for most of the century.[23] But Brazil was so enmeshed in the world market that diplomatic initiatives or invasions were not necessary to convince Brazilians to trade or to open Brazil's resources to foreigners.

The Brazilian state's reliance on foreigners was based on more than diplomatic and military necessity. Limited state capacity resulting from three centuries of concentration on international commerce and an interior ruled by independent *fazendeiros* dictated that foreign trade and loans rather than taxes on land, labour or internal commerce would serve as the foundation of imperial finances. It was possible to erect a state that was recognised from abroad without having to conquer the acquiescence of the Brazilian landed elite. Where in Europe 'war made the state and the state made war', in Brazil trade made the state and allowed the state to avoid internal wars.[24]

As Miguel Centeno points out in this volume, Brazil's experience conformed to the general Latin American pattern in that the military was not strong. Dom João's army and then Pedro I's army were staffed largely by Portuguese career military men and led by Portuguese officers. Their objectives, particularly in the Banda Oriental (Uruguay), were more closely related to Portuguese goals than Brazilian nation building. Warfare led to state-building in Brazil, not in the sense of creating strong armed forces and internal tax extractive apparatus, but in the sense that regional, often race-based revolts convinced regional elites to acquiesce in central government authority while retaining their own military authority through the national guard. It was the failure of that military arrangement, manifested in the bloody war against Paraguay (1865–70), which led to demands for the modernisation of state and armed forces, and eventually to the founding of the republic.

The weak military and tax institutions would lead to economic policies that were liberal — 'para Ingles ver' ('for the English to see') — in the ports and that fell very far short of liberalism in the interior. Such a combination turned out to be something of an advantage in the short run. The hollow state of *Brasil independente* did not have to transform the fiscal system, unlike independent Mexico,

---

[23] M.P. Macdonald, *The Making of Brazil: Portuguese Roots, 1500–1822* (Sussex, 1996), pp. 460–4; Stephen Haber and Herbert S. Klein, 'The Economic Consequences of Brazilian Independence', in S. Haber (ed.), *How Latin America Fell Behind* (Stanford, 1997), pp. 245–53. For a discussion of the next trade treaty, see Steven Topik, *Trade and Gunboats* (Stanford, 1996).

[24] Charles Tilly, *The Formation of National States in Western Europe* (Princeton, 1975), p. 42.

which would require painful adjustments because it inherited an ancien regime tax system based in good part on taxing internal trade and establishing monopolies.

The imperial regime in Rio found it much easier to tap international resources than to extract revenue internally. To maintain access to overseas funds, the empire had to follow policies that were essentially liberal. Despite the apparent contradiction between a slave-based monarchy and liberalism — an idea 'out of place' according to Roberto Schwartz — it was not a contradiction with *economic* liberalism. (Indeed, European observers considered its constitutional monarchy liberal as well.)[25] Officially, the country was on the gold standard. Although currency was inconvertible early on because Dom João took the Banco do Brasil's gold reserves back to Portugal with him in 1830, and Brazil had had to pay large indemnities to Portugal in return for recognition of independence, monetary policy was orthodox in order to maintain the value of the milreis. Except for some spurts, as during the 1820s and during the Paraguayan War, the per capita money supply grew about at the pace of the economy. For most of the period the treasury (rather than private institutions or individuals as in most of Latin America) had the monopoly of issue and found maintaining its credit more valuable than paying its bills with depreciated currency. Indeed, for most of the 1870s and 1880s the real money supply actually declined.

Consequently the value of the Brazilian milreis remained surprisingly stable after 1830, generally fluctuating between 20 and 30 pence to the milreis.[26] By one calculation prices between 1850 and 1889 barely doubled despite the Paraguayan War and were stable between 1870 and 1889. In a country whose urban population was quite dependent upon imports, this meant that there was little inflation and few urban revolts of the dangerous classes.[27]

The strong performance of the milreis allowed Brazil to enjoy better credit in London than any other Latin American country, and almost any country outside Europe — indeed better than parts of Europe. While the great crash of 1824 closed the City to most Latin Americans, Brazil continued borrowing throughout the empire's lifetime, taking 15 loans worth about £40 million. By 1889 Brazil had the largest foreign debt in Latin America and was still able to float loans on London. Price stability meant that the government was successful in placing internal loans in milreis, mostly from foreign merchants. The ability to borrow allowed the empire to distribute patronage, pay off the army and service the debt, while avoiding greater taxes on the planters. Brazil largely escaped the ravages of *caudillismo* and *pronunciamientos* that so weakened Spanish American states and societies because its relatively peaceful independence

---

25   Roberto Schwartz, 'As ideias fora do lugar', *Estudos CEBRAP*, no. 3 (1973).

26   IBGE, *Separata do Anuario Estatístico do Brasil, 1939/40*, p. 63.

27   Raymond W. Goldsmith, *Brasil 1850–1984. Desenvolvimento financeiro sob um seculo de inflação* (São Paulo, 1986), pp. 30–1.

movement did not militarise society. This, combined with the tax base and the stability of the milreis, allowed the treasury to pay off the armed forces.

But while the ability to borrow abroad strengthened the state's autonomy vis-à-vis the domestic elite, the great debt dictated continued orthodox monetary policies which very much restricted the treasurer's policy alternatives. He had to maintain the value of the milreis and thereby prevent the rise in the cost of debt servicing. Tight money was undertaken at the expense of the many indebted planters, who would have preferred to see inflation diminish the real value of their debt, and the nascent domestic manufacturers and artisans, who would have happily greeted the protection from imports that a weaker currency would have afforded. The restricted money supply also hurt internal commerce since coin was almost unknown in the interior and even provincial cities often found themselves short of money.[28]

Of course this system of external support for the state required sufficient taxes on external trade. Coffee came to the rescue in the wake of the decline of gold and then sugar. In the last 60 years of the nineteenth century coffee sales abroad grew 800 per cent and Brazil became the world's largest producer of coffee, the world's second or third most valuable internationally-trade commodity. Large exports also enabled Brazil to enjoy very high imports. But the fiscal necessities of debt servicing meant that the treasurer could not charge high customs duties. Even after the treaty with the British expired in 1843 and Brazil went through almost half a century with no trade agreements, the country continued what was essentially a policy of free trade, using customs for revenue until almost the end of the empire.

Brazil's post-Independence experience contrasted sharply with that of Mexico and most of Spanish America. The Mexican state was undermined by foreign powers, foreign trade and foreign investment rather than being sustained by them. The failure of debt policies in Mexico was intimately related to the fact that it was a militarily weak, politically unstable and debt-ridden state, even though the internationally-respected peso maintained its value until the 1870s. Mexico's disastrous experiences with first the 1825 and 1826 loans, then the infamous Jecker bonds that provided the excuse for the French intervention and finally Juárez's moratorium on debt repayment made the country an international pariah for much of the nineteenth century.[29] Only in the 1880s did Mexico begin to restore its credit by reaching an agreement with British bondholders in 1886 and then organising the great £10.5 million conversion loan of

---

[28] C.F. Van Delden Laerne, *Brazil and Java. Report on Coffee-Culture in America, Asia and Africa* (London, 1885), p. 209.

[29] For more on this see Carlos Marichal, *A Century of Debt Crises in Latin America: from Independence to the Great Depression, 1820–1930* (Princeton, 1989) and Steven Topik, 'When Mexico had the Blues; a Transatlantic Tale of Bonds, Bankers, and Nationalists, 1862–1910', *American Historical Review*, vol. 105, no. 3 (June 2000), pp. 714–38.

1888. Not only past history, but continuing trade deficits (which averaged US$ 3.5 million in the 1880s) tarnished Mexico's credit. In 1888 Mexico's foreign debt stood at US$70.8 million, about one-half of Brazil's. But because of lower exports, it required a marginally larger share of national exports to service it. Debt repayment jumped to one-quarter of the budget once debt servicing was normalised two years later and remained at about that level over the next two decades, approximately the same share as in Brazil.

The eagerness of Brazilian and Mexican politicians to borrow abroad even when possessing small or non-existent trade surpluses clearly meant that trade alone could not service the debts. Even Brazil's merchants and bankers, despite healthy commercial surpluses, shipped far more money out of the country than trade brought in.[30] The only means of assuring that their foreign drafts did not bounce was either to borrow more, which they did, or attract foreign risk capital. The imperial state was certainly not anti-capitalist since it so depended upon the international economy for its lifeblood. Urban merchants were given free reins to conduct business. This liberal policy was an elegant solution for a state that could not assert its will in the countryside, but did not need to because those distant planters were exporters whose goods could be taxed at the ports.

To the Englishmen on whom it depended, the imperial state showed its liberal face. Not only did it follow free trade and orthodox monetary policies, it recognised property as individual held in fee simple. There was no communal property, and the state did not arbitrarily seize or tax property, nor did it force loans as was common in Mexico for many decades. The same laws applied to all free men, no corporate privileges applied even to the aristocracy nor Jim Crow laws to people of colour. This was a legal system in which Europeans felt comfortable (unlike in Asia, Africa or even Mexico for much of the century). State monopolies remained only in unimportant areas such as Brazilwood. Although the state maintained its control over mineral rights, these were easily leased out to private and often foreign companies. The few state enterprises of note that existed were mixed enterprises that were intended to serve the private sector. They were limited to the outward-looking face of Brazil. In particular, state enterprises, which only began after mid-century, concentrated on developing and subsidising the export economy through railroads, shipping and banks. The mixed enterprise Banco do Brasil has been the largest bank in the country for most of the time since the 1850s. The state also owned and operated over one-third of the largest railroad network in Latin America by 1890 and had important interests in a number of private lines as well.

The empire was able to finance the growing infrastructure because Brazil sustained an enviable credit rating, burgeoning trade and, after mid-century, substantial amounts of foreign capital. Foreign, largely British, capital rose from

---

[30] Castro Carreira's figures in *História Financeira*, vol. 2, pp. 738–41 imply that Brazil sent to Europe some US$20 million a year between 1880–88 in excess of export earnings. Although this was only about four per cent of GNP, it was one-fifth of exports.

some £40 million at mid-century to over £100 million in 1889. Very few countries in the world received so much European capital at that point.

Yet why did so many Brazilian liberals criticise the empire for opposing private enterprise, for dampening the spirit of enterprise, for being backward and tradition-bound? The trouble was not so much precapitalist bureaucrats as the other face of Brazil. Internally, the state was never successful in effecting the non-market preconditions of the market. Yes, money was reliable, prices stable, the exchange rate steady, property respected by the state. But in the countryside this was far from a bourgeois regime of rule of law. The state barely trespassed onto the plantation. In the interior clan force and influence not capital and entrepreneurship dictated success.

In contrast to Mexico, where the state successfully titled and sold communal and Church lands after the middle of the century, land in Brazil was not a commodity. The vast majority of Brazil's vast virgin lands officially belonged to the state, but they were never surveyed nor did the state have means of controlling access to them. Efforts to do so began during the last years of the colonial period but came to nothing. At Independence state land grants, *sesmarias*, were abolished by the landlord-dominated parliament and no other means of distributing land was legislated for 27 years. Even the 1850 law, intended to reassert the state's control over the countryside in order to attract European immigrants and raise funds through land sales, failed miserably. The planter elite preferred uncertain boundaries which enabled the landlords to employ their own private armies and local political influence to seize adjoining territory. For this reason, until the early 1880s slaves rather than real estate secured loans, and personal relationships were fundamental for business transactions. The expansion of Brazilian agriculture more resembled military campaigns against indigenous and neo-European people than bourgeois market decisions. This was, in its truest sense, frontier-society primitive accumulation.[31] Only gradually was land commodified; surveys and titles were more a consequence of a flourishing export sector and an imposition of the financial sector than creations of the state.

Not only land titles remained vague. Weights, measures and time conventions, as Witold Kula points out, have historically been 'an attribute of authority', indeed a key dimension of sovereignty.[32] Yet the greatest chaos existed in Brazil's interior, and even in the ports only foreign merchants were able to standardise practices. The metric system took two decades legally to implement and provoked revolts and much resistance for decades more.[33]

[31] Warren Dean, *With Broadax and Firebrand: The Destruction of the Brazilian Atlantic Forest* (Berkeley, 1995), pp. 146–51; Emilia Viotti da Costa, *The Brazilian Empire, Myths and Realities* (Chicago:, 1985).

[32] Witold Kula, *Measures and Men*, trans. by R. Szreter (Princeton, 1986), p. 18.

[33] Laerne, *Brazil and Java*, pp. 208, 209; Ridings, *Business Interest Groups*, pp. 296–7; Roderick Barman, 'The Brazilian Peasantry Reexamined: The Implications of the Quebra-Quilo Revolt, 1874–1875', *Hispanic American Historical Review*, vol. 57 (Aug. 1977), pp. 401–24.

For landlords the uncertainty of titles had some obvious disadvantages. Land markets were slow to develop, mortgages were few, and land prices remained low. On the average *fazenda*, land constituted a minor part of total assets. But this system that hindered the creation of bourgeois relations and a farmer class in the interior was not inconvenient for powerful landlords. Virgin land, which was plentiful in the dynamic south-east and was rapaciously worked and then abandoned after 30 years, was not a patrimony, nor the collateral for loans. Technological demands were low, and coffee could be grown successfully on a small scale. Under these circumstances, the key for maintaining hierarchy and concentration of wealth was the control (not ownership) of land and labour and privileged access to credit. The credit system was based upon the personal reputations of individuals; credit could not be impersonal because laws prevented foreclosure on rural mortgages, so it was a man's — and occasionally a woman's — personal reputation, not their property that secured loans. Yet an individual's reputation was itself based upon clan power, political influence and number of slaves owned. Clans exerted much patrimonial power because the arbitrary political and judicial systems required the less influential squatters and hangers-on to have powerful landed protectors, and because of a labour system based on slavery that made the owners' word law. Economic and political power were intertwined. The (incorrect) perception of the imperial state's opposition to enterprise and corporations is best explained by the intransigence of planters who feared losing their clan power rather than by the precapitalist mentality of the state's bureaucrats. This was not a tradition-bound precapitalist state fighting against the bourgeoisie, but rather a liberal state with too few bourgeois allies and hence reliant on the disbursal of patronage.

Ironically, the opposition to the monarchy complained not of an impotent state, but — unlike anywhere else in Latin America — of an excessively powerful state: it was too centralised; the bureaucracy was too large and expensive; and policy shackled capital markets while hindering entrepreneurship. To be sure, there was some truth in their analysis. The imperial state was the most centralised in Latin America aside from Paraguay. In the fiscal realm, most important tax sources were reserved to the central government as were most important powers. The provinces and municipalities combined often earned less than one-quarter of the income of the central government and the Church was impoverished.[34]

Critics of the imperial state also inveighed against the treasury's presence in capital markets. The only bank in the country from 1808 until it folded in 1829 was the state-dominated Banco do Brasil. The treasury continued to play an important role in capital markets after the Banco do Brasil closed. Government bonds were one of the few safe investments in Brazil in the first half of the century.[35] In Mexico and the rest of Spanish America, land and mines were much

---

[34] F.J. Santa-Anna Nery, *Le Bresil en 1889* (Paris, 1889), p. 450.

[35] Carreira, *História Financeira* p. 742; Manuel Carlos Pelaez and Wilson Suzigán, *História monetária do Brasil* (Rio de Janeiro, 1976), p. 82.

more attractive to capitalists than government bonds, reducing the state's access to capital. The banking system was much slower to develop in Mexico and to a greater extent remained under the control of private oligarchical groups.[36]

A Brazilian banking law was passed as part of a greater expansion of state activity after 1850 aimed at fostering the growth of the private sector and helping finance the expansion of state capacity. The date is significant because it reveals the overwhelming importance of slavery for the Brazilian social formation. When the Atlantic slave trade was finally ended in 1850 (and while coffee exports had slumped for more than a decade) the state attempted to initiate far-reaching reforms to aid the now inevitable transition to free labour. To encourage European immigration it passed a land law and established an agency to register titles, planned the first national census and created a civil registry of births and deaths. To foster business, it authorised a new private Banco do Brasil and passed a commercial code.[37] The state attempted not only to institutionalise, secularise and standardise the economy (in 1852 the first effort to institute the metric system was passed) but also to strengthen the hand of private enterprise. The commercial code empowered commercial associations to establish standard business practices in each commercial centre and form commercial courts. This collation of business laws and practices was years ahead of British jurisprudence and certainly ahead of Mexico.[38] However, Brazil was not yet ready for this state-led move towards more capitalist relations and institutionalised rule. Planter patriarchal power was still too strong. Most of the reforms would have to wait almost four more decades to be put into practice when the economy had brought more bourgeois practices.

The crown was, nevertheless, able to increase its economic role, which would unwittingly undermine the colonial pact that sustained the hollow state. Relative internal peace after the middle of the century meant that the crown could turn its attention and its resources more to economic matters. Real per capita expenditures

---

[36] Carlos Marichal, 'El nacimiento de la banca mexicana en el contexto latino-americano: problemas de periodización', in Leonor Ludlow and Carlos Marichal (eds.), *Banca y poder en México*, pp. 231–66; and Marichal, 'Obstacles to Capital Markets in Mexico', in Haber (ed.), *Why Latin America Fell Behind*, pp. 118–45. Stephen Haber, 'Financial Markets and Industrial Development', in *Why Latin America Fell Behind*, pp. 146–78; Steven Topik, 'Brazil's Bourgeois Revolution?' and 'Introduction' to *The Americas*, vol. XLVIII, no. 2 (Oct. 1991), pp. 131–8 and 245–71.

[37] Barman, *Forging of a Nation*, pp. 235–6.

[38] Laerne, *Brazil and Java*, p. 208; Eugene Ridings, *Business Interest Groups in Nineteenth Century Brazil* (Cambridge, 1994), pp. 286–8; and Eugene Ridings, 'Business Organizations in Nineteenth Century Brazil and England: Some Preliminary Comparisons', paper presented at 'The Brazilian State and Business' Anglo-Brazilian Business History Conference, Business Research Unit of the London School of Economics, 10 March 1995.

tripled between the 1840s and the 1880s and total central government outlays grew by nearly 500 per cent. Consequently, total real central government expenditures for economic development multiplied twenty-fold between mid-century and the end of the empire so its penetration of society grew.[39] The state was able to expand outlays not so much because it had intensified its political hegemony nationally (the empire's overthrow in 1889 demonstrated its weak basis of support), as because the economy thrived after mid-century. Brazil was able to take advantage of an unprecedented boom in the world economy which saw a 260 per cent growth in international trade between 1850 and 1870. The country's coffee exports alone multiplied six-fold between the 1840s and the 1880s, and rubber became a very important commodity. Brazil was similarly able to reap the benefits of the great growth of European overseas investments.

Politicians undertook important measures in the empire's last years to develop a capitalist society because of changes in the world economy. They succeeded in abolishing slavery gradually, first ending the slave traffic in 1850; then the law of the free womb in 1871 declared slave children free; the Septuagenarian Law of 1884 emancipated slaves over the age of 60; and finally, on 13 May 1888, all forms of slavery were abolished. The Brazilian state, lord of the largest slave society the world had known, had over four decades succeeded in emancipation without compensating the owners and without provoking the civil wars that bloodied and fragmented the states in Cuba, Haiti and the United States. This reflected both the development of the state's relative autonomy from the slavocrats *and* the dependence of the Brazilian social formation on the international context. Europeans had first transported Africans to tropical America; their opposition had first doomed the Atlantic slave trade and then the slave system itself. Even Brazilian *fazendeiros* had to accept this reality.[40]

State aid helped smooth the transition to free labour. To replace slaves, the state of São Paulo, and then after 1889 the federal government, attracted more European immigrants than any other Latin American country save Argentina. Brazil became the only country in the world to convince millions of southern Europeans to work on large semi-tropical plantations. Clearly, many Europeans thought well enough of Brazil not only to lend its state money, but to make it their home. As a result, coffee export statistics did not skip a beat with emancipation. Indeed, coffee enjoyed its greatest prosperity precisely in the late 1880s

---

[39] José Murilo de Carvalho, 'Elite and State Building in Imperial Brazil', PhD diss. Stanford University, 1974), pp. 578, 580–1; Nathaniel Leff, 'Government and the Economic Development of Nineteenth-Century Brazil', Columbia University of Graduate School of Business, Research Working Paper, no. 179A, p. 12.

[40] Robert Slenes, Pedro Carvalho de Melo and Rebecca Scott have demonstrated that slavery's demise was politically instigated; it was still a dynamic and profitable economic system in its last years.

and early 1890s. Brazil was still coffee — it was alone responsible for three-quarters of the explosive growth of world coffee production in the nineteenth century — but as the saying went, coffee was no longer the Negro slave.

At the same time that parliament made all Brazilians free, it also began to tie the country together into a nation. It initiated a national railroad system that was the largest in Latin America and one of the largest in the developing world (greater than the systems in either China or all of Africa), and strung up thousands of kilometres of telegraph lines. Unlike in Mexico, where the railroads were foreign-owned and mostly extensions of US lines, the railroads in Brazil connected major port cities or entrepots with their spreading hinterlands and many of the most important lines were financed by Brazilian private and public capital.[41] Trains facilitated the rapid marshalling of federal troops to quell revolts but, as Porfirio Díaz discovered, trains ran both ways and could be appropriated by rebels. Also, many of the revolts occurred in areas distant from tracks, such as Canudos in the interior of Bahia or Quintana Roo, Yucatán. The main contribution of the railroad to state-building was less the rapid transporting of the forces of repression, than pushing the growth of internal commodity and labour markets and advancing communications.

The foreign connection allowed the Brazilian state to invest in infrastructure. The treasury tapped capital markets by borrowing as well as through taxation. Despite a large jump in revenues, the Rio treasury experienced 36 deficits in 40 years because of the growth of state activity and because planters refused to allow an adequate modification of the taxation system. They preferred to be the state's creditors by holding treasury bonds to being its debtors as taxpayers. Thus, the treasury had to continuously borrow, mostly at home. Between 1850 and 1885 the internal debt grew twice as fast as the external debt, which it far outweighed. The result was a sevenfold swelling of the public debt between mid-century and the end of the empire. In contracting it, the treasury secured a large portion of the country's capital. The consolidated internal debt in 1889 was fully 75 per cent more than all of the deposits in all of the banks in the country. Until the last year of the empire, the majority of stocks and bonds traded on the Rio Bourse were treasury bonds.[42] This reflected the success of the empire's orthodox monetary policy that allowed inconvertible currency to reach par in 1888 because there was general faith in the treasury's probity. In

---

[41] Sandra Kuntz Ficker, *Empresa extranjera y mercado interno: el Ferrocarril Central Mexicano, 1880–1907* (Mexico City, 1995); Sandra Kuntz Ficker (ed.), *Ferrocarriles y vida económica en México, 1850–1950* (Mexico City, 1996), and Paolo Riguzzi and Steven Topik, *The Political Economy of the Brazilian State* (Austin, 1989).

[42] Calculated from APEC, *A Economia Brasileira*, vol. 13 (Rio de Janeiro, 1974), p. 20; Manuel Carlos Pelaez and Wilson Suzigan, *História monetária do Brasil* (Rio de Janeiro, 1976), p. 449; 'Ato da Seção do Conselho de Estado', Rio de Janeiro, 12 March 1885 in Instituto Histórico e Geográfico Brasileiro, Coleção Instituto Histórico Pasta 55, lata 545.

Brazil, unlike Mexico or the rest of Latin America, capitalists preferred to invest in government bonds than in land reflecting the institutionalisation of the urban economy and the limited reach of the state's protection of property rights in the countryside. Much, perhaps the majority, of the treasury milreis-denominated bonds were purchased by foreign merchants resident in Brazil. Rather than repatriate profits, they reinvested a significant share in Brazil because they trusted the currency and the government's respect of property.

The central government's deficits led it to borrow foreign exchange abroad as well. The foreign debt grew 400 per cent between 1850 and the end of the empire. The need to finance the debt explains a good deal of the restrictive nature of the financial policy that was criticised.

Brazil's greater statism was not, however, a sign of the state's overpowering of private initiative, of its continuation of the Portuguese patrimonial tradition as principal merchant and lender. The state was relatively poor and its economic resources limited. State enterprises were limited to the Dom Pedro Segundo railroad and some smaller lines and the domestic telegraph system. The state did not directly intercede in the accumulation process. Land and labour were left to market forces or private coercion. Despite considerable bureaucratic support for the end of slavery, introduction of European immigrants, land reform and industrial promotion, such actions were only taken when international pressures made them inevitable.

The Brazilian state's presence as an economic regulator and actor was felt most acutely in the most capitalistic sector. In order to protect the international value of the currency and the treasury's credit it had to interfere in commercial laws, the money supply and international commerce. These actions were not taken so much as signs of obeisance to the traditionalist landed class (many of whom were in fact also merchants and stock investors) as efforts to guarantee the continued functioning of the export economy. The Brazilian state always had one eye on the interior and one on the City of London.

Conclusion

Ironically, the imperial state was overthrown in 1889 for being too strong and too centralised. The growing dissatisfaction with Dom Pedro II's regime centred on liberals who believed that their party and principles had been subordinated to the conservatives ever since the Paraguayan War (1865–70). Since politics and economics were closely linked in the empire's patronage system, contempt for centralised conservative rule soon found its way into criticism of economic policy. The attacks were phrased in economically liberal language. Protegés of the liberals began measuring Brazilian economic policy by the standards of the increasingly liberal British, and found their own wanting. The most famous Brazilian entrepreneur of the nineteenth century, the viscount of Mauá, began denouncing state economic actions as 'undue government intervention' when he fell out of favour after decades of being a principal beneficiary of them.[43] The rise of economic liberalism in Brazil resembled the Mexican experience, although in neither case were these close imitations of European liberalism. They recognised that state interventionism was necessary because of the superiority of European state power and capital and the under-formed markets of the New World. As Richard Weiner has pointed out, liberals in Mexico were quite suspicious of market forces. This was also true of Brazil.[44]

Europeans did not greet the fall of the house of Bragança as a triumph of modern capitalism and democracy. They feared that Brazil would revert to a Spanish American caudillo-style system ruled by rural warlords. It had been the monarchy that maintained a veneer of European civilisation over this tropical land; once it was removed the state would crumble. José Murilo de Carvalho has eloquently stated this position in his discussion of the 'dialectic of ambiguity', the heterodox hybrid of European monarchy and New World slavery. Referring to Clifford Geertz's study of *Negara*, Carvalho characterises the imperial regime as 'theatre'.

> The imperial system is characterised [by Joaquim Nabuco] as a trick of appearances, of false realities, of fiction. The theatrical metaphor is tied to a metaphor of shadows. The government would be the shadow of slavery ... imperial politics would be shadow boxing ... Nabuco's apparent paradox follows in that imperial power, the shadow of slavery, was a giant phantasmagoria, but only it was able to abolish slavery. Nonetheless, in abolishing slavery, as Nabuco had foreseen and Cotegipe as well, the king broke the spell that sustained the entire system.[45]

Conventional wisdom holds that the demise of the empire brought the deterioration of the Brazilian state as if the monarchy alone had papered over the contradictions of the Brazilian social formation, using smoke and mirrors to project a much stronger state than actually existed. As the country came out of its spell, as the wizard was revealed as simply a small-town charlatan, the true, almost ungovernable Brazil and the hollow state came into view. According to this interpretation, the agrarian-based *coronelismo* of the First Republic, founded on a strange mix of patriarchy and laissez faire, represented the take-over of the real Brazil. This is the opposite trajectory of Mexico, which at the same time was treading its way through minefields of civil wars, invasions and local revolts to regain its international standing and patch together a muscular national state. Porfirio Díaz reassembled the state and asserted its authority.

---

[43] Irineo Evangelista de Sousa, Visconde de Mauá, *Autobiografía* (Rio de Janeiro, 1942), p. 235.

[44] Richard Weiner, 'Battle for Survival: Porfirian Views of the International Marketplace', *Journal of Latin American Studies*; vol. 32, no. 3 (Oct. 2000), pp. 645–70. Steven Topik, 'La Revolución, el estado y el desarrollo económico en México,' *História Mexicana*, vol. XL, no. 1 (1990), pp. 79–144.

[45] Carvalho, *Construção da ordem, Teatro de Sombras*, pp. 387–8.

Neither of these views is entirely convincing. In fact, as I have argued elsewhere, Brazil's republican state was fairly strong and well articulated. Victor Nunes Leal has pointed out how *coronelismo* continued after the abolition of slavery to link symbiotically the notable families of the interior with the cosmopolitan coastal elite and government bureaucrats.[46] State capacity and penetration grew as private Brazil became incorporated into public functions. Foreign trade, investment and state revenues all continued to grow.[47] Although republican leaders pretended to respect provincial leaders, they actually exercised greater authority than had the emperor, though they did it with less splendour.[48] They maintained sufficient sovereignty to nationalise much of the railroad and intervene in one of the world's most important commodity markets: coffee. The empire had, in fact, been built on a solid foundation. Not only did the emperor and slavery sustain the system, but, equally importantly, the foreign umbilical cord nourished the regime. Without the monarchy and slavery, the regime fell, but the state and nation both remained strong and continued to grow stronger. While establishing sovereignty early on because of foreign recognition and support; precluding the need to extract resources from planters in the interior by mounting a large bureaucracy and army, the official Brazil of the court came increasingly to penetrate the real Brazil of the interior. This was theatre based not only on imagination but on transformation.

---

[46] Topik, *The Political Economy of the Brazilian State*; Victor Nunes Leal, *Coronelismo, voto e enxada* (São Paulo, 1975). Also see Paul Cammack, 'Brazil: Old Politics, New Forces', *New Left Review*, vol. 190 (Nov./Dec. 1991), pp. 21–58.

[47] Joseph Love, 'Federalismo y regionalismo en Brasil, 1889–1937', in *Federalismos latinoamericanos: México, Brasil, Argentina* (Mexico City, 1993), pp. 213–19.

[48] Topik, *The Political Economy of the Brazilian State*. For a different view see Victor Nunes Leal.

CHAPTER 6

State and Society in Nineteenth-Century Goiás*

David McCreery

'The central state's presence there was a dim shadow, more of a future
project than an actual reality.'[1]

From the arrival of the first European settlers until at least the Estado Novo,
Brazil's central regime had notoriously limited purchase on the country's vast
interior. In Professor José Murilo de Carvalho's characterisation, 'the bureaucracy of the state was a *macrocefálica*: it had a huge head and short limbs. It was
active in the *Corte* but did not reach the municipalities and hardly touched the
provinces.'[2] Yet all agree that it was the empire that in the nineteenth century
undertook for the first time a serious 'state-building' project away from the
coast. From new laws and taxes to a reorganised administrative apparatus to
railroads and the telegraph, the state sought to tighten control and standardise
its presence in the *sertão* (interior). This chapter will examine how these efforts
played out on Brazil's remote western frontier. What did the central state
attempt to control? What were its policies and instruments? How successful was
it and why? Although revenue collection and expenditure are particularly good
indicators of pre-industrial state effectiveness, data for Goiás are incomplete
and will allow us only limited conclusions. Instead, the focus here will be on the
efforts of the provincial regime to control or repress the activities of groups
thought to threaten state power or the interests of those aligned with the state.
These included black slaves, Indians and criminals. Goiás was the edge of the
empire, and its nineteenth-century history provides a useful limit case for evaluating the effectiveness of the state policies and actions on the frontier.

Gold seekers from São Paulo and Minas Gerais introduced a Luso-Brazilian
and African population into Goiás beginning in the second decade of the eighteenth century, initiating a handful of settlements scattered across a wide area
and linked by only a few precarious trails.[3] Modest at best, the gold boom

* The author wishes to thank the Conselho Nacional de Pesquisa (CNPq) of Brazil for
a Visiting Professorship/Research grant that helped to enable this work.
[1] Fernando Uricoechea, *The Patrimonial Foundations of the Brazilian Bureaucratic
State* (Berkeley, 1980), p. 120.
[2] José Murilo de Carvalho, O *teatro de sombras; a política imperial* (Rio de Janeiro,
1988), p. 163.
[3] See Luis Palacín, O *século de ouro em Goiás* (Goiânia, 1979), Gilka V.F. de Salles,
Economia e escravidão em Goiás colonial (Goiânia, 1992), and Marivone Matos Chaim, *A
sociedade colonial goiana* (Goiânia, 1978).

peaked at mid-century and was plainly over by the 1780s, throwing the province into a half century of crisis. Not until the 1830s and 1840s did Goiás begin to revive, with an economy based on small-scale agriculture and, increasingly, the sale of cattle and horses to neighbouring provinces and coastal markets.[4] But a sparse population, poor quality soils, immense distances and dependence on middlemen to handle the sale of the provinces' products condemned Goiás to the condition of a backwater even as the coffee boom engulfed the centre-south. To many it seemed that 'all Brazil turns its back on Goiás'. Even distant Mato Grosso and the remote Amazon had river communications, while Goiás continued to rely on mule trains and ox carts well into the twentieth century.

Goiás in the nineteenth century does not fit easily into standard typologies of frontiers.[5] It did not exhibit the 'moving line' between 'barbarism' and 'civilisation' familiar to students of North America and Argentina, and there was no massive influx of settlers during the nineteenth century to displace the indigenous population and 'close' the frontier. The chief commercial activity was cattle raising, but Goiás's economic and social structures shared little with the gaucho cattle culture of Rio Grande de Sul or the Pampas. Its cattle and horses, while vital to the local economy, were marginal to the nation. The northern part of Goiás had much in common with Brazil's north-eastern *sertão*, but it was spared the periodic droughts and the extraordinary levels of violence characteristic of the interior of Bahia or Pernambuco in these years.

Goiás as a frontier is best understood in terms of two characteristics. First, until the end of the empire the province remained an area where no individual, group or institution successfully monopolised violence. Instead, a generalised resort to private violence to deal with the differences predominated. But because no group could gain the upper hand, problems were not resolved and resources not definitively apportioned. A balance of weakness prevailed. Conflict was endemic to Brazil, but in Goiás it remained at low levels and never burst into larger conflagrations, as happened in other parts of the empire.

---

4   Euripides Antônio Funes, *Goiás 1800–1850: um período de transição de mineração a agropecuario* (Goiânia, 1986); David McCreery, 'A economia de Goiás no século XIX' (forthcoming), Federal University of Goiás.

5   There is a surprisingly extensive literature on the frontier in Latin America. For a sample, see Donna J. Guy and Thomas Sheridan (eds.), *Contested Ground: Comparative Frontiers on the Northern and Southern Edges of the Spanish Empire* (Tucson, 1998); David J. Weber and Jane M. Rausch (eds), *Where Cultures Meet: Frontiers in Latin American History* (Wilmington, 1994); David Harry Miller and Jerome O, Steffen (eds.), *The Frontier: Comparative Studies*, vol. 1 (Norman, OK, 1977); Alistair Hennessy, *The Frontier in Latin American History* (Albuquerque, 1978); Martin T. Katzman, 'The Brazilian Frontier in Comparative Perspective', *Comparative Studies in Society and History*, vol. 17, no. 3 (July, 1975), pp. 266–85; and Silvio R. Duncan Baretta and John Markoff, 'Civilization and Barbarism: Cattle Frontiers in Latin America', *Comparative Studies in Society and History*, vol. 20, no. 4 (Oct. 1978), pp. 587–620.

Second, Goiás for most of the nineteenth century was an 'unsuccessful frontier'.[6] Its failure to attract capital or large numbers of settlers was both cause and effect of its inability to develop economic activities that adequately integrated the province into larger national and international economies. This failure, in turn, deprived the state of the financial resources necessary to establish control over the province and to link it effectively to the larger state enterprise.

What could 'state-building' mean in this distant outpost? It is useful to think of state control in terms of political and ideological hegemony. 'Political hegemony rests directly on the threat or use of force or coercion, whereas ideological hegemony implies the achievement of policy ends based on willing, or apparently willing, compliance, on shared ideas and values.'[7] Both forms of hegemony are always partial and they commonly encounter — indeed they generate — resistance. And despite much recent emphasis on 'consent', it is well to remember that states can rule by force alone, as the history of much of nineteenth-century Spanish America makes clear.[8] By contrast, the nineteenth-century Brazilian state enjoyed a high degree of acceptance, of ideological hegemony, in the interior, and among elites and the mass of the population alike. Key to this was the role of the emperor as symbol and national unifier.[9] As many have remarked, the emperor provided the Brazilian polity a source of legitimacy that Spanish Americas' caudillos lacked. State agents consciously worked to build up this sense of community by emphasising an 'otherness' apart from their Spanish American neighbours, with rituals of voting and the distribution of symbols such as flags and pictures of the imperial family and by following the activities of the court. Equally, the state sought to standardise everything from laws and language to weights and measures across the empire.

Evidence of the empire's legitimacy was the general absence of alternative foci of loyalty, apart from unthreatening local attachments or occasional outbursts of self-defeating messianic religion. Goiás's governors, year after year, and in almost exactly the same terms, praised the *boa indole* (good disposition) of the *goianos* and their commitment to the institutions of the empire. For most of the century elections were largely unproblematic celebrations of civic enthusiasm. Education and schools, key instruments in the institutionalisation of citizenship, gained a growing share of the provincial budget and after 1850 were usually the largest item in that budget [see Table 1].

---

6   Emilio Willems, 'Social Change on the Latin American Frontier', in Miller and Steffen (eds.), *The Frontier*, p. 260.

7   David McCreery, 'Hegemony and Repression in Rural Guatemala', *Peasant Studies*, vol. 17, no. 3 (Spring 1990), p. 157.

8   For discussions of the role of 'consent' and hegemony see essays by Joseph/Nugent, Roseberry, and Mallon in Gilbert M. Joseph and Daniel Nugent (eds.), *Everyday Forms of State Formation* (Durham, NC, 1994).

9   Roderick Barman, *Citizen Emperor: Pedro II and the Making of Modern Brazil, 1825–1891* (Stanford, 1999).

A sense of 'Brazilianness', if always tinged with a local colour, permeated all layers of society, but one imagines that this was in part precisely because the state's presence weighed so lightly upon Goiás. Accompanying such a commitment was a broad willingness to accept as legitimate an elite-defined national and nationalising project, something the indigenous populations of Mesoamerica or the Andes, for example, rejected peremptorily. This agreement was less than absolute, of course. By definition slaves were left out, as were Indians, but both were a declining presence in most of Brazil after 1850, and ex-slaves and 'civilised' Indians were undeniably citizens. Where the state's centralisation and development schemes did meet with serious resistance, — for example, when the regime attempted civil registration of birth and deaths in the early 1850s — the government backed down or was willing to go slow with changes, as in the wake of the *quebra quilos* riots in the 1870s.[10]

However, on at least one point the elite project did encounter sustained resistance: the reluctance of the non-slave poor to enter voluntarily into wage work on terms defined by the employers. The 'laziness' of the ex-slaves and the mixed blood rural population was a staple item of upper class and state discourse throughout the period: 'The people of Goiás are little industrious,' an official explained, 'not because they lack natural resources but because they let themselves be dominated by indolence and give themselves without restraint to the pleasures of the senses.'[11] Still, the Brazilian state made no serious effort forcibly to incorporate the mass of the free poor into wage labour and undertook nothing comparable to the vagrancy schemes of the neighbouring Argentine Republic or the peonage systems of Peru or Mesoamerica.[12] This relative freedom from forced wage labour constituted a large part of what the free poor gained from the national pact that legitimated the empire. The state and the elites could allow such slippage precisely because an influx of European immigrants helped to satisfy the labour demands of the more dynamic regions of the country. One key result of this was that the imperial state had almost no direct or day-to-day contact with the mass of the population. Even demands for taxes or military service were mediated through local elites.

It was exactly those rural landowning elites, rather than the poor, that most commonly disturbed public order under the empire, with their land and family

---

10   For example, see President of Goiás, *Relatório–1852*, p. 4.

11   Luis d'Alincourt quoted in Augusto Saint-Hilaire, *Viagêm a Província de Goiás* (Belo Horizonte/São Paulo, 1975), note 19, pp. 54–5.

12   On Argentina, see Richard Slatta, 'Rural Criminality and Social Conflict in Nineteenth-Century Buenos Aires Province', *Hispanic American Historical Review*, vol. 60, no. 3 (August, 1980), pp. 450–72. For a survey of Brazil's nineteenth-century labour laws, which were weak and rarely enforced, see Maria Lucia Lamounier, 'O trabalho sob contrato: a lei de 1879', *Revista Brasileira de História*, vol. 12 (1986) and 'Formas de transição de escravidão ao trabalho livre', Mestrado, UNICAMP (1986).

disputes fought out by hired gunmen.[13] However, apart from border areas such as Rio Grande do Sul where other factors intervened,[14] intra-elite conflicts remained largely within the established sociopolitical system. They did not threaten the empire, except where they opened the way for the eruption of the lower orders into politics, or to the extent that private, unregulated violence delegitimised the state and its agents. These were not the problems in nineteenth-century Goiás.

It was just as well that the central state enjoyed such widespread acceptance, for the instruments available to it to enforce political hegemony were limited. A citizens' militia, the national guard, replaced the old *Segunda Linea* and *ordinanças* in 1831 as the regime's chief vehicle for internal control.[15] In Goiás, and in most of the interior, the guard never proved satisfactory. During the 1830s and early 1840s provincial presidents reported that there was no guard or that if it existed they had no information about it.[16] Once in place, the guard continued to be characterised by poor organisation and lack of discipline and to suffer from shortages of equipment and arms. Observing national guard troops called to duty in 1840 at Natividade to repel a possible invasion of Balaiada guerrillas, an observer found 'a hundred and forty men, most armed only with their hunting shotguns, and without muskets, powder or shot. Those who did not have guns came armed with knives tied to sticks.'[17] The guard's general 'uselessness' continued to beleaguer state agents, and provincial presidents repeatedly dismissed it as 'disarmed' and in 'disarray'.[18]

Apart from serving as a local security force where police were not available, the guard's duties included transporting prisoners and government funds, protecting the courts when they were in session and imposing peace on election days. Occasionally, and very reluctantly, guard detachments relieved regular troops at frontier garrisons or spearheaded expeditions against marauding Indians or rebels. They were not particularly effective: 'Guard detachments got themselves together slowly because the members were reluctant to leave their

[13] See, for example, the violence surrounding a disputed inheritance: President of Goiás, *Dsicurso [sic]–1837*, pp. 6–7.

[14] John Charles Chasteen, *Heroes on Horseback: A Life and Times of the Last Gaucho Caudillos* (Albuquerque, 1995); Astolfo Serra, *A Balaiada* (Rio de Janeiro, 1946).

[15] For information on the Segunda Linea in Goiás just prior to the creation of the national guard, see Archivo Histórico do Estado de Goiás [AHEG], Documentação Avulsa [Doc. Avulsa], Box [Cx] 17, package [Pac.] 1, 20 March, 1830; on the creation of the national guard in general, see Jeanne Berrance de Castro, *A milícia cidadã: a Guarda Nacional de 1831 a 1850* (São Paulo, 1977).

[16] President of Goias, *Dsicurso (sic)–1837*, pp. 32–3 and *Relatório–1839*, pp. 23–4.

[17] George Gardner *Viagem ao interior do Brasil (1836–1841)* (Belo Horizonte/São Paulo, 1975), p. 171.

[18] President of Goiás, *Relatório–1841*, p. 8, *Relatório–1854*, p. 13 and *Relatório–1854*, 3rd, p. 15.

own affairs, they did not have the proper arms, and since there was no secrecy, it was useless to attempt to catch anyone.'[19] Potentially the guard's most important task was to guard tax collection points when regular troops were not available and to back up fiscal agents, particularly at the isolated river crossings upon which the province depended for much of its revenues.[20] But because they, or their superiors, were themselves often heavily involved in tax evasion and smuggling, guard members did not always perform anti-contraband activities with the zeal or the impartiality for which the government hoped.[21]

Despite, or perhaps because of, the guard's notorious inefficiency, the citizens of Goiás accepted its legitimacy and the state's right to call upon them to serve. They just wanted someone else to go. 'They lack the necessary discipline and zeal for service, which they give almost always reluctantly', complained a provincial president.[22] More fundamentally, by relying on a self-financing control apparatus headed by local notables, by 'privatising' the repressive function, the state forfeited its ability to discipline those that it called upon to discipline the general population.[23] The state delivered power into the hands of a group likely to misuse it, but, at least in Goiás, to misuse it within and not against the state. This was the best trade-off available at mid-century.

The problem of control should have been at least partially resolved in 1858 with the creation of a provincial police force.[24] Even had this agency functioned as proposed, the 60 men provided for in the original law could hardly have adequately policed a population of some 120,000 spread over more than 600,000 square kilometres. In the event, the poor wages offered, together with eruption of the Paraguayan War, kept the force a paper entity until the 1870s.[25] In 1874, and in the wake of reforms that stripped the national guard of all but ceremonial functions, a new provincial law authorised a police force of 100 men and 18 officers. By 1879 80 had been recruited, but wages were low and the quality of the recruits evidently lower still. In 1885 the provincial chief of police reported that he still had only 80 men, 43 stationed in small detachments around the

---

[19]   President of Goiás, *Relatório–1848*, pp. 37–8.

[20]   President of Goiás, *Relatório–1855*, p. 7; AHEG, Documentação Diversa [Doc. Diversa], volume [Cdx] 337, 'Correspondência da Presidência da Provincia com Autoridades Policiais', 24 Feb. 1860.

[21]   David McCreery, 'Smuggling and the "Internal Economy" of Nineteenth Century Goiás', *The Americas*, vol. 53, no. 3 (Jan., 1997), pp. 333–51.

[22]   AHEG, Doc. Diversa, 'Correspondência do Governo Provincial com o Ministério de Justiça', 12 Mar. 1858.

[23]   Uricoechea, *Patrimonial Foundations*, p. 81.

[24]   *Correio Oficial*, 13, 20 and 24 Nov., and 3 Dec. 1858; President of Goiás, *Relatório–1859*, pp. 43–45 and *1859* 2nd., p. 36.

[25]   President of Goiás, *Relatório–1866*, p. 7, *Relatório–1867*, p. 16, and *Relatório–1871*, p. 6.

province and the rest involved in various tasks such as guarding prisoners and gathering state revenues from the various fiscal stations.[26] Rarely were men available to hunt criminals or to patrol to prevent crimes. In the wake of a disturbance the chief of police would round up a detachment and send it to the trouble spot, but as often as not the men only further inflamed the situation, by drinking and trouble-making or by openly siding with one faction or another.[27] Until the end of the empire Goiás's provincial government lacked even the semblance of an adequate or independent police force in the rural areas.

The president also had at his disposal a portion of the regular army, the 20th battalion, composed typically of two companies of infantry, one of cavalry and two of *pedestres* (poorly equipped garrison troops). In the 1840s the battalion was supposed to total some 350 men and by the 1850s almost 600, but rarely was it up to strength, both because of recruiting and desertion problems and because the minister of war repeatedly detached elements for service in Mato Grosso.[28] The regular army paid its men better than the police, but, again, its numbers and their disposition did little to guarantee the peace. The president kept about half of the troops in the capital, as a strategic reserve, for a presidential guard and to reinforce the municipal police. The rest were scattered about the province in small garrisons and at *presídios* (forts) in the north.[29] While these detachments may have helped calm local fears, in reality there was not much they could do to discourage bandit raids or Indian attacks or to combat the smuggling that plagued the countryside. To the extent that these troops fell under the sway of local elites, they too became implicated in political disputes and protecting criminals.[30] On other occasions they were simply drunk and annoying.[31] The *presídios* were even more problematic. They did little to thwart Indian raids, and service there tended to destroy what discipline the *pedestres* might have acquired. According to one commander, the troops in the *presídios* lost their 'soldierly habits' and 'confused themselves with the rural mixed bloods'.[32]

---

[26] *Correio Oficial*, 1 Aug. 1874 and 4 June 1879, pp. 1–2; President of Goiás, *Relatório–1879*, p. 4; AHEG, Doc. Diversa, Cdx 442, 'Secção Militar', 1881; AHEG, Doc. Avulsa, Cx 347, Commander, Goiás Provincial Police–President, 10 June 1885. Compare Paul Vanderwood, *Disorder and Progress: Bandits, Police, and Mexican Development* (Lincoln, NE, 1981).

[27] See, for example, the events in Duro (Niquelândia) during the 1880s: Paulo Bertran, *Memoria de Niquelândia* (Brasilia, 1985), chap. VII.

[28] President of Goias, *Relatório–1842*, p. 4; *Relatório–1846*, p. 6; and *Relatório–1859*, p. 41.

[29] President of Goiás, *Relatório–1861*, p. 79.

[30] For example, see AHEG, Municípios, Goiás, Juiz de Direito, San José do Tocantins — Vice-President, 15 Nov. 1885. On *coronelismo*, see footnote no. 92.

[31] For example, AHEG, Municipalities, Paraná, Cx 1, Police Delegate–Provincial Chief of Police, 9 Dec. 1876.

[32] AHEG, Doc. Diversa, Cdx 442, 'Secção Militar', 1881.

The empire's chief representative in Goiás was the provincial president, appointed directly from Rio de Janeiro. Presidents were generally law school graduates, and after the mid-1840s none was locally born. In Goiás the office suffered a high turnover: for the years of the empire presidents averaged only slightly more than 13 months in office, and the circulation increased after mid-century as communications improved.[33] The empire found it difficult to fill these positions in the interior. Appointment to a district judgeship was preferred to a presidency, and up to mid-century a shortage of trained personnel gave applicants some leverage in negotiations.[34] Even by the standards of the *sertão*, Goiás's poverty and isolation made it an unattractive assignment: only bachelors could be sent there because the overland trek was thought to be too arduous for women.[35] Anyone with reasonably good connections could hope for something better, and those named to Goiás sometimes stalled months while they manoeuvred for a better assignment.

The provincial president's chief job was to mediate between the bureaucratic demands of the state and the interests of locally powerful. This could be a frustrating and thankless task. One president, previously a successful judge in the province, simply quit with the candid admission that he was not up to the task.[36] Before an 1870s reform that banned multiple job holding, the president often was gone from the province for months at a time serving as a deputy in the National Assembly, and others took extended leave to attend to private concerns. With the president absent, the vice-president, always a Goiás native, replaced him. Vice-president João Bonifácio Gomes de Siqueira, for example, served as acting president five times, for a total of 44 months, between 1862 and 1871.[37] Although Gomes de Siqueira was a lawyer, and eventually became an appeals court judge, the substitutes typically lacked legal training and few had had upper level administrative experience. All were deeply enmeshed in local affairs. As such, they were dubious instruments for the imposition of central authority, at least as this might conflict with provincial or class interests.

Working with the president was the Provincial Assembly and the chief of police. The assembly met briefly during the dry season [April-September] and did little.[38] Apart from overseeing the municipalities and passing the occasion-

---

[33] *Cronologia dos governantes de Goiás — de 1772 a 1975* (Goiânia, 1977).

[34] Thomas Flory, *Judge and Jury in Imperial Brazil* (Austin, 1981), pp. 40–43. On recruitment to bureaucratic offices, see Eul-Soo Pang and Ron L. Seckinger, 'The Mandarins of Imperial Brazil', *Comparative Studies in Society and History*, vol. 14, no. 2 (March, 1972), pp. 215–48 and Richard Graham, *Patronage and Politics in Nineteenth-Century Brazil* (Stanford, 1990).

[35] Graham, *Patronage and Politics*, p. 231.

[36] President Dr Francisco Mariani, 1853–54: President of Goiás, *Relatório–1854*, p. 12.

[37] *Cronologia dos governantes.*

[38] On the politics of the period see Maria Augusta Sant'anna Moraes, *História de uma oligarquia: os Bulhões* (Goiânia, 1974).

al law, the assembly's chief task was to vote the provincial budget. But chaos dominated revenue collection and state spending, budgets were commonly in deficit, and the assembly was unwilling or unable to resolve these problems. Effectively a 'council of local notables', the assembly could not directly contravene imperial directives, but it did work to shield the provincially powerful from the more extravagant designs of the central government and its agents. Pressured, for example, to pass a cattle-production tax in 1870 and a land tax later in the decade, the assembly acquiesced but allowed both to quickly wither for lack of enforcement.[39] Efforts by the imperial regime to obtain information about economic activity in the province, with the possible goal of taxing it, or to register land titles met with a similar lack of success.[40] The empire's situation in Goiás was effectively a holding action, while it tended to more urgent problems or more promising opportunities in other regions.

The chief of police, also a law graduate and appointed by the president, oversaw a network of *delegados* (marshals) and *subdelegados* (deputies) who were the main law enforcement officers in the province. More than any other official, it was the *delegado* that linked central authority to local interests, custom to law. The position was unpaid, but in compensation offered considerable local power, especially after reforms in the 1840s stripped the elected justices of the peace of most of their powers.[41] *Delegados* and *subdelegados* could expect help from the provincial police or the army only rarely, and then with considerable delay, forcing them to rely instead on the national guard or, more broadly, on the power that accrued to them as members or agents of the local elite. It was the classic instance in nineteenth-century Brazil of reliance on 'private' power to enforce 'public' law, and the individual and the position were caught up in all of the contradictions this implied. Because local politics commonly opposed several clan or family factions, the *delegado* or *sub-delegado* often found himself at odds with other local officials: in one instance, a travelling Italian doctor found himself caught in a conflict at Palma that pitted the *delegado* against a *sub-delegado* and divided the town's other officials.[42]

The chief functions of the *delegado* were to investigate possible crimes, to gather evidence and present this to the district judge (*juiz de direito*) to determine if a prosecutable offence had occurred. If so, he was to capture the culprits, find witnesses, gather additional evidence and turn these over to the public prosecutor (*promotor*) for presentation to a jury. Where possible he also was to act pre-

---

[39] AHEG, Municipalities, various censuses of cattle production, 1870–1873; Cavalcante Cx 1, Collector-Inspector, Treasury, 9 July 1879; *A Tribuna Livre*, 3 May 1879.

[40] AHEG, Doc. Diversa, Cx 226, 'Relatório sobre o estado da lavoura na provincia de Goyaz …, 24 Jan. 1874'.

[41] Flory, *Judge and Jury*, p. 172; Graham, *Patronage and Politics*, p. 53.

[42] *O Publicador Goyano*, 31 Oct. 1885.

emptively to prevent crimes and forestall disruptive or suspicious behaviour. Not all the *delegados* and *sub-delegados* were competent or particularly assiduous. One, for example, ruled a death to be an accident when further investigation showed that the unfortunate victim had been 'strangled with the cover of his own shotgun, castrated while still alive and then had rocks piled on his stomach until he expired'.[43] But just as the *delegado* balanced public and private, law and custom, he was himself poised between advantage and peril. There was the simple physical danger of having to arrest armed and dangerous criminals with limited resources. Faced with such a situation, a subdelegate in the town of Rio Verde instead took refuge in his house, only to be joined there shortly by the presumed criminal himself, now pursued by an angry lynch mob.[44] Officials also had to weigh the political dangers of attempting to enforce the law. Some offenders were themselves local elites or enjoyed powerful patrons. In November of 1878, for example, a subdelegate in the countryside near Rio Verde reported that he could not investigate a murder because of the population's 'terror' of Colonel Joaquim Bernardo de Oliveira, who was thought to have ordered the killing.[45]

In other cases, the only 'crime' alleged was violence connected with political or family or land disputes.[46] To elites and gunmen alike, the idea of impartial law and blind justice made no sense, especially when it ran against their interests or came at the hands of a member of an opposing faction. Justice often seemed, and was, little but vengeance and retribution or a vehicle for personal gain. The office of *delegado* could add to an individual's power and status in the local community but it also could be burdensome and dangerous, and each year dozens of *delegados* and *sub-delegados* petitioned to be relieved.[47]

The chief legal authority in the district (*comarca*) was the district judge. All were law school graduates and most hoped for upwardly mobile careers in the state bureaucracy or electoral politics. Through schooling and a centralised bureaucratic structure the state sought to socialise these judges to national values and to a view of law and public administration that served the empire.[48] But

---

[43] AHEG, Municipalities, Piracanjuba Cx 2, Delegate-Provincial Chief of Police, 11 March 1853.

[44] AHEG, Municipalities, Itumbiara [Santa Rita Paranayba], Cx 3, Subdelegate-Provincial Police Chief, 19 April and 10 May 1892.

[45] AHEG, Doc. Diversa, Cx b03, 'Correspondência da Presidência da Provincia ao Ministério de Justiça', 11 Nov. 1878.

[46] Among dozens of such comments, see President of Goiás, *Relatório–1852*, 2nd., 4 and AHEG, Doc. Avulsa, Cx 184; Vigario, Santa Rita do Paranaiba-? [Reservado], 12 Jan., 1868; and Municípios, Natividade Cx 1, Subdelegate-Provincial Chief of Police, 24 March 1871; and *Provincia de Goyaz*, 2 July 1870.

[47] For example, President of Goiás, *Relatório–1874*, p. 6.

[48] Pang and Seckinger, 'Mandarins', Graham, *Patronage and Politics*.

patronage and politics as much as competence determined the judges' professional fate, placing them too at the intersection of 'public' and 'private' power. Goiás was not a sought-after posting for ambitious young law graduates and at no time during the empire did the province have trained lawyers sitting in all of its districts. The imperial system of appointments aggravated the situation by constantly shuffling judges between posts and moving them to other administrative positions. A judge, like a president, could delay taking up his office for months and many did, in hope of a better post. Once in place, judges often escaped at the first opportunity to a better district or on temporarily leave. After 1873 Goiás gained an appeals court (*relação*), and district judges sometimes had to be called up when insufficient *desembargadores* (appeals courts judges) were available.

If the district judge was not available or could not serve, a substitute (*suplente*), appointed by the provincial president from among the locally prominent, replaced him. Although most had had experience as municipal judges, few of these men enjoyed any formal legal training and they were not provided with books or other materials to orient them in deciding cases.[49] Some were grossly ignorant or only semi-literate. Others 'mixed in politics, indifferent to the evils this causes and became involved with the persons to whom they are supposed to dispense justice'.[50] Not a few *suplentes* seized the opportunity to settle old scores or build their clientele. Why, a provincial president inquired of one judge, did you chose only jurors that would give you the decision you desired, try to intimidate the jury, arrange for all of the defendants to have your brother-in-law as their defence lawyer and allow those who were obviously guilty to go free?[51]

A persistent problem for central control was the inability of the imperial or the provincial governments to collect enough revenue to recruit, train and maintain an adequate bureaucracy or to fund state programmes. In many years Goiás ran a budget deficit, as did the imperial government and other provinces evidently more prosperous than Goiás.[52] Provincial budget records for the period are scattered and incomplete, but nevertheless revealing.

Spending for public education was impressive, rising dramatically over the course of the century as a percentage of the total budget, but that for public works, in a province that complained constantly of poor roads, seems low. That

---

[49] Flory raises but does not pursue this problem: Flory, *Judge and Jury*, p. 69. Goiás's presidents complained constantly of the ignorance of the law among the substitute judges: AHEG, Doc. Diversa, Cdx 162, 'Ofícios diregidos à Secretaria da Justiça', 31 May 1844 and 3 Aug. 1844, among dozens more.

[50] President of Goiás, *Relatório–1840*, p. 10 and see *Relatório–1848*, p. 8.

[51] AHEG, Doc. Avulsas, Cx 297, President-Bac. Bernardo Joaquim da Silva Guimares, 25 Nov. 1861 and various other associated letters.

[52] On national budgets, see Leslie Bethell (ed.), *Colonial Brazil* (Cambridge, 1987), p. 80; Murilo, *Teatro*, p. 173. For a comparison to Goiás, see Katia M. de Queiros Mattoso, *Bahia: século XIX* (Rio de Janeiro, 1992), ch. 14.

is because much of the funding for projects of this nature came from federal grants. Indicative too is the spending on Indian pacification (*catequese*), falling from ten per cent of the budget in 1835 to less than one tenth of a per cent in 1875 and disappearing entirely a decade later, as the Indian menace receded. Administrative costs, including the assembly and revenue collection, remained comparatively low and declined as a percentage of the budget. Despite such evidence of fiscal responsibility salaries commonly ran months and years behind, and often the government had to resort to loans to pay its employees.[53]

Table 1: Selected Provincial Expenses (in milreis)

Category	1835	1845	1854	1865	1875	1885
Total	53:135	58:562	47:442	149:100	203:259	233:365
Assemblea	4:982	5:224	2:337	9:053	8:547	9:218
Presidência	4:550	3:300	4:150	9:800	11:080	12:208
Instruçao	6:300	11:652	11:760	30:600	53:650	64:660
Hospital	1:600	2:900	1:800	6:800	8:700	10:000
Obras Públicas	8:000	7:000	4:000	23:750	15:000	14:000
Catequese	5:000	4:600	1:000	1:000	500	
Revenue exps.	14:124	11:503	29:129	28:533	30:000	

Source: From presidential *Relatórios*.

The imperial government routinely voted funds to supplement those collected in the province, but, apart from the military payroll, these were never certain and remained a source of anxiety for provincial administrators.[54] Initially, subsidies arrived as sheets of copper to be stamped into coins.[55] However, problems with transportation and counterfeiting quickly put an end to that, and by the 1840s they took the form of credits in the budgets of specific imperial min-

---

53 President of Goiás, *Relatório–1850*, p. 51; *Coleção das leis da Provincia de Goiás*, T. 50, Law 796.

54 Paulo Bertran, *Formação econômica de Goiás* (Goiânia, 1978), p. 71; AHEG, Doc. Avulsa, Cx 185, Minister of Agriculture–President of Goiás, May 1868.

55 *A Matutina Meiapontense* (Meia Ponte) [Pirinópolis], 8 June 1830.

istries. Precisely because they were uncertain, such transfer payments from the central regime did not usually register in the provincial budgets voted and printed each year.[56] In 1862, however, President Alencastre provided a complete breakdown of credits granted for the fiscal year 1861–62.

The funds from the Ministry of Justice covered the salaries of the district judges and the chief of police, that of empire paid, among other things, the salary and expenses of the provincial president; the treasury funded imperial tax collection, and the Ministry of Agriculture subsidised roads and bridges. By far the largest amount went for the military, and this would have been the case most years. By comparison, the income anticipated from all provincial revenue sources for 1861 was 142:946 $000 milreis, or slightly more than half what the central government spent on the province's military force alone. Goiás was not a money-making enterprise for the empire.

Table 2: Imperial Subsidies, 1861–62

Ministry	Amount
Empire	50:990$000
Justice	41:900$000
War	287:609$294
Treasury	34:177$232
Agriculture	36:527$000

Source: President of Goiás, *Relatório–1862*, p. 106.

Until mid-century the most important source of revenue for the provincial government was the *dízimo* (tithe), a 5–10 per cent tax on the production of agricultural goods and animals. *Dízimos* were the scourge of the small farmer, as provincial presidents recognised: 'these taxes are always vexing and onerous for the taxpayer, especially for the most wretched and needy, frequently the victims of various abuses of the collectors'.[57] In a marginal economy any tax was a problem, but *dízimos* were particularly burdensome because of the manner in which they were assessed and collected. *Dízimos* were based not on actual output but on what the tax collector anticipated the farmer or rancher would produce. Accompanied by proper pomp and ritual,[58] the tithe agent each year inspected

---

56 Regarding the need for a subsidy from the imperial treasury, see AHEG, Doc. Diversa, Cdx 134, 'Correspondência da Presidência da Provincia para Diversos, 1835–1842', Provincial Assembly, 19 Aug. 1837,

57 President of Goiás, *Relatório–1859*, p. 60.

58 *A Matutina Meiapontense*, 6 Oct. 1831.

the area the farmer had under cultivation and from this estimated the likely yield. At harvest time a district committee made up of farmers and merchants agreed upon the prices of agricultural commodities, and from these, and using each producer's estimated output, the tithe agent calculated what each owed. A similar process applied to ranchers, although in those cases the prices were set province-wide. Bad weather or an attack of predators could ruin a year's work overnight, while the farmer's tax liability remained unaltered. Those that suffered the effects of natural disasters could petition for a reduction in tithes, but the process was lengthy and stacked against them. Equally vexing was the fact that tithe payments had to be made in cash, even though the farmer, if he found a market for his goods, could expect to sell them only on credit terms. Not surprisingly, producers evaded the tax where they could, engaging in a wide and imaginative array of frauds and collections ran years behind.[59]

As mid-century approached and cattle production increased, provincial income came to depend less on tithes than on taxing animals that were exported from the province.[60] Taxes of this sort had existed from the colonial period and served two purposes. On the one hand, they were intended to limit the shipment of animals from the province, in order to build up local breeding stocks. For this reason taxes were higher on cows than steers. On the other, the taxes were a source of revenue, and an increasingly important one. As exports grew, the provincial government in 1856 abolished the tithe, raised the taxes on animals and set up *registros* (check points) along Goiás's borders to ensure collection. It supplemented this with a five per cent levy on the value of food items sold in the towns or to travellers along the roads. This was only collected regularly in the main market of the provincial capital, but it nevertheless quickly became second in importance to that earned from exports. Though producers found it relatively easy to evade these taxes, and smuggling and tax fraud flourished,[61] the reforms produced substantial gains in revenues: provincial income doubled in constant terms between 1855 and 1865.[62] Spending kept pace, however, as did budget shortfalls.

Persistent fiscal problems were doubly damaging to the province. A shortage of resources limited what the state could do, whether paying public officials on time, policing the countryside or building adequate roads and bridges. It also pointed up

---

[59]   On the difficulties and abuses of tithes, see, for example, AHEG, Doc. Avulsa, Cx 17, pac. 1, 'Ministerio de Estado dos Negócios da Fazenda — Artigos de Officio, Repartição dos Negócios da Fazenda', 5 June 1829, Cx 18 pac. 2, Vereador Pedro Gomez Machado, 16 Nov. 1829; *A Matutina Meiapontense*, 28 Jan., 13 April and 10 June 1830; Cx 17 'Opiniões dos Senes. Conselheiros sobre Dízimos', 19 April 1831.

[60]   For a survey of provincial taxes, with methods of collection, etc., that remained more or less valid until the end of the Empire see: *Livro da Lei Goiana–1869*, 3a parte.

[61]   McCreery, 'Smuggling.'

[62]   AHEG, budget records.

the general weakness of the state. While the population of Goiás largely accepted the state's right to collect taxes, most sought to avoid paying some or all of what they were said to owe. They understood and agreed that the government needed adequate revenues to operate successfully, and there was broad agreement too on the purposes to which the regime put this money, it was just that they wanted someone else to provide it. The most successful tax evaders were the elites themselves, cutting revenues and legitimising popular resistance to state demands.

Few groups in nineteenth-century Brazil seemed as threatening to the fledgling state as did the country's African slaves, a population replenished regularly from overseas right up to mid-century.[63] During these years several of Goiás's neighbours suffered slave revolts or popular uprisings that swept up the slaves together with the free population.[64] In the 1860s the Paraguayan War disrupted the whole centre-west and loosed numbers of runaway slaves and army deserters. By the mid-1880s many areas of Brazil were experiencing massive slave flight. If all of this had remarkably little impact on Goiás, that had not always been the case. During the eighteenth century there were many reports of *quilombos* (runaway slave settlements) in the captaincy and of army attacks and popular expeditions against them.[65] As late as the mid-1830s an expedition pursuing Indians in the north of the province had orders to be on the lookout for *quilombos*.[66] However, evidence of fear that escaped slaves might threaten settled populations are noticeably absent from most nineteenth-century Goiás documents.[67] This contrasts with neighbouring Mato Grosso, where *quilombos* figured prominently in presidential reports right up to and after the declaration of the republic.[68] A similar lack of concern about capturing runaway slaves is also evident in provincial records. Occasionally notices appeared in newspapers, and criminal and jail records sometimes mention recaptured slaves, but the correspondence of the provincial police chief with the *delegados* and that of the municipalities with the provincial president seldom touched on the subject.[69]

---

[63] On the waning days of the African slave trade see Leslie Bethell, *The Abolition of the Brazilian Slave Trade* (Cambridge, 1970), and on the tensions involved, see Dale T. Graden, 'An Act "Even if Public Security": Slave Resistance, Social Tensions, and the End of the International Slave Trade to Brazil, 1835–1856', *Hispanic American Historical Review*, vol. 2, no. 76 (May 1996), pp. 249–82.

[64] A good summary of the unrest in this period is Bethell, *Brazil*, pp. 68–76.

[65] Mary Karasch, 'Os quilombos do ouro na Capitania de Goiás', *Liberdad por um Fio: história dos quilombos no Brasil* (Rio de Janeiro, 1996); see also Palacín, *Século de ouro*, pp. 79–80.

[66] President of Goiás, *Relatório–1835*.

[67] For a rare exception, see AHEG, Municipalities, Parana, Cx 1, Report [incomplete, undated but from late 1840s].

[68] See, for example, President of Mato Grosso, *Relatório–1853*, 28 and *Relatório–1872*, p. 18.

[69] *Correio Oficial*, 26 January and 13 July 1878; *A Tribuna Livre* (Goiás), 26 April and 22 November 1879.

Why were the owners not worried about slaves escaping, and, more broadly, how could slavery function on an 'open' frontier? Part of the answer is demographics. By mid-century there were not many slaves in Goiás, either in numbers or as a percentage of the population.

Table 3: Slave Population of Goiás[70]

1804	19,285	38 per cent of total population
1872	10,652	7 per cent of total population
1885	5,194	3.5 per cent of total population

It was more than a question of numbers. Once mining collapsed it became prohibitively expensive to import slaves into Goiás, and suggestions that the central state subsidise such a traffic met with no favour.[71] Not only were there no new slave levies, but there was a small but steady sale of slaves out of the province, mainly to Mato Grosso before 1850, and then to the areas of export coffee production after mid-century.[72] An 1847 export tax intended to keep slaves in Goiás was easily evaded.[73] Other slaves were stolen and taken out of the province.[74] A creole slave population tended toward a more balanced sex ratio than was common when slaves were brought in from Africa, and sales and thefts drained off at least some of the more active young men. As a result, the 1885 *matrículas* (slave registries) showed that older women and men and children predominated among Goiás's slaves.[75] This was not a population likely to revolt or to escape and form *quilombos*.

Other factors militating against overt resistance included the physical openness of Goiás, the nature of the local economy, patterns of labour relations and the relative ease with which slaves could free themselves legally. One might argue that the

---

[70]   Maria de Sousa França, *Povoamento do Sul de Goiás: 1872–1900 — estudo da dinâmica da ocupação espacial* (Mestrado, UFG, 1975); Funes, *Goiás*, p. 116; Moraes, *Os Bulhões*, p. 64; AHEG, Doc. Avulsa, Cx 347, Table of Slave Population by Municipalities, 9 Dec. 1885. Percentages do not include the Indian population.

[71]   AHEG, Doc. Diversa, Cdx 8, 'Correspondência do Governo e Autoridades Fora da Provincia, 1808–1809', 30 December 1808; AHEG, Doc. Diversa, Cdx 36 'Correspondência dos Negócios do Reino, 1820–1824', 8 April 1820.

[72]   AHEG, *recebedorías*, Santa Rita do Paranaiba and Rio Grande/Araguaia.

[73]   AHEG, Doc. Diversa, 'Correspondência da Provedoria da Fazenda Provincial, 1847–1850, Cdx 200, 28 April 1847.

[74]   Judy Bieber Freitas, 'Slavery and Social Life: Attempts to Reduce Free People to Slavery in the Sertão Mineiro, Brazil, 1850–1871', *Journal of Latin American Studies*, vol. 26 (1994), p. 603.

[75]   Archivo do Museu da Bandeira (Goiás), 1885 slave registries.

very size of Goiás and its small population should have made it easy for slaves to form runaway communities. In fact, far from isolating themselves, *quilombos* in Brazil had a history of symbiosis with nearby free settlements. The relative absence of evidence for such interactions suggests that at the very least there were few escaped slave settlements in nineteenth-century Goiás,[76] and where they existed they had little economic or military importance.

Labour shortages in Goiás were such that slaves seem to have been relatively well treated and to have worked together with other types of labour under similar conditions. Mid-century censuses, for example, showed free wage workers, *agregados* ('attached' or resident workers) and slaves mixed together on many small and medium-sized properties, and there were no large slave-based agricultural operations comparable to the coastal plantations.[77] Travellers commonly reported that from looking at housing and clothing, it was often difficult to tell the slave from the master.[78] On the ranches slave cowboys were common and worked apart on their own much of the time and few seem to have tried to escape.[79] Instead, notary records show a steady stream of manumissions, most of these through self-purchase, suggesting that the slaves took advantage of opportunities such as free-lance gold mining to earn money and to liberate themselves through the legal system.[80] Especially after the Free Birth Law in 1871, the day-to-day situation of slaves may not have been all that different from other workers nor have been experienced as such. And if not more than 10–20 per cent of the population of even the capital could be classified as 'white', slaves, free workers, and masters must have looked very much alike.[81] In general, then, a slave's chances to gain freedom within settled society seem to have been good, whether by purchase or gift or by slipping away to another property to be taken on as an *agregado*. By contrast, to escape into the wild not only involved entering an environment with which creole slaves had little experience but risked falling into the hands of an indigenous population that generally killed blacks.

Far from seeing slaves as a threat, state agents and landowners in nineteenth-century Goiás complained repeatedly of a shortage of captive workers and

---

[76] Which is not to say there were none. As late as the early 1990s a previously unknown settlement of the descendants of escaped slaves was reported in the Goiás press: Mary Karasch, 'Interethnic Conflict and Resistance on the Brazilian Frontier of Goiás, 1750–1890, in Guy and Sheridan (eds.), *Contested Ground*, p. 126.

[77] See, for example, AHEG, Doc. Diversa, Cdx 229, 'Arrolamento dos habitantes da Freguesia da Vila de Corumbá, 1850–1851' and Cdx 235, 'Recensamento da Freguesia do Bomfim, 1851.'

[78] For example, Saint-Hilaire, *Goiás*, p. 110.

[79] For an area in which slave cowboys played a major role, see Heloisa Selma Fernandes Capel de Ataídes, *Flores de Goiás: tradição e transformação* (Mestrado, 1990).

[80] Cartórios de Notas, Goiás, Santa Cruz de Goiás and Formosa.

[81] Paulo Bertran (ed.), *Notícia Geral da Capitania de Goiás* T. 1 (Goiânia, 1997), p. 113.

argued that this was one of the main causes of the province's 'decadence' and economic decline. They blamed it for the fall off in the province's mining economy and for rising food prices.[82] What comes across dramatically in provincial newspapers and government correspondence is the extent to which, even on this far frontier and even though slavery played such a small part in the local economy, the free population stuck unswervingly to the assumption of the need for bound labour. It is a quite astonishing triumph of ideology over reality and aggravated the province's problems by distracting attention from more creative ways of addressing the economic, and specifically the labour, situation. The attitude could persist because the development of extensive cattle raising and the lack of markets for large-scale commercial agriculture limited labour requirements. Employers may not have found labour as cheap as they would have liked, but an absolute shortage of workers was not a major impediment to the development of the provincial economy.

More threatening than the slaves, in real and imagined terms, were the activities of criminals and Indians. Remembering that 'crime' is defined and enforced by those with power, it is useful to distinguish among its several categories, roughly in terms of the potential threat to the state. Most evident in the police chiefs' annual reports were murder, woundings and physical assault. Comprehensive statistics are not available, but a few examples show a clear pattern:

Table 4 Crime Statistics

Year	Murder	Attempted Murder	Woundings	Robbery
1838	17	5	4	1
1847–48	20		10	1
1850	30	2	6	2
1864	23	6		
1874	16	4	9	1

Source: President of Goiás, *Relatório-1838*, pp. 123-34, *Relatório-1851*, np, and *Relatório-1874*, p. 7; AHEG, Doc. Avulsa, Cx 186, Report, Provincial Chief of Police, 1868.

The chiefs of police only sometimes detailed the specifics of crimes, but it is clear that most did not threaten the state or the elites as a class. There were career criminals, such as Sebastião José de Lacerda, 'Dedão', a 'scourge on

---

[82]   AHEG, Doc. Avulsa, Cx 117, Provincial Police Chief-President, 10 Jan. 1858.

humanity',[83] but most of this crime fits a pattern common to rural Brazil: individual and unplanned violence, albeit often underlaid by years of personal or family tensions. Occasionally something more premeditated occurred — in June of 1854, for example, the district judge of Porto Imperial was shot in an ambush, the victim of an escalating conflict that involved most of the local elites — and there were several killings of *delegados* and *sub-delegados*. In one well-publicised case, a provincial deputy was murdered in broad daylight in Vila Boa as the result of a political dispute.[84] But these were exceptional.

Drink, sexual conflicts and 'honour' provoked violence among the lower orders, and sometimes among their betters too, but in the case of the elites disentangling the motives for murder is more difficult. Local notables played so many different political, economic and social roles that it was often impossible to know in what capacity they were acting when they killed or were killed. From the perspective of state control, it did not matter. Unless these crimes got out of hand and threatened to spread or to engage large numbers of the population, they did not endanger the regime. If they appeared to be headed in such a direction, provincial authorities could muster a force sufficient to pacify at least temporarily the situation and the disputants. What they could not do was maintain day-to-day order independent of reliance on local elites and their private armed forces. As a result, the state had to tolerate intra-elite local violence, if not on the order of the infamous north-east and not at the levels that would be characteristic of the Old Republic.[85]

The military and the provincial police were too few to have much impact in the countryside on a day-to-day basis, but their officers became enmeshed in local factions and disputes. Products of the same culture, the upper ranks of the police and military generally subscribed to the same code of personal justice as did rural elites. Many possessed or assumed family connections that drew them into disputes. The rank and file of the police and army, for their part, could not escape, or even imagine escaping, the demands for obedience and personal loyalty made on them by a hierarchical society, demands that superseded institutional loyalties. In a typical case, soldiers from the garrison at Formosa acted as hired gunmen with others from Burity (Minas Gerais) to kill Captain Vicente Xavier da Silva at Flores in 1855 as part of a dispute between border smugglers.[86]

---

83 AHEG, Municipalities, Catalão, Cx 2, Delegate-Provincial Police Chief, 11 Dec. 1870.

84 AHEG, Doc. Diversa, Cdx 79, 'Correspondência da Presidência a Junta da Fazenda, Autoridades Civis e as Camaras, 1824–1826', 17 March 1826; President of Goiás, *Relatório–1854*, 3rd., p. 7; for the background for this see *Relatório–1854*, pp. 4–5. On the murder of the deputy, see AHEG, Doc. Diversa, Cdx 136, 'Juizes de Paz, 1835–1852', 28 April 1839.

85 The most notorious of the local bosses, whose violent career spanned the late Empire and the Old Republic as well as eastern Goiás and western Bahia was Abilio Wolney: Nertan Macedo, *Abilio Wolney — um coronel da Serra Geral* (Rio de Janeiro, 1975).

86 AHEG, Doc. Diversa, Cdx 262, 'Correspondência do Governo com o Secretaria dos Negócios da Justiça, 1853–1856', 11 Dec. 1855; President of Goiás, *Relatório–1856*, pp. 4–5.

If the crime statistics indicate a high murder rate for these years (and they almost certainly understated the actual number of killings), they also show an astonishingly small number of property crimes. For example, they rarely mention the theft of cattle and horses. These are crimes common to most frontiers, and Goiás's ranchers claimed that rustling was rampant.[87] We know that *delegados* executed warrants that included charges of stealing animals, but police correspondence almost never mentions criminals sought or arrested solely or chiefly for theft. They were rare too in the court reports or jail statistics.[88] This was perhaps not entirely because the inhabitants of the province were as law abiding as their presidents and chiefs of police liked to suggest, though it does seem that much of the cattle rustling was carried out by gangs from the *sertão* of Bahia and Piauí.[89]

Bringing itinerant or home-grown rustlers to justice was not easy. Given the extensive nature of cattle raising in the province and the limited labour force employed, many ranchers had only a vague idea of how many animals they owned, and even a half dozen gone missing might not be noticed. It is not at all clear, in any event, that juries would have convicted a poor man for stealing a steer for his family's consumption. Nor, at the other extreme, would jurors be likely to take on powerful local ranchers even if these were engaging in large-scale, systematic theft. In all, the most common solution was probably that favoured by many ranchers in present-day Goiás: thieves caught in the act might be summarily shot, without recourse to institutions of state justice.

Violence potentially more threatening to the state was that resulting from local political feuds. Although *coronelismo* (boss rule) only reached full flower in the Old Republic with the innovation of elected state governors, most of the elements were in place and functioning at the local level well before 1889.[90] But at no time during the empire did local elites in Goiás threaten to overturn the provincial regime or even seriously dispute state power. In part this was because province-wide parties did not develop until late in the 1870s, and before the twentieth century even these were little more than tentative family alliances.[91] Without parties it was impossible to mobilise a stable power bloc on a provincial or even regional basis, and local conflicts did not spread. Still, uncontrolled

---

[87] President of Goiás, *Relatório–1836*, p. 9; AHEG, Doc. Avulsa, Cx 285, President–Provincial Chief of Police, 12 Feb. 1879.

[88] For a description of a reputed professional cattle thief, see Gardner, *Viagem*, p. 145.

[89] See, for example, *O Commércio* (Goiânia), 24 April 1880.

[90] On *coronelismo* see, in a large literature: Nunes Leal, *Coronelismo*, Matia Isaura Pereira de Queiroz, *Mandonismo local na vida política brasileira*, and Eul-Soo Pang, *Bahia in the First Brazilian Republic: Coronelismo and Oligarchies, 1889–1934* (Gainesville, 1979); for Goiás see F. Itami Campos, *Coronelismo em Goiás* (Goiânia, 1987).

[91] Moraes, *Os Bulhões*; Campos, *Coronelismo em Goiás*; Maria Luiza Araujo Rosa, *Dos Bulhões aos Caiados: um estudo da história política de Goiás, 1899–1909* (Goiânia, 1984).

violence, even if only low level, worried the presidents, because it threatened to undermine respect for state power.

The chief centres of such turbulence were along the province's frontiers, in municipalities such as Boa Vista, Catalão, Duro and Rio Verde/Jataí. The district judge of Catalão as early as 1839 remarked that 'the state of the town is not far from anarchy', and some of the worst and most persistent violence occurred at Boa Vista, in the far north.[92] Conflict grew in part out of struggles among local elites for control of the lucrative inter-provincial smuggling traffic, especially the illegal export of untaxed cattle. The absence of an effective state monopoly on violence offered employment to those whose profession was its private practice. Aggravating the problem was the ease with which ranchers and gunmen moved across provincial boundaries to evade justice; not until the 1930s did the provinces sign 'hot pursuit' agreements. It is important to repeat, however, that these conflicts had little or no ideological content. They were not separatist movements and, although by the 1880s some groups were calling themselves liberals or even republicans, the causes of conflicts and the goals of struggles were always local. Provincial presidents repeatedly sent army and police troops to suppress outbreaks of fighting in one municipality or the other, but they understood, and consistently pointed out, that so long as these conflicts could be kept to a reasonable level they did not endanger the state.

Sedition, by contrast, is a direct challenge to the legitimacy and power of the state. Such threats were extremely rare in nineteenth-century Goiás and none took serious root. In 1822 there was a short-lived attempt to separate the north of the province from the south.[93] It failed, but the perceived differences between the regions persisted, as did repeated calls for separation. In 1831 there were anti-Portuguese riots in the capital, parallel to those in much of Brazil at this time, and the Portuguese-born chief judge of the Comarca of the North was murdered in Flores, reportedly by individuals from Bahia.[94] After mid-century there were several instances of gangs of armed men seizing and burning recruiting records and even killing recruiting officers, but no broader uprisings or popular movements.[95] In part, Goiás owed its tranquility to its isolation: the

---

[92]   AHEG, Doc. Diversa, Cdx 124, 'Livro 1o Correspondência dos Juizes de Direito e Municipais, 1833–1847', Interim District Judge, Catalão-President, 17 Oct. 1839; President of Goiás, *Relatório–1839*, pp. 140–1. See also part 1 of Luis Palacín Gomez, Nasr Fayad Chaul and Juárez Costa Barbosa *História Política de Catalao* (Goiânia, 1994); Luis Palacin Gomez, *Coronelismo no extremo norte de Goiás* (Goiânia, 1990).

[93]   AHEG, Doc. Diversa, Cdx 36, 'Correspondência da Secretária dos Negócios do Reino, 1820–1824', [President-Secretary], various; Maria de Sousa França, 'Povoamento do Sul de Goiás: 1872–1900' (Mestrado, 1975), p. 32.

[94]   AHEG, Doc. Diversa, Cdx 99, 'Registro de editais, bandos e proclamaçoes expedidas pela Secretaria do Governo, 1827–1872', *bando* of 21 July 1831.

[95]   *Correio Oficial*, 4 Aug. 1880; AHEG, Doc. Avulsa, Cx 197, Report, Provincial Chief of Police, 15 July 1870.

telegraph arrived only in the 1890s and the railroad after 1900, and before the 1870s only the government newspaper circulated. Goiás lacked any profile in imperial politics, sheltering it in part from national-level disputes.

Banditry was a form of criminality that did plague parts of the province and was difficult to disentangle from boss and clan violence. It is important to point out that banditry in Goiás had no 'social' overtones. The majority of the province's population accepted the right of the state to rule and did not see bandits as protectors of popular interests or avengers of social injustices. Rather, they experienced them to be vicious criminals, and often agents of competing elite-dominated factions, that robbed, raped and murdered the poor with impunity. This was hardly unique to Goiás or even Brazil, and much recent research has called into question the whole concept of 'social banditry',[96] but it does underline the extent to which bandits operated with the acquiescence, and even in the employ, of the locally powerful. Put another way, who was a 'bandit' depended on where or with whom you stood. Even in cases where gangs worked more or less independently, they did so only by permission of the elites and were quickly eliminated if they troubled local bosses.

Apart from an obvious challenge to the legitimacy of a state that could not bring this sort of violence under control, banditry also caused economic problems. Continuing violence ruined small ranchers and farmers, and it was linked, too, to smuggling and tax evasion, depriving the state of valuable revenue. Provincial administrations could not always keep control of even key border crossings: the priest of Santa Rita do Paranayba reported in 1868 that the town was a 'nest' of criminals engaged in all manner of illegal activity and protected by 'certain people' in the district.[97]

Most frightening for the inhabitants of Goiás's small towns and rural properties were the unsubdued Indians that roamed large swathes of the province. Estimates from the mid-1860s put their numbers at 20,000–25,000.[98] Attacks, and the fear of such attacks, emptied large areas of the north of settlers during the first half of the century, and after 1850 Indian-rancher conflict slowed settlement of Goiás's southwest.[99] The chief threat in the north came from the Canoeiros, who terrorised the

---

[96] For a useful introduction to the state of 'bandit studies' in Latin America, see Gilbert Joseph, 'On the Trail of the Latin American Bandits: A Reexamination of Peasant Resistance', *Latin American Research Review*, vol. 25, no. 3 (1990), pp. 7–53 and comments in *Latin American Research Review*, vol. 26, no. 1 (1991), pp. 145–74.

[97] AHEG, Doc. Avulsa, Cx 184, Vigario, Santa Rita Paranayba– (reservado), 12 Jan. 1868.

[98] AHEG, Doc. Diversa, Cdx 383, 'Correspondência com o Ministério de Agricultura, 1861–1873', President-Ministry of Agriculture, 12 Jan. 1862. This is a very extensive report on the general situation of Indians and Indian-Brazilian relations in the province.

[99] See any of the annual presidential *Relatórios* for these years. For example, President of Goiás, *Dsicurso (sic)–1837*, pp. 12–17.

countryside and were notorious for torturing their unfortunate victims.[100] They apparently attacked the settlers in what proved to be a vain hope of permanently clearing the Luso-Brazilian invaders and their cattle out of the area between the lower Tocantins and Araguaia rivers. Less fearsome but also liable to assault northern ranches and towns were the Xavantes and the Xerentes. In the south the most active were the Caiapó. From the colonial period the state and settlers had pursued three strategies in attempting to deal with the province's indigenous population: *aldeias* (administered villages), *presídios* and *bandeiras* (anti-Indian expeditions). All failed. As a provincial president explained in 1881, 'the history of Indian relations ... can be compared without exaggeration to that of Bahús in the recent war, a never interrupted succession of failures'.[101]

For a century and a half provincial administrators founded, abandoned and refounded *aldeias*, most of them in the north of the province. After the government had selected a likely spot, a priest or lay administrator, accompanied by a detachment of troops, would lay out a village and attempt to persuade Indians to settle there, offering gifts (*brindes*) or protection from their enemies. The goal was to 'civilise' the Indians by introducing them to Christianity and to European material culture and work habits.[102] But most of these villages soon collapsed or metamorphosed into mixed blood settlements, Indian in name only.[103] The *aldeias* failed for evident reasons: the inhabitants died of unaccustomed diseases or from attacks by unsubdued Indians or they fled the abuses of administrators: one old man remembered years later how 'they tormented us, with blows, stocks, chains, the whip and collar'.[104] Those who escaped took back into the bush a better understanding of Luso-Brazilian ideas and military tactics, new weapons and tools and a deep suspicion of Christians. The province recruited Capuchins in the mid-nineteenth century to found and run *aldeias* but only one or two of these had any success, and at least one friar fled precipitously to Mato Grosso to avoid being sent to a village. Lay administrators tended to see an appointment to an *aldeia* as an invitation to exploit the Indians. Most observers would have agreed with one president's comments, that 'the system of Indian

---

[100] Antonio Theodoro da Silva Neiva, 'Os Canoeiros: aspectos da cultura goiana' (Mestrado, 1971). Today this group is called the Ava-Canoeiro.

[101] President of Goiás, *Relatório–1881*, p. 5.

[102] John Hemming, *Amazon Frontier: the Defeat of the Brazilian Indians* (Cambridge, 1987), chs. 10 and 19.

[103] See, for example, the fate of São José Duro: *Correio Oficial*, 25 Nov. 1837; AHEG, Doc. Diversa, Cdx 645, 'Correspondência da Província Relativa a Catequese dos Indios', President-Director General of the Indians, 19 March, 1879; 'Restaurar', '1879–1883 Livro de editais, termos' [in fact, is correspondence of Ministry of Agriculture], President-Ministry of Agriculture, 3 Nov. 1879. For Pedro Afonso, see Wells, *Three Thousand Miles*, vol. 2, pp. 218–19.

[104] President of Goiás, *Relatório–1856*, p. 27.

settlements is bad, without providing the means to sustain them, without establishing the necessary rules and without showing the Indians the advantages of a social life instead of wandering in the forest'.[105]

To deal with the Indians that would not be attracted to *aldeias* the state deployed *presídios* and *bandeiras*. *Presídios* were military garrisons or colonies located at what were thought to be key points in the north, to impede Indian raids and to protect settlers. Small detachments of *pedestres* or, less often, national guards manned the forts, surviving on their own subsistence farming and irregular shipments of supplies from the capital.[106] Gradually small civilian populations grew up around the forts. Though the province lacked sufficient funds to carry out the sort of 'rationing' system used on some frontiers to buy off hostiles, the garrisons did attempt sporadically to enter into peaceful exchange with the Indians and offered them gifts of cloth and tools.[107] *Presídio* troops typically responded to Indian depredations only after they had received reports of an attack, and they rarely made any serious effort to patrol, because of their small numbers and because of the poor quality of weapons and limited munitions available to them. Because provincial authorities regularly drafted criminals to fill out *presídio* garrisons the soldiers did not have a good reputation for competence or courage, and they generally lived up to this.[108]

It is hard to know what the Indians thought of the *presídios*. At times they attacked the posts,[109] but at others they traded with the soldiers and settlers, or they simply ignored and bypassed the forts, easily enough done. The *presídios* were too strong to be readily taken by direct assault but too weak to impede Indians activities in surrounding areas. On more than one occasion troops crossed a trail or saw smoke in the distance but were afraid to seek out the source.[110] When they did

---

[105] Instituto Histórico e Geográfico de Goiás, Documentos, Pasta 2, Documento 52 'Livro 4o para o Império, Estrangeiros e Marinha, 1829–1832', Miguel Lino de Moraes, President — José Clemente Pereira, 25 Aug. 1829. When he wanted to reinforce his point about the uselessness of aldeas, the President of Mato Grosso pointed to the example of Goiás: President of Mato Grosso, *Relatório–1837*, p. 19.

[106] AHEG, Doc. Avulsa, Cx 347, President-Treasury Inspector, Goiás, 6 March 1885.

[107] On rationing systems, see Kristine L. Jones, 'Comparative Raiding Economies: North and South', in Guy and Sheridan, *Contested Grounds*, pp. 87–114. For budgets for Indian relations, see President of Goiás, *Relatório–1880*, pp. 36–44. By the 1880s the effort was to shift from gifts to the exchange of items for labour: AHEG, Doc. Avulsa, Cx 304, Minister of Agriculture–President of Goiás, 17 Aug. 1881.

[108] AHEG, Doc. Diversa, Cdx 202, 'Secretaria da Justiça, 1847–1853', 31 Oct. 1849 and Doc. Diversa, Cdx 395, 'Juiz Municipal', various letters remanding prisoners to the *presídios*.

[109] *Correio Oficial*, 7 May 1889.

[110] For example, AHEG, Doc. Diversa, Cdx 211, 'Correspondência da Presidência para as Camaras Municipais, 1848–1853', São José do Tocantins, 27 Aug. 1850.

venture to explore they typically found nothing, turned back in fear when it looked as though they might find Indians or fell into ambushes. The posts did little to stop Canoeiro or Xavante attacks. Still, the system persisted until the fall of the empire, because the settlers demanded it and because it profited others.

Less formal than *presídios* and more routinely abusive were ad hoc revenge expeditions mounted by the national guard and local citizens, and called rather grandly *bandeiras*, after the famous seventeenth- and eighteenth-century *paulista* expeditions. The 1845 Imperial law that governed relations with Indians forbade such attacks, but the Luso-Brazilians of Goiás continued to mount them at least until the 1880s. A central problem for the expeditions was leadership. Most of the non-Indian inhabitants of nineteenth-century Goiás were not at home in the forest or familiar with the wilderness the way the first generation of adventurers had been. Instead, they had transferred from São Paulo and Minas Gerais to the interior of Goiás a particularly destructive complex of slash and burn agriculture and extensive cattle raising, and most remained alienated from, and frightened of, their natural surroundings.[111] Once the gold rush passed there was little subsequent exploration of the province, except for occasional attempts to open new smuggling routes. Proposed *bandeiras* repeatedly found themselves paralysed for lack of a skilled tracker, while others lost their way or the members panicked when it appeared that they might in fact catch up with the Indians they were pursuing.[112] At best, or worst, they generally managed only to round up a few hapless Indian women and children whom they divided among themselves or sold to others, to be 'civilised'. In fact, *bandeiras* increasingly became little more than excuses for enslaving Indians to substitute for the Africans the settlers could no longer afford.[113] One official suggested that the only effect these attacks had was to increase the Indians' contempt for the Luso-Brazilians.[114]

Each dry season the Canoeiros assaulted travellers, ranches and communities, and they forced the abandonment of dozens of properties in the Amaro Leite area and threatened settlers as far south as the outlying districts of Santa Luzía. Refugees huddled together in a few towns, and workers in the fields and slaves sent to the river for water needed armed guards.[115] Small holders that could or

---

[111] On Brazilian agricultural techniques and their impact on the forest, see Warren Dean, *With Broadax and Firebrand: The Destruction of the Brazilian Atlantic Forest* (Stanford, 1995).

[112] President of Goiás, *Dsicurso (sic)– 1837*, pp. 6–7 and 16–17, and *Discurso–1838*, pp. 12–17.

[113] Pohl, *Viagem*, pp. 213–14; Francis Castelnau, *Espedição as regiões centrais da America do Sul* T.1 (Rio de Janeiro, 1940), p. 362.

[114] President of Goiás, *Discurso–1838*, p. 13.

[115] On armed guards to protect the women getting water, see Castelnau, *Espedição*, T1, pp. 359–60 and T2, p. 8.

would not abandon their properties courted death. The Indians typically killed or kidnapped Luso-Brazilians and their black slaves but on other occasions simply mocked them. After mid-century Canoeiro attacks tapered off, perhaps because their number had declined from the effects of disease or because of inter-tribal conflicts, but more likely because a renewed settler thrust in the north drove the Indians west of the Araguaia River. The Xerente and the Xavante continued to attack travellers on the lower Tocantins and to raid isolated homesteads around Boa Vista. In between they made war on other Indian groups, capturing children whom they traded to the settlers for iron and alcohol.[116]

In the south it was the Caiapó that occupied the attention of the state and the ranchers. Several thousand roamed the plains and mountains south and west of Vila Boa and across the Araguaia into Mato Grosso. For a time, several hundred Caiapó had lived in the best known of the *aldeias*, São José de Mossâmedes, southeast of the capital.[117] But with the death of their remarkable leader Damiana da Cunha in the early 1830s the settlement collapsed, and by the 1850s the Caiapó were raiding throughout the south-west, from the new ranches of the Rio Verde/Jataí region to the gold and diamond diggings of the Rio Bonito and Rio Claro. Less bloodthirsty than the Canoeiro, the Caiapó seem to have assaulted mule trains and ranches chiefly to obtain the tools and iron.[118]

To most of Goiás's Luso-Brazilian population, the Indians' abandonment of the *aldeias* and their attacks on settlers proved their barbarism and were adequate reason to exterminate them. The failure of the state to 'do something about' the Indians was a clear indictment and a constant challenge to its legitimacy. From the perspective of the state, the need to protect the ranchers and farmers from Indian attacks, attacks they had as often as not had brought upon themselves, was a constant drain on scarce resources. Many among the settlers were so poor and, as a result, so poorly armed, that they could do little to defend themselves, or so they constantly complained. The cowardice and lack of discipline characteristic of the national guard aggravated the situation. Presidents of Goiás generally had scant regard for the martial abilities of the province's inhabitants: 'Our ancestors confronted hordes of Indians but today a half dozen warriors of any small tribe spread terror in our towns, and the people imagine that only the army can save them.'[119]

---

[116] AHEG, Doc. Diversa, Cdx 308, 'Correspondência da Presidência com o Ministério do Império, 1857–60', p. 21 Feb. 1858.

[117] Mary Karasch, 'Damiana da Cunha: Catechist and *Sertanista*', in David G. Sweet and Gary B. Nash (eds.), *Struggle and Survival in Colonial America* (Berkeley, 1981), pp. 102–201; IHGG, Documents, Pasta 2, Document 52 'Livro 4o para o Imperio, Estangeiros e Marinha, 1829–1831', Miguel Lino de Moraes–José Antônio da Silva Maia, 24 May 1831.

[118] AHEG, Municipalities, Caiapônia [Rio Claro] Cx 1, Police Delegate-Provincial Chief of Police, 9 Aug. 1879.

[119] President of Goiás, *Relatório–1853*, 2nd., p. 10; see also Pohl, *Viagem*, pp. 213–14 and 224.

Fear of Indian attacks restricted the areas open for cattle or agriculture. For example, some of the best land was along riverbanks, but farmers shied away because of the danger of assault by water-borne raiders, and instead crowded around a few towns where they overworked the land. Indian attacks hampered subsistence production, aggravating the province's periodic food crises, raising costs and reducing tax revenues.[120] *Presídios* and *aldeias* were expensive and accomplished little, and *bandeiras* were brutal and largely fruitless.

There can be few better demonstrations than the history of Goiás that on the frontier 'civilisation creates barbarism.' Almost from the beginning contact involved violence, driven by European slaving and murderous wars of extermination intended to open the way for the miners and cattle ranches: 'the difficulty', one president remarked, 'is not that the Indians hate the whites but that the whites hate the Indians'.[121] The decline of mining aggravated the situation. A partial withdrawal of whites and slaves and the decay of towns, especially in the north, seem to have animated the Canoeiro, and a desperately bloody *bandeira* in 1819 sharpened their anger. But until at least the 1890s neither side could gain a sustained monopoly, or even predominance, of violence or muster enough strength to deliver a deciding blow.

What was in theory a centrally appointed, bureaucratised and hierarchical state apparatus staffed by trained specialists socialised into a rational national outlook, was something altogether different on the frontier. Untrained and partisan *suplentes* replaced qualified judges, and local bosses dominated the posts of law officers. Family-based political squabbles often determined 'justice'. Public prosecutors typically were incompetent and juries intimidated. Nevertheless, the system and the state persisted, while much of the continent fell apart into war and division. The system persisted because it served the interests of all concerned — slaves and Indians excepted, of course. The imperial state functioned as a compromise between local and national power that kept the peace for the majority of the population with a minimum of cost, a maximum of local/class control and at least a modicum of deference to the central state. No group mounted a serious or sustained challenge to public authority or state legitimacy. Rather, elites successfully manipulated the power and symbols of empire to reinforce their own positions. At one level the central state enjoyed a high degree of autonomy and encountered in Goiás few political barriers to its centralising project: local elites, one observer remarked, fought to be on the side of the government.[122] At the same time, however, by relying on these elites to

---

[120] For example, AHEG, Municipalities, Traíras, Cx 1, Tax Collector-Superintendent of the Treasury, 21 Sept. 1842; Pirinópolis [Meia Ponte], Cx 2, Tax Collector, Palma (sic) — Superintendent of the Treasury, 17 Jan. 1847.

[121] President of Goiás, *Relatório–1877*, p. 11.

[122] Virgilio M. de Melo Franco, *Viagems pelo interior de Minas Gerais e Goyaz* (Rio de Janeiro, 1888), pp. 145–50.

carry out the centralising project, the state risked becoming so drawn into local society as to be in danger of losing any separate identity.

Goiás was a frontier without wishing to be. Despite the romance and ideas of freedom popularly attached to some frontiers, and this was certainly not the vision of the *sertão* in nineteenth-century Brazil, most of Goiás's inhabitants wanted not independence but integration into the central state and what they imagined this would provide them: cheaper imports, better access to markets for their products and protection from, or perhaps persecution of, their enemies. At least as important, they longed to be, and to be taken to be, part of the civilised world, as their slavish attempts to copy often quite inappropriate fashions emanating from the centre make clear. Ironically, had state central control functioned more effectively, the provincial economy might well have collapsed, as the widespread resort to smuggling suggests. The population of Goiás, poor and elites alike, wanted a strong state to protect them from Indians and criminals and a weak state that could intervene in the economy only so as to advance their interests. For most of the empire they got instead a state that was too weak to do the first but too strong, for their tastes, as regards the second.

CHAPTER 7

The Political Economy of State-Making:
The Argentine, 1852–1955

Colin M. Lewis

In the case of the Argentine, much of the literature on state-formation has conformed to a sharply-demarcated, politically-determined chronological interpretation. This identifies a sequence of inter-connected phases from 'national consolidation' to 'mass politics' and beyond. Bench-mark events include the promulgation of the 1853 Constitution (effective with the re-incorporation of the province of Buenos Aires into the Argentine Confederation in 1862); the federalisation of the city of Buenos Aires in 1880; electoral reform in 1912 (which inaugurated 'mass' political participation); the military coup of 1930 (widely regarded as signalling institutional fragility); the election of Perón in 1946 (the *peronato* was a polity that both united and divided Argentinians); increasing institutional instability and political violence reflected in a cycle of alternating military and civilian administrations in the 1950s, 1960s and 1970s, which culminated in the 1976 military government; and, finally, the return of democracy in 1983, since when elections have followed the prescribed, constitutional timetable.[1] Too often, this chronology is presented as a conflict between order and 'barbarism', between accountability and authoritarianism, between inclusive and exclusive structures or between evolutionary and radical solutions to issues of governance and (un-)governability.

Such a framework of nation-state formation is being revitalised by new contributions to the literature of political history and a revival of the growth-economics tradition (rational choice theory) among institutionalist economic historians. Advancing beyond Weberian definitions of the state that are centred on its control of legitimate force within a designated territory, recent research has presented statehood in terms of a dependence on the consent of the governed and capacity to act. Emphasis is placed on sovereignty as a concept that subsumes the internal and the external.[2] Consolidating domestic order — 'internal'

[1] For recent examples see D. Rock, *Argentina, 1516–1982* (London, 1986); L. Bethell (ed.), *Argentina since Independence* (Cambridge, 1993); M.C. Angueira, *El proyecto confederal y la formación del estado nacional (1852–1862): el problema de la organización estatal* (Buenos Aires, 1989); H. Sabato, *La política en las calles: entre el voto y la movilización, Buenos Aires (1862–1880)* (Buenos Aires, 1998); C.A. Floria and C.A. García Belsunce, *Historia política de la Argentina contemporánea, 1880–1983* (Buenos Aires, 1988).

[2] D.A. Smith, D.J. Stolinger and S.C. Topik, 'Introduction', in D.A. Smith, D.J. Stolinger and S.C. Topik (eds.), *States and Sovereignty in the Global Economy* (London, 1999) p. 2.

sovereignty — was critical to obtaining external recognition, the first step to secure 'international' sovereignty. Ensuring that the writ of the state ran throughout the national territory discouraged external intervention: internal security facilitated the defence of national boundaries and reinforced sovereignty. International recognition and national integration might, in turn, facilitate the influence of the state beyond the frontier, further forestalling the possibility of external agents compromising security and sovereignty. For Oszlak, domestic order (and hence sovereignty) depends on a capacity to contain conflict within the institutions of the state. This feature is the bed-rock of state formation. It enables the state to externalise authority through a monopoly of the means of coercion, to differentiate control through legitimate, layered institutions and to internalise a collective identity by means of symbols and sentiments that foster social solidarity and national consciousness — a shared ideology, the most effective mechanism of control, domination and state survival.[3]

Growth-economists connect state structure and growth. Echoing modern political science literature, they implicitly identify economic growth as legitimising the state. Growth generates support, consolidates structures and delivers survival. Unsurprisingly, the more recent historical growth-economics literature compares Latin American states unfavourably with their North Atlantic and East Asian counterparts, attributing the poor economic record of the continent to state failure rather than market failure, more particularly, to the formation of the 'wrong' type of states. Variously depicted as repressive, interventionist or predatory (or a combination of all three), these regimes frustrated initiative: 'the institutional environment in Latin America ... dampened growth through the eighteenth and nineteenth centuries'.[4] Coatsworth asserts that the economic history of modern Latin America has to address two fundamental questions: 'First, why did the region fail to achieve sustained economic growth before the last quarter of the nineteenth century? Second, why has the region failed to grow fast enough to catch up since then?'[5]

Commenting on state formation in Eurasia, Bin Wong emphasises 'challenges', 'capacities', 'claims' and 'commitment',[6] language that has begun to permeate the discussion about the supply of public goods as a contract between state and society. State consolidation and survival depend on an ability to

---

[3]   O. Oszlak, *La formación del estado argentino* (Buenos Aires, 1982), p. 15.

[4]   S. Haber, 'Introduction: Economic Growth and Latin American Economic Historiography', in S. Haber (ed.) *How Latin America Fell Behind: Essays on the Economic Histories of Brazil and Mexico, 1800–1914* (Stanford, 1997), p. 20.

[5]   J.H. Coatsworth and A.M. Taylor, 'Introduction', in J.H. Coatsworth and A.M. Taylor (eds.), *Latin America and the World Economy since 1800* (Cambridge, MA, 1998) p. 1.

[6]   R. Bin Wong, *China Transformed: Historical Change and the Limits of European Experience* (Ithaca, NY, 1997) pp. 83–8.

mobilise resources and exert control. However, there are different ways of real-
ising resources and exercising control. Coercion and violence may be effective.
They are also expensive. Contractual or exchange mechanisms may be more
efficient in the long-run, particularly in an environment of state competition.
Thus ideology — the creation of a system of beliefs in the morality or desirability of a particular kind of social order — and the market — rendering services in exchange for exactions — may enhance state survival.[7]

Arguing from the premise that growth derives from market rules and that it
is the responsibility of the state to embed those rules, rational choice theorists
appraise the extent to which states secured property rights and thereby the
smooth functioning of the market. Extending the approach, the role of the state
can be presented as stabilising private property rights through the rule of law
and guaranteeing the supply of — and access to — public goods.[8] The provision of public goods promotes the consent of the governed and empowers the
state. This echoes the views of nineteenth-century Argentinian state-builders
who saw state formation and market formation as inter-connected and mutually reinforcing phenomena. Public goods represent the state, and bind together its disparate components thereby permitting the 'occupation' of national
space. The consumption of public services in distinct regions and by various
groups forge the nation. Public goods are a tangible manifestation of national
identity, imparting substance to concepts of nation and state. Systems of transport and communication integrated the market and enhanced the coercive
power of the state as much as a national army. National currency extended and
deepened the market. National education and national justice similarly reinforced the authority of the central state above that of its regional and local
counterparts. Schools and courthouses (and police barracks) were the physical
images of intangible public goods: they were the places where progress and
order were given substance. They represented state 'presence'.

The view that the market became critical for state and society in the nineteenth century is not unchallenged in the literature on the Argentine. Salvatore
argues that nineteenth-century liberals saw the market as ill-suited to the task
of nation-building. The achievement of constitutional order, territorial unity,
political stability and international economic insertion were prioritised over the
consolidation of national markets. Constructing constitutional order required a
coercive — certainly, an active — state.[9] This interpretation of nineteenth-century Argentinian ideologues of state formation like Alberdi and Sarmiento pres-

---

[7] *Ibid.*, pp. 74–5.

[8] J. Adelman, *Republic of Capital: Buenos Aires and the Legal Transformations of the
Atlantic World* (Stanford, 1999), pp. 6, 112.

[9] R. Salvatore, 'The Strength of Markets in Latin America's Sociopolitical Discourse,
1750–1850: Some Preliminary Observations', *Latin American Perspectives*, vol. XXVI, no.
1 (1999), pp. 24, 30–1.

ents the 'national' (self-regulating) market not so much as a necessary if insufficient condition for statehood but, rather, as an aspiration to be realised only after
political consolidation had been achieved. Oszlak also speculates about the links
between constructing the state and constructing the market — processes that are
not mutually exclusive but often defy fixing a neat causality. He does, however,
recognise that the tyranny of distance and difficulties of communication inhibit-
ed both market and state consolidation.[10] Halperín Donghi offers a more
nuanced view. He argues that from the middle of the nineteenth century, with the
development of an open, export-led economy, the laws of the market were not
questioned. Acceptance of the importance of clearly defined property rights did
not result in slavish recourse to liberal economics. On the contrary, '… faith in the
laws of the market appeared compatible with the recognition of a more complex
policy role for the state than that of demolishing the legal barriers inherited from
the past'.[11] The orthodox (and neoliberal) response, rooted in precepts of economic rationality and factor homogeneity would be to vaunt the 'civilising'
(integrating) role of the market, particularly in the process of nation-formation.
Little wonder that some nineteenth-century liberals saw the market as a force for
social peace, political harmony and material abundance.[12] The market forged the
nation; the state guaranteed the market.

Drawing on arguments advanced in the institutionalist literature, this chapter will consider state-formation in the Argentine between the collapse of the
Rosas regime in 1852 and the *revolución libertadora* that marked the end of the
first Perón presidencies. It will pay particular attention to the supply of public
goods — notably transport and communications and money — in order to
map and weigh the growth of the Argentinian state. Contemporaries and historians have devoted considerable attention to the provision of economic infrastructure, almost invariably quoting the preamble to the 1853 Constitution that
required the state to promote railway construction.[13] If there was agreement

---

10   O. Oszlak, 'The Historical Formation of the State in Latin America', *Latin American Research Review*, vol. XVI, no. 2 (1981), pp. 3–4, 19, 20.

11   T. Halperín Donghi, 'Argentina: Liberalism in a Country Born Liberal', in J.A. Love and N. Jacobson (eds.) *Guiding the Invisible Hand: Economic Liberalism and the State in Latin American History* (New York, 1988), p. 105.

12   R. Weiner, 'Competing Market Discourses in Porfirian Mexico', *Latin American Perspectives*, vol. XXVI, no. 1 (1999), p. 44.

13   República Argentina, Ministerio de Relaciones Exteriores y Culto *Constitution of the Argentine Republic* (Buenos Aires, 1926) p. 20. For a contemporary view see J.B. Alberdi, *Obras completas. vol. III. Bases y puntos de partido para la organización de la República Argentina* (Buenos Aires, 1886), pp. 433–5. Many historians, particularly economic historians, correlate growth, market integration and state outreach with the expansion of
the railway network in the late nineteenth and early twentieth centuries. See C.F. Díaz
Alejandro, 'The Argentine State and Economic Growth: a Historical Review', in G. Ranis,

about the modernising role of railways, there was less consensus about the means: was government or the private sector to assume primary responsibility? Agonising about the organisation of transport services in the nineteenth century prefigures later debates about the emergence of the 'corporate' state during the *peronato*. In the railway sector, the state was active during the mid-nineteenth century as promoter of private initiative and direct agent. Later the state retrenched, only to 're-appear' in the second quarter of the twentieth century. Who were the actors and what were the expectations driving the formation of the national railway network? What did it deliver?

New institutionalists depict currency regimes as a 'contract between state and society'. During the period studied here, the Argentine may be viewed as moving fitfully from a condition of monetary anarchy towards one of currency stability and, subsequently, from 'hard' to 'soft' money. The mid-nineteenth century witnessed a sustained, relative decline in monetary volatility and a quest for virtue. While loose money policies can be observed in the late 1880s, stability was soon restored and prevailed for more than half a century. How are these shifts to be explained and what light do they shed on state formation and state behaviour? Who were the actors driving these shifts and how were they influenced by ideas about the role of the state in the monetary sphere?

Applying these premises to the period addressed, the collapse of Rosas can be interpreted as a shift from a coercive to a persuasive regime — from a system based on plunder to one offering ideology (liberalism and the market). This implies the provision of public goods, including railways and currency stability, in exchange for exactions. Similarly, the *peronato* can be presented as a breakdown of the consensus that had emphasised economic stability above equity and a willingness to trade macroeconomic stability for (re)distribution and welfare? Was soft money perceived, as in the 1880s, as an effective means of re-constructing the state?[14]

Infrastructure and Modernisation: Expectations and Performance

For Roca, victor of the 'desert' Indian campaigns, installed as president in 1880, the railways and the telegraph — along with the Remington rifle — were instru-

---

Government and Economic Development (New Haven, 1971), pp. 219, 222, 228, 231 and *Essays on the Economic History of the Argentine Republic* (New Haven, 1970), pp. 1–66 (esp. pp. 2, 6–7, 13, 16–19, 28–35, 45), 135, 287–8; R. Cortés Conde, *El progreso argentino, 1880–1914* (Buenos Aires, 1979), pp. 58, 78–140, 176–84; R. Cortés Conde and E. Gallo, *La formación de la Argentina moderna* (Buenos Aires, 1967), pp. 43–50, 56; R.M. Ortiz, *El ferrocarril en la economía argentina* (Buenos Aires, 1958), pp. 26–8; V. Vásquez-Presedo, *El caso argentino: migración de factores, comercio exterior y desarrollo, 1875–1914* (Buenos Aires, 1971), pp. 11, 48–53, 143, 166–9, 210–25.

14 J. Adelman, *Republic of Capital: Buenos Aires and the Legal Transformation of the Atlantic World* (Stanford, 1999), pp. 281, 283, 292.

ments of order.[15] The communications revolution of the late nineteenth century enabled the central state to promote 'peace and administration'. Recalcitrant provincial caudillos were subdued. The Indian menace was finally eradicated, opening the central pampas and southern territories to settlement, bringing them into the national space and the market economy.

Railways and education were the first economic and social public goods provided by the reunited Argentine Confederation — either directly or by the private sector as a result of 'enabling' state action. Several explanations have been advanced to account for the growth of state corporations in non-socialist economies. They substitute for private investment when markets are weak and can assume a pioneer role. In the case of natural monopolies, state enterprises may be preferable to private companies. Government firms can perform socially or sectorally beneficial redistributive functions and serve as mechanisms for macroeconomic management and/or global efficiency. Albeit plausible and 'scientific', these explanation neglect the predominance of the political in driving the growth of the Argentinian corporate-state and the haphazard course of the sectoral proliferation of state companies.[16]

At the beginning of the twentieth century (1900–04), current and capital public expenditure represented 16.3 per cent of GDP. In 1940–44 the figure was 19.5 per cent and in 1950–54 28.5 per cent.[17] The near ten point increase in state size registered between the early 1940s and 1950s can be explained by the transfer of enterprises from the private to the public sector. What this data disguises, however, is the growing weight of public corporations — particularly railways — in the global budget in the 1940s, 1950s and 1960s. By the early 1980s, publicly-owned enterprises had come to constitute the largest component of the Argentinian state and a significant proportion of the economy.[18]

---

15 C.M. Lewis, 'La consolidación de la frontera argentina a fines de la decada del 70: los indios, Roca y los ferrocarriles', in F. Ferrari and E. Gallo, *La Argentina del ochenta al centenário* (Buenos Aires, 1980), p. 491; Oszlak, *La formación del estado* p. 106; Floria and García Belsunce, *Historia Contemporánea*, p. 70.

16 A. Porto, 'Una revisión crítica de las empresas públicas en la Argentina', in P. Gerchunoff, *Las privatizaciones en la Argentina* (Buenos Aires, 1992), pp. 168–9, 172.

17 Banco de Análisis y Computación, *Relevamiento estadístico de la economía argentina, 1900–1980* (Buenos Aires, 1982) pp. 16, 109. Data elaborated from CEPAL original estimates.

18 For Ugalde, government corporate activity represented about six per cent of GDP and public enterprises some 28 per cent of gross fixed investment in the early 1980s: see A.J. Ugalde, *Las empresas públicas en la Argentina: cuántas son; sus orígenes; dimensión económica; sus problemas* (Buenos Aires, 1984), p. 9. Porto estimates the participation of public enterprises in GDP as averaging seven and eight per cent in the 1970s and 1980s and around 21 per cent gross investment: see Porto, 'Una revisión crítica', p. 205. Responsible for between 30 and 43 per cent of total public expenditure during the 1960s, 1970s and 1980s, public corporations represented a larger 'proportion of the state' than the federal administration or the combined weight of all provincial administrations and the municipality of Buenos Aires: see Porto, 'Una revisión crítica,' pp. 187, 189.

Writing at a time when the economic outreach of the state stood at its greatest extent, and acknowledging that government intervention increased dramatically after 1945, Martelliti found that, following Independence, banking was the major area of state corporate action. From the foundation of the Banco de Buenos Aires in 1822, state banks multiplied later in the century. Government presence was further strengthened with the creation of the Central Bank, in 1936, the National Re-Assurance Agency, 1946, and various investment and development banks to stand alongside already dominant federal and provincial commercial banks. Yet, relatively early in the third quarter of the nineteenth century, railways had become the principal area of state activity and remained so for the whole of the period studied.[19] However, the importance of official involvement in other sectors such as oil production, power generation, commerce and, indeed, manufacturing should not be ignored.[20]

Railways

A few observations confirm the contemporary political and economic importance attached to railways. Between national reunification (1862) and the eve of

---

[19] J.A. Martelliti et al., *Las empresas del estado en la economía argentina* (Buenos Aires, 1973), pp. 39–40.

[20] There is dispute about the timing of federal government activity in the oil industry. Some sources date the initiative from 1907, when oil was discovered in the national territories in Patagonia, others from 1910, with the creation of the Petroleum Board. The first wells came on-stream in 1913. Most accept that sustained government involvement in the oil sector began in 1922 when Yacimentos Petrolíferos Fiscales (YPF) was established. The beginning of government activity in manufacturing is usually dated with greater precision: the Dirección Nacional de Industrias del Estado (DNIE) was founded in 1945 to administer property seized from enemy aliens at the end of the Second World War. The Dirección General de Fabricaciones Militares (DGFFMM), the successor to DNIE, soon became one of the largest military-industrial complexes in Latin America. As a dependency of the armed forces, DGFFMM was not officially categorised as a state corporation. The state iron and steel corporation, SOMISA, was founded in 1947 but did not begin production for some considerable time. During the 1970s, several industrial enterprises threatened with bankruptcy were taken into state ownership, including SIAM Di Tella (consumer durables and capital goods), La Emilia (textiles), La Palmas (sugar refining) and Swift (meat packing). State presence in the utility sector grew haphazardly from the late nineteenth century: initially a municipal entity, the Buenos Aires Water Works (Obras Sanitarias de la Nación) was created in 1869; the Gas Corporation (Gas del Estado) was nationalised in 1945; electricity supply and generation facilities were nationalised between 1947 and 1958; telephone services were nationalised in 1946–47; the national airline, shipping company, coastal fleet and port authorities date from 1945–47; radio and television companies followed. Some of these utility companies were newly created enterprises, most were nationalised. See C.E. Solberg, 'YPF: the Formative Years of Latin America's Pioneer State Oil Company, 1922–39', in J.D. Wirth (ed.), *Latin American Oil Companies and the Politics of Energy* (Lincoln, NE, 1985) p. 51; Porto, 'Una revisión crítica,' pp. 165–213; Martelliti, *Las empresas del estado*, p. 42–44; Ugalde, *La empresas públicas*, pp. 15–38.

the first Baring Crisis (1889), Martínez calculates that government developmental expenditure totalled $133.4 million *pesos fuertes*. Of this figure, $57.4 millions, around 43 per cent, had been spent on the construction of state railways and the payment of subsidies to private companies through profit guarantees.[21] This was the single most important individual item, exceeded only by the general category 'public works'. Official estimates show that $254.9 million had been invested in railways by 1889.[22] This figure was almost exactly the same as the overseas trade of the republic that year, $254.7 million, or approximately 70 per cent of the federal consolidated debt, $354.1 million.[23] In 1938, before external debt repatriation during the Second World War, the historical value of the investment in railways was around $2,000 million (notionally expressed in 'hard pesos'), approximately seven times the value of outstanding federal debt.[24]

Between the 1880s and the 1920s, an expanding railway network meant that the national market came to occupy virtually the whole of the national territory. By the time the frontier of settlement closed in the 1920s,[25] there was an approximate correspondence between nationally occupied economic space and the international boundaries of the country. Contemporaries and historians have agonised about the role of the state in the railway sector and the consequences of the growth of private (notably foreign) initiatives.[26] At mid-nine-

---

[21] A. Martínez, *El presupuesto nacional* (Buenos Aires, 1890) cited in Oszlak *La formación del estado* p. 218. The main items of development expenditure, besides miscellaneous general public works ($63.7 million) and railways, were subsidies for immigration and colonisation ($7.5 million), construction of telegraphs ($4.8 million) and agriculture ($0.1 million). The hard peso (*peso fuerte*) was a unit of account.

[22] República Argentina, *Segundo censo de la República Argentina* (Buenos Aires, 1898), vol. III, pp. 465–6.

[23] E. Tornquist, *The Economic Development of the Argentine Republic in the Last Fifty Years* (Buenos Aires, 1919), p. 140; *Parliamentary Papers* 1911 XC 32, public debt in 1890.

[24] República Argentina, Dirección General de Ferrocarriles, *Estadísticas de los ferrocarriles en explotación* (Buenos Aires, 1944); V.H. Ruíz, *Evolución de la deuda pública federal interna y externa documentada con valores desde 1935 hasta 1973* (Buenos Aires, 1974). Guesstimates based on 'gold' value of railway investment and US dollar value of the external debt.

[25] A. Ferrer *The Argentine Economy* (Berkeley, 1967), pp. 135; G. Di Tella and M. Zymelman, *Las etapas del desarrollo económico argentino* (Buenos Aires, 1967), pp. 88–9, 104; Tulio Halperín Donghi, *The Contemporary History of Latin America* (Durham, NC, 1993), p. 173.

[26] The presidential message of 1887 typifies assessments and assumptions during the railway mania of the period. Reviewing market and statist theories, the report identifies the main reasons for and against government operation of railways. The potentially greater efficiency and flexibility of private companies is acknowledged. Similarly, the adverse affects of 'developmental' public works on government credit are recognised. (pp. 17–22). On the other hand, it is argued that some projects may be beyond the capacity of

teenth century, there appeared to be three options: exclusively official intervention; wholly private funding; a combination of both public and private investment. Given the volume of capital required, the first option was hardly feasible. The second was not in keeping with the spirit of the age. A marriage of the public and the private seemed to offer the best chance of promoting new companies. But how was the balance between private funding and state participation to be struck? After several false starts, profit guarantees (and a hefty measure of direct government investment) emerged as the main form of state support.[27] This arrangement signalled that the lumpy nature of railway investment was beyond the savings capacity of the national economy.[28]

With merchant investors (rather than landowners) acting as midwife, private capital implied both local and foreign funds. Yet progress was slow, despite the inauguration of the first line in 1857. The basic problem was finance followed closely by lack of consensus about the nature of state assistance and the price to be paid for that aid in terms of regulation. Procuring investment, however, was the most pressing concern. Having promoted and operated the FC Oeste (FCO), the first railway in the province of Buenos Aires, without a profit guarantee but with a great deal of direct state funding, merchant capital withdrew and the line passed to the provincial government. Private commitment was sustained in the province by two companies franchised in the 1860s, the Buenos Ayres Great Southern Railway Company Limited and the Buenos Ayres and San Fernando Railway Company Limited (later renamed the Northern) and the Central Argentine Railway Company Limited, a concession granted by the federal government for a line to connect the cities of Rosario and Córdoba.

Yet the momentum of railway building faded within a few years. Between 1876 and 1880 not a single mile of new private track was inaugurated. For almost 20 years after 1870, the greater part of the expansion of the Argentinian railway system was accounted for by state construction. Substantial accretions to the non-state sector did not occur until the period 1886–93. Subsequently, the 'railway mania' of the late 1880s, reflected in a concessions frenzy as the federal government and provincial legislatures franchised new guaranteed compa-

---

the private sector. States need to safeguard against private monopolies and strategic, national interest may also compel governments to act. Italy appears as an example: underdeveloped national commerce, infant industries and national defence require easy, cheap and speedy communications, pointing to the public service functions of railways. (pp. 11–13) See República Argentina, *Mensaje del presidente de la república al abrir las sesiones del congreso argentino en mayo de 1887* (Buenos Aires, 1887).

[27] Lewis, *British Railways*, pp. 9–12, 29–32, 98–101, C.M. Lewis, 'The Financing of Railway Development in Latin America, 1850–1914', *Ibero-Amerikanisches Archiv*, vol. IX nos. 3/4 (1983), pp. 255–78.

[28] R. Cortés Conde, *La economía argentina en el largo plazo, siglos XIX y XX* (Buenos Aires, 1997), p. 146, *Progreso y declinación de la economía argentina* (Buenos Aires, 1998), p. 20.

nies and sought funding for additions to state-owned networks, ended in fiscal and financial collapse. The reckless issuing of railway guarantees, along with the credit policies of official banks, contributed to the spiral of inflation, exchange depreciation, sleaze and crisis of confidence that brought down the government and brought the boom to an end.[29]

With the liquidation of a large part of the government network after the Baring Crisis, private participation rose. The absolute significance of the private sector also grew between 1900 and 1914 as total route mileage doubled, expansion being particularly rapid after 1907. The period immediately prior to the First World War witnessed a 'railway boom' even greater than that of the 1880s. National and provincial government re-entred the field in the pre-First World War period and several administrations sought to re-activate continental European interest in Argentine railway development.[30] Thereafter, government initiative predominated. After the mid-1920s, enterprises operated by federal government and provincial administrations (then representing about 15 per cent of the network) accounted for an increasing share of new building: every mile of new track opened after 1935 was completed by the state railway executive.

Alternating, sometimes over-lapping, cycles of private and government initiative can be explained by funding problems and contemporary expectations. Access to funds clearly conditioned the building programmes of all lines. The state tended to construct where private firms would not. Official construction may have been consciously counter-cyclical; at least it represented a desire to sustain the pace of construction for political or economic reasons when flows of new private investment faltered. Early private companies built in regions where there was already considerable commercial activity, demand for transport services was predictable and, notwithstanding profit guarantees, a strong possibility of traffic growth existed. These railways were substitutive: they were not built to foster new traffic.[31]

---

[29]   H.S. Ferns, *Britain and Argentina in the Nineteenth Century* (Oxford, 1960), chapter XIV, esp. pp. 441–2, 445–65; Floria and García Belsunce, *Historia política* p. 83; Cortés Conde, *Dinero, deuda y crisis*, pp. 174–204; E.A. Zalduendo, *Libras y rieles: las inversiones británicas para el desarrollo de los ferrocarriles en Argentina, Brasil, Canadá e India durante el siglo XIX* (Buenos Aires, 1975), p. 326; E. Gallo, 'Society and Politics, 1880–1916', in L. Bethell (ed.) *Argentina since Independence* (Cambridge, 1993), p. 99.

[30]   In 1891 French-owned lines accounted for 8.5 per cent of total railway investment: the proportion was 10.6 per cent by 1913. A. Regalsky, 'Foreign Capital, Local Interests and Railway Development in Argentina: French Investment in Railways, 1900–1914,' *Journal of Latin American Studies*, vol. XXI, no. 3 (1989) pp. 417, 427–30, *Las inversiones extranjeras en la Argentina, 1860–1914* (Buenos Aires, 1986), p. 30.

[31]   P.B. Goodwin, 'The Central Argentine Railway and the Economic Development of Argentina, 1854–1881', *Hispanic American Historical Review*, vol. LVII, no. 4 (1977), pp. 613–32; C.M. Lewis, 'Railways and Industrialisation: Argentina and Brazil,' in C. Abel and C.M. Lewis (eds.), *Latin America: Economic Imperialism and the State* (London, 1991), p. 202.

Private railway initiatives in the 1850s and 1860s may also be presented as state retreat. Before the coming of the railways, what passed for highways had been provided and maintained by the state. Users of modern transport facilities now had to cover the capital and operating costs of infrastructural services. Was there a corresponding fiscal saving from the privatisation of the supply of formerly public goods? Conversely, it is open to question whether the surge in federal and provincial railway construction in the 1870s and 1880s (or rail and highway construction after 1918) constituted a re-socialisation of the costs of infrastructural investment that benefited the few — producers and shippers served by 'developmental' state railway companies that ran deficits, presumably providing transport services at less than operating costs.[32] The increasing role of government from the 1920s until the nationalisation of all foreign-owned railways in 1947 reflected changing attitudes to the role of the state in the provision of public goods. State railway building and a programme of national highway construction inaugurated by the federal authorities in the 1930s signalled a change in ideology and in the outreach of the state.[33]

The struggle to promote infrastructural development in the 1850s and 1860s illustrates a further aspect of state formation. At that point two state 'models' were contending for supremacy: the first was represented by the secessionist province of Buenos Aires; the other by the Argentine Confederation. The former projected itself as a modern, organised, liberal state. The latter, dominated by the *entrerriano* caudillo General José de Urquiza, with its seat of government in the city of Paraná, appeared a loose confederation held together by a network of personal loyalties.[34] An entrepreneur as much as a conventional rural strongman, Urquiza had invested heavily in meat-salting plants, steamship lines, colonisation companies and

---

[32] For a variety of opinions, see L.A. Huergo, *Ferrocarriles económicos para la República Argentina* (Buenos, 1872); R.J. Cárcano, *Historia de las medias de comunicación y transporte en la República Argentina* (Buenos Aires, 1893); E. Schickendantzá, *Los ferrocarriles argentinos en 1910: historia de su desarrollo* (Buenos Aires, 1910); E. Rebuelto, *Historia del desarrollo de los ferrocarriles argentinos* (Buenos Aires, 1911); A.E. Bunge, *Ferrocarriles argentinos: contribución al estudio del patrimonio nacional* (Buenos Aires, 1918); C.E. Corti, *Investigaciones: algunos problemas ferroviarios* (Buenos Aires, 1926); E. Dickman, *Nacionalización de los ferrocarriles: un problema tecnico-económico argentino* (Buenos Aires, 1938); R.M. Ortiz, *El ferrocarril en la economía argentina* (Buenos Aires, 1958); R. Scalabrini Ortiz, *Historia de los ferrocarriles argentinos* (Buenos Aires, 1958); H.J. Cuccorese, *Historia de los ferrocarriles en la Argentina* (Buenos Aires, 1969); W.W. Wright, *British-owned Railways in Argentina: Their Effect on the Growth of Economic Nationalism, 1854–1948* (Austin, 1974); C.M. Lewis, *British Railways in Argentina, 1857–1914* (London, 1983).

[33] R. García Heras, *Automotores, norteamericanos, caminos y modernización urbana en la Argentina, 1918–1939* (Buenos Aires, 1985).

[34] J.R. Scobie, *La lucha por la consolidación de la nacionalidad argentina, 1852–1862* (Buenos Aires, 1964); J. Lynch, 'From Independence to National Organisation', in L. Bethell (ed.), *Argentina since Independence* (Cambridge, 1993) p. 39; J. Adelman, *Republic of Capital*, p. 213.

'model estancias': he appreciated the political as well as the economic importance of railways.[35] Hence the 1850s witnessed a scramble — as well as a struggle — to promote railways.[36] Franchises were hawked around Europe and the local merchant community by administrations in both Buenos Aires and Paraná. The difference was that the provincial government was judged able to honour promises of support while contemporaries doubted the viability of projects proposed in Paraná and, indeed, of the confederation itself.[37]

Buenos Aires was economically and financially 'large', more populous and more institutionalised. Growth in the interior was sluggish and the confederation administration unable to guarantee either order or the co-operation of provincial governments where proposed lines would be located, The province promised — and delivered — massive capital resources to the FC Oeste; the confederation encountered great difficulty in providing material (a land grant) and financial (a profit guarantee) assistance for the projected Central Argentine Railway. It was a matter of public confidence and state competence. As a political entity, the province was credible: the confederation was not. In 1859, the provincial government was able to crow over the success of the FC Oeste.[38] Prospects for railway promotion in the confederation remained dire until the reunification of the country, when a Buenos Aires-dominated national administration pledged the funds necessary to underwrite railway guarantees. At this point, the financial muscle of Buenos Aires was made available to interior provinces and included an equity stake in the Central Argentine Railway.[39]

Issues of confidence and credibility surfaced again during the railway mania of the 1880s. Until the mid-1880s, the country lacked an integrated network. Besides a handful of short standard gauge lines located in the mesopotamian provinces, there were two skeletal regional systems: an embryonic pampaen broad gauge network centred on the city of Buenos Aires operated by state and private companies; a trunk route from the river port of Rosario to the north-west composed of broad

---

[35] M. Macchi, *Urquiza: el saladerista* (Buenos Aires, 1971), pp. 249–80.

[36] Lewis, *British Railways in Argentina*, chapter I; V. Blinn Reber, *British Merchant Houses in Buenos Aires, 1810–1880* (Cambridge, MA, 1979), pp. 124–7; Zalduendo, *Libras y rieles*, pp. 264–318.

[37] *The Commercial Times*, 10 June 1861; W. Wheelwright, *Introductory Remarks on the Provinces of La Plata and the Cultivation of Cotton: Paraná and the Cordoba Railway, Report of Allen Campbell: Proposals for an Interoceanic Railway between the Río de la Plata and the Pacific. Being a Paper Read at a Meeting of the Royal Geographic Society, 23rd January, 1860* (London, 1881); Zalduendo, *Libras y rieles*, pp. 265–74, 286–98; Cuccorese, *Historia de los ferrocarriles*, pp. 9–14, 17–24. For a general comment on provincial and confederation finances during this period, see Cortés Conde, *La economía argentina*, pp. 99–106.

[38] Provincia de Buenos Aires, *Mensage [sic.] del poder ejecutivo a la sesta legislatura constitucional del estado de Buenos Ayes [sic.]* (Buenos Aires, 1859), pp. 29–31.

[39] Cuccorese *Historia de los ferrocarriles*, pp. 21–4; Zalduendo, *Libras y rieles*, pp. 288–9, 290, Adelman, *Republic of Capital*, p. 283.

and metre gauge lines operated by private companies and the federal government. Both were strategic systems that originated, respectively, in schemes conceived in the province of Buenos Aires and the Argentine Confederation in the 1850s. One of the objectives of the administration of Juárez Celman, president from 1886 to 1890, was to unite the country by connecting the systems.

The network was forged from several links between the existing trunk routes that threaded across the pampas, south into northern Patagonia, the scene of Roca's recent victory against nomadic Indians and Chilean territorial pretensions, west to the frontier with Chile and north-west and north towards the *altiplano* and national territories. Regime stability — the arrangement represented by the Partido Autonomista Nacional (PAN) that had emerged in the 1870s and had presided over Roca's presidential success in 1880 —[40] would be enhanced by construction beyond the province of Buenos Aires. Railways would bind together the loose confederation of provincial oligarchies, dignified by the sobriquet 'the league of governors' and deliver the perceived benefits of infrastructural modernisation already enjoyed by Buenos Aires. A liberal franchising of lines supported with federal profit guarantees would also consolidate the position of Celman, who was attempting to establish his own faction within the PAN. National railway guarantees represented federal subsidies for the provinces — and friends of the government — on whom the administration depended.[41]

The guaranteed railway concessions game was unsustainable. By the late 1880s alarm was being voiced in the business community, the *porteño* political class and sections of the regime.[42] From 1883 to 1886, the federal government had paid out £365,000 to guaranteed railway companies; between 1887 and 1888, £760,000; and, by 1891, had assumed annual liabilities exceeding £900,000.[43] Unfortunately for the administration, the delivery of one public good — railways for the inte-

---

[40] N. Botana, *El orden conservador: la política argentina entre 1880 y 1916* (Buenos Aires, 1977); J. Arce, *Roca, 1843–1914: su vida y su obra* (Buenos Aires, 1960); E. Gallo and R. Cortés Conde, *La república conservadora* (Buenos Aires, 1972).

[41] H.S. Ferns, *Britain and Argentine in the Nineteenth Century* (Oxford, 1960), p. 410; Botana, *El orden conservador*; Floria and García Belsunce, *Historia política*, pp. 67, 70; Adelman, *Republic of Capital*, pp. 290; Zalduendo *Libras y rieles*, pp. 326–37; A.M. Regalsky, *Las inversiones extranjeras en la Argentina, 1860–1914* (Buenos Aires, 1986), p. 29; Paula Alonso, *Between Revolution and the Ballot Box: The Origins of the Argentine Radical Party* (Cambridge, 2000), pp. 50–1.

[42] A. del Valle, *La política económica argentina en la década del 80* (Buenos Aires, 1905), p. x; Ferns, *Britain and Argentina*, pp. 438–9; Zalduendo, *Libras y rieles*, pp. 326, 409 (note 146); Lewis, *British-owned Argentine Railways*, pp. 111–23; Alonso, *Between Revolution and the Ballot Box*, pp. 51–68.

[43] M.G. and E.T. Mulhall, *Handbook of the River Plate* (Buenos Aires, 1892), p. 26; *The Economist*, 28 November 1891, XLIX 1526; *South American Journal*, 3 October 1891, XXXI, p. 391; República Argentina, Congreso Nacional, *Diario de sesiones de la cámara de diputados, 1891* (Buenos, 1891), vol. I, pp. 281–2.

rior — undermined confidence in another, money. While railway route mileage more than doubled between 1885 and 1892, the public debt tripled and the stock of money in circulation increased almost fourfold. The federal fiscal gap widened: expenditure appeared to be out of control by 1888–89. The gold premium which had remained fairly stable from 1885, when convertibility had been abandoned, until late 1888, rose rapidly thereafter.[44] Inflation triggered social unrest and threatened to unpacked the PAN, circumstances that were fatal to the administration and potentially dangerous for the state. The administration of Juárez Celman went and the regime re-consolidated itself.[45]

Nevertheless, the size of the sums that the administration was prepared to pledge to subsidising railway construction in the west and north-west demonstrates the scale of the commitment to cementing regime and state. Market integration was a spin-off. Conventionally, the modernisation of wine and sugar production in Cuyo and the north, sectors that now benefited from effective communications with the burgeoning littoral, has been offered as evidence of the emergence of a national marketplace.[46] Recently, Rocchi has argued convincingly that larger processes were at work. Both Buenos Aires industrialists and sections of the regime had clamoured for developmental, market-expanding railway construction, and took advantage of it. Particularly after the turn of the century, manufacturers looked to the interior for markets. The campaign to 'conquer' national economic space reflected an element in entrepreneurial ideology. Opening up the interior was economically rational and corresponded with the national mission of modernising manufacturers.[47]

As suggested, it was a much more confident state that reconnected with infrastructural provisioning at the start of the twentieth century. This was signalled by new regulatory initiatives, the first since the abrogation of railway guarantee legislation in the 1890s, and a willingness to confront the predominance enjoyed by British-owned companies. Several factors influenced the revision of railway legislation. One was the proximate expiry of some early railway concessions. Another was the complicated juridical position of many lines, sections of which had been franchised at different times and, possibly, by different authorities. Yet another was the sluggish pace of railway construction over the previous dozen years — a peri-

---

[44] A.G. Ford, *The Gold Standard, 1880–1914: Britain and Argentina* (Oxford, 1962); R. Cortés Conde, *El progreso argentino, 1880–1914* (Buenos Aires, 1979).

[45] Ferns, *Britain and Argentina*, pp. 451–6, 470–1; Floria and García Belsunce, *Historia política*, pp. 83–8.

[46] Lewis, *British-owned Argentine Railways*, p. 88; Wright, *British-owned Railways in Argentina*, pp. 39, 56; W.J. Fleming, 'Mendoza y el desarrollo de la red ferroviarria nacional entre 1854 y 1886,' mimeo; R.M. Ortiz, *Historia económica de la Argentina, 1850–1930* (Buenos Aires, 1964), pp. 228–9; Zalduendo *Libras y rieles*, pp. 323–4, 354–67.

[47] F. Rocchi, 'Manufacturing Modernity in an Agrarian Economy: Industrial Growth in Argentina during the Export Boom Years, 1870–1930' (unpubl. manuscript), ch. IV.

od when the agricultural frontier had caught-up with railway 'over-build' in the 1880s. It was felt that the Argentine was being displaced in world commodity markets by other producers because, looking back from 1906, there had been virtually no substantial new private investment in the sector since the late 1890s. It was hoped that the Mitre Law, as the 1907 codification of railway legislation became known, would encourage the formation of new companies and attract investment from a wide range of sources, particularly from non-British sources.

The drive to codify railway regulation in the early twentieth century represented both state competence and a search for transparency in the sphere of state-corporate relations. As the burden of railway guarantees had spiralled on the eve of the Baring crisis, the federal government had threatened to intervene in various aspects of company operations. In some quarters, this was interpreted as more than a cynical ploy to renege on guarantee payments. Rather, it was regarded as a repudiation of economic liberalism, prefiguring a general attack on property rights.[48] The new regulatory framework was, in part, designed to reassure the private sector by resolving conflicts between the government and the companies that had emerged around the turn of the century.[49] Openness, order and stability in the regulatory framework would promote confidence.

Between 1907 and 1913 the Argentine became the most popular destination for new British overseas investment, sometimes absorbing over 13 per cent of total annual outflows.[50] Between 1907 and 1916 (when projects initiated before the war were completed) railway route mileage increased by more than one half. More mileage was inaugurated in these years than the whole of the 1857–1891 period.

As stated above, this was also a period of some diversification in sources of funding and expansion of state-owned lines. Regalsky shows that state construction and the promotion of French investment in the province of Buenos Aires resulted from conflict between *estancieros* and established British companies over the pace and direction of extension building. As in the Mexican oil sector, government action derived from a deliberate policy to promote competition among foreign companies in order to counter the preponderance enjoyed by one group of overseas investors.[51] In the official mind, diversity of finance

---

[48] Argentine Republic, *Message of the President of the Republic at the Opening of the Congress Session of 1888* (Buenos Aires, 1888), pp. 4–5; *The Railway Times,* 14 July 1888, vol. LIV, no. 50, 21 September 1889, vol. LVI, no. 372; Cuccorese, *Historia de los ferrocarriles,* pp. 88–90; Ferns, *Britain and Argentina.*

[49] Regalsky, *Las inversiones extranjeras,* pp. 37, 123–9; Lewis, *British-owned Argentine Railways.*

[50] Sir George Parish, 'The Export of Capital and the Cost of Living', *The Statist Supplement,* 14 February 1914, no. LXXIX.

[51] Regalsky, 'Foreign Capital, Local Interests', pp. 417, 428–30. See also *PP* 1912/3 XCIX 107; *The Times,* 8 October 1913, 19f; *The Economist,* 22 September 1923, no. XLXII, p. 442.

and new construction became inter-linked objectives. Labour unrest also triggered official intervention after 1907. The federal government became increasingly involved in the sector, particularly with regard to wages, levels of employment and worker welfare, a tendency that grew under radical administrations of the 1910s and 1920s and did not diminish under the more authoritarian political arrangements of the 1930s.[52] These measures, seeking more diverse sources of funding and intervention in the sphere of worker-employer relations, again reflected a determination and an ability to act. They also connect issues of sovereignty and social order.

By the 1920s it was being argued that the dominance of private (foreign) interests in the supply of railway services, and the corresponding retreat of the state, had produced a number of structural defects; an over-concentration of lines in the central pampas; an imbalance between trunk and branch routes; and a road deficit. For example, in 1917–18, the province of Buenos Aires contained a little under a quarter of the total population but over one-third route railway mileage.[53] In well-endowed provinces such as Buenos Aires and Santa Fé the density of railway provision increased from ratios of 19.6:1 and 10.3:1, respectively, in 1889 to 6.9:1 and 6.8:1 in 1939. In less well provided provinces like Corrientes, ratios only improved from 101.5:1 to 72.4:1 over the same period.[54] These factors, and the changing nature of the state itself associated with radical electoral victories in 1916, account for greater intervention. Government action, as well as regulation, was back on the political agenda.[55] Nationalism and statism provided the ideological underpinning. The critical question was how to effect nationalisation. Initially, it was proposed to create a mixed corporation (*sociedad mixta*) to oversee a phased transfer of ownership from private foreign companies to the state.

A scheme to establish a mixed corporation, with both state and private capital, was peculiar neither to the railways nor the Argentine. Similar arrangements were envisaged in Brazil and indeed the Argentine itself to promote the development of domestic iron and steel production.[56] Although mixed corporations rarely progressed beyond the planning stage, the device undoubtedly encapsulated ideolo-

---

[52] Bunge, *Ferrocarriles argentinos*, chs. XII and XIII; P.B. Goodwin, *Los ferrocarriles británicos y la UCR, 1916–1930* (Buenos Aires, 1974); J. Horowitz, *Argentine Unions, the State and the Rise of Perón* (New York, 1990).

[53] Tornquist, Economic Development, pp. 8, 121; Bunge, Ferrocarriles.

[54] DGNFF (Buenos Aires, 1944).

[55] P.B. Goodwin, *Los ferrocarriles británicos y la UCR, 1916–1930* (Buenos Aires, 1974).

[56] *Review of the River Plate*, 30 May 1947, p. 15; M. Panaia and R. Lesser, 'Estrategias militares frente al proceso de industrializacion (1943–47)', in M. Murmis et al. (eds.), *Estudios de los origenes del peronismo* (Buenos Aires, 1973), p. 151. For preliminary discussion to establish the Volta Redonda integrated iron and steel mill in Brazil, see J. With, *The Politics of Brazilian Development, 1930–1954* (Stanford, 1970), pp. 118–29; S. Hilton, 'Vargas and Brazilian Economic Development, 1930–45: A Reappraisal of his Attitudes towards Industrialisation and Planning', *Journal of Economic History*, vol. 4, no. 2 (1975), pp. 754–78.

gies in vogue in the 1940s. Embracing state and private capital and allegedly harmonising the interests of producers, consumers and government, the mixed corporation epitomised *peronista* efforts to construct a third path that was nationalist, Keynesian and distributionist but not anti-capitalist nor autarchic.[57]

Administrations in Brazil and the Argentine recognised after 1945 that the creation of domestic iron and steel production required large amounts of capital, technology and managerial expertise. Similar considerations applied in the case of the railways. In the immediate post-war period, it was unlikely that large amounts of new capital could be raised in London to modernise the railway system. This was hardly an issue, given substantial blocked sterling balances accumulated at the Bank of England by the Argentinian government as the result of war-time sales to the Allies. Rather, the critical factor was access to vital imports in order to maintain and modernise the railway system. At a time of frosty relations with the USA, the flotation of a mixed corporation to effect railway refurbishment and gradual nationalisation was initially viewed as a virtue and a necessity.[58] The arrangement combined the ideological and the pragmatic. In the final event, the foreign-owned railways were nationalised outright — a gesture that proclaimed state competence and chimed with nationalist aspirations.

Money and the Market

The early monetary history of the republic was one of confusion. Different regulations applied and distinct currencies circulated in various provinces, a result of the tenuous authority of the central government and the general scarcity of money. In the north, and some central provinces, Bolivian silver pesos constituted the principal coinage and issuing institutions denominated their notes accordingly. Chilean coins were to be found in the western provinces. In the province of Buenos Aires most domestic transactions were conducted in paper, but in up-country districts paper money was virtually unknown. The Argentinian silver peso (*peso fuerte*), first introduced during the revolutionary period, was rarely seen and served only as a unit of account. External transactions were conducted in gold — bullion or specie — and foreign coins had the status of legal tender though normally only encountered in Buenos Aires.[59] The first formal issue of currency notes occurred in 1822. Thereafter the volume and variety of paper in circulation grew massively. Most series were held in dubious regard, even nominally convertible

---

[57] J.C. Torre and L. de Riz, 'Argentina since 1946', in L. Bethell (ed.), *Argentina since Independence* (Cambridge, 1993), pp. 248–51.

[58] Wright, *British-owned Railroads in Argentina*, pp. 251–2.

[59] F.S Pérez, *Bancos y moneda en la Argentina* (Buenos Aires, 1944), p. 17; R.M. Ortíz, *Historia económica de la Argentina* (Buenos Aires, 1964), vol. I, p. 143; Cortés Conde, *Dinero, deuda y crisis*, pp. 19–23.

notes.[60] Paper money bore the stamp of several issuing authorities, notwithstanding half-hearted attempts to retire old issues and unify series. Only paper — bonds and currency notes — issued by the Buenos Aires authorities and subsequently the Provincial Bank, were generally accepted, notwithstanding currency depreciation. However, these series were confined almost exclusively to the city and province. In short, there were competing monies and different monetary authorities sought to secure the primacy of their respective currencies.

Before the first serious attempt to establish a national monetary system in the 1860s,[61] several categories of notes circulated. Namely, those issued by the Banco de Buenos Aires (1822–26), the Banco de las Provincias Unidas de Río de la Plata (1826–36), the Casa de la Moneda (1836–53) and the Banco y Casa de Moneda (1859–61). Banks only in name, the principal function of these agencies was to print currency notes and bonds to cover the fiscal deficit of administrations established in the city of Buenos Aires. Collectively, these agencies had issued notes valued in excess of 400 million paper pesos. It is also possible that some forced loan certificates issued by revolutionary governments of the 1810s and 1820s (and accepted as currency) may have continued in circulation along with tokens (*vales*) passed out by merchants and *estancieros* at times of acute monetary scarcity.[62] Circumstances were hardly different in other provinces, save that the volume of emissions was more modest and the existence of institutions even more precarious. Between the mid-1860s and mid-1870s, seven banks had been floated and failed in the province of Santa Fé alone.[63]

Following reunification, strenuous efforts were made in 1862 to establish a national currency and to promote monetary order. A bimetallic standard, based on the gold ounce (*onza de oro*), which was held to equal 16 silver ounces (*pesos fuertes*), was established. One silver (hard) peso was to equal 25 paper pesos. This gave the *onza* an official value of $400 paper (approximately, the price of gold then prevailing in the market).[64] The re-constituted Banco de la Provincia de Buenos

---

[60]   H.H. Hipwell, 'Banking, Currency and Finance', in British and Latin American Chamber of Commerce, *Commercial Encyclopedia* (London, 1922), p. 24; S.E. Amaral, 'El descubrimento de la financiación inflacionaria: Buenos Aires, 1790–1830', *Investigaciones y Ensayos* XXXVII (1988).

[61]   A common national currency with the exclusive status of legal tender throughout the country would not appear until 1881. See Cortés Conde, 'The Growth of the Argentine Economy', p. 64; Gallo, 'Society and Politics' p. 82.

[62]   A.M. Quintero Ramos, *A History of Money and Banking in Argentina* (Río Piedras, 1965), pp. 28–41.

[63]   C.A. Jones, 'Personalism, Indebtedness and Venality: the Political Environment of British Firms in Santa Fe Province, 1865–1900', in *Ibero-Amerikanisches Archiv*, vol. 9, nos. 2/3 (1983), pp. 385–6.

[64]   J.A. Difrieri, *Moneda y bancos en la República Argentina* (Buenos Aires, 1967), p. 102; Adelman, *Republic of Capital*, pp. 270–1.

Aires was charged with establishing a schedule of equivalences for foreign currencies. In 1863 several 'definitive' lists were devised: the sovereign was valued at 4.90 silver pesos; the French (20 franc) napoleon at 3.90 pesos; the Brazilian 20 milreis piece at 11.00.[65] The quest for monetary unity and stability during the 1860s was aided by export growth and an influx of foreign investment associated with a new wave of railway construction in the pampas which in turn fostered expansion of production and overseas trade. Official commitment to the new order was enhanced by political stability resulting from reunification and reflected in efforts to reduce the volume of notes in circulation and to limit future emissions.[66]

These conditions were not to last. Currency stability was subsequently undermined by the outbreak of war against Paraguay in 1865 — the War of the Triple Alliance — and the world crisis of 1866.[67] New monetary emissions to finance the war coupled with contracting world markets and declining prices ended any possibility of sustaining currency convertibility and frustrated efforts by the Conversion Office (Oficina de Cambios), set up as a division of the Banco de la Provincia in 1867 to build up a metallic reserve. In 1872, with the creation of the National Bank, there was a further attempt to sustain order and to establish a stable national currency. The experiment came to an end in 1876 when the Buenos Aires provincial government suspended convertibility of provincial bank notes, forcing the federal government to free the National Bank from its obligations.[68] Among other things, the breakdown of convertibility confirms the continuance of 'currency competition' between the federal and Buenos Aires provincial authorities.

Nevertheless, as overseas trade and inward investment picked up at the end of the 1870s some politicians and officials re-stated the case for convertibility. This led to yet another currency project in 1881.[69] The 1881 Act broke new ground on several fronts. It set a more realistic mint ratio between gold and silver. Foreign coins were gradually to lose their legal tender status, obviating the need for a complicated schedule of official values and curtailing the supply of competing foreign currencies that sat ill with claims of national monetary sovereignty. The proposal attempted to link the peso to a modified form of the system operated by the Latin Monetary Union (originally formed by France, Italy, Belgium and Switzerland, and later Romania and Greece) then gaining acceptance in Latin America.

---

[65] Ortíz, *Historia*, vol. I, p. 145; Quintero Ramos, *Money and Banking*, pp. 41–3, 47–8.

[66] Ortíz, *Historia*, vol. I, pp. 144–5; Difrieri, *Moneda*, pp. 100–1; Cortés Conde, *Dinero, deuda y crisis*, pp. 39, 45–6.

[67] J.C. Chiaramonte, *Nacionalismo y liberalismo económico, 1860–1880* (Buenos Aires, 1971), ch. II.

[68] Difrieri, *Moneda*, p. 117; Quintero Ramos, *Money and Banking*, p. 61; Cortés Conde, *La economía argentina*, pp. 131–2.

[69] Quintero Ramos, *Money and Banking*, pp. 70–5; Cortés Conde, *Dinero, deuda y crisis*, p. 158.

Reference to an external model validated the domestic project. More relevant for confidence-building, the final settlement of differences with the province of Buenos Aires marked the complete domestic sovereignty of the federal government and lent weight and credibility to its monetary project. For the first time there would be a common unit of currency for the whole country.[70]

For a few years the system worked fairly well. Export growth and foreign borrowing increased reserves. Gold coins entered into circulation. Old notes were gradually retired and the size of the fiduciary issue and supply of fractionary notes tightly regulated. However, by the end of 1884 the system was beginning to unravel. The balance of trade deteriorated and the external accounts were further pressured by rising interest charges. Convertibility was suspended in 1885 and the country embarked upon a debt-led boom that ended with the Baring Crisis. Monetary emissions mushroomed, overseas borrowing rocketed and direct foreign investment soared.[71]

Table 1: Money Supply and Purchasing Power

	Money Supply (millions of pesos)	Gold Cover (per cent)	Purchasing Power (1900=100)
1900–04	335	*14.7	100.03
1905–09	565	48.1	89.03
1910–14	773	62.6	82.81
1915–19	1,069	57.4	59.89
1920–24	1,354	77.8	52.49
1925–29	1,334	78.1	60.46
1930–34	1,246	51.6	71.20
1935–39	1,314	–	67.97
1940–44	1,981	–	60.63
1945–49	6,141	–	36.89
1950–54	22,086	–	12.82
1955–59	60,360	–	5.79

* 1901/4

Source: Elaborated from FIAT Concord, Dirección de Planificación y Estudios, *Argentina económica y financiera* (Buenos Aires, 1966), pp. 316-22, tables 258, 260, 263, 266.

---

[70] E. Gallo, 'Society and Politics, 1880–1916', in L. Bethell (ed.), *Argentina since Independence* (Cambridge, 1993), p. 82.

[71] The classic accounts of the causes and course of the Baring Crisis remain A.G. Ford, 'Argentina and the Baring Crisis of 1890', *Oxford Economic Papers* VIII (1956), pp. 127–50 and Ferns, *Britain and Argentina*, chs. VIII and XIV. See also Cortés Conde, *Dinero, deuda y crisis*, pp. 162–7, 209–43, Ferns, 'The Baring Crisis Revisited', *JLAS*, vol. 24, no. 2 (1992), pp. 241–73; C. Marichal, *A Century of Debt Crises in Latin America*, chs. V and VI.

In the 1890s, following agreement with foreign creditors, government expenditure was subject to tighter control and more orthodox attitudes to banking, finance and currency prevailed. Having rejected debt repudiation and economic isolation in 1889 — an option momentarily contemplated by a section of the elite — a final effort was made by the government to join the gold club.[72] By this point, large supplies of overseas credit and cheap labour were demonstrably available. In narrower terms, the dramatic growth in export volumes — as the agricultural frontier 'caught up' with the railways frontier — coupled with price improvements both eased the cost of currency reform and threatened to drive up the value of the peso. In 1899 when the Argentine began operating a gold exchange standard, the choice was no longer between currency stability and exchange depreciation but between stability and currency appreciation.[73]

For the next half century the country experienced a period of remarkable monetary stability. Notwithstanding the effect of inflation during the First World War, the general suspension of the gold standard by most major trading nations in 1914, and a piecemeal return to gold during the 1920s followed by the final breakdown of the system in the early 1930s, the Argentinian peso remained relatively firm. This stability was reflected in foreign exchange markets. As the table above indicates, from the 1900s until the 1940s currency supply was tightly controlled — possibly excessively so — and the external value of the peso carefully managed.

The growth in the volume of notes and coins in circulation during the early decades of the twentieth century barely kept pace with the huge expansion in economic activity. A massive growth in exports, coupled with positive trade balances and a foreign investment boom before 1914 enabled the Exchange Office to accumulate a substantial stock of gold. In compliance with the 1899 conversion law, the fiduciary issue was reduced and gold cover rose progressively from the 1900s to the 1920s. For much of the First World War, and at various points during the 1920s, the peso stood above par against the currencies of most of the country's major trading partners. Throughout this period, the stock of money was tightly controlled. Bullion reserves only fell sharply in 1931 before gold exports were banned and sales of foreign exchange regulated.[74]

Both on and off the gold standard the modest changes in currency supply from 1916 until 1944 accounted for exchange stability and the prestige enjoyed

---

[72] Ferns, *Britain and Argentina*, pp. 455, 471–4.

[73] J. Panettieri, 'La ley de converción de 1899 en el marco de formación de la Argentina moderna', *Desarrollo Económico*, vol. XXI, no. 82 (1981), pp. 231–56; Quintero Ramos, *Money and Banking*, pp. 117–24.

[74] *Revista de economía argentina* (June 1927), p. 488; Quintero Ramos, *Money and Banking*, pp. 125, 153, 175, 207; R. Cortés Conde, *Progreso y declinación de la economía argentina* (Buenos Aires, 1998), pp. 34–5, 40–1.

by the Argentinian peso in neighbouring countries. From a 1914 par value against sterling of $11.4545, the paper peso slipped to $17.21 in September 1931, only to recover thereafter as the pound itself came under pressure. In December 1939 the free market rate on London was $17.27 against an official selling rate of $17.00. In December 1939 the dollar bought $4.39 on the free market against an official selling rate of $4.23 and an official 1914 parity of $2.35 paper pesos. The story after the late 1940s was very different, with multiple rates of exchange, repeated abrupt devaluations and a widening gap between the free market and official rates. The Central Bank maintained an official selling rate of $4.23 on the dollar until 1948. In 1949 the average was $4.85. From 1951 to 1954 the official selling price was held at $7.50. In 1955 the average rate was $10.12 to the dollar. An official rate of $18.00 was defended from 1956 until 1958. By 1959 the dollar bought $80.63.[75] As the final column of Table 1 confirms, the near collapse in the external value of the peso was reflected in changes in internal purchasing power.

Virtue and violence account for this progress to and from monetary stability. Echoing an earlier work, Tilly establishes the connection between states and violence (or coercion and state-formation).[76] 'Monetary violence' may be depicted as a threat to flood the market with money; 'monetary coercion' with the struggle for a state monopoly of issue. Both phenomena have a large impact — on households, groups and sectors. As shown above, various forms of money circulated within the River Plate region in the middle third of the nineteenth century. This reflected competition among the different state 'models' that were on offer at the time. During the third quarter of the century, competitive currencies were gradually displaced by 'national money'. The campaign to establish a national monetary regime corresponded with the quest for monetary stability and is only loosely co-terminus with the period of 'national consolidation' that has received much attention in the conventional literature.

Conventional histories of money tend to address more the issue of 'how' rather than 'why' currency stability was achieved in the Argentine. Standard works identify two principal signposts on the journey towards monetary virtue: ideology and exports. Jones has shown how discussions of monetary policy were influenced by events and imported ideology — 'mimicry': in an inversion of Gresham's Law, 'good' institutions drove out 'bad'.[77] The survival and success

---

[75] Vásquez-Presedo, *Estadisticas*, vol. II, pp. 280–3.

[76] C. Tilly, *Coercion, Capital and European States, A.D. 990–1990* (London, 1990), p. 1.

[77] C.A. Jones, 'The Transfer of Banking Techniques from Britain to Argentina, 1862–1914', *Révue International d'Histoire de la Banque*, vol. XXVI, no. 7 (1983), pp. 255–61. See also C.A. Jones, 'The Fiscal Motive for Monetary and Banking Legislation in Argentina, Australia and Canada before 1914', in D.C.M. Platt and G. Di Tella (eds.), *Argentina, Australia and Canada: Studies in Comparative Development, 1870–1915* (London, 1985); D. Joslin, *A Century of Banking in Latin America: Bank of London and South America Limited, 1862–1962* (London, 1963). Villela provides a convincing analysis of this hypothesis in his

of British houses in periods of turmoil, when state and national private banks collapsed, offered a compelling model of banking and monetary orthodoxy. As stated, rapid export expansion around the mid nineteenth century and again during the 1890s underwrote and sustained monetary order. The road to gold was paved with export growth and diversification and improving terms of trade.[78] This suggests that the commitment to monetary virtue was conditional: it was dependent on international commercial and financial opportunities and was as much pragmatic as ideological. Chiaramonte shows that powerful forces were aligned against liberal economics.[79] Nevertheless, most of the early contributions to the history of money adopt a whiggish or simplistic approach, subsuming monetary stability within a larger project to conform Argentinian practices with prevailing liberal-internationalist norms.

Panettieri was among the first to offer an explicit explanation of currency stability. He accepts that buoyant export conditions facilitated efforts to establish the currency on a metallic basis — successively a silver system, a bi-metallic arrangement and, finally, gold. However, he argues persuasively that convertibility was a mechanism to prevent peso appreciation.[80] Currency stability was a second-best alternative to a soft monetary regime but preferable to currency appreciation. This analysis is rooted in the assumption that monetary policy was largely shaped by the agro-exporting elite of the pampa.

A number of recent contributions to the study of the history of Argentinian monetary policy have drawn upon on the new institutionalism.[81] The primary

---

work on banking and monetary policy in Brazil. See A.A. Villela, 'The Political Economy of Money and Banking in Imperial Brazil, 1850–1870', unpubl. University of London doctoral dissertation (1999): the hypothesis is set out in the Introduction, pp. 13–15.

[78] J.C. Chiaramonte, *Nacionalismo y liberalismo económico, 1860–1880* (Buenos Aires, 1971); H. Sabato, *Agrarian Capitalism and the World Market: Buenos Aires in the Pastoral Age, 1840–1890* (Albuquerque, 1990); J.H. Williams, *Argentine International Trade under Inconvertible Paper Money, 1880–1900* (Cambridge, MA., 1920); A.G. Ford, *The Gold Standard, 1880–1914: Britain and Argentina* (Oxford, 1962).

[79] J.C. Chiaramonte, *Nacionalismo y liberalismo, La crítica ilustrada de la realidad* (Buenos Aires, 1982). See also D. Bushnell, *Reform and Reaction in the Platine Provinces, 1810–1852* (Gainesville, 1983) and T. Halperín Donghi, *Proyecto y construcción de una nación: Argentina 1846–1880* (Caracas, 1980). Halperín's history of ideas is one of the few contributions to political history that bridges conventional divides, namely 1852 and 1862.

[80] J. Panettieri J., *Devaluaciones de la moneda (1822–1935)* (Buenos Aires, 1983), pp. 102–5, 153–4; 'La ley de conversión monetaria de 1864 y la oficina de cambio de 1867: causas y consequences economicos-sociales', *Desarrollo Económico*, vol. XX, no. 79 (1980), pp. 383–412; 'La ley de conversión monetária argentina de 1899 en el marco de formación de la Argentina moderna', *Desarrollo Económico*, vol. XXI, no. 82 (1981), pp. 237–8.

[81] Jones, 'The Fiscal Motive for Monetary and Banking Legislation'; R. Cortés Conde, 'Fiscal Crisis and Inflation in Nineteenth-century Argentina', pp. 1–46 (mimeo); G. della

interest of much of this research lies in the operation of capital markets and there is a tendency to project back into the period before 1950 issues deriving from analyses of the current monetary system — the 'return' to gold in 1899 being used as a 'laboratory' for the study of the 1991 Convertibility Plan. Nevertheless, drawing extensively on concepts of 'credibility' and 'confidence' in the conduct of monetary and fiscal policy, the approach resonates with analyses of state-formation such as those of Bin Wong. Neo-institutionalist historians imply that an orderly monetary system restored 'neutrality' to the currency and so was a means of avoiding distributional conflicts often associated with loose-money regimes. Stable money enhanced the arbitrational capacity of the state and its ability to manage dispute within the existing institutional framework. Irigoin and Bordo and Vegh employ rational-choice theory to analyse changes in pre-1862 monetary regimes that point to the success of state-building.[82] Loose monetary regimes signal state weakness or states in formation. Inflationary methods of financing could only be discarded after effective consolidation.[83] This analysis suggests that efforts to impose monetary order in the 1860s and the early 1880s demonstrate state strength. The realisation (and maintenance) of relative currency stability for almost the whole of the first half of the twentieth century, notwithstanding shocks such as world war and global depression, signals the achievement of state authority.

Monetary stability was increasingly regarded as essential to the liberal project and implied greater fiscal efficiency.[84] As the 1890 crisis confirmed, the opportunity cost of monetary anarchy was high, limiting access to funds necessary to secure the supply of other public goods. The Baring Crisis also revealed the discretionary nature of banking regulation. The so-called guaranteed banks had played fast and loose with note issue requirements. Limits on issue had been

---

Paolera, 'Experimentos monetarios y bancarios en Argentina, 1861–1930', *Revista de Historia Económica*, vol. XII (1994), pp. 539–89; 'The Economic History of Monetary and Financial Markets in the Nineteenth and Early Twentieth Century in Argentina: Observers, Actors and Outcomes', pp. 1–12; G. della Paolera and A.M. Taylor, 'Finance and Development in an Emerging Market: Argentina in the Inter-war period', in J.H. Coatsworth and A.M. Taylor (eds.), *Latin America and the World Economy since 1800* , pp. 139–70.

[82] M.A. Irigoin, *Moneda, impuestos e instituciones en el estado de Buenos Aires, 1850–1860* (Buenos Aires, 1995); M.D. Bordo and C.A. Vegh, 'What If Alexander Hamilton had been Argentinean: a Comparison of the Early Monetary Experiences of Argentina and the United States', National Bureau of Economic Research Working Paper no. 6862 (Cambridge, MA., 1998).

[83] Bordo and Vegh, 'Alexander Hamilton', pp. 3–4.

[84] C. Marichal, 'Liberalism and Fiscal Policy: The Argentine Paradox, 1820–1862', in V.C. Peloso and B.A. Tenenbaum (eds.), *Liberals, Politics and Power: State Formation in Nineteenth-Century Latin America* (Athens, GA, 1996), p. 102; Cortés Conde, 'Fiscal Crisis and Inflation', *Dinero, deuda y crisis*.

breached, often with the connivance of officials.[85] After the crash, there was both a perceived need and a willingness to overhaul the monetary and banking order. Monopoly of issue was initially conferred on a reconstructed Banco de la Nación Argentina but transferred at the end of the century to the Conversion Office (Caja de Conversión), charged with restoring currency convertibility. Originally established as a mixed corporation in 1891, so as to prevent political control, the bank became an exclusively state institution. By then orthodoxy in theory and practice was the norm. Before 1914 the Banco de la Nación was already the dominant institution in the local market and gained in importance thereafter. On the eve of the First World War the Banco held almost half the reserves of the whole banking system.[86] This dominance, and the reserves accumulated by the Caja, were the mechanisms by which monetary order was sustained. The two organisations symbolised the new institutional order which, as indicated above, was consolidated with the creation of the Central Bank and survived until the 1940s. The arrangements were credible and operated with a considerable degree of transparency in the Buenos Aires money market. While the creation of the Central Bank permitted greater flexibility in the monetary sphere, it followed a broadly orthodox approach.[87] Stable money validated the state.

Public Service Provision: Actors and Preferences

Given the notorious difficulty experienced in raising direct taxes, state options in the nineteenth and twentieth centuries have been presented in stark terms — inflation-financing or borrowing, but rarely effective direct taxation.[88] Confronted with an inability to obtain fiscal resources by physical coercion or exchange, states will resort to monetary violence — monetising the fiscal deficit until conditions permit an alternative. Yet borrowing assumes a degree of

---

[85] Ferns, *Britain and Argentina*, ch. XIV, and 'The Baring Crisis Revisited', p. 258; Cortés Conde, *Dinero, deuda y crisis*, pp. 202–4; Rock, *Argentina, 1516–1982*, p. 159; Alonso, *Between Revolution and the Ballot Box*, pp. 58–60.

[86] Quintero Ramos, *Money and Banking*, p. 138.

[87] Cortés Conde, *Progreso y declinación*, pp. 43–44.

[88] Adelman, *Republic of Capital* pp. 267; Amaral, 'El descubrimento'; J.H. Coatsworth, 'Economic and Institutional Trajectories in Nineteenth-Century Latin America', in J.H. Coatsworth and A.M. Taylor, *Latin America and the World Economy*, p. 36; R. Cortés Conde and G. MacCandless 'Argentina: From Colony to Nation (Eighteenth and Nineteenth Centuries): Fiscal and Monetary Experience', Universidad de San Andrés, Documentos de Trabajo, Economía (1998); della Paolera, 'The Economic History of Monetary and Financial Markets'. For Cortés Conde, the period from the turn of the century until 1930 was exceptional. During these years the fiscal compact between state and society (and between the federal government and the provinces) was explicit, facilitating growth and governability. The state financing was based on indirect taxes (import duties) and borrowing. See Cortés Conde, *Progreso y declinación*, pp. 21–2.

commitment on the part of the state and the need for confidence-building. Notwithstanding limits on direct taxation, 'successful' borrowing pre-supposes a demonstrable capacity to sustain or expand the fiscal base, possibly through indirect taxation. Consequently, an ability to tax, or to capture a share of the fruits of growth, reduces 'country risk'.[89] This was the arrangement that forged a virtuous spiral, the elements of which were state consolidation, debt-financed infrastructural modernisation, export expansion, indirect taxation and monetary order. (Indirect taxes were the means by which the state captured a share of additional resources generated by growth resulting from the supply of public goods.) But what was the sequencing of these elements: which came first? Conventionally, a commitment to monetary orthodoxy is associated with dependence on external funding. All other things being equal, a stable (or possibly modestly appreciating) exchange rate equates with monetary virtue, reassures foreign creditors and facilitates access to overseas money markets. State performance in domestic and overseas capital markets tend now to be treated similarly, as a failure to perform in one reduces confidence in the other. In short, states that borrow are assumed to favour a stable monetary regime. Those that do not — or cannot — may have other preferences or more limited options.

In the nineteenth century and beyond, agro-exporting interests, as well as the producers of non-internationally traded goods and services and domestic debtors are thought to have favoured soft monetary policies to fund infrastructural provision and credit expansion. For agriculturalists and exporters, whose incomes were either received in, or linked to, hard currencies, an expansionary monetary regime offered declining costs of production. In addition, access to cheap credit and market extension through monetisation and railway building was positive for domestic groups involved in supplying the home market, so long as inflation did not choke market growth. Currency depreciation also offered added protection to domestic producers whose goods had a low import content.

According to the modern development literature, foreign investors have an ambivalent attitude to monetary orthodoxy, preferring a 'soft' exchange when investing in host economies and 'hard' monetary policy when remitting and repatriating capital. These are preferences that nineteenth-century critics would categorise as those of speculators. During periods of currency inconvertibility, opponents of monetary orthodoxy invariably viewed the tendency of corporations and commercial houses to remit during the harvest season (when the exchange rate rose) and import capital during the back half of the year with suspicion. Following their domestic counterparts, foreign interests involved in the supply of non-tradables are thought to have supported 'developmental' monetary policies.

While public works generated jobs, those dependent on salaries and wages can be assumed to have favoured monetary stability. They could not hedge against inflation. In addition, those who relied on wages and salaries were dou-

---

[89]   Cortés Conde and MacCandless, 'Argentina'; della Paolera, 'The Economic History of Monetary and Financial Markets'.

bly dependent on the market — for the supply of basic wage goods, which were often imported, as well as employment. These groups, who were largely urban and may be classified as non-investing classes, became increasingly politically important during the period under review. A particularly significant sub-category of this group were immigrants, who were prominent savers and remitters. Savers and remitters shared a similar preference for monetary order. Immigrants may not have had a vote but certainly had a voice and they had legs. Wage and salary earners and savers are, thus, assumed to have favoured 'liberal orthodoxy' — exchange stability and economic openness.

In the conduct of railway and monetary policy, how did the state accommodate the preferences of these groups? What does the supply of public goods suggest about state formation? For Adelman and Cortés Conde, critical features of reunification in 1862 and the federal settlement of 1880 were the ability of the federal government to enhance the supply of public goods in the interior and a willingness on the part of the *porteño* capitalist class to underwrite the provision of those goods — railways, credit and currency.[90] Writing on the pre-1900 period, Sabato points to a broadening of political participation, notably the incorporation of a larger spectrum of urban society into the electoral game.[91] For Rock, this process was extended further with electoral reform and an abandonment of abstentionism by the Radical Party.[92] While the radicals may have favoured expanding the state sector, their commitment to monetary orthodoxy was manifest during the First World War and the 1920s. Perhaps this was because their principal competitor for urban votes, the Socialists, were equally committed to economic orthodoxy as a means of defending consumer interests.[93]

These tendencies suggest the 'representation' of a wider spectrum of regional and social interests within the state as understood by Oszlak. Resolving tensions within the structure of the state contributed to its consolidation and durability. Adelman, Cortés Conde and Irigoin attribute a fiscal dimension to the processes: the state became a mechanism for fiscal bargaining and groups that had previously avoided taxes were now prepared to assume a fiscal burden — in

---

[90] Adelman, *Republic of Capital*, pp. 269–71, 273–4, 283; R. Cortés Conde, *Dinero, deuda y crisis: evolución fiscal y monetária en la Argentina, 1862–1890* (Buenos Aires, 1989); *La economía argentina en el largo plazo, siglos XIX y XX* (Buenos Aires, 1994), pp. 171–99, *Progreso y declinación*, pp. 21–2.

[91] H. Sabato, 'Citizenship, Political Participation and the Formation of the Public Sphere in Buenos Aires, 1850s–1880s', *Past and Present*, vol. CXXXVI (1992), pp. 139–63; see also Sabato, *La política en las calles*.

[92] Rock, *Argentina, 1516–1982*, pp. 188–90. See also D. Rock, *Politics in Argentina, 1890–1930: The Rise and Fall of Radicalism* (Cambridge, 1975).

[93] Gallo, 'Society and Politics', p. 96. See also R.J. Walter, *The Socialist Party in Argentina, 1890–1930* (Austin, 1977).

exchange for public services.[94] 'Democratisation' did not signal taxation with representation but a relatively less unequal distribution of the fiscal burden. The emergence of a political class, implicit in the writing of Sabato, corroborates the view of a state standing above society and, thus, better able to arbitrate the supply of public goods. The 'separateness' of economic and political elites required — and enabled — the state to respond to demands emanating from sectors other than pampan pastoralists.

Finally, the impact of the Baring Crisis cannot be exaggerated. Variously presented as a crisis of development, corruption and confidence, above all it was associated with the provisioning of public goods. A systemic shock, the Crisis induced support for orthodoxy and a degree of transparency. It is not without significance that two devices were swept away after 1890 — the guaranteed banks and guaranteed railways regimes. 'Free', guaranteed banking, instituted in 1887, represented a major policy reversal — the struggle to centralise note issue that had been fitfully applied up to that point and had seen provincial banks progressively deprived of the right of issue. Thereafter, the conferment of a monopoly of issue on an autonomous central agency was conceived as the most effective means of promoting monetary stability. The Mitre Law was designed to deliver similar stability to the franchising (and regulation) of railways in place of the *ad hoc* (and discretionary). Both implied 'neutrality' delivered by a secure state committed to exchange for exactions. And, notwithstanding shocks such as world war and global depression or regimes 'shifts' in 1916, 1930 and 1943, both institutional arrangements survived well into the 1940s.

---

[94] Adelman, *Republic of Capital*, pp. 11, 14; Cortés Conde, *Progreso y declinación*, pp. 21–22; Irigoin, 'Part III'.

CHAPTER 8

Liberalism and Nation-Building in Mexico and Spain during the Nineteenth Century

Guy Thomson

Mexico and Spain began and ended the nineteenth century with much in common. In 1800 they shared the same king, the same godless enemies, the same rational, Bourbon administrative blueprints, the same reforming clergies, the same reigning philosophies of applied economic and political liberalism, even the same name. Eighty years later, flexible, cacique-based, modernising, administrative autocracies, installed by Porfirio Díaz and Antonio Cánovas, were functioning well. Mexico's formerly persecuted Catholic Church had substantially recovered the prominent position in society that it had retained throughout the century in Spain. Mexico and Spain now possessed national railway networks and expanding, modern industrial sectors. Yet beneath their surface glitter, both countries scored badly on any checklist of modernity: poor health standards and low per capita incomes, idle internal markets, under-funded public education and high levels of illiteracy, low levels of political participation and high degrees of alienation from cacique-dominated regimes, manifested in the mounting popularity of 'socially corrosive' doctrines: anarchism, republicanism, socialism and radical liberalism.

This chapter considers how two countries, which began and ended the nineteenth century with so much in common, diverged so markedly in the intervening decades. The nature of this divergence goes some way to explaining the different — almost asymmetrical — courses which Mexico and Spain followed during the twentieth century. Of course, between 1820 and 1870 the two countries continued to have much in common, being heirs to the same legacy of the Spanish Enlightenment and the Bourbon revolution in government. During this period, both countries underwent comprehensive liberal revolutions, profoundly affecting property relations, the relationship between government and society and the shape and function of the state. Liberal political economy, the retreat of the Catholic Church to the spiritual sphere, the rise of a secular, centralising and reforming state, the belief in the inevitability and desirability of progress were unspoken assumptions about the proper shape of society and government. Mexico and Spain also shared the experience of territorial dismemberment (Mexico's loss of one half of its territory in 1848 and Spain's loss of its American empire in 1825) and regional separatism (Mexico's Caste Wars and Spanish Carlism), which re-enforced the determination of liberal regimes to centralise power and to impose the uniform codes of the secular state. The two countries also shared the experience of frequent civil wars, continual military intervention in politics, frequent constitutional tinkering and experimentation, a politicised and interventionalist Catholic Church and crash programmes of ecclesiastical and civil disentailment. Yet, in spite of these similarities, the everyday experience of liberalism, and the allied phenomenon of nation-building, diverged dramatically.

In this chapter I discuss four overlapping areas of difference.

i) *Desamortización*. Mexico and Spain underwent common programmes of corporate and common land privatisation but with significant differences in timing, socioeconomic and political impact and longer-term consequences. In Spain, *desamortización* was accompanied by a successful transition to rural capitalism without significant agrarian complications. In Mexico, by contrast, *desamortización* provoked both immediate and longer-term agrarian conflict.

ii) Liberal constitutionalism and the legacy of the 1812 Constitution of Cadiz. Spanish absolutists and moderate liberals prevailed over much of the period between 1812 and 1868, and they were resolutely inflexible in their resistance to pressures for popular representation, and regional and local autonomy. Mexican liberals, by contrast, were constitutionally adventurous and more responsive to pressures from below and from the regions.

iii) Church and State. Spanish moderate liberals were reluctant to relinquish the historic association between the Catholic Church and the state, in spite of a secular decline in church attendance and religiosity. This contrasts with the Mexican experience of precocious secularisation, religious toleration and, after 1859, official anti-clericalism, despite a much greater persistence of Catholic religious observance and popular religiosity.

iv) The nation-state. From the outside nineteenth-century Mexico and Spain look equally weak. While for Mexico this appearance is largely accurate, for Spain, it is deceptive. For the nineteenth century (and much of the early twentieth), the state in Mexico was weak; able to maintain a narrow margin of authority only by conceding large measures of regional and local autonomy. In Spain, by contrast, the state was much stronger, able to withstand challenges from regional movements and democrats and federal-republicans at home, and from Cuban insurgents and Moroccan tribesmen abroad. Apart from their relative strengths as states, Mexico and Spain also differed in the way that the 'Nation' was constructed symbolically. Here, paradoxically, the weaker Mexican state hid behind a progressive, secularising, liberal-patriotic discourse of nationhood which achieved a precocious ascendancy after 1867. In Spain, by contrast, a much stronger state, particularly after the Bourbon Restoration in 1876, revealed a declining interest in defining a common discourse of nationhood or in embracing a modern set of secular national symbols and rituals.

'*Historia Patria*' in Nineteenth-Century Mexico and Spain

The levels of adult literacy found in Mexico and Spain at the turn of the twentieth century — almost everywhere below 40 per cent — were very low compared with France, Germany or the United States, and suggest that neither state had placed much emphasis upon public education as a medium for introducing children to modern ideas of citizenship and nationhood.[1] Yet, such an impression is belied by the commitment of the Bourbon state in the late eighteenth century to encouraging secular schooling as the key to forming new, rational and productive citizens, and its declared intention to relieve the Church of its sole responsibility to moralise the young.[2] In 1814 a draft law was issued to create a national — empire-wide — educational system. Liberals in Cadiz believed that public instruction 'creates good family men, honourable citizens and faithful, zealous and illustrious servants of the State; inspires in all respect for the law and submission to legitimately constituted powers, and thus tightening social bonds, assures the internal peace of nations'. [3] The restoration of absolutism, insurgency and civil war prevented this law from being implemented, yet Spain's 'Ley Moyano' in 1857 and Mexico's Law of Public Education in 1867, reiterated that ambitious design. Both established obligatory primary education for all boys and girls, to be provided free for the poor. Yet, by the end of the century, the reforming thread had somewhere been lost.[4] It is interesting, then, to see how differently the intention to form citizens through literacy was expressed in the two countries.

In 1861, Ignacio Ramírez, Mexico's minister of education, proposed that Nicolás Pizarro's 1858 *Catecismo político constitucional* be assigned to all of Mexico's public schools. The catechism was a comprehensive, but easily comprehensible guide to the small-print of Mexico's radical 1857 Constitution, listing the rights and duties of citizens (freedom of conscience, expression, association, male universal suffrage, obligatory service of males in the national guard, etc.). For the first time, a constitutional catechism explained the historical con-

---

[1] Adult illiteracy was estimated at between 55 and 60 per cent in Spain in 1900, comparable to rates in Southern and Eastern Europe but well below those of Britain, Germany and France. Adult illiteracy in most parts of Mexico in 1910 exceeded 70 per cent. Carolyn P. Boyd, *Historia Patria: Politics, History, and National Identity in Spain, 1875–1975* (Princeton, 1997), p. 8; François-Xavier Guerra, *Le Mexique de l'ancien régime à la Révolution* (Paris, 1985), vol. I, pp. 378–9.

[2] Dorothy Tanck Estrada, *La educación ilustrada (1786–1836)* (Mexico City, 1977); Ministerio de Educación y Ciencia, Madrid, *Historia de la educación en España, del despotismo ilustrado a las Cortes de Cádiz* (Madrid, 1985).

[3] Quotation taken from Boyd, *Historia Patria*, p. 3.

[4] Vaughan argues Mexican liberals' commitment to universal education foundered on weak municipal finances, Mary Kay Vaughan, 'Primary Education and Literacy in Nineteenth-Century Mexico', *Latin American Research Review*, vol. 24 (1990), pp. 42–55, and 'Economic Growth and Literacy in Late-Nineteenth-Century Mexico: The Case of Puebla', in Gabriel Tortella (ed.), *Education and Economic Development since the Industrial Revolution* (Valencia, 1990). For the failure of nineteenth-century mass education in Spain, see José Antonio Piqueras, *El taller y la escuela* (Valencia, 1988).

text within which the rights had been achieved (by the heroic sacrifices of Mexico's liberal-patriots since the first insurgency against Spain).[5]

In the same year, in southern Spain, Antonio Guerola, civil governor of Malaga, having made a pastoral visit to more than one half of the province's 204 primary schools, insisted that every poor child in be given a free copy of Alejandro Oliván's *Manual de agricultura y cartilla agraria*. The governor considered this practical farmer's encyclopaedia to be ideal for instructing children in the practice of reading aloud and of learning by heart, with the additional advantage that the knowledge it contained could be applied to the improvement of agriculture upon the child leaving school. Productive agricultural employment would also protect Malaga's young men from falling prey to village democrats (of whom, during the rebellion of Rafael Pérez del Alamo in July 1861, the provincial governor had become the principal scourge). The only other books Guerola recommended for Malaga's primary schools were Ripalda's catechism of Christian doctrine and a Castillian grammar (*Prontuario de ortografía y gramática castellana de la Academia de la Lengua*).[6] In Mexico, the emphasis was upon forming active, patriotic citizens; in Spain, productive but politically passive subjects.

The emphasis in Mexico upon encouraging active citizenship began even before Independence. Long before the shattering experience of defeat in 1848 convinced younger liberals in Mexico of the urgent need to teach patriotic history in schools, federal, state and municipal governments were budgeting for constitutional manuals to inform Mexican children about their state and nation. These moral and political catechisms (of which at least 40 were published in Mexico between 1808 and 1861) instructed children on the merits of republican government, and on why the break with Spain was necessary (often using the analogy of the grown up child having to leave the parental home), on the need to temper liberty with duty and obedience, and on the meaning of the Mexican *nación/patria*. Some of these catechisms alluded to the source of the *patria* in an ancient, pre-hispanic past, others to its peninsular roots, but most were silent about the past, preferring to look ahead to the near future when all Mexicans would enjoy their rights and perform their duties as citizens. The manuals usually combined constitutional exercises with instruction on public and private morality, as well as *urbanidad* (manners). Until the separation of Church and state in 1857, most manuals invoked the moral authority of the Catholic Church and treated Catholicism as an integral part of the Mexican *patria*.[7]

---

5   A letter of approval from Ignacio Ramírez prefaced the second edition of Pizarro's *Catecismo constitucional* in 1861, Eugenia Roldán, 'The Making of Citizens: An Analysis of Political Catechisms in Nineteenth-Century Mexico', unpubl. M.Phil diss., Department of History, University of Warwick (1996), pp. 25–6, 68–9.

6   Antonio Guerola, *Memorias (Málaga)* (Seville, 1995), vol. II, p. 192.

7   Roldán, 'The Making of Citizens'.

After the liberal triumph over the conservatives in 1861, Mexican constitutional catechisms became more secular, partisan and more detailed about specific individual rights. But they were fewer in number and were used less in schools. After all, now that the rights had now been formally won, the centralising liberal state was less keen to remind citizens about how many of those rights were still not being respected.[8] Instead, more emphasis was placed in school curricula upon *Historia Patria*, a version of Mexican history designed to demonstrate the genealogy of liberal patriotism. Children were invited to trace back the pantheon of national heroes from living, seemingly permanent liberal deities, such as Porfirio Díaz, through the martyrs of the liberal revolution, such as Benito Juárez and Melchor Ocampo, to the martyrs of the independence struggle, such as Miguel Hidalgo and José María Morelos, to the martyrs of the Aztec struggle against the the Spanish, above all Cuauhtémoc.[9] So successful was this liberal version of the past that even conservative authors of history textbooks such as Tirso Córdoba's *Historia Elemental de México* —[10] broadly adopted the liberal vision of the past as the price for ensuring that Catholicism still kept a prominent place in the nation's history.[11]

The liberal state in Mexico moved beyond the schoolroom to dramatise its presence in public patriotic rituals and festivals which jostled with saints days in an already crowded festival calendar. Again, before 1857, the Baroque symbolism of the ancien regime suffused post-Independence patriotic ceremonies.[12] Most political and military acts were sacralised by religious oaths;

---

[8]   During the 1870s Pizarro's *Catecismo del Moral* was banned from Mexico's state Preparatory School by its positivist director, Gabino Barreda, who found its anticlericalism and 'vague and incoherent deism', to jar with his positivist convictions, Charles A. Hale, *The Transformation of Liberalism in the Late Nineteenth Century Mexico* (Princeton, 1989), p. 149.

[9]   Eugenia Roldán, 'The Making of Citizens', and 'Conciencia histórica y enseñanza; un análisis de los primeros libros de texto de historia nacional, 1852–1894', unpubl. BA thesis, Faculty of Philosophy and Letters, UNAM, Mexico (1995). See also the pioneering Josefina Vázquez de Knauth, *Nacionalismo y educación en México* (Mexico City, 1970); Fernando Escalante Gónzalbo, *Ciudadanos imaginarios* (Mexico City, 1993); Anne Staples, 'El catecismo como libro de texto durante el siglo XIX', in Roderic A. Camp, Charles A. Hale and Josefina Zoraida Vázquez (eds.), *Los intelectuales y el poder en México* (Mexico City and Los Angeles, 1991), pp. 491–506.

[10]   During the European Intervention Tirso Córdova established a secondary school in the Puebla Sierra district capital of Zacapoaxtla, a conservative town that, nevertheless, sports a proud liberal-patriotic pedigree. This perhaps explains his receptivity to a liberal heroology, Roldán, 'Conciencia histórica y enseñanza', p. 191.

[11]   Roldán, 'Conciencia histórica y enseñanza', p. 182.

[12]   Annick Lempérière, '¿Nación moderna o república barroca? México 1823–1857', in François-Xavier Guerra and Mónica Quijada, *Imaginar la nación* (Hamburg, 1997), pp. 135–77.

grander occasions, such as patriotic victories, by Te Deums.[13] This seemingly comfortable *convivencia* came to a sudden end after the Three Years' War between liberals and conservatives from 1857–61, in which the Catholic Church was seen to take the side of the latter. The privatisation of corporate and communal property in 1856, followed by the confiscation of all Church wealth (including the funds of the confraternities that organised most festivals) in 1859, culminating in an amendment to the constitution in 1861 which removed religious instruction from schools and forbade any external celebration of the religious cult, left the liberal state as the only 'master of ceremonies'. [14]

During the European Intervention, Emperor Maximilian almost succeeded in appropriating this role. Concerned to distract attention from his Habsburg, hence, embarrassingly neo-colonial, genealogy, he made much of Independence day (stage-managing the 1865 celebrations in the birthplace of Independence at Dolores), paid respect to liberal heroes (while ignoring conservative ones) and, adopted the Aztec eagle upon a cactus, symbol of Anahuac, for his imperial flag and coat-of-arms.[15] Maximilian's reverence for Mexican mythology and symbolism was not enough to save him from execution after military defeat. Juárez justified the death sentence because of France's attack upon Mexico's national sovereignty and in terms of the Habsburg attempt to return the country to colonialism. Juárez chose to view the Second Empire as an aggression against the 'nation of Anahuac', for the defence of which he, as 'heir to Cuauhtémoc', was now responsible. The execution of Maximilian was presented as a just revenge for the murder by the Conquistadores of the last Aztec emperors, Moctezuma and Cuauhtémoc.[16]

After the restoration of the republic in 1867, federal, state and municipal governments constructed a full secular calendar of patriotic festivals to commemorate important rites of passage in the history of the Mexican nation.[17] Most towns and

---

[13] An exception to this was the Independence day celebration which Michael Costeloe finds to be 'almost entirely unreligious … (with) … the role and intervention of the clergy always kept to a minimum', Michael Costeloe, 'The Junta Patriótica and the Celebration of Independence in Mexico City, 1825–1855', *Mexican Studies/Estudios Mexicanos*, vol. 13 (1997), p. 51.

[14] Annick Lempérière, '¿Nación moderna o república barroca?', pp. 175–7.

[15] Robert H. Duncan, 'Embracing a Suitable Past: Independence Celebrations under Mexico's Second Empire, 1864–66', *Journal of Latin American Studies*, vol. 30 (1998), pp. 249–78.

[16] Brian Hamnett, 'La ejecución del emperador Maximiliano de Habsburgo y el republicanismo mexicano', cited in Enrique Florescano, *Etnia, estado y nación* (Mexico, 1998), pp. 435–6.

[17] William Beezley, Cheryl English Martin and William E. French (eds.), *Rituals of Rule, Rituals of Resistance. Public Celebrations and Popular Culture in Mexico* (Wilmington, 1994), pp. i–xxvii.

villages acquired brass bands that carried the *himno nacional* and a patriotic reper-
tory to the remotest parts.[18] Civic monuments, republican statuary and band
kiosks replaced crosses in streets and public squares, now named after patriotic
heroes instead of Catholic Saints. The best example of the appropriation of public
space is Mexico City's Paseo de la Reforma. Two miles of chronologically arranged
statues of national and provincial liberal heroes demonstrated the territorial com-
prehensiveness of the liberal 'theatre state'. Dwarfing the statue of Columbus, the
massive figure of Cuauhtémoc and the Independence monuments symbolised
both Mexico City's historic claim over Anahuac (the central Mexican tableland)
and beyond and the nation's rejection of Spain as its original source.[19]

In contrast the liberal state in nineteenth-century Spain reveals a remarkable
austerity in its use of the school, modern national symbols or secular ceremoni-
als and rituals for political ends. Throughout the century, successive governments
had to be reminded, in plaintive opposition speeches in Parliament or by street
demonstrations, that many Spaniards considered the Second of May (the start of
the national uprising against the Napoleonic invasion in 1808) to be the source of
the modern nation-state. Before 1868, the ruling moderates feared that banquets
organised for the Second of May by their progressive opponents might spill over
into revolutions. After the Restoration in 1875, the growth in popularity of
International Labour Day (the First of May) among socialists and anarchists, only
added to official anxiety about the beginning of spring.

Reticence over commemorating the nation's birthday was matched by failure to agree upon a national anthem and coyness over the national flag.
Throughout the period of predominantly absolutist and moderate rule between
1823–68, singing of the *Himno de Riego* was considered subversive. Even after
the Restoration, when the state ostensibly became more tolerant, striking up the
Himno de Garibaldi in a café in Seville could result in arrest — during the 1860s
Garibaldi had become a surrogate national hero in Spain's 'mezzogiorno' where
villagers awaited his liberating presence.[20]

The nation-state in Spain could survive without a national anthem, but not
without a flag. The red and yellow flag was only devised in 1785 to distinguish
Spanish ships from others carrying the Bourbon flag. *Exaltados* (progressive liberals) briefly adopted the red and yellow during the *Trienio Liberal* (1820–23).
This was enough to ensure its disfavour during the Ferdinand VII's absolutist

---

[18] Guy P.C. Thomson, 'Bulwarks of Patriotic Liberalism: The National Guard,
Philharmonic Corps and Patriotic Juntas in Mexico, 1847–88', *Journal of Latin American
History* (1990), pp. 51–61.

[19] Barbara A. Tenenbaum, 'Streetwise History: The Paseo de la Reforma and the
Porfirian State, 1876–1910', in William Beezley et al. (eds.), *Rituals of Rule, Rituals of
Resistance*, pp. 127–50.

[20] Federico Suárez (ed.), *Memorias del Gobernador Antonio Guerola, Sevilla, 1876–78*
(Seville, 1993) vol. III, p. 671.

regime. Only in 1843 was the yellow and red flag re-adopted; now as a triumphalist gesture by moderate liberals under Ramón María Narváez, flushed from their victory over the local militias of their progressive liberal rivals. The Spanish flag was not required to be flown over public buildings until 1908.[21] The seeming indifference to the advantages of deploying the symbolism and imagery of the modern nation-state as a focus of national unity is chalked up as another of Spain's 'failures' (to industrialise, to have a proper bourgeois revolution, to modernise, to secularise, to democratise ...).[22]

Spanish reluctance to adopt the symbolism of the modern nation-state was reflected in history textbook writing. In *Historia Patria: Politics, History and National Identity in Spain, 1875–1975* Carolyn Boyd analyses the content of these textbooks to see for what their authors (mainly high-school teachers) considered to be appropriate versions of Spanish national history. Peter Sahlins has shown how illiterate Pyrenean peasants became increasingly aware of their 'Spanishness', in opposition to the 'Frenchness' of their fellow Catalan neighbours of the same Cerdanyan valley. The same peasant preference for clear boundaries is not evident among the authors of these history textbooks. Of the 30 or so published under the Restoration Monarchy (1875–1923), Boyd observes that only one contained a map of Spain and none the national flag, which was seen as 'a partisan and, thus, divisive symbol...'[23]

Beyond omitting a map and the flag, Boyd found that, in spite the range of ideological viewpoints of their authors (from Catholic absolutists, to moderates, to republicans), the versions of Spanish history in these textbooks shared common elements. Most focused on the period before the expulsion of the French in 1814 and commented little on the period of liberal revolutions and civil wars between 1820 and 1875.[24] For Mexican liberals, of course, the secular pantheon of national heroes was born between 1808 and 1875, when the liberal *patria* and nation were forged. Mexican patriotic histories and catechisms distilled this seemingly chaotic period into a set of exemplary tales of civic virtue and patriotic self-sacrifice, designed to ensure children's emotional attachment to a liberal republic no more democratic than Cánovas' Restoration Monarchy.[25]

---

[21] Carolyn P. Boyd, *Historia Patria*, pp. 88–9.

[22] Borja de Riquer i Permanyer, 'La faiblesse du processus de construction nationale en Espagne au XIXe siècle', *Revue d'Histoire Moderne et Contemporaine* (1994), pp. 2, 42, 351–66. For a criticism of the historiography of the 'pathology of failure' approach, David R. Ringrose, *España, 1700–1900: el mito del fracaso* (Madrid, 1996).

[23] Peter Sahlins, *Boundaries: The Making of France and Spain in the Pyrenees* (Berkeley, 1998).

[24] To the middle ranking intellectuals of the Restoration Monarchy who wrote these textbooks, this period was an ideological minefield over which they chose to draw a veil, Boyd, *Historia Patria*, pp. 86–7.

[25] Boyd sees the failure of secondary school historians to draw useful lessons from Spain's 60 years of liberal revolution, above all their silence over the unstable First Republic (1874)

Spanish history textbooks were also vague about national geography and silent about provincial history. Probably seeking to avoid offending regional sensibilities, authors scripted simple narratives that depicted Spain as an eternal unity, forged from ancient times by crown and cross, aided by fearless bearded warriors.[26] This geographical imprecision contrasts with the reverence shown in Mexican patriotic histories for the small provincial towns and villages from where so many national heroes — Ramírez, Altamirano, Juárez, Díaz — were drawn.

Apart from their preference for the more distant past and their geographical vagueness, Restoration textbook writers were shy in depicting the ordinary Spanish people — the *pueblo* — who only began to attract the attention of historians and ethnographers after 1898. Even then, the lament (at least from José Ortega y Gasset) was that, ever since the Visigothic invasions, Spain had suffered from having too much 'pueblo' and too few 'distinguished minorities':

> Here the 'pueblo' has always done everything, and what the 'pueblo' has been unable to do, has not been done ... the 'pueblo' can only exercise the elemental functions of life; it cannot do science, the higher arts, nor create a civilisation equipped with complicated techniques, nor organise a state with any long-term consistency, nor distil the magic emotions of an elevated religion.[27]

Compare such pessimism with the liberal Ignacio Ramírez's optimistic view of a Mexican *pueblo* in 1846 (on the eve of the American invasion):

> When I see the semi-barbaric *vecinos* of a town gathered to organise a popular festival, allotting different commissions, one to purchase fireworks, another to hire the costumes, another to negotiate with the local priest ... and, as a result of their efforts, they enjoy a superb public function ... I ask myself, is it the same people that are unable to plan public lighting, the construction of a school or the cleaning of public spaces? We assume that they are ignorant, and that ignorance kills the spirit of association. But I have demonstrated the opposite. A society that does not take care of its own necessities is dead.[28]

---

and 'sexenio revolucionario' (1868–74), as having fatal long-term consequences for the success of Second Republic in 1932. 'By omitting discussion of the recent past, authors deprived their readers of any knowledge of the historical process by which the liberal state had taken shape and discouraged children from seeing the present as a continuation of the past. Few of the books attempted to draw young readers into a national tradition in which they might imagine themselves as historical actors.' *Ibid.*, p. 86.

[26] Silence over regional and local contributions to national history was not because such histories were lacking. There was boom in the writing of provincial histories between the 1840s and 1860s, Paloma Cirujano, Teresa Elorriaga and Juan Sisinio (eds.), *Historiografía y nacionalismo español 1834–1868* (Madrid, 1985), pp. 58–9.

[27] José Ortega y Gasset, *España invertebrada* (Madrid, 1922), p. 166.

[28] Ignacio Ramírez, *Obras Completas* (Mexico City, 1984), I, pp. 210–12.

Boyd speculates that Spanish popular culture was 'too regionally diverse ... too intertwined with Catholic culture ... to fit the idealised vision of a unified, modern nation'.[29] With no *pueblo*, there could be no truly popular heroes, certainly no recent ones. The heroes that reappear in every textbook — Cid El Campeador, Pelayo of Asturias, Columbus — were too remote in time and too morally neutral to serve as avatars for the modern age. Moreover, Boyd concludes, 'writers failed to bring them to life or to present them in moral conflict'. After the French invasion of 1823 the absence of recent heroes or villains in these texts was partly a result of the absence of a serious external enemy, denying Spain that inducement to national self-definition which Colley sees as so instrumental in the forging of British national identity.[30] Spanish textbook writers were also limited, Boyd argues, by 'the transactional character of the Restoration settlement that eliminated the option of vilifying the internal enemies of the liberal regime'. [31]

Mexico's liberal historians suffered no such political constraints, possessing many of the inducements that Spanish lacked, such as an abundance of foreign and internal enemies. After soundly defeating the conservatives and the French, and constitutionally silencing the Church, Mexican liberal historians could make the century their own, ransacking the recent past for their own ends. 'We come from the village of Dolores. We descend from Hidalgo,' declared Ignacio Ramírez, the minister for public instruction, claiming to speak for the whole Mexican nation.[32] The modern, secularising message of Mexico's liberal patriotism acquired additional appeal through its ability to connect with sub-currents of popular anti-clericalism, anti Spanishness and anti-Americanism.[33]

Aside from these differences in the content of textbooks, Mexican and Spanish history teaching during the later nineteenth century had much in common. There were no nationally prescribed history textbooks in either country until the twentieth century. Hence, national history for schools could be constructed by a small number of intellectuals who enjoyed considerable freedom in each country to determine the content of the curriculum.[34] Although there are notable examples of *Historia Patria* being taught in Mexican primary

---

[29] Carolyn Boyd, *Historia Patria*, p. 83.

[30] Linda Colley, *Britons: Forging the Nation, 1707–1837* (London, 1996).

[31] Boyd, *Historia Patria*, p. 90.

[32] Quoted in D.A. Brading, *The First America: The Spanish Monarchy, Creole Patriots, and the Liberal State* (Cambridge, 1991), p. 662.

[33] D.A. Brading, *The Origins of Mexican Nationalism* (Cambridge, 1985), pp. 100–1; Alan Knight, 'Peasants into Patriots: Thoughts on the Making of the Mexican Nation', *Mexican Studies*, vol. X (1994), pp. 145, 152–3; Frederick C. Turner, *The Dynamic of Mexican Nationalism* (Chapel Hill, 1968), pp. 22–61.

[34] There was probably more intellectual freedom for textbook writers in Spain than in Mexico where the official anti-clericalism of the Porfirian regime contrasted with the greater tolerance of the Restoration monarchy.

schools from the 1870s, in general, in Mexico, as in Spain, little history appears to have been taught at the primary level, where the emphasis remained upon instruction in 'the three Rs'.[35] The pedagogy was also the same in Spain and Mexico: children confronted equally tedious memorising techniques and positivist curricula despite the important differences, both in how *Historia Patria* was written and in how effectively the patriotic message was received.[36]

Spanish history textbooks were written by 'institutos catedráticos', whose prime concern was to impress each other and to compete for textbook prizes. They were mostly, Boyd claims, 'indifferent to their audiences ... What distinguished Spanish (history) schooling was the relatively inert quality of the material to be learned.'[37] By contrast, several of Mexico's most popular *Historias Patrias* were written by prominent liberal statesmen, with already established literary reputations, several of whom had taken part in, or had closely observed during their childhood, the great events that their histories described. The *Historias Patrias* of Guillermo Prieto, Manuel Payno or Justo Sierra, contained clearer, fresher and more immediate moral messages. There was no equivalent in Spain to the figure of Benito Juárez, whose memory was contested by rival historians throughout the *Porfiriato*, when every Mexican school child would have been familiar with some of the details of his life.[38]

Of course, there were many other nineteenth-century Spains in which quite different versions of national history were constructed, most notably during the Nationalist renaissance in Catalonia and the Basque country, and in the work of writers such as Fernando Garrido, Francisco Pi y Margall and E. Rodríguez Solís. The democratic-republican version of Spanish history was much closer to that of the Mexican liberal *patria* — concerned above all with the nineteenth century, internationalist (particularly in its debts to the French revolutionary tradition and the Italian *Risorgimento*), anchored as much in the regions and the countryside as in Madrid and, finally, well populated by vernacular heroes and martyrs.[39] But these progressive liberal and republican writers did not have

---

[35] Guy Thomson, '"La République au Village" in Spain and Mexico, 1848–1888', in Hans-Joachim König and Marianne Wiesebron, *Nation Building in Nineteenth Century Latin America* (Leiden, 1998), pp. 59–60.

[36] Liberal *Historia Patria* was well embedded in the primary school curriculum of the Puebla Sierra by the early Porfiriato. G.P.C. Thomson, *Politics, Patriotism and Popular Liberalism in Mexico. Juan Francisco Lucas and the Puebla Sierra, 1854–1917* (Wilmington, 1999), ch. 1.

[37] Boyd, *Historia Patria*, p. 76.

[38] Charles A. Hale, *The Transformation of Liberalism*; Charles A. Weeks, *The Juarez Myth in Mexico* (Tuscaloosa, 1987); Brading, *The First America*, pp. 663–7.

[39] Fernando Garrido, *La España contemporánea. Sus progresos morales y materiales en el siglo XIX*, 2 vols. (Barcelona, 1865), and *Historia del reinado del último Borbón de España. De los crímenes, apostasías, opresión, corrupción, inmoralidad, despilfarros, hipocresía, cru eldad y fanatismo de los gobiernos, que han regido España durante el reinado de Isabel de*

the privileged access to children, through state or private schools, enjoyed by moderate liberals and Catholics.[40] Their ideas were spread through a national network of night schools, libraries, workers associations and the branches of the Socialist International.[41] For Spaniards on the left it must have been hard not to feel discouraged by the lessons of the nineteenth century.

Democratic-republican regional martyrology is well exemplified in the cult of Mariana Pineda, publicly garrotted in Granada in 1831 for the crime of having embroidered a flag for conspirators opposed to Ferdinand VII's despotism.[42] During the 1850s and 1860s, democrat and progressive leaders in Granada and Malaga took strength from the stoicism of Mariana Pineda in their struggles against the tyranny of Narváez and the moderates. Wives of village Democrats adopted 'Mariana' as a nickname.[43] Much later, in the dying months of the liberal monarchy and the early years of the Primo de Rivera dictatorship, Federico García Lorca became obsessed with setting the Mariana Pineda legend to a play (as much, Ian Gibson wonders, for her impossible love for a cousin as for her involvement with the liberal cause).[44]

Mexico's ruling liberal elites were, then, successful in constructing a modern nationalist mythology, rooted in contemporary history. In Spain, by contrast, the century provided little comfort even to conservatives, let alone republicans or regional nationalists. Only the moderate liberals (who held power for most of the period between the end of absolutism in 1833 and the Revolution of 1868) devised a nationalist mythology, most clearly manifested in Modesto Lafuente's 30 volume *Historia General de España* published between 1850 and 1859 (the first general history of Spain published since Padre Mariana's *Historia*, written in the seventeenth century).[45] But, as Boyd points out, moderate historiography was hardly modern:

Borbón; Francisco Pi y Margall and Francisco Pi i Asuaga, *Historia de España en el siglo XIX*, 6 vols. (Barcelona, 1902); Enrique Rodríguez Solís, *Historia del partido republicano español*, 2 vols. (Madrid, 1892–93).

[40]   Boyd cites only one textbook written from a radical progressive perspective, first published in 1871 by Esteban Paluzie who 'managed to condense into a small space an unusually pluralistic and "popular" perspective on the national past', Boyd, *Historia Patria*, pp. 95–6.

[41]   Clara Lida, 'Educación anarquista en la España del ochocientos', *Revista de occidente*, vol. 97 (1971), pp. 33–47; Carolyn Boyd, 'The Anarchists and Education in Spain, 1868–1909', *Journal of Modern History*, vol. 48 (1976), pp. 125–72; José Antonio Piqueras, *El taller y la escuela* (Valencia, 1988).

[42]   Luis Morell y Terry, *Efemérides granadinas* (Granada, 1892), pp. 85, 89, 167, 278.

[43]   Antonio Guerola, *Memorias (Málaga)*, vol. III, p. 1173.

[44]   Ian Gibson, *Federico García Lorca* (London, 1989), pp. 130–1.

[45]   Modesto Lafuente's History is judged by Paloma Cirujano et al. as 'la primera historia nacional con una difusión y valoración nacional', *Historiografía y nacionalismo español*, p. 81.

nationalist historiography produced by the dominant moderados was essentially retrospective and conservative; it invoked the national past from a position of 'arrival', of general satisfaction with present arrangements ... it represented Spanish history as a teleological journey toward territorial, political and religious unity whose culmination was the constitutional monarchy of the Isabelline era ... Moderado historians legitimated the constitutional monarchy not by dramatising its differences from the old order, but rather its affinities with it.[46]

The providentialism and self-confidence of the moderate position, which rested upon the claim that only those with considerable wealth should enjoy political representation, collapsed with the Isabelline regime in September 1868.

How were Mexican liberals able to construct an effective national mythology from their contemporary history while their counterparts in Spain were obliged to turn back beyond the nineteenth century to revive past glories? The answer lies in how differently Mexico and Spain responded to 'applied liberalism' between the late eighteenth century and the 1870s, when Porfirio Díaz and Antonio Cánovas arrived to establish stable administrative oligarchies. These differential responses to applied liberalism are now examined under three headings: *desamortización*, liberal constitutionalism and Church-state relations.

Desamortización

Liberal regimes in Spain and Mexico accepted civil and ecclesiastical *desamortización*, and the inauguration of a regime of private property, as necessary preconditions for economic modernisation. In spite of resistance from the Church and Carlists in Spain, and from the Church and Indian communities in Mexico, the programme contributed crucially to the development of commercial agriculture, the leading sector in both countries during the nineteenth century. However, in their timing, manner of execution, political contexts, economic impact and longer-term social consequences, Mexico and Spain's passages to private property differed enormously. After 1910 Mexico spiralled into 30 years of agrarian revolution. By contrast, Spain's twentieth-century agrarian structure has remained quite stable. Agrarian reform never achieved the same popular appeal as in Mexico, with the exception, perhaps, of Andalusia.[47]

That the privatisation of common and corporate land in Spain was accompanied by less social conflict, and provoked less agrarian longing than in Mexico, probably tells us more about differences in the strengths of the two states, than in popular attitudes towards the liberal revolution in land-ownership.

---

[46] Boyd, *Historia Patria*, p. 71.

[47] And even there, according to Mintz and Martínez Alier, landless workers saw the 'reparto' as a distant and improbable outcome of their labour struggles, rather than a panacea. See Juan Martínez-Alier, *Labourers and Landowners in Southern Spain* (London, 1971), pp. 103–23; Jerome R. Mintz, *The Anarchists of Casa Viejas* (Bloomington, 1982).

Desamortización was applied earlier and more generally in Spain than in Mexico. It was implemented by less democratic and more centralised administrations. It was also more discriminatory in its social impact. Why, then, was there less opposition to it in Spain than in Mexico?

The *desamortización* in Spain was implemented under moderate liberal (conservative) regimes, when Spanish towns were tightly controlled by centrally appointed *alcalde corregidores* and municipal corporations elected under a very narrow property franchise, representing only the *mayores contribuyentes* (major tax papers).[48] Most land privatisation in Spain had been completed by the late 1850s, before universal male suffrage was achieved and before towns had regained some of their autonomy.[49] In Mexico, by contrast, although *desamortización* was applied in peripheral states such as Yucatan, Chiapas and Sonora as early as the 1820s (with the catastrophic consequence of provoking Indian wars), it was not until after the liberal victory against the French in 1867 that civil *desamortización* (particularly the sale of village commons) was carried out throughout most of central Mexico.[50] In areas where there was local resistance, the process was postponed until even later.[51]

Desamortización in Spain was administered from the centre by the 'Royal Fund of Desamortización', through the *diputaciones provinciales*. The revenues it generated were used to fund colonial and Carlist wars. In Mexico each municipality handled its own *desamortización*, under the supervision of *jefes políticos*. Municipalities, moreover, were permitted to retain the revenues from land privatisation, which they could use for building schools, buying musical instruments for wind bands or for improving their *palacios municipales*.[52] Village *ejidos* (grazing commons) were also exempted from privatisation.[53]

---

[48] Although *desamortización* was implemented by moderate liberals, under a limited suffrage, the legislation was introduced by the progressive liberals, Juan Alvarez Mendizabal in 1837 (ecclesiastical) and Pascual Madoz in 1855 (civil).

[49] There is a massive literature on *desamortización* in Spain. The most significant English language contribution is Richard Herr, *Rural Changes and Royal Finances in Spain at the End of the Old Regime* (Berkeley, 1989).

[50] José Velasco Toro, *Política y legislación agraria en México. De la desamortizacón civil a la reforma campesina* (Jalapa, 1993).

[51] Michael Ducey, 'Tierras comunales y rebeliones en el norte de Veracruz antes del Porfiriato, 1821–1880: el proyecto liberal frustrado', *Anuario* (Jalapa, Veracruz), vol. VI (1989), pp. 209–30; José Luis Blanco Rosas, 'La muerte de Quihuikolo. Territorialidad de tres municipiuos totonacos del siglo XX', in Victoria Chenaut (ed.), *Procesos rurales e historia regional (Sierra y Costa Totonaca de Veracruz)* (Mexico City, 1996), pp. 103–30.

[52] An example of this flexibility is Frank Schenk, 'La desamortización de la tierras comunales en el estado de México (1856–1911). El Caso del Distrito de Sultepec', *Historia Mexicana*, vol. XLV (1995), pp. 3–37.

[53] Robert J. Knowlton, 'El ejido mexicano en el siglo XIX', *Historia Mexicana*, vol. XLVVIII (1998), pp. 71–96.

Desamortización was often more discriminatory in its social consequences in Spain than in Mexico. Most seigniorial and common land in Andalusia went to the existing nobility, their tenants and administrators, much less to medium farmers and none to the majority of the labouring population that remained landless, losing even the right of access to former commons and *dehesas* (wastes).[54] Political channels for protest under the absolute monarchy and later, under the moderates, did not exist. The countryside was well policed by municipal guards and after 1843, by the centrally organised civil guard. The few rebellions with agrarian pretensions were put down swiftly and ruthlessly by the army.

Apart from being less centralised and fiscally oppressive, the Mexican *desamortización* appears often to have been more socially inclusive and democratic. Recent studies have revealed that liberal leaders, in order to reward villagers' support in civil and patriotic wars, recognised their claims of 'entitlement' to common lands.[55] And throughout much of rural Mexico, it was small farmers as much as great landowners (*hacendados*), who benefited most from the *desamortización*.[56] That 'ranchero' group provided many revolutionary leaders after 1910.

We can deduce from the ubiquitous agrarian movements in Mexico of the 1910s and 1920s, that, however socially inclusive or even democratic, Mexico's *desamortización* ultimately had more explosive consequences. Spain's nineteenth-century *desamortización* often left a legacy of agrarian discontent, but remarkably little will or tactical capacity on the part of the peasantry and landless labourers to press for a fairer *reparto*. As already suggested, this divergence can be explained in part by differences in the political context of *desamortización*. It can also be better appreciated by observing the distinct ways in which liberal land reform in Mexico and Spain affected regions with strong traditions of communal agriculture and regions where larger estate agriculture prevailed.

As we have seen, the division of village commons in most parts of Mexico occurred much later than in Spain. By the 1870s, when the *desamortización* was applied to most parts of Central Mexico, the territories of the colonial *pueblos de indios* had fragmented into a myriad of much smaller municipalities. Had the ter-

---

[54] A.M. Bernal, *La lucha por la tierra en las crisis del antiguo regimen* (Madrid, 1979); for the effects upon a single town in the province of Seville, David Gilmore, 'The Class Consciousness of the Andalusian Rural Proletarians in Historical Perspective', *Ethnohistory*, vol. 24 (1977), pp. 149–61.

[55] Florencia E. Mallon, *Peasant and Nation. The Making of Postcolonial Mexico and Peru* (Berkeley, 1995), pp. 88–131.

[56] Ian Jacobs, *Ranchero Revolt: The Mexican Revolution in Guerrero* (Austin, 1982); Frans Shryer, *The Rancheros of Pisaflores: The History of a Peasant Bourgeoisie in Twentieth Century Mexico* (Toronto, 1980); Luis González, *Pueblo en vilo: microhistoria de San José de Gracia* (Mexico City, 1972); Mathew Butler, 'The "Liberal" Cristero: Ladislao Molina and the Cristero Rebellion in Michoacán, 1927–1929', *Journal of Latin American Studies*, vol. 31 (1999), pp. 645–72.

ritorially extensive Indian communities of the late colonial period been convinced, under benign Bourbon guidance, to shift to private ownership, they might have managed the transition without too much loss of land to outsiders. However, a hundred years later, Indian *pueblos* were much smaller territorial entities; and more directly exposed both to outsiders and to non-Indian competitors within their midst.

The main beneficiaries of common land privatisation in Mexico were the liberal, non-Indian, 'peasant bourgeoisie' that had usurped local political control, formerly exercised by Indian authorities, and who provided so many revolutionary leaders. These leaders were concerned in part with keeping agrarian reform out of their patches although they were prepared to pay lip-service to its principles.[57] A northern variant of this process of loss of communal control over land can be observed in the declining position of the military colonies first established by the Bourbons as a defence against encroachment by *indios bárbaros*.[58] Here, revolutionary leaders were able to tap communal frustrations over recent land loss and encroachments upon political autonomy by bringing agrarian reform to the top of the political agenda. Both factors — 'serrano' conservatism in central Mexico and 'serrano' agrarianism in the north — contributed to rural violence throughout the 1910s and 1920s. For Spain, Herr and others have shown how in regions with strong communal traditions, although at first many titles accrued to urban rentiers and nobles, over the longer term, community members were effective at recovering titles to much of village land, and even at regaining some community control over former commons.[59] Such developments encouraged popular compliance with *desamortización*.

In areas of larger estate agriculture, there are also interesting contrasts in the way the *desamortización* was implemented which help to explain popular compliance/resignation in Spain and popular unrest in Mexico. In Andalusia, Spain's main area of *latifundismo*, the *desamortización* was implemented between the 1780s and 1850s over extensive municipal territories, which, because of the sur-

---

[57] For example, Frans Schryer, 'A Ranchero Elite in the Region of Huejutla (The Career of General Juvencio Nochebuena of Atlapexco)', in Wil Pansters and Arij Ouweneel (eds.), *Region, State and Capitalism in Mexico: Nineteenth and Twentieth Centuries* (Amsterdam, 1989), pp. 158–73; Keith Brewster, 'Gabriel Barrios Cabrera: The Anti-agrarian Friend of the Campesino', *Bulletin of Latin American Research*, vol. 17 (1998), pp. 263–84; Butler, 'The "Liberal" Cristero'.

[58] Daniel Nugent, *Spent Cartridges of Revolution. An Anthropological History of Namiquipa, Chihuahua* (Chicago, 1984); Ana Maria Alonso, *Thread of Blood: Colonialism, Revolution and Gender on Mexico's Northern Frontier* (Tucson, 1995); Friedrich Katz, *Pancho Villa* (Stanford, 1998).

[59] Herr, *Rural Change and Royal Finances*, pp. 749–51; Michael Kenny, *A Spanish Tapestry Town and Country in Castile* (London, 1961), pp. 15–35; William Christian, *Person and God in a Spanish Valley* (Princeton, 1988), pp. 18–28; Carmelo Lisón-Tolosana, *Belmonte de los Caballeros. A Sociological Study of a Spanish Town* (Oxford, 1996), pp. 15–53.

vival of absolutism until 1833 and a narrow property franchise thereafter, resisted the territorial fragmentation signalled by the concession by the 1812 Cortes of Cadiz of the right of smaller settlements to form new municipalities. Hence, the existing nobility, or the *señoritos* (as the former administrators, now proprietors, of seigniorial, Church and municipal lands came to be known), became the principal beneficiaries of the *desamortización*, at the expense of the absentee nobility, the clergy and smaller tenants of municipal commons. In most areas, the polarised social structure existing before the liberal land reform changed little, although greater commercial dynamism stimulated the peasant sector and opened up more employment for the growing army of day labourers. For the day labourers (*jornaleros*), the *desamortización* brought no substantial changes in agricultural or employment practices. Indeed, the resulting commercial expansion, for a time (before population growth began to outstrip the demand for labour), strengthened the bargaining position of day labourers.[60]

The process of land privatisation, and commercial expansion that accompanied it, is correctly interpreted as Spain's variant of a 'bourgeois revolution'. Most scholars now rate Spain's liberal property revolution as an economic success, facilitating the emergence of a class of modern agricultural entrepreneurs. It was also a political success; by underpinning the pre-eminence of the moderates before 1868, and by contributing to the stability of Cánovas' liberal monarchy after 1875. Spain's *desamortización* was also a social success: the loss of rights of access to common land was not accompanied by serious social unrest.[61] Recent studies show that the most important factor accounting for popular compliance with the liberal property revolution in Andalusia was the economic opportunity provided by agricultural expansion, not only to the new class of agricultural proprietor-entrepreneurs, but also to peasant farmers and wage labourers. Not until population began to outstrip employment opportunities at the turn of the twentieth century did local prospects seriously deteriorate. Then, the result was mass emigration rather agrarian revolution.[62]

---

[60] Gilmore, 'The Class Consciousness of the Andalusian Rural Proletarians', p. 153, and Martínez-Alier, *Labourers and Landowners*, pp. 124–73.

[61] Gilmore, 'The Class Consciousness of the Andalusian Rural Proletarians', p. 155.

[62] For the global picture in Spain, Herr, *Rural Changes and Royal Finances*. For the impact of the *desamortización* in the mountainous borderlands of Malaga and Granada, Manuel Martínez Martín, *Revolución liberal y cambio agrario en la Alta Andalucía* (Granada, 1995); A Ferrer Rodríguez, *Paisaje y propiedad en la tierra de Alhama (Granada siglos XVIII–XX)* (Granada, 1982); M. Gómez Oliver, *La desamortización de Mendizábal en la provincia de Granada* (Granada, 1983); M. Gómez Oliver, *La desamortización de Madoz en Granada* (Granada, 1985); Rodrigo Fernández-Carrión, 'Antequera a mediados del siglo XIX. Estudio de Estructuras y Comportamientos Sociales', *Revista de Estudios Antequeranos*, vol. IV, nos. 1–2 (1996), pp. 11–80; Antonio Parejo, 'Revolución liberal y élites locales. Dos ejemplos antequeranos de la segunda mitad del siglo XIX', in Antonio Gómez Mendoza and Antonio Parejo (eds.), *De economía e historia. Estudios en homenaje a José Antonio Muñoz Rojas* (Malaga, 1998), pp. 139–84.

In Mexico's regions of large estate agriculture, lacking a territorial or juris-
dictional aristocracy to be disentailed, the *desamortización* was less a bourgeois
revolution, and more an opportunity for existing members of the landed elite,
joined by new members (often immigrants), further to extend the boundaries
of large estates at the expense of communal agriculture. Memories of this displacement fuelled later agrarian struggles.[63] Meanwhile, peonage and *latifundismo* provided easy targets at the turn of the twentieth century for agrarian
reformers seeking to redress the country's economic backwardness and to deep-
en its shallow democracy.[64] Their counterparts in Spain were greeted by a much
less enthusiastic response 20 years later.[65]

If nineteenth-century Spain is judged to have failed in the construction of a
modern nation-state, her agriculturally-based, 'bourgeois' revolution can be
viewed as a 'success'. Mexico, by contrast, provides an example of the successful
construction of a modern, secular, nation-state, but on the foundations of an
agrarian structure which would not weather the first decade of the twentieth
century. This tension between the ideals and symbols of Mexico's precocious
construction of nationhood, and unresolved tensions in her social structure, is
clearly visible in the way the late nineteenth-century Mexican state regarded
Indianness. On the one hand, during the *Porfiriato*, and even more after the
Revolution, the Indian past and present moved to the centre of the official
national identity and mythology.[66] On the other, it is evident that one of the
principal consequences of liberal reforms, particularly the *desamortización*, was
to erode the already beleaguered political and economic position of Indian
communities. The *desamortización* in Spain posed no such profound a cultural
dilemma. Instead, the liberal property revolution accommodated itself to, or
partially modified, a traditional social hierarchy that proved quite resilient, even
after the liberal state came under greater strain during the 1920s and 1930s.

Liberal Constitutionalism

Spain and Mexico both inherited eighteenth-century, Bourbon centralising traditions. In Spain moderate liberals applied this French model to the highly centralised Constitution of 1845, which determined the administrative shape of Spain
until the Second Republic. The architect of the *Moderado* state was Javier de

---

[63] For the most famous agrarian struggles resulting from this process, John Womack,
Zapata and the Mexican Revolution (New York, 1969); Paul Friedrich, *Agrarian Revolt in
a Mexican Village* (Chicago, 1970).

[64] The best known critique of the pre-revolutionary agrarian system is Andrés Molina
Enríquez, *Los grandes problemas nacionales* (Mexico City, 1909).

[65] Mintz, *The Anarchists of Casas Viejas*, pp. 279–82.

[66] Mauricio Tenorio-Trillo, *Mexico at the World's Fairs. Crafting a Modern Nation*
(Berkeley, 1996).

Burgos, As minister of development in 1833, he called for the 'omnipresence of the administration ... removing at once all the obstacles and promoting, with a single and enlightened impulse, great prosperity ... Those charged with doing this must form a chain which starts with the head of the administration and ends with the last local policeman.' He also decreed the abolition of Spain's 34 historic provinces, replacing them with 49 provinces modelled on the French departments.[67]

Moderates succeeded in defeating the attempts in 1840–43 and 1855–56 by progressives to restore provincial and municipal liberties, lost under the early Habsburgs, the recovery of which had been hinted at in the Constitution of 1812. Also vanquished in the chaos of the First Republic were the democrats and republicans who, inspired by Swiss federalism and Mazzinian internationalism, sought to rebuild a democratic and reunited Iberia (to include Portugal) from the bottom up.[68] However, the ability of the moderate vision of a centralised state to prevail over competing projects owed less to the successful transferral of French fiscal or administrative efficiency, more to the continuing utility of Madrid as a centre of court intrigue and of financial and political corruption. The *moderado* state was also bolstered by the success of the army under generals Ramón María Narváez and Leopoldo O'Donnell in defeating internal enemies, such as the Carlists and democrats, as well external foes (especially the much trumpeted Spanish triumph over Moroccan tribesmen in 1859–61, signalling the renewal of Spain's civilising mission).

In Mexico, the Bourbon centralised vision foundered almost immediately upon Independence. Mexican provincial elites drew far more from the experience of the 1812 Constitution of Cadiz than their Spanish counterparts, especially regarding provincial representation, just as non-elite Mexicans, especially Indian communities, were attracted by the constitution's concession of the right of smaller settlements to form autonomous municipalities. The provincial representations of 1812, revived in 1820 after the Cadiz mutiny and combined with the example of the United States, became the basis of Mexican federalism. In Mexico's first federalist revolution of 1824 against the empire of Agustín de Iturbide, the provincial elites decided to construct the nation from an association of 'free and sovereign states'. This was the 'bottom up' constitutional rebuilding of the state that eluded Spanish progressives, democrats and republicans throughout the nineteenth century.[69]

Mexico's equivalent to Spain's *moderados* were the conservatives, who were inspired by the same ideal of a centralised, administrative republic in the Central Republic of 1835–46.[70] Like the *moderados*, the conservatives relied heavily on the army created during the Independence Wars. But Antonio López

---

[67] Quoted in Adrian Schubert, *A Social History of Modern Spain* (London, 1992), pp. 170–1.

[68] María Victoria López-Cordón, *El pensamiento político internacional del federalismo español, 1868–1874* (Barcelona, 1975).

[69] Timothy E. Anna, *Forging Mexico 1821–1835* (Lincoln, NE, 1998).

[70] Michael P. Costeloe, *The Central Republic in Mexico, 1835–1846. Hombres de Bien in the Age of Santa Anna* (Cambridge, 1993).

de Santa Anna was less successful than either Nárvaez or O'Donnell in confronting Mexico's external and internal enemies. Moreover, Mexico City, largely because of its economic decline, was also a less effective national capital than Madrid for holding together a troubled country.

The liberal triumph against the conservatives in the Revolution of Ayutla in 1854 was only in part a consequence of the weakness of the conservative centralism in Mexico. Rising liberalism was also able to take advantage of wide margins of regional and local political autonomy, which simply could not be accommodated in the repressive and centralised politics of nineteenth-century Spain. Liberal triumphs in Mexico, first against the conservatives, then against the European Intervention, were a consequence of the ability of leaders to harness the potential of locally controlled national guard units. During these two decades of civil and patriotic warfare, a new liberal army embodied regional as much as central power (Porfirio Díaz succeeded in reigning in regional caciques only during the 1880s). Spain's army, although highly politicised and prone to revolt, never grew to embody regional or local power and remained at the service of the central authority. Spain's equivalent to Mexico's national guard — the *Milicias Nacionales/Voluntarios de la Libertad* — were always disbanded within weeks of being formed, denying regions the capacity to negotiate with the central power. In each of Mexico's liberal triumphs (1854, 1861, 1867 and 1876), leaders further strengthened their claim to be defending the Mexican *patria* against its foreign and domestic enemies. The Spanish *patria*, by contrast, remained the property of the moderates until 1868, while their opponents could be presented as unpatriotic agents of the British, Mazzini, Garibaldi or Bakunin.

When the Franco-Austrian army left Mexico in 1867, Mexico's liberals could claim that they had saved the *patria* and constructed a new state on the basis of armed municipalities engaged in a successful struggle to secure a charter of individual liberties, against the combined opposition of the Church, the conservatives and European monarchists.[71] Of course, once installed in the national palace, Benito Juárez and his team of liberal lawyers resumed the task of Bourbon centralisation. But they did so in the face of constitutional guarantees, institutions and power structures that ensured, for the time being, high levels of regional autonomy. Only after 1876 was Porfirio Díaz successful in curbing regional autonomy. Yet he achieved this without needing to tamper with the sacred charter of Mexicans' liberties in the Constitution of 1857 (except in the small matter of 'no re-election'). Also left untouched, indeed to be greatly enhanced, was the mythology of a people's republic, heir to the nation of Anahuac, led in its moment of triumph by the impassive 'Zapotec Buddha', Benito Juárez.[72]

---

[71] For an optimistic interpretation of this process, Alicia Hernández Chávez, *La tradición republicana del buen gobierno* (Mexico City, 1993).

[72] The term 'secular Zapotec Buddha' was used by Francisco Bulnes to describe Juárez in his critical biography, *El verdadero Juárez y la verdad sobre la intervención y el imperio* (Mexico City, 1867), cited in D.A. Brading, *The First America*, p. 666.

Church and State

Only recently has Spain emerged from a pattern of Church–state relations in which the state had made full use of the Church's ideological and institutional armoury, a pattern formalised in the Concordat of 1851. Even more recently, Mexico has emerged from a century and a half of extreme, official anti-clericalism with its roots in the Three Years' War (1857–61). The reticence of Spanish liberals to separate Church and state, despite their early determination to close down monasteries and divest the Church of its land and urban property, can be explained by the pragmatism of moderate liberals who sought to use the moralising influence of the clergy to combat the secularism and radicalism of their progressive and democratic opponents. Moderates also feared presenting the Carlists with a political ally in an aggrieved Roman Catholic Church. Queen Isabel's close relations with neo-Catholics and support for the papacy during the Italian Risorgimento provided an additional ideological and diplomatic dimension. In general, the Church, as a symbol of Spanish unity and as a day to day moraliser in the face of the invasion of subversive and impious foreign doctrines, was too valuable an ally for the *moderados* to sacrifice.

The Mexican Church at first offered similar ideological props for independent nationhood, and it was used in political catechisms to re-enforce the state's appeal to citizens' loyalties. As distinct from its Spanish counterpart, it also figured prominently in early evocations of patriotism and nationhood, with its roots in the Marian cult of Guadalupe and the myth of Saint Thomas/Quetzalcoatl. Mexican clerics were prominent in the insurgency, in the culmination of Independence in 1821 and in the birth of the Federal Republic. Thereafter, however, relations between liberals (moderates and radicals) and the Roman Catholic Church deteriorated, and the Church–state conflict acquired a political dynamic of its own. Liberals justified their anticlericalism through imputations, soon all too clearly proven, of the Church's disloyalty to the *patria* and political support for the conservatives.

The political risks of anti-clericalism for Mexican liberals were much less than for their Spanish moderate counterparts, while the attractions of the separation of Church and state were much greater. In Spain, the Church was more strongly embedded socially, with Roman Catholic piety and institutional life already undergoing a revival by the 1840s and 1850s, due in part to energies of charismatic catechists, such as Antonio María Claret, whose missions were helped greatly by 'the support they received from moderate notables and the prosperous men of property dominating local governments'.[73] In Mexico, the great landowners had no such uncontested control of local government.

---

[73] W.J. Callahan, *Church, Society and Politics in Spain, 1750–1874* (Oxford, 1979), pp. 231–40.

The Spanish Church also deployed itself in politics more effectively, particularly through the court and the monarch (Father Claret was Queen Isabel's confessor). In Mexico, the Church and its conservative allies became increasingly isolated and 'de-patriated', once they had allied themselves with the European Intervention. By the time of Mexico's 'second revolution of independence' in July 1867, martial liberalism, patriotism, republicanism and rhetorical anti-clericalism had become irresistibly fused. Liberals had also learned how to take advantage of a popular indifference to the clergy, found throughout much of rural Mexico. This 'folk anti-clericalism' had grown since the eighteenth century as a response to the Church's renewed campaign against popular religion and idolatry.[74] In this respect, Francisco Bulnes's irreverent labelling of Benito Juárez as a 'secular Zapotec Buddha' who was tapping into the residual Catholicism of the Mexican people, 'who always look for an image, a cult, a piety for social emotion', is not too wild an image.[75] Popular liberalism had already become a secular religion in certain pockets of rural Mexico by the late 1860s.[76] By contrast, the popular constituency in Spain was already being courted and accommodated by the Catholic revival, or by secular religions of Mazzinian internationalism, anarchism and socialism, none of which would present much competition for Mexico's official ideology of patriotic-liberalism until the early twentieth century.[77]

Conclusions

Mexicans still wrestle with a sense of nationhood — and with a nation-state — that liberal patriots constructed during the nineteenth century. Liberal patriotism was a powerful mythology that exalted the leaders of the struggles against Spain, the conservatives, the Catholic Church and foreign invaders. During the 1920s and 1930s, this secular religion was given additional cultural and social substance by revolutionary nationalists. Liberal patriotism and revolutionary nationalism have enjoyed such enduring success because they have served states with active secularising and reforming agendas. By engaging emotionally with Mexico's youth, and by being at the disposal of politically active regional and local elites, they have shaped the political imagination of most Mexicans.

---

[74] This phenomenon is explored by William Taylor in *Magistrates of the Sacred. Priests and Parishioners in Eighteenth-Century Mexico* (Los Angeles, 1996).

[75] Brading, *The First America* , p. 666.

[76] The case of the Methodist congregation of the Villa del Cinco de Mayo (Xochiapulco) is explored in Guy Thomson, "'La République au village" in Spain and Merxico, 1848–1888', in Hans-Joachim König and Marianne Wiesebron (eds.), *Nation Building in Nineteenth Century Latin America* (Leiden, 1998), pp. 37–62; see also Jean-Pierre Bastian, *Los disidentes: sociedades protestantes y revolución en México, 1872–1911* (Mexico City, 1989).

[77] Clara Lida and Carlos Illades, 'El anarquismo europeo y sus primeras influencias en México', unpubl. paper, El Colegio de México and the Universidad Autónoma Metropolitana-Iztapalapa (1999).

In this chapter I have argued that the success of liberal patriotism in Mexico during the nineteenth century lay in the way it that it served as a useful, nation-building ideology for a succession of liberal leaders who sought to consolidate their control, and to pursue progress, by applying a wide-ranging, and potentially highly divisive, package of liberal reforms. Through these reforms — the secularisation of education and the teaching of *Historia Patria*; a decentralised and democratic (and ultimately socially explosive) *desamortización*; a radical, social rights-based constitution; a flexible territorial division; the partial rebuilding of the national army from a citizen's army (the national guard); the corralling and political neutralisation of the Catholic Church — liberal leaders succeeded in penetrating a vast national territory, creating allies in the regions and localities and providing the means for these allies to consolidate their economic and political hold.

If in Mexico the nation-state derived much of its strength and durability from the fusion of liberalism and patriotism, in Spain the state was able to retain control over the national territory only by suppressing regional patriotism, by postponing the application of central elements of the liberal programme (such as universal suffrage, the secularisation of education and the separation of Church and state) and by favouring a version of the Spanish nation and *patria* that was retrospective and religious, rather than modern and secular. However, Spain's privileged Church and conservative political class, which so successfully kept the spectre of 1812 at bay during the nineteenth century, eventually abandoned the liberal state for the greater certainties of dictatorship during the 1920s and after 1939. Yet, since the restoration of democracy following the death of Franco in 1975, Spain at least has not had to free itself from the burden of a dominant modernising national mythology established during the nineteenth-century. No such mythology was ever constructed. Instead, a repertoire of 'failures' has served as a useful bank of experience for what must qualify as one of Europe's more adaptable nation-states.

CHAPTER 9

The Weight of the State in Modern Mexico

Alan Knight

During the 1980s, a decade of aggressive 'state-shrinking' in Latin America and elsewhere around the world, a school of political science told us that we should devote ourselves to 'bringing the state back in'.[1] So while the state in the real world shrunk, the intellectual-academic-Platonic state was puffed.[2] Mexico, not for the first time, tended to buck both trends. Under President Salinas the executive power of the state appeared to burgeon, while academic students of Mexican history and politics needed no exhortation to 'bring the state back in', because it had never been shown the door. The state had been a major theme of Mexican inquiry — historical and political — for decades. Indeed, in the realm of historiography (where, of course, the state is also the major supplier of raw, archival data), the revisionist turn of post-1968 had re-emphasised the role of the state, while at the same time tending to demonise it. That is to say, the comfortable notion of a revolutionary state enacting the popular will (hence of a state that was progressive, benign and in tune with society) gave way to the image of an aggressive, centralising, corrupt and authoritarian state, which betrayed the revolution, conned the peasantry, shackled organised labour, created the bourgeoisie, thwarted democracy, and feathered its own particularist nest. Even social historians who set out to rescue neglected groups from the 'enormous condescension of posterity' placed their collective heroes and heroines against the bleak backdrop of a powerful, expanding, aggressive and oppressive state.[3] Local and regional historians, whose efforts have greatly enhanced our understanding of modern Mexico, likewise depicted the overweening central (Federal) government as both villain and victor in an essentially Manichaean political drama. Social scientists — sociologists as well as politólogos — also contributed to this inflation of the state. Thus, by the 1980s, it had become a standard view that the Mexican state — or, in naively personalised form, the Mexican president — enjoyed pervasive and untrammelled power.[4]

[1] Peter Evans, Dietrich Rueschmeyer and Theda Skopcol, *Bringing the State Back In* (Cambridge, 1989) is a central text. For a critique, see Paul Cammack, 'Review Article: Bringing the State Back In', *British Journal of Politics*, vol. 19 (1989), pp. 261–90.

[2] Albert Fishlow, 'The Latin American State', *Journal of Economic Perspectives*, vol. 4, no. 3 (1990), p. 61.

[3] For example, Marjorie Becker, *Setting the Virgin On Fire* (Berkeley, 1995).

[4] Alan Knight, 'The Mexican Revolution: Bourgeois? Nationalist? Or just a "Great Rebellion"?', *Bulletin of Latin American Research*, vol. 4, no. 2 (1985), p. 11.

Of course, this statolatrous view did not go unresisted. Historically, there exists an old tradition of lamenting the weakness of the Mexican nation-state. Nineteenth-century elites saw Mexico as a mere geographical expression, lacking true citizens or patriots.[5] Twentieth-century revolutionaries echoed the refrain, proclaiming the need to 'forjar patria', to bring into the fold the 12 million or so Mexicans who languished 'on the fringe of civilization', as Calles put it.[6] Social scientists, too, picked up on the theme of Mexico's deep-rooted parochialism. Redfield, echoed by Whetten, saw Mexico's Indians — 29 per cent of the population according to the 1921 Census — locked into their 'little isolated worlds'; in the 1940s, Sol Tax found that the Indians of the deep south regarded Mexico (City) as if it were Tibet.[7] Not only national integration, but also Mexico's potential for democracy, were thereby compromised.[8]

These contrasting views can to some extent be squared by means of chronological distinctions: *juarista* Mexico was a collage of parochial *patrias chicas*, lacking sentiments of national integration; the *Porfiriato* advanced the task of *forjando patria*, which the Revolution triumphantly consummated. But spokesmen — such as Calles — had their doubts. Recent historians, too, have questioned this neat teleological advance, with its Whiggish focus on the onward and upward rise of the state.[9] So have some younger political scientists who, alert to historical and anthropological evidence, adopt a more critical and nuanced tone, querying the post-revolutionary state's supposed exercise of seamless centralised power.[10] The ensuing debates — between 'statolaters' and their critics, between 'traditional' and 'revisionist' views of the Revolution and 'its' state, between 'top-down' and 'bottom-up' views of Mexican history — are too well-known and not worth rehearsing in this context. Rather, my aim in this chapter is more neutral, methodological and, perhaps, consensual. It is to consider how these debates are conducted, and how they might be better conducted. For a remarkable feature is the lack of agreement about basic strategies of investigation. This results in conceptual confusion: what is the state; how should it be defined or disaggregated? How is the casual binary

5   Fernando Escalante Gonzalbo, *Ciudadanos imaginarios* (Mexico City, 1992).

6   Manuel Gamio, *Forjando patria* (Mexico City, 1982; first pubd. 1916); Eyler N. Simpson, *The Ejido: Mexico's Way Out* (Chapel Hill, NC, 1933), p. 253, quoting Calles.

7   Nathan Whetten, *Rural Mexico* (Chicago, 1948), pp. 53, 57, 536, quoting Sol Tax; see also Simpson, *The Ejido*, pp. 244–5, quoting Noriega Hope.

8   Whetten, *Rural Mexico*, p. 535; compare Frederick C. Turner, *The Dynamic of Mexican Nationalism* (Chapel Hill, NC, 1968), p. 10, citing Robert Scott.

9   Daniela Spenser and Bradley A. Levinson, 'Linking State and Society in Discourse and Action: Political and Cultural Studies of the Cárdenas era in Mexico', *Latin America Research Review*, vol. 34, no. 2 (1999), pp. 227–45, reviews recent work on the 1930s.

10   Jonathan Fox, *The Politics of Food in Mexico* (Cornell, 1992); Jeffrey Rubin, *Decentering the Regime* (Durham, NC, 1997).

'nation-state' to be disaggregated?[11] How is state strength to be evaluated and what are the benchmarks against which the strength — or 'weight' — of the state should be judged? And are there quantitative data which can be used in order to arrive at calibrated — as opposed to merely 'impressionistic' — conclusions, which may be amenable to comparison across time and space? In short, I am trying to respond to Stephen Haber's call for a more 'scientific' approach to (Mexican) history; although I do not wish to reduce 'scientific' to 'quantitative' in the way that Haber sometimes seems to do.[12]

Measuring the State

One aspect of the 'scientific' historical inquiry which Haber rightly favours is careful definition. The proliferating assertions of state 'strength' rarely embody a definition of either 'the state' or of 'strength'. For the sake of simplicity, we can start with a roughly 'organisational' definition of the state, derivative of Weber, which denotes the state as an institution or set of institutions which exercises a 'monopoly of the legitimate use of physical force within a given territory'.[13] Clear and conventional though this may be, it poses two problems. First, it is an ideal-type, which by no means corresponds to historical reality. For the twentieth-century Mexican state, like many others, allows — perhaps even encourages — a measure of illegitimate violence, perpetrated sometimes by its own agents, sometimes by 'private' agents who enjoy state tolerance (*pistoleros, halcones, guardias blancas, defensas sociales*, etc.).[14] Furthermore, the inclusion of the crucial qualifier 'legitimate' obliges analysts to appraise the legitimacy of states — on the grounds that states which lack legitimacy are not 'proper' Weberian states. This is difficult — more difficult than many happy users of the concept ('legitimacy') seem to realise.[15] Extremes of legitimacy and illegitimacy may be readily discernible (compare, say,

---

[11]   I take it that this question is at the heart of the debate between Heraclio Bonilla ('The Indian Peasantry and 'Peru' during the War with Chile') and Florencia E. Mallon ('Nationalist and Antistate Coalitions in the War of the Pacific: Junín and Cajamarca, 1879–1902') in Steve J. Stern (ed.), *Resistance, Rebellion and Consciousness in the Andean Peasant World: 18th to 20th Centuries* (Madison, 1987), pp. 219–31, 232–79.

[12]   Stephen Haber, 'Introduction: Economic Growth and Latin American Economic Historiograph,' in Stephen Haber (ed.), *How Latin American Fell Behind* (Stanford, 1997), ch. 1.

[13]   Ralph Miliband, *The State in Capitalist Society* (London, 1973), pp. 46–7. On 'organisational', as against 'functional', models of the state, see Patrick Dunleavy and Brendan O'Leary, *Theories of the State* (Basingstoke, 1987), pp. 1–4.

[14]   Alan Knight, 'Habitus and Homicide: Political Culture in Revolutionary Mexico', in Wil G. Pansters (ed.), *Citizens of the Pyramid. Essays on Mexican Political Culture* (Amsterdam, 1997), ch. 4.

[15]   Juan Molinar Horcasitas, *El tiempo de la legitimidad* (Mexico City, 1991) is a good study of the electoral decline of the PRI, but it does not explain the concept which graces the title.

Switzerland and East Timor), but subtle calibration of the vast universe of intermediate cases is as rare as it is difficult. Some states seem to survive and function, doing the things that states do — taxing, extracting resources, conducting foreign policy — despite sizeable 'legitimacy deficits'.[16]

Furthermore, some schools of thought would cavil at the very notion of legitimacy, preferring to recast it as 'hegemony' or even 'false consciousness'. Or they may choose to ditch it altogether, on the grounds that states are no more than glorified protection rackets; states and mafias differ in scale rather than basic *modus operandi*.[17] This is a point to which I will return in my conclusion. Initially, given the problems inherent in the notion of 'legitimacy', I propose to separate out this crucial qualifier and to use a stripped-down Weberian definition, omitting, for the time being, the question of legitimacy. However, as my analysis suggests, legitimacy — or something like it — cannot be permanently banished from the discussion. Indeed, any evaluation of the state — its weight, stamina and capacity — inevitably leads to an analysis of state-society relations. I will therefore start with the state, while alerting the reader that the exclusion of society is a temporary, tactical gambit.

This initial, stripped-down definition invites an analysis of state capacity: that is, the ability of the state to affect society, which in turn implies an ability to collect information (Whitehead's 'cognitive capacity'),[18] to influence people and to control resources. Such activities would seem to be reciprocally reinforcing: a state which accurately collects socioeconomic information is in a better position to tax; a state which educates its citizens enjoys a measure of influence as well as a means to collect information; a state which effectively taxes has the ability to deploy resources in education. I am not assuming here that state capacity necessarily enhances legitimacy, accumulation or redistribution.[19] It may do none of these things. I am separating organisation from function and focusing on the more limited question of state power. (A second minimal Weberian definition: power is an actor's capacity to 'carry out his will despite resistance').[20] Another way of conceptualising power is to switch the focus from

---

[16] Of course, they may not do so indefinitely, hence the time scale becomes important. Maybe in the long term illegitimate regimes always collapse. But, like individuals, all regimes are dead in the end. The acute reader will note that I am tending to conflate 'state' and 'regime' (see fn. 126 below).

[17] Charles Tilly, 'War and State Making as Organised Crime', in Evans et al., *Bringing the State Back In*, pp. 169–91; for St Augustine's anticipation of this argument, Alexander Passerin D'Entrevès, *The Notion of the State* (Oxford, 1967), p. 22.

[18] Laurence Whitehead, 'State organisation in Latin America since 1930', in Leslie Bethell (ed.), *Cambridge History of Latin America*, vol. 6/2 (Cambridge, 1994), pp. 46–7.

[19] Evelyne Huber, 'Assessments of State Strength', in Peter H. Smith (ed.), *Latin America in Comparative Perspective* (Boulder, 1995), pp. 167–8.

[20] Quoted in Dietrich Rueschmeyer, *Power and the Division of Labor* (Cambridge, 1986), p. 11.

the state to its subjects/citizens and to ask what impact the state has on their lives. Are those lives barely touched by the state? Or is the state a pervasive force? And, if so, which state agencies impinge upon them? Again, I am not initially trying to evaluate the quality, the benefits or the popular estimation of state intervention. Redeploying Whitehead's term, we could say we are measuring the 'cognitive impact' of the state (how much do people know about it?), not its 'affective' foundation (how much do people value, endorse or approve state authority?).

Some rough statistical evidence can be marshalled. Such evidence has the obvious merit of facilitating comparison: instead of venturing vague 'impressionistic' judgements (the revolutionary state was stronger than the Porfirian; the Mexican state is stronger than the Bolivian), we can attempt calibrated comparisons. Significantly, as the century progressed, the Mexican state itself became an assiduous collector of statistics — and information more generally. The scope of the registro civil widened;[21] the agrarian reform involved herculean tasks of counting, measuring and mapping; agents of the state, such as schoolmasters, were set prodigious — sometimes, it seems, self-defeating — tasks of data collection.[22] The quality of such data, of course, is questionable. Like many rural folk, especially those familiar with the ravages of forced military recruitment, Mexicans were reputedly hostile to data collectors ('Mexican antipathy to statistics is profound', Stuart Chase observed in the early 1930s).[23] Village hostility to outsiders — which in some cases the Revolution had exacerbated — made the work of census-takers, tax-gatherers, teachers and surveyors difficult, if not risky.[24] In the eyes of the rancheros of El Llano Grande (Jalisco),

---

[21] Elsie Clews Parsons, *Mitla: Town of Souls* (Chicago, 1936), p. 114; Whetten, *Rural Mexico*, pp. 376–8, gives (1940) figures of couples married by civil ceremony (alone, or in conjunction with a religious ceremony) as a percentage of all couples: <20 year-olds: 6%; 20–39 year-olds: 6%; >40 year-olds: 6%.

[22] Simpson, *The Ejido*, p. 346, on the 'endless reports' required by the ejidal bureaucracy. Note also Luis González, *Pueblo en vilo: Microhistoria de San José, de Gracia* (Mexico City, 1972), p. 179; and Elsie Rockwell, 'Schools of the Revolution: Enacting and Contesting State Forms in Tlaxcala, 1910–30', in Gilbert M. Joseph and Daniel Nugent (eds.), *Everyday Forms of State Formation* (Durham, NC, 1994), p. 189. Gamio, *Forjando patria*, pp. 33–6, was a staunch advocate of statistical collection. A related feature, scarcely studied, is the imposition of standard metric measurements of weight, quantity and distance, in place of the old colonial units, which were still widely in use at the time of the Revolution: note Engracia Loyo, Cecilia Greaves and Valentina Torres (coords.), *Los maestros y la cultura nacional, 1920–52*, t. IV, Centro (Mexico City, 1987), p. 48.

[23] Stuart Chase, *Mexico. A Study of Two Americas* (New York, 1931), p. 232.

[24] Frank Tannenbaum, *The Mexican Agrarian Revolution* (Hamden, CT, 1929), pp. 47–51; Mary Kay Vaughan, *Cultural Politics in Revolution* (Tucson, 1997), p. 125 notes how at Zacapoaxtla (Puebla), 'the revolution provoked a turning inward, a rejection of outside linkages and innovations'.

the state was 'muy listo, muy listo ... nomás quiere chingar'.[25] Data also became part of the endless and ancient battle for patronage and promotion. Officials wanted to tell superiors the right story; leaders wanted to inflate the numbers of their followers (especially where payrolls were concerned). Some statistical series entered the realms of fantasy — and I am not referring simply to the early, amateurish efforts of the 1920s.[26] Electoral returns were, until recently, highly 'alchemical' in quality; so, too, were figures of mass organisations — such as the Confederación Regional de Obreros Mexicanos (CROM), whose claimed membership of some two million (1928) was grossly inflated.[27] At the grass-roots level, data collection was not only patchy, but also counter-productive. A Secretaría de Educación Pública (SEP) school inspector in Veracruz (1934) regretted that he could not furnish accurate figures relating to the *campaña anti-alcohólica*, since, he expained, 'now that the production of alcohol is repressed, bootlegging is all the greater and therefore the statistics one can provide will be inaccurate'.[28] Thus, as Haber is surely aware, the quantitative data on which we seek to base our firm cliometric conclusions are flawed, and sometimes grossly flawed. That said, what do the data, warts and all, tell us?

Several series indicate a progressive growth in state activity during the postrevolutionary period. Central government spending as a percentage of GDP, hovering around four per cent in the late *Porfiriato*, reached six per cent by 1930 and eight per cent by 1940; the 1940s represent a plateau (1945: 8.1 per cent; 1950: 8.2 per cent); while the 1950s and '60s saw a gradual but not inexorable increase (1955: 9.9 per cent; 1960: 12.6 per cent; 1965: 13.7 per cent; 1970: 11.9 per cent). The 1970s saw a decisive shift (upwards): 1975: 20.0 per cent; 1980: 23.5 per cent.[29]

---

[25] José Eduardo Zárate Hernández, *Procesos de identidad y globalización económica. El Llano Grande en el sur de Jalisco* (Zamora, 1997), p. 175.

[26] P. Lamartine Yates, *Mexico's Agricultural Dilemma*, pp. 271–9, which lists statistical horror stories (e.g., a census of farm land for the state of Campeche which exceeded the total area of the state; or an increase in the ass population of San Luis from 5 to 97,638 in five years). Luis Alfonso Ramírez C., *Chilchota*, p. 115, suggests that the 1980 census undercounted by some 26% at Chilchota.

[27] Marjorie R. Clark, *La organización obrera en México* (Mexico City, 1979; first pubd. 1934), pp. 59–60, which points out that in 1926–27 CROM membership dues totalled 13,505 pesos, which meant that only some 13,000 of the organisation's alleged 1.8m members (one in 138) were paying dues. Ejidal censuses — the necessary prerequisites for ejidal grants — were also liable to inflation (if they occurred at all): Kaja Finkler, *Estudio comparativo de la economía de dos comunidades de México* (Mexico City, 1974), p. 72; Paul Friedrich, *Agrarian Revolt in a Mexican Village* (Chicago, 1977), pp. 91–2, describes how the legendary agrarista leader Primo Tapia conned Naranja's Catholics into signing a petition requesting the appointment of a parish priest, which was then used as an ejidal petition.

[28] Manuel Malpica to Matías López, 10 July 1934, SEP Archive/Depto de Escuelas Rurales, Caja 1071, Exped. 4 (Veracruz).

[29] James W. Wilkie and Adam Perkal, *Statistical Abstract of Latin America*, vol. 24 (Los Angeles, 1985), p. 875. The figures for 1981 and 1982 are given as: 42.7% and 35.9%.

As a result, per capita central government spending (pesos of 1950) rose from 32 pesos in the last decade of the *Porfiriato* to 56 pesos under Obregón; 68 under Calles; 85 under Cárdenas; 113 under Avila Camacho; 147 under Alemán; 181 under Ruiz Cortines; 256 under López Mateos; 348 under Díaz Ordaz; 517 under Echeverría; and 1,082 under López Portillo.[30] In crude terms, the 'impact' of the state, measured in spending per capita, was 19 times greater under López Portillo than it had been under Obregón. This belated increase, incidentally, brought Mexico roughly into line with several Latin American countries, such as Chile and Peru.[31]

Consider, too, the 'weight of the state' in terms of its payroll, of the agents it could deploy to enforce its will. Was the perception of a 'pervasive officialdom', called into being to run the Six Year Plan (1934), justified?[32] Or, in grander theoretical terms, does the 'Bonapartist' image of an 'enormous bureaucracy, well-gallooned and well-fed' fit the Mexican reality?[33] It certainly fits the 1970s better than any previous period. Indeed, what is remarkable concerning earlier decades is the relatively low and constant level of state employment. In 1932 there were 98,000 federal government employees in a population of 17.2 million, making a ratio of one employee per 176 Mexicans. In 1950, after nearly two decades of state-strengthening, there were 147,000 federal employees in a population of 25.8 million, making a ratio of one employee to 176 Mexicans. By 1970 the ratio had dropped to 1:80 (616,000:49.36m); by 1976 it stood at 29 (2.1m:60.06m); by 1983 one in 22 Mexicans was a government employee (3.3m:71.71m).[34]

This does not mean, of course, that government capacity stagnated between 1930 and 1952 (no more does it mean that government capacity surged ahead after 1970). In education, for example, per capita spending increased during the 1930s; schooling underwent an important process of federalisation; texts and

---

[30]   Wilkie and Perkal, *Statistical Abstract of Latin America*, p. 876.

[31]   Wilkie and Perkal, *Statistical Abstract of Latin America*, p. 699, gives central government spending as a percentage of GDP (1980) as: Chile, 20.9%; Peru, 23.4%. These are on the high side for Latin America (compare: Argentina. 15.4%; Brazil, 9.2%; Colombia, 10%).

[32]   The phrase is taken from a long report, 'Latin America: International, Economic and Social Developments', Institute of Public Affairs, University of Virginia, 4 July 1935, in British Foreign Office Records, PRO, London, FO 723/172.

[33]   Quoted in Knight, 'The Mexican Revolution', p. 5.

[34]   José, E. Iturriaga, *La estructura social y cultural de México* (Mexico City, 1951), p. 224. See also Luis González, *Historia de la revolución mexicana, período 1934–40. Los artífices del cardenismo* (Mexico City, 1979), p. 71, which gives a lower figure of federal employees (80,000). For recent data: Miguel Angel Centeno, *Democracy Within Reason. Technocratic Revolution in Mexico* (University Park, PA, 1994), p. 82, where figures relate to 'public servants', rather than Federal government employees. However, the difference should not affect the general argument. See also Whitehead, 'State organisation', pp. 34–5, which suggests ratios (of public sector employees to total population) of 1:83 in 1960 and 1:25 in 1980.

curricula were standardised; and — particularly in relatively 'open' communities — federal schools became key centres of social and political organisation.[35] Now, for the first time, Mary Kay Vaughan notes, the SEP 'acquired the size, jurisdiction and experienced talent to conduct meaningful dialogue with the peasantry'.[36] In particular, federal schools were set up in hitherto remote and marginal *pueblos*, to which novice *maestros* had to trek, usually on horseback, in the face of formidable natural and human hazards.[37] The new schools frequently acted in close conjunction with the new *ejidos* which, apart from providing peasants with land, fostered sentiments of empowerment and citizenship: 'ejidatarios have a stake in the community; they own something about which they can make plans. In a word, however slow the process, these ejidatarios are on the road to becoming something new in rural Mexico — citizens'.[38] The 1930s also witnessed the rise of the Banco Nacional de Crédito Ejidal as a key interlocutor between the state and the burgeoning population of *ejidatarios*. Ejidal communities were therefore structurally linked to the state. For better or worse, they had to reckon with state power; the 'cognitive impact' of the state was unavoidable. Integration into 'statist' circuits of power, however, did not necessarily mean across-the-board 'integration' (into national and international labour markets, for example); on the contrary, ejidal grants *could* foster a degree of economic introversion, as the reconstituted peasantry — literally — 'cultivated its own garden'.[39]

At the same time, the emerging system of labour arbitration gave the central government significant powers in the realm of industrial relations, particularly in the major industries, where national unions now came to the fore, and in the major industrial centres, where the implementation of Mexico's advanced

---

[35] Vaughan, *Cultural Politics*; James W. Wilkie, *The Mexican Revolution. Federal Expenditure and Social Change since 1910* (Berkeley, 1973), pp. 160–1, gives per capita education spending (1950 pesos) as: 1900: 1.1; 1910: 2.5; 1920: 0.3; 1930: 6.9; 1940: 11.3; 1950: 12.2.

[36] Vaughan, *Cultural Politics*, p. 189.

[37] Loyo, *Los maestros*, pp. 21, 96ff.

[38] Simpson, *The Ejido*, p. 108. Alicia Iwanska, *Purgatory and Utopia. A Mazahua Indian Village of Mexico* (Cambridge, MA, 1971), p. 101, sees a similar organisational and empowering effect of the *ejido*.

[39] Finkler's dyadic comparison of two *ejidos* (Itel and Nalcan: pseudonyms for, I think, Tezontepec de Aldama and Caltimacan in the Valle del Mezquital, Hidalgo) notes how the recipients of irrigated ejidal land at Itel forged a community which, though tightly linked to the government, via powerful local political brokers, was relatively isolated from the national and international economy; while Nalcan, a landless community of migrant workers, was more economically integrated, 'extrovert' (my phrase) and open to outside influences in general (e.g., trucks and modern medicine): Finkler, *Estudio comparativo*. The phenomenon of post-land-reform peasantries who experience — opt for? — a form of involution is not, of course, confined to Mexico.

labour legislation (always subject to ample discretionary leeway) tended to be more effective.[40] Thus, as in most Latin American countries, the post-1930 period saw a marked enhancement of central state power.[41]

However, this process can easily be exaggerated or misunderstood. Federal government agencies often had a skeletal existence. The Banco Nacional de Comercio Exterior (BNCE), for example, serviced only 14 per cent of *ejidatarios* in 1945; the rest had to look to private sources of credit.[42] In the same year, only seven per cent of *ejidatarios* had access to government health programmes.[43] Many schools remained poor, primitive and under-funded; dynamic mobilisation in some communities contrasted with suspicion and stagnation in others; and, after 1940, some *cardenista* educational programmes lost momentum or were wound up.[44] Furthermore, state agencies did not necessarily pull together. Teachers and BNCE officials feuded; Federal initiatives were swallowed up in the quicksands of village factionalism.[45] The impact of the state, therefore, varied greatly from place to place (and, to a lesser extent, from time to time). An increase in quantifiable resources was potentially, but not necessarily, significant.

As for state regulation — of labour relations, for example — there is no doubt that it increased during the 1930s, and did not abate in the 1940s. But regulation is hard to measure and, more particularly, it begs the questions: regulation for what, in whose interests? Likewise, bald figures of expenditure (even assuming they are accurate), tell us little about legitimation, accumulation or redistribution: first, because they neglect the relationship of the state to (civil) society; second, because they are largely silent concerning the direction and consequences of state activity. We are saying, in effect, that the state has built up some impressive muscle; but we do not know how that muscle is used — whether for constructive labour, showy callisthenics or acts of grievous bodily harm. We therefore have to look beyond the state itself.

Measuring Civil Society

If we seek to relate state activities to civil society we encounter a major methodological problem.[46] While it may be possible to make a rough assessment of

---

[40] Nora Hamilton, *The Limits of State Autonomy. Post-Revolutionary Mexico* (Princeton, 1982), pp. 134, 148–52, 172–5.

[41] Whitehead, 'State Organisation', pp. 13, 58, 62, 64–5, 69, 74. The period also witnessed an accentuation of metropolitan primacy: Mexico City comprised 4.3 per cent of the national population in 1920 and 6.3 per cent in 1930; over the next four decades the share rose constantly: 7.9, 11.1, 14.1, 17.8 (Wilkie and Perkal, 'Statistical Abstract', p. 87).

[42] Whetten, *Rural Mexico*, p. 195.

[43] *Ibid.*, p. 353. Nearly half of these were in the Laguna region.

[44] Vaughan, *Cultural Politics*, pp. 65, 119, 168, 179, suggests the variety of outcomes.

[45] *Ibid.*, p. 86.

[46] We may also encounter definitional problems. What is 'civil society'? Gramsci, who

state activities — to estimate the 'weight of the state' — equivalent calculation of the 'weight' or 'density' of civil society is difficult, if not impossible. Though there are plenty of off-the-cuff generalisations,[47] attempts at careful assessment are rare and, even in the case of the contemporary United States, open to serious question.[48] Carlos Forment's pioneering analysis of civil society in four nineteenth-century Latin American countries illustrates some of the problems.[49]

Furthermore, even if we could make some headcount of civil society, measuring its cohesion and density, what would that tell us about the state? The relationship between state and civil society — between the two notional indices, the 'weight of the state' and the 'density' of society — is not necessarily a zero-sum game.[50] If it were, we would have to conclude that civil society has experienced a global decline throughout most of the twentieth century and, within the capitalist world, probably reached its nadir in social-democratic Scandinavia. This is scarcely credible. Save in extreme cases, such as Stalin's Russia, the state does not necessarily 'squeeze out' civil society, in the way that some economists believe that public investment squeezes out private. Some states exist in mutual synergy with civil society. The successful state draws strength from a dense civil society (in Michael Mann's terminology, the state acquires 'infrastructural power');[51] dense civil society benefits from the existence of a functioning state (in Tarrow's words: 'it was the expansion and consolidation of the national state which prod-

---

has strongly influenced a later generation of scholars, 'did not succeed in finding [sic] a single, wholly satisfactory conception of "civil society" or the State': Quintin Hoare and Geoffrey Nowell-Smith, 'Introduction', in Antonio Gramsci, *Selections From the Prison Notebooks* (London, 1982), p. 207. Rockwell, 'Schools of the Revolution', p. 171, sees 'civil society' as being 'formed by the historically constituted relationships which make public, collective action possible'.

[47] Usually to the effect that Mexico has historically languished under authoritarian regimes (Aztec, Spanish and national), hence the majority of Mexicans suffer from 'Indian-Spanish inertia' and the country consequently lacks a strong, dense, efficacious civil society: for example, Octavio Paz, *The Labyrinth of Solitude. Life and Thought in Mexico*, transl., Lysander Kemp (New York, 1961,), pp. 11–12, 127.

[48] E.g., Robert Putnam, 'Bowling Alone: America's Declining Social Capital,' *Journal of Democracy*, vol. 6 (1993), pp. 65–78.

[49] Carlos Forment, work in progress, Princeton University; in particular, see Forment's chapter in Miguel Angel Centeno and Fernando López-Alves (eds.), *The Other Mirror*.

[50] Sidney Tarrow, *Power in Movement. Social Movements, Collective Action and Politics* (Cambridge, 1994), pp. 62–3.

[51] Michael Mann, *States, War, and Capitalism* (Oxford, 1992), pp. 1–11, which contrasts 'infrastructural' with 'despotic' power; however the same author's *The Sources of Social Power* (Cambridge, 1986), pp. 6–10, offers a more complex (and, to my mind, more opaque) typology.

ded the social movement into existence').[52] Thus, in Mexico, the Federal school — an agency of the state — sometimes successfully fostered sociability, consciousness, organisation and mobilisation among local communities.[53]

Conversely, state and civil society may share a common condition of weakness or anomie: for example, in frontier regions where a predatory 'state of nature' prevails (Amazonia, the Putumayo, the Selva Lacandona). Take those two old Mexican protagonists, the Catholic Church and the secular state. Sometimes, their relationship has a zero-sum quality. In post-revolutionary Jalisco, especially Los Altos, the strength of the Church implied a corresponding repudiation of the state; so, too, in parts of Puebla, state educational initiatives were regarded as 'satanic' in inspiration.[54] Meanwhile, in new communities, produced by the market and migration, where Church and tradition were weak, state agencies, like the school, afforded basic organisation and social cohesion: for example, along the left bank of the Yaqui Valley in Sonora.[55] In contrast, there were regions where Church and state shared a *common* condition of marginality: in the Porfirian northern borderlands, where communities like Tomóchic rejected Church and state alike, or, at the other end of Mexico, in revolutionary Quintana Roo, where 'tribal' communities similarly spurned both authorities.[56] More generally, it seems, Mexican cities have accepted the authority of *both* Church and state to a greater degree than Mexican villages; the latter, possessed of their own rooted customs and practices, may be resistant to both macro-institutions, to both carriers of the Great Tradition.[57] There is evidence, too, that in recent years Church and state have penetrated marginal zones in tandem, rather than in zero-sum competition.[58]

Church and state offer a particularly good example of the multiple interactions — from zero-sum to mutually reinforcing — which link the state and (parts of) civil society; not least because they tend to define themselves dis-

---

[52] Tarrow, *Power in Movement*, p. 65.

[53] Vaughan, *Cultural Politics*, pp. 178–9; Rockwell, 'Schools of the Revolution', p. 201; Simpson, *The Ejido*, pp. 107–8.

[54] Jean Meyer, *La cristiada* (Mexico City, 1973–74), t.1, *La guerra de los cristeros*, pp. 169–81; t. 3, *Los Cristeros*, pp. 162–72; Vaughan, *Cultural Politics*, p. 67.

[55] Vaughan, *Cultural Politics*, pp. 169, 178–9, 187.

[56] Paul Vanderwood, *The Power of God against the Guns of Government* (Stanford, 1998), chs. 3, 4; Robert Redfield, *The Folk Culture of Yucatan* (Chicago, 1941), pp. 101–2.

[57] I base this on the admittedly slim — but quantitative — evidence that church and civil marriages have tended to be more common in the city than the countryside, where free unions have been more common: Whetten, *Rural Mexico*, p. 375.

[58] Frank Cancian, *The Decline of Community in Zinacantán* (Stanford, 1992), pp. 108–13, notes the parallel growth of civil and religious offices/institutions at Nachig (Chiapas) in the late 1960s and 1970s.

tinctly, even antagonistically, and, as the institutions of civil society go, the Church is relatively clear and visible. In other cases, such interactions are harder to fathom.[59] If calibrating the state is tricky, the measurement of 'civil society' is difficult, at times impossible. Since the associations of civil society are by definition voluntarist, their economic presence is shadowy: their members may pay dues, but they do not (usually) receive salaries. The Church does not show up in figures of national acounts — indeed, in Mexico the Church has no juridical presence. *Cofradía* expenses can be calculated, in some particular cases,[60] but no national accounting is possible. Calibration of civil society would therefore have to involve head-counting, rather than monetary reckoning, but this, too, is tricky. The great mass organisations of twentieth-century Mexico — CROM, CTM, CNC, PNR/PRM/PRI — recalcitrantly resist weighing. Their numbers, we have seen, are subject to wild inflation; furthermore, even if we could agree on deflated figures, we would fool ourselves if we thought we were weighing genuine, autonomous mass organisations. For the cited organisations are closely tied to the apron-strings of the state, hence their very status as indices of the density of civil society is doubtful.

There is, too, a more basic problem with headcounting. A host of formally assembled individuals hardly constitutes a dense civil society (recall Marx's description of the French peasants as a sack of potatoes: whatever the historical truth of the remark, the image suggests that a collection of homologous units, grouped under a common rubric, may enjoy scant cohesion or solidarity). Since the notion of a vigorous civil society implies dense, closely-woven relationships between citizens, not a simple accumulation of individuals, it is presumably *relationships-within-society* that we should be counting — transactions rather than units, synapses rather than neurons. But, methodologically, where would we begin? We can calibrate the growth of, say, postal services, telegraphs or telephones.[61] But there are several problems with this approach. First, do, say, telephones indicate a dense civil society or an atomised one? Second, do they actually function? This is a twofold question: (a) 'do they work?' (San José, de Gracia's telephone line, installed in 1935, suffered from 'continual break-

---

59 For example, the interaction between 'state' and 'market' which, as noted above (see fn. 39), may not be mutually supportive and may even constitute a zero-sum game.

60 Cancian, *Decline of Community*, pp. 172–5.

61 E.g., ratio of population to telephones:

	Mexico	Cuba	Argentina
1913	362	153	106
1930	173	59	–
1940	109	77	–
1950	90	52	21

Source: B.R. Mitchell, *International Historical Statistics. The Americas and Australasia* (Detroit, 1983), pp. 746–51.

downs')';[62] and (b) 'do they actually serve to integrate people?' (in Mitla, about the same time, there was 'a telephone which rings quite often but to which nobody pays attention').[63] And, thirdly, to what extent are these new means of communication serving the state, rather than civil society?[64]

Even if it were possible to establish the density of civil society and the cohesion of its constituent networks, it would still necessary to take into account: (i) the units of society under consideration (that is, the level at which 'density' or 'cohesion' is measured); (ii) the rationale of these units — what makes them tick; and (iii) the implications of (i) and (ii) for state-society relations. These questions, even if they cannot be answered, merit some brief consideration.

First, we have noted that many Mexican communities were — for good historical reasons — hostile to state interference. Yet outward hostility was quite compatible with inward cohesion; indeed, there may well be a positive correlation between these two attributes. The classic 'closed corporate peasant community' enjoyed a high level of internal cohesion, while displaying a diffident — 'inhospitable, unsociable and suspicious' — face to the outside world.[65] The Mexican village, Whetten observed in the 1940s, 'facilitates informal gatherings, such as the play group among children, visiting among adults and mutual aid in times of trouble, sorrow or great need'.[66] Such demonstrations of mutual support and sociability were not confined to 'traditional' or Indian nucleated settlements; they were also to be found in more scattered *ranchero* and mestizo communities — which could present similarly a hostile face to the outside world.[67] If the unit of analysis is the rural community, therefore, a dense civil society may well imply a host of locally circumscribed, introverted and politically indigestible lumps within national society.

---

[62] González, *Pueblo en vilo*, p. 185. Likewise Oscar Lewis, *Life in a Mexican Village. Tepoztlán Restudied* (Urbana, 1963), p. 35: 'Tepoztl n has had a telephone and a telegraph service since before the Revolution but the lines have rarely functioned'.

[63] Parsons, *Mitla*, p. 171.

[64] It is worth noting that in the 1940s over half of Mexican telephones (55 per cent) were to be found in the DF, where the telephone-to-population ratio stood at 17.8, compared to the national average of 109; the ratio for the state of Guerrero was 9,772: Whetten, *Rural Mexico*, pp. 301, 608. Tepoztlán's phone, repaired in the 1930s, was chiefly used 'for official business' until, following the opening of a bus service to Cuernavaca, demand — presumably spurred by commerce — began to increase: Lewis, *Life in a Mexican Village*, p. 35.

[65] Simpson, *The Ejido*, p. 247, citing an educational inspector's report from the 1920s. The 'closed corporate peasant community' is, of course, a disputed concept (even Eric Wolf, its intellectual parent, sought to qualify some of its cruder applications). However, there is something to the concept; and part of that something is a Janus tendency, implying a measure of inward cohesion (hence a dense micro-civil society?) and outward alienation (hence a fragmented macro-civil society?).

[66] Whetten, *Rural Mexico*, p. 47.

[67] On *ranchero* collective work and reciprocity: Loyo, *Los Maestros*, vol. IV, p. 45; and introversion: González, *Pueblo en vilo*, p. 135.

Second, the rationale of these 'lumps' bears consideration. It is a common assumption — deriving from Tocqueville — that a rich or healthy civil society embodies a large number of voluntary, non-state organisations; that such organisations positively offset the centralising ambitions of the state; and that, in consequence, they may be conducive to democracy.[68] In other words, a dense civil society makes for — that is, favours the establishment and maintenance of — a legitimate democratic state. But this overlooks cases, not difficult to find, in which voluntary associations, the building blocks of civil society, are authoritarian, undemocratic or patriarchal; and in which voluntary associations derive their strength from their members' deep antipathy to other voluntary associations. In other words, a 'dense' civil society may be populated by organisations indifferent or downright hostile to democracy; and it may also be riven by feuds and factions, by class, ethnic and ideological divisions. Mexican communities have frequently been so riven. The permutations of factionalism are numerous: political/clientelist factions (ins against outs); cultural/ideological factions (*tontos* against *correctos*, Catholics against anticlericals, *mochos* against *ateos*, *hombres de palabras* against *hombres de pistola*);[69] class factions (*ricos* against *agraristas*, 'sandal' against 'shoe', *La Seda* ['the silk'] against *La Hilacha* ['the rags']);[70] spatial factions (barrio against barrio; the 'centre' against the 'outskirts'; *cabecera* against *sujeto*).[71] A classic form of factional polarisation, which often embodied these elements, while suggesting parallels with, say, France or Spain, was school against church, *maestro* against *cura*, red against black. Such divisions, while they fostered cohesion among the 'in-group', did so precisely by confronting the 'out-group'. Hence cohesion and solidarity at one level generated hostility and dissension at another. In addition, many of these voluntary organisations have been deeply authoritarian and most are patriarchal. Popular leftist organisations — *agrarista* groups and *sindicatos* — are no exceptions: Paul Friedrich's 'Princes of Naranja' are quintessentially tough, ruthless, macho and male-chauvinist.[72]

---

[68] For example, Huber, 'Assessments of State Strength', p. 174, states: 'the existence of a dense civil society with autonomous organisations of subordinate classes increases the chances that democracy will be installed and consolidated'. However, this may well be a distortion of, or departure from, Tocqueville's own thought; for Tocqueville was no 'ardent advocate' of democracy; and he valued intermediary societal organisations precisely as checks on centralised government, democratic government included: Jack Lively, *The Social and Political Thought of Alexis de Tocqueville* (Oxford, 1965), p. 104ff.

[69] Lewis, *Life in a Mexican Village*, p. 430 (*tontos*); Manuel Jiménez Castillo, *Huáncito. Organización y práctica política* (Mexico City, 1985), p. 144 (*ateos*); Vaughan, *Cultural Politics*, p. 121, (*hombres de palabras*, referring to Zacapoaxtla).

[70] Simpson, *The Ejido*, ch. 20 (*ricos*); Guillermo Ramos Arizpe and Santiago Rueda Smithers, *Jiquilpan, 1895–1920* (Jiquilpan, 1984), p. 328 (*la Seda*).

[71] Oscar Lewis, *Pedro Martínez* (London, 1969), pp. 52 ('centre'), 188 (sandal); Parsons, *Mitla*, p. 4, Zárate, *Procesos de identidad*, p. 138 (*barrios*).

[72] Paul Friedrich, *The Princes of Naranja* (Austin, 1986).

What does this imply for state-civil society relations? The existence of a dense but authoritarian civil society does not necessarily undermine 'the state' (indeed, it may bolster an authoritarian state); it simply impedes the formation of a particular kind of state or regime, namely the democratic, consensual and inclusionary kind which is nowadays seen as normatively preferable and, perhaps, more conducive to legitimacy. Irrespective of regime type, however, the existence of chronic factionalism in civil society is likely to weaken the state, except — and this is a key qualifier — to the extent that the state capitalises on such divisions, according to the principle of *divide et impera*. Such a perspective on civil society therefore raises two quite different analytical alternatives: first, a state based on and bolstered by a dense, 'synergetic' civil society (the supposed Tocquevillean norm); and, second, a state which, unable or unwilling to achieve such a relationship, foments divisions, capitalises on factionalism, marginalises some groups and favours others.[73] Colonial models — which raised *divide et impera* to an art of government — spring to mind. We could call the first the consensual/inclusionary model, the second the colonial/exclusionary model. Both can generate stable governance; and they can co-exist within the same body politic. Indeed, Mexico typically contains both elements; and the longevity of the regime since the Revolution depends not only on successful integration of 'society' into the state, but also on 'successful' marginalisation, exclusion and the manipulation of factionalism. Thus, state survival — though not necessarily state efficacy — may involve juggling these contrasting relationships with civil society: one that is consensual/inclusionary and another that is colonial/exclusionary. Several analytical conclusions flow from this: we are dealing with a schizoid state, not one displaying seamless homogeneity;[74] it is a state which defies neat definition (democratic, authoritarian, etc.);[75] and it is not amenable to analysis couched in terms of a single definable 'political culture'.

State, Economy and Infrastructure

A second relationship is also worth exploring and, if possible, measuring: the relationship of the state to the economy. States depend on communications, military power and the extraction of resources, especially in the form of taxa-

---

[73] Oral testimony from Tepalcingo, Morelos, suggests three principal mechanisms whereby the PRI (i.e., the regime) has maintained control: deterring opposition parties; offering certain material benefits; and 'encouraging disunity, keeping up the confrontation between the two main factions (centre and outskirts)': Elena Azaola Garrido and Esteban Krotz, *Los campesinos de la tierra de Zapata* (Mexico City, 1976), t. III, *Política y conflicto*, p. 146.

[74] Alan Knight, 'México bronco, México manso: una reflexión sobre la cultura cívica mexicana', *Política y gobierno*, III/i (1996), pp. 5–30.

[75] Mexico has regularly perplexed political scientists who favour a dichotomous approach to democracy and authoritarianism; hence their recurrent use of 'semi', 'quasi' and other qualifiers: Samuel P. Huntington, *The Third Wave. Democratization in the Late Twentieth Century* (Norman, OK, 1991), pp. 48, 76, 120, 275, 282.

tion.[76] It is usually supposed that the speed and reliability of communications enhance state power.[77] In Mexico's case, the establishment of a railway and telegraph system conferred advantages on the Porfirian state which its predecessors had lacked.[78] Railways also benefited the state militarily and materially. Trains could shift troops — including artillery and machine guns — in greater numbers at greater speed, facilitating counter-insurgency campaigns against political rebels and peripheral Indian groups — the campaigns in which the generals of the Porfirian army won their laurels and made their names. As Díaz put it: 'the steel of the rails would complete the task begun by the steel of bayonets: national unity'.[79] Trains also made possible the Porfirian export boom, which the state tapped to its own advantage, raising taxes and deploying new forms of economic patronage.[80] The state's triumph over every rebellion for 35 years bred a climate of complacency which, by 1910, was shared by most informed observers of Mexico.

The Revolution did not disprove the state-building potential of railways, telegraphs, artillery and machine guns. True, remote guerrilla *focos*, sustained by genuine local support, could not be easily snuffed out, especially as their number multiplied in 1910–11. But when the tyro rebels tried their hand at conventional warfare, they proved vulnerable (as at Casas Grandes in February 1911).[81] The compromise peace of 1911 — in part a product of this military stalemate — postponed the issue to 1913–14, when the northern armies — and even to a degree Zapata's more unconventional forces — had to make the painful and costly transition to conventional warfare.[82] Guerrilla campaigns gave way to pitched battles — if the Revolution was to defeat the old regime. Eventually, therefore, Villa's Division del Norte turned the state's advantages against itself: Villa won control of the northern railroads, exported raw materi-

---

[76] The British case has been well studied: John Brewer, *The Sinews of Power: War, Money and the English State, 1688–1783* (New York, 1989); Mann, *States, War and Capitalism*, ch. 3.

[77] In Mann's chosen terminology: 'logisitical penetration of territory has increased exponentially [sic] over the past century and a half'. *States, War and Capitalism*, p. 24; Anthony Giddens, *The Nation-State and Violence* (Berkeley, 1987), p. 172 ff., sees this as a process of 'time-space convergence'.

[78] In 1877 Mexico had only 570 km of railway track, compared to Argentina's 2,262, Peru's 2,030 and Chile's 1,624; by 1910 Mexico, with 20,000km, was second only to Argentina: Paolo Riguzzi, 'Los caminos del atraso: tecnología, instituciones e inversión en los ferrocarriles mexicanos, 1850–1900', in Sandra Kunz Ficker and Paolo Riguzzi (coords.), *Ferrocarriles y vida económica en México (1850–1950)* (Mexico City, 1996), pp. 31–3.

[79] Riguzzi, 'Los caminos del atraso', p. 62.

[80] John H. Coatsworth, *Growth Against Development. The Economic Impact of Railroads in Porfirian Mexico* (DeKalb, IL, 1981) remains the best overview, although some of the (economic) findings are queried by Kunz Ficker and Riguzzi, *Ferrocarriles*.

[81] Alan Knight, *The Mexican Revolution*, 2 vols. (Cambridge, 1986), vol. I, p. 187.

[82] Knight, *Mexican Revolution*, vol. I, p. 228; vol. II, pp. 41–2, 141–2, 149–50.

als in bulk to the USA and imported the guns and ammunition with which he fought and won the decisive battle of Torreón in April 1914.[83] Obregón did likewise, if less spectacularly, on the west coast. These were the last examples of local forces, created from the bottom up, making a successful transition to conventional warfare. Subsequent rebellions either pitted rival conventional armies against each other (the battles of the Bajío in 1915, the Agua Prieta and De la Huerta rebellions of 1920 and 1923–24) or they involved the federal (conventional) army fighting localised guerrillas (Cristeros in the 1920s and 1930s; the radical guerrillas of the 1960s; today's EZLN and ERP).

Meanwhile, the technological quality of guerrilla warfare changed. Although the pioneer insurgents of 1910 were often poorly armed, they were not hugely disadvantaged when it came to backwoods skirmishing with the federal army. They could ride and shoot — sometimes better than their regular army opponents, who found themselves fighting in a strange land against an elusive enemy. This — we could call it the Boer War syndrome — characterised the campaign against the Tomochic rebels in 1891, many of the early skirmishes of the Revolution and much of the Cristero War.[84] Time and technology eroded this rough equality. While railways stopped at the railheads (and cautious Federal commanders, fearful of a bullet in the back, often stopped there too), roads were eventually cut through the backwoods, making possible the entry of military trucks, even tanks.[85] Air power, which had been hazarded to little effect during the Revolution, became more significant during and after the 1920s: planes were used to crush the Cristeros and helped to end the age-old insurrection of the Yaquis in 1926.[86] Though roads and air power (including helicopters), coupled with radio, have not eliminated the possibility of guerrilla rebellion, they make such rebellion riskier. It is not military inadequacy so much as political calculation which prevents the Mexican army from marching on the last Zapatista redoubts in Chiapas.

---

[83] Knight, *Mexican Revolution*, vol. II, pp. 141–4; Friedrich Katz, *The Life and Times of Pancho Villa* (Stanford, 1998), pp. 306–7.

[84] Vanderwood, *The Power of God*; Knight, *Mexican Revolution*, vol. I, pp. 175–83, and vol. II, p. 147 (noting Obregón's interest in the Boer War). Jean Meyer, *La cristiada*, t. 1, *La guerra de los cristeros*, pp. 279–80, comments on 'the tactical superiority of the Cristeros, with their scant munitions, over numerous, well-armed troops of the line'.

[85] Railways could be easily targeted by insurgents, who blew up bridges (and sometimes entire trains): Meyer, *La cristiada*, v. I, pp. 279–80; John Womack Jr., *Zapata and the Mexican Revolution* (New York, 1969), pp. 269–70. Hence governments — like Huerta's — adopted Boer-war-style countermeasures: building blockhouses, cutting back vegetation alongside the track or simply shooting suspicious people seen in the vicinity of the line: Knight, *Mexican Revolution*, vol. II, p. 361.

[86] David C. Bailey, *Viva Cristo Rey! The Cristero Rebellion and the Church-State Conflict in Mexico* (Austin, 1974), p. 237; Adrian Bantjes, *As If Jesus Walked on Earth. Cardenismo, Sonora and the Mexican Revolution* (Wilmington, 1998), p. 37.

Improved communications thus favoured the state in military terms. Did they also strengthen the state politically? It depends what sort of 'strength' is at issue. The capacity to exert force was clearly enhanced: more people could be more easily and rapidly intimidated. Thanks to the telegraph and telephone, orders could be despatched more expeditiously.[87] But it does not follow that those orders were more expeditiously carried out; the old practice of *obedezco pero no cumplo* ('I obey but do not carry out') did not die with the colony (as I note below). Furthermore, if 'strength' is equated with, or inferred from, 'longevity' or 'durability', then the effect of improved communications would seem to be ambivalent. A glance at other Latin American states does not suggest a clear correlation between logistical integration and political stability (stability being defined in terms of regime survival and the absence of violent protest/revolt/coup). One obvious problem is that logistical integration makes military takeovers easier. While the military remains loyal, integration may redound to the advantage of the (civilian) state; when the military is disloyal, integration may become a liability. Military coups have occurred in South America's most developed and integrated states: Chile, Argentina and Uruguay. What is more, in certain circumstances, popular insurrections can — following the cited precedent of Villa's División del Norte — take advantage of logistical integration. The Cuba in which Castro and the 26th of July Movement seized power was relatively developed and integrated; the Bolivian Revolution — in its short, sharp, insurrectionary form — depended on the urban centres and transport links generated by the mining industry. Integrated systems, therefore, are hostages to fortune: while they generally favour central governments — and probably make old-style regional rebellions, the classic *cuartelazos* and peasant insurrections of the nineteenth century, harder to mount — they are capable of being captured by 'modern' insurgents, especially the military. This may help explain why military governments — of the 'bureaucratic-authoritarian' kind — reached their peak in the third quarter of the twentieth century, and in relatively 'developed' countries. Mexico, of course, slimmed its military establishment dramatically during the 1920s and 1930s and, as a result, the civil government could enjoy some of the benefits of integration without fearing praetorian intervention.

Systems of integration also affect society at large. The railways not only bolstered solvent government; they also differentially affected regions, while knit-

---

[87] Political leaders also enjoyed a new mobility: Calles received prominent visitors to his Sonoran retreat, who arrived via a local airstrip; Governor Tomás Garrido Canabal flew to, from and around Tabasco in a striking red and black plane ('El Guacamayo': 'the macaw'); Cárdenas, as PNR presidential candidate, winged into Tabasco in a trimotor airplane. Convenience aside, this resort to the air was also, I think, an affirmation of the power of science and technology (back in 1911, Madero had been ridiculed by the press for taking a flight in a biplane). But it also carried risks: Cárdenas' chief rival for power in the state of Michoacan, Benigno Serrato, was conveniently removed by a fatal airplane crash in December 1934, the day after Cárdenas took office as president.

ting all regions together in a tighter national market. Some towns and regions boomed; in certain cases, new settlements — even entire cities like Torreón — sprang up alongside the tracks or at key railway junctions.[88] Other communities, however, were bypassed by the railways; they suffered economic decline, which in turn generated or aggravated tensions with rival communities.[89] This watershed did not escape popular perception: people talked of the 'time before the railway'.[90] The chief change wrought by the railways was, I think, economic, rather than cultural or psychological. The railways facilitated the movement of goods in bulk, especially for export. Market production grew relative to subsistence production and exports grew relative to GDP.[91] Passenger traffic was less significant; and we should be careful not to exaggerate the immobility of the Mexican people prior to the railway watershed — when markets, pilgrimages, military campaigns and seasonal labour migration had prompted movement on foot or by mule.[92] Nor should we underestimate the scale of foot-and-burro mobility which necessarily complemented rail transport.[93]

---

[88] Knight, *Mexican Revolution*, vol. I, p. 11; Luis Aboites Aguilar, *Norte precario. Poblamiento y colonización en México (1760–1940)* (Mexico City, 1995), pp. 100–2, 111. For a lesser example, from the other end of Mexico, Redfield, *Folk Culture of Yucatán*, pp. 40, 43 (Dzitas).

[89] Such as Mocorito, Sinaloa, which was 'greatly prejudiced by being left isolated by the railway line': Alfonso Dollero, *México al día* (Mexico City, 1911), p. 386.

[90] Redfield, *Folk Culture of Yucatán*, p. 69.

[91] Coatsworth, *Growth Against Development*; William Summerhill, 'Transport Improvements and Economic Growth in Brazil and Mexico,' in Haber, *How Latin America Fell Behind*, pp. 93–117, which shows that in Brazil, as compared to Mexico, railways did not necessarily favour the foreign over the domestic market.

[92] For example, Redfield, *Folk Culture of Yucatán*, p. 14; and Iwanska, *Purgatory and Utopia*, p. 46, which reports 'emic' corroboration of this fact, i.e., recurrent reminders (to the visiting anthropologist) that 'Mazahuas have been traditionally great travellers'. While hard-and-fast, positivistic measuring would be difficult, further 'anecdotal' exploration of 'pre-industrial' mobility in Mexico might be feasible and rewarding.

[93] The odysseys of *maestros rurales* in the 1930s have been mentioned (fn. 37); these were exacerbated by the sheer frequency of moves from school to school ('another sad leave-taking and more wandering throgh the villages and hamlets of ... Michoacan', as one recalled: Loyo, *Los Maestros*, t. I, p. 69). Daily treks — on foot — were also a feature of popular life long after the onset of the railways: take the case of Doña Zeferina, who in the 1930s would, every week, carry 300 eggs from Hueyapan to Atlixco, returning the next day (a round trip of some 19 hours); round trips were also made to Yecapistla and Ocuituco, making a total of some 39 hours on the road, per week: see Judith Friedlander, 'Doña Zeferino Barreto: Biographical Sketch of an Indian Woman from the State of Morelos', in Heather Fowler-Salamini and Mary Kay Vaughan (eds.), *Women of the Mexican Countryside, 1850–1990* (Tucson, 1994), p. 139.

However, economic integration certainly favoured central government in several respects: it boosted revenue and gave government new powers of logistical control and economic patronage. Favoured regions, communities and interests benefited from infrastructural investment (railways, ports, telegraphs); within an integrated market, the award of concessions and allocation of tariffs counted for more. Díaz's authority depended in good measure on the manipulation of such economic patronage.[94] But, again, this was not a one-way street. Market integration, we have seen, generated inter-regional tensions — and, often, provincial resentment against 'the centre'. During the *Porfiriato*, as during the late colony, prospering provincial bourgeoisies chafed at the impositions of the 'centre'; a richer, denser civil society, while it might yield more tax revenue, might also generate more political dissent.

Such tensions did not end with the Revolution; sometimes, indeed, they were exacerbated by the aggressive revolutionary reconstruction which began in the 1920s. From Sonora to Yucatán policies of centralisation and social reform raised provincial bourgeois hackles.[95] In Jalisco, the old antipathy to Mexico City was exacerbated by Callista centralisation and anticlericalism; in Nuevo León the Monterrey group successfully resisted the authority of Cárdenas and the Confederación de Trabajadores de México (CTM); in Puebla, Cárdenas had to defer to the Avila Camacho clan and their conservative allies, such as William Jenkins.[96] The processes of economic integration did not, therefore, uniformly favour the central state. Sometimes, in fact, these processes bolstered provincial power and bourgeois resistance. And provincial elites were quite capable of turning the new means of communication and control to their own advantage; the central government did not enjoy a monopoly of modernity. Provincial elites sponsored or suborned the press, patronised mass organisations — such as state labour confederations — in opposition to those of the centre, and even wove their own webs of ideological hegemony.[97] Ostensibly centralising agencies — the party, the Federal bureaucracy — were successfully colonised by provincial bourgeois interests. Popular interests could play the same game: that is, they played

---

[94] Knight, *Mexican Revolution*, vol. I, pp. 19–22, 28; François-Xavier Guerra, *Le Mexique de l'ancien régime à la Révolution* (Paris, 1985, 2 vols.), vol. I, pp. 214–16.

[95] Bantjes, *As If Jesus Walked on Earth* (Sonora); Ben Fallaw, *Cárdenas Compromised: The Failure of Reform in Postrevolutionary Yucatán, Mexico, 1934–40* (Durham, NC, 2001).

[96] Alex Saragoza, *The Monterrey Elite and the Mexican State, 1880–1940* (Austin, 1988), ch. 8; Wil G. Pansters, *Power and Politics in Puebla. The Political History of a Mexican State, 1937–87* (Amsterdam, 1990). There is, to my knowledge, no general study of politics and state-centre relations dealing with Jalisco: a major and inexplicable gap.

[97] The best, but by no means the sole, example, would be Monterrey: Saragoza, *The Monterey Elite*, pp. 102, 141, 146, 167 (the press); pp. 129–30, 182ff (labour); and pp. 143–5, 180 (hegemony/discourse); see also Pansters, *Politics and Power*, and Bantjes, *As If Jesus Walked on Earth*, especially ch. 7 (labour).

federal agencies off against each other, manipulated federal resources to their own advantage and thereby managed to maintain a measure of autonomy.[98]

The story was not, therefore, one of inexorable centralisation. Processes of economic change could enhance provincial as well as central power. The relations between these — grandly reified — entities was fluid and contingent. A great deal depended on the policies and projects of the central government. During the 1920s and 1930s (years of reform and innovation, especially at the Federal level) centre-periphery tensions ran high; provincial elites resisted what they saw as an alien radicalism; while popular interests sought the patronage of a sympathetic 'centre'. After 1940 such tensions diminished. But their diminution reflected not the definitive triumph of the central government, as often supposed, but rather the establishment of a new modus vivendi between centre and periphery, involving mutual collaboration between the state and the bourgeoisie, both provincial and metropolitan. The Mexico-Puebla axis — exemplified by two poblano presidents, Avila Camacho and Díaz Ordaz — was a classic instance.[99] Meantime, popular interests came to regard the centre as a source less of patronage and support than of control and repression

An important and neglected aspect of this process of ambiguous centralisation is road-building. Historians have dedicated a good deal of time and energy to the railroad revolution of the late nineteenth century, particularly its economic impact. Roads, in contrast, have been bypassed.[100] This, no doubt, reflects the long time-lag associated with archival research; but it also derives, I suspect, from the fact that, while railway-building was a massive centralised operation, road-building — and its necessary corollary, the development of road transport (cars, buses and trucks) — tended to be a more messy, decentralised, piecemeal process. Thus, the railway system depended on huge government subsidies; came under close government regulation (well before the Revolution); produced a powerful centralised sindicato; and provided the central

---

[98]   Friedrich, *Princes of Naranja*, is a classic study of the general phenomenon of (popular/populist) *caciquismo*; on which see also Alan Knight, 'Caciquismo and Political Culture in Mexico,' paper given at the conference on Mexican Political Culture, Center for US–Mexican Studies, UCSD, April 1998 (publication forthcoming in volume edited by Eric Van Young). *Caciquismo* may not be the only vehicle for such local, popular appropriation of federal resources (the 'new social movements' are also candidates); but, over time, it has probably been the most common.

[99]   Pansters, *Politics and Power*.

[100]   It is not overly fussy or linguistic-philosophical to note that the very idea of 'a road' is quite tricky: whereas railway lines are clearly definable and measurable, in terms of both time and space, roads have existed since before the Conquest and come in varied forms, from rutted mule tracks through (intermittently) viable dirt roads to tarmacked highways. Hence measuring the extent and impact of 'roads' is far from straightforward. See, for example, David Skerritt, 'El ranchero: génesis y consolidación', in Esteban Barragán López et al. (coords.), *Rancheros y sociedades rancheras* (Zamora, 1994), p. 143.

government — especially the Ministry of Communications and Public Works (SCOP) — with a capacious porkbarrel of patronage as well as a wide network of spies and informers.[101] Of course, central government initiatives were crucial in developing Mexico's road system, beginning in the 1920s and gathering speed in the 1930s and 1940s, during which time railway-building stagnated.[102] The railway revolution now gave way to the automobile revolution, particularly the bus revolution.[103] Mexicans became 'Ford-conscious'; villagers, perhaps for the first time, resorted to wheeled vehicles; they also began to carve *huaraches* from car tyres and to convert old Ford engines to power corn mills.[104] Buses soon began to play a part in political mobilisation: elections, rallies, demonstrations.

Roads completed the pioneering economic integration undertaken by the railways; if the rail lines were, in a sense, the principal arteries, the roads supplied the dense capillaries. In terms of narrow, military control, roads (coupled with the mechanisation of the army) extended the reach of government forces, facilitating cental control; for this reason, some communities and caciques strenuously resisted road access.[105] Certainly, the new road network, like the old rail network, favoured some communities at the expense of others.[106] But resistance to the tidal

---

[101] The information-gathering role of railway employees is clearly evident in the papers of Francisco Múgica, minister of communications and public works under Cárdenas, which are held at the Centro de Estudios de la Revolución Mexicana 'Lázaro Cárdenas', Jiquilpan, Michoacan.

[102] The railways took 60% of public investment in 1926, 20% in 1950; however, throughout the period, the system lacked investment in line and rolling stock, hence suffering what Kuntz Ficker and Riguzzi call a 'premature block'. Track increased from approximately 20,000 km in 1910 to 23,000 in 1950; however, only 600 of those new kilometres were within the (publicly-controlled/owned) Ferrocarriles Nacionales: Kuntz Ficker and Riguzzo, *Ferrocarriles y vida económica*, pp. 292–3, 300–1.

[103] Parsons, *Mitla*, p. 50, suggests that the automobile revolution may have been accelerated by the heavy loss of horses and burros during the Revolution. Mitchell, *Historical Statistics*, p. 716 gives figures of vehicles which show a steady (per capita) increase and, more interestingly, a shift in favour of commercial vehicles over private cars through the first generation (1920s–50s, as the initial luxury cars are outsold by trucks and buses), followed by a trend back to private cars post-1950s:

	1925	1935	1945	1955	1965	1975
commercial vehicles as a percentage of total	25	32	42	44	35	27

[104] Simpson, *The Ejido*, p. 315; Chase, *Mexico*, pp. 4, 133, 162.

[105] Redfield, *Folk Culture of Yucatán*, pp. 52, 55; Finkler, *Estudio comparativo*, p. 208.

[106] Redfield, *Folk Culture of Yucatán*, p. 37 (Dzitas); Cancian, *Decline of Community*, pp. 101–2, 127, on the impact of roads in Chiapas, hence the intense politicking surrounding road programmes. Another major federal proramme — irrigation — had a similar discriminatory and polarising effect, not only between communities but also within them: for example, employers who feared a rise in wage rates resisted the introduction of irrigation: Finkler, *Estudio comparativo*, p. 208.

force of road transport had a Canute-like quality, since it meant opposing the combined and inexorable force of both state and market. For roads had a decisive effect in deepening markets, including labour markets. Communities remote from railways now had recourse to the bus.[107] Frontier regions, like the Chiapas interior, could be opened up.[108] Nascent *ejidos* found new market outlets and villagers could commute en masse into neighbouring towns.[109] As one prosperous *ejidatario*, the beneficiary of a new (1954) road, panegyrised: 'today we live in glory. In the past, life was impossible, until they built the roads. Once the road was built, there was progress; without roads there is none.'[110] Speed and flexibility of transport meant that producers could better maximise profits; rich merchants could buy in bulk and undercut their lesser competitors.[111] Road-building and bus-driving created new jobs and new sources of patronage.[112] Income and, perhaps, horizons expanded. By the 1980s, as road-building and commerce transformed Chiapas, a muleteer-turned road-builder and construction-worker, could opt to take a bus from Tuxtla to Villahermosa to have his teeth fixed.[113]

   In some respects, therefore, the road did for the postrevolutionary *ejido, rancho* and 'smallholding' what the railway had done for the Porfirian hacienda. Like the railways, roads also generated new interests and local (as opposed to provincial) power-holders, who could obstruct as well as bolster the state. They could also stimulate change, conflict and instability. Coffee production in Oaxaca and the Huasteca created small fortunes, generated land disputes and provoked factional violence.[114] New local elites — commercial and political — came to power:

---

[107] Lewis, *Life in a Mexican Village*, p. 35; González, *Pueblo en vilo*, pp. 206–7, which again reminds us that road-building, like cathedral construction, can be a long intermittent business; hence precise dates of completion may prove elusive.

[108] See Thomas Benjamin, *A Rich Land, A Poor People. Politics and Society in Modern Chiapas* (Albuquerque, 1989), pp. 165–6, 181, 183–4, 227–8. Every governor of Chiapas from the 1920s to the present — including radicals like Vidal (1925–27) and conservatives like Grajales (1933–36) — appears to have given a high priority to road-building: economic and strategic considerations have conspired with the quest for political legitimacy and, perhaps not least important, the provision of patronage. Chiapas' roads thus neatly embody the four rationales of state action outlined in the conclusion (pp. 21–2).

[109] Simpson, *The Ejido*, pp. 314–15.

[110] Finkler, *Estudio comparativo*, p. 150.

[111] Parsons, *Mitla*, p. 403; Azaola Garrido y Krotz, *Los campesinos*, pp. 134–5.

[112] González, *Pueblo en vilo*, pp. 206–7; US Consul Goforth, Matamoros, to State Department, 30 April 1937, US State Deparment Records, RG M 1370, 812.00/Tamps./305, on the multiplier effect of public works, especially roads.

[113] Cancian, *Decline of Community*, p. 62. We can compare this easy mobility with the travails of the itinerant *maestros rurales* of the 1930s (see fn. 37).

[114] James B. Greenberg, *Blood Ties. Life and Violence in Rural Mexico* (Tucson, 1989); Frans J. Schryer, *Ethnicity and Class Conflict in Rural Mexico* (Princeton, 1990), p. 161 ff.

merchants, money-lenders, retailers, bus magnates (Carlos Hank is, of course, the biggest and best example).[115] While the buses ferried voters and demonstrators around, bus magnates acquired a good deal of local and regional clout. In Zinacantan the truckers' faction became a key player in local politics.[116] In a sense, therefore, the road revolution favoured that part of civil society we call the private sector. Government — Porfirian and revolutionary — had closely regulated — and, at times, directly managed — Mexico's railways. But road transport fell into the domain of private enterprise.[117] Furthermore, while the railwaymen's union was a bastion of independent organised labour (which the government chose to break in 1948), road transport was comparatively weakly unionised. In crudely schematic terms, the railway era (c. 1880–1920) bolstered government, the era of road transport (post-1940) favoured the private sector.

There is a possible parallel here with what some people may wish to call 'symbolic' — as opposed to 'material' — communication. If trains and trucks were alternative means of shifting goods and people, newspapers, film and radio were alternative ways of shifting ideas and information. Again there is a watershed during the postrevolutionary period. The mass circulation press took off during the *Porfiriato* and grew following the Revolution. Radio appeared in the inter-war period and flourished during and after the 1940s, by which time it was commonplace to see 'radio antennae protruding from makeshift huts' in the Mexicali Valley.[118] The successive generations of the *Porfiriato* and Revolution placed an inordinate faith in the power of the printed word (Vasconcelos' school textbooks were perhaps the extreme case); radicalism and literacy supposedly went hand-in-hand.[119] The Alemanista generation — and its successors — nurtured a more lowbrow faith in radio, film and later television. The older generation, somewhat in the style of the Spanish anarchists, stressed the transforming and emancipatory power of literacy; the younger generation tended to see

---

[115] Roderic Ai Camp, *Mexican Political Biographies, 1935–81* (Tucson, 1982), p. 146 (which, as they say, reveals only the tip of the iceberg). An earlier revolutionary entrepreneur who partly built his fortune on road construction was Juan Andreu Almazean: Saragoza, *The Monterrey Elite*, p. 125.

[116] Cancian, *The Decline of Community*, pp. 88, 128, 138–9; truckers and bus factions also appear in Lewis, *Pedro Martínez*, p. 54 and Finkler, *Estudio comparativo*, p, 184.

[117] Of course, government paid for the roads (until the ill-fated privatisation programme of the 1990s). But the 'rolling stock' was privately-owned; and road construction provided enormous opportunities for the private sector. Furthermore, it was the Mexican private sector which benefited, whereas railway construction had depended heavily on foreign investment.

[118] Whetten, *Rural Mexico*, p. 301.

[119] Simpson, *The Ejido*, p. 108. Alan Knight, 'Popular Culture and the Revolutionary State in Mexico, 1910–40', *Hispanic American Historical Review*, vol. 74, no. 2 (1994), pp. 393–444, ventures some thoughts about the revolutionary cultural project and its impact.

literacy in narrower functional and economic terms (getting city jobs); and when they read for pleasure, they spurned Vasconcelos' classics in favour of comic books (*pepines*).[120]

More specifically, the different media were subject to different degrees and kinds of state control. The Porfirian press was closely, if not always effectively, censored; the loopholes which allowed *Regeneración* or the 'penny press' to circulate were politically significant. The victorious revolutionaries could not impose blanket censorship (although leaders like Carranza certainly tried); instead, they promoted a subtle combination of rewards and sanctions: subsidies, paid advertisements, control of the supply of newsprint, sporadic repression — all of which survived until recent years.[121] The press was not thereby rendered wholly inert or docile. When confronted with a radical president like Cárdenas, the Mexico City press could be outspokenly critical. But criticism from the right was more common and unconstrained than criticism from the left; as a result, given the trend of government policy during the Maximato and again after 1938, relations between the regime and the print media were generally congenial, even incestuous. In the regions, too, political elites exercised substantial control over the provincial press.[122] As a result, the power of the press — and, we may cautiously infer, the power of literacy — did not pose a threat to the regime and tended, perhaps, to enhance state power.

The 'electronic' media — radio, film and televison — were scarcely subversive either. But, like road transport, they represented a bastion of private enterprise, relatively autonomous of state power. Government efforts to enlist radio — by creating government radio stations or broadcasting 'official' programmes (the *horas antialcohólicas* of the 1930s; the *hora nacional* of the post-war period) — were not to conspicuously successful. Listeners preferred *ranchero* ballads and, later, rock music. A comparable trend was evident in the cinema, which began in the late *Porfiriato*, burgeoned in the interwar period and boomed after 1940. State promotion of official, nationalist themes in the 1930s had limited success; meanwhile, Hollywood invaded Mexico technically, commercially and symbolically.[123] Neither radio nor film (nor, later, television) con-

---

[120] Anne Rubenstein, *Bad Language, Naked Ladies, and Other Threats to the Nation* (Durham, NC, 1998), p. 18 ff; Armando Bartra, 'The Seduction of the Innocents: The First Tumultuous Moments of Mass Literacy in Postrevolutionary Mexico', in Joseph and Nugent, *Everyday Forms of State Formation*, pp. 305–6; Oscar Lewis, *Life in a Mexican Village*, p. 40.

[121] Ernest Gruening, *Mexico and its Heritage* (London, 1928), pp. 355–7, 372–4; William A. Orme, Jr., *A Culture of Collusion. An Inside Look at the Mexican Press* (Miami, 1997).

[122] Saragoza, *The Mexican Elite*, pp. 140–1; Bantjes, *As If Jesus Walked on Earth*, pp. 72–3.

[123] Seth Fein, 'Everday Forms of Transnational Collaboration: US Film Propaganda in Cold War Mexico', in Gilbert M. Joseph, Catherine C. LeGrand and Ricardo D. Salvatore, *Close Encounters of Empire. Writing the Cultural History of US–Latin American Relations*

stituted a direct challenge to the power of the state, or of the Partido Revolucionario Institucional (PRI) regime; the state and electronic media established a cosy modus vivendi, which, to a degree, still exists. However, the electronic media were certainly not tools of the state; they were not subject to the same direct influence that the press experienced; they displayed a distinct independence of the official line when it suited them (e.g., film production in the 1930s); and — like the road transport system — they spawned new private sector elites who could, by turns, defy, influence and manipulate state actors. Emilio Azcárraga (senior), doyen of the Monterrey group, began as a humble cigarette and shoe salesman and went on to build an economic empire based on records and radio, which his son, Emilio Junior, parlayed into the massive TV conglomerate, Televisa (ABC, CBS and NBC rolled into one, as it has been called).[124]

Over time, therefore, improvements in material and symbolic communication have — as the early revolutionary leaders hoped — enhanced aspects of state power. But it is arguable that the chief beneficiary, especially since the 1940s, has been the private sector rather than the state. The recent neoliberal turn in economic policy has therefore accelerated, or clarified, a much older trend; while the recent neoliberal revamping of official Mexican discourse — its history and heroes — suggests, again, that the state's role in moulding Mexican minds is somewhat capricious in character and limited in effect. This leads to the final, grand and intractable question: the rationale of the state.

State, Society and Legitimacy

The argument so far strongly suggests that any attempt to analyse state efficacy (power) or state longevity (regime survival and reproduction) rapidly leads to an analysis of state-society relations. This in turn broaches the question of legitimacy — or whatever we wish to call the kind of consensual state-civil society relationship which raises state power above the level of mere coercion. Legitimacy, efficacy and longevity, though analytically separable, are therefore historically bound up with each other. In particular, legitimacy helps explain longevity. Some Latin American states have demonstrably had more muscle than the Mexican (according to the rough statistical criteria already advanced).[125] But they have not displayed the durability of the Mexican state which, as every schoolboy knows, has

---

(Durham, NC, 1998), pp. 400–50. For examples of the early cinema in provincial Mexico: González, *Pueblo en vilo*, p. 185, and Simpson, *The Ejido*, p. 271, which notes, however, that local peasants could not attend the early shows in Actopan and Ixmiquilpan (c. 1933), 'because of their poverty and ... the distance from their houses to the towns mentioned'.

[124] Marjorie Miller and Juanita Darling, 'The Eye of the Tiger: Emilio Azcárraga and the Televisa Empire', in Orme, *Culture of Collusion*, pp. 60, 63.

[125] Roger D. Hansen, *The Politics of Mexican Development* (Baltimore, 1971), gives government revenue as a proportion of GNP (1965) thus: Mexico, 10%; Argentina, 1%; Peru, 2%; Chile, 26%; Brazil, 30%.

experienced no violent change of government (or regime) in nearly 80 years.[126] Thus, however much we may wish to qualify the 'strength' of the Mexican state in terms of its efficacy, there can be little doubt about its 'strength' in terms of longevity, stamina and endurance. Analysis of legitimacy and longevity, it seems to me, demands some consideration of the thrust of state policy. Returning to a previous metaphor: it is not enough to measure the muscle-power (resources, agencies, payroll) of the state; it is also necessary both to evaluate its stamina (its capacity for survival and self-reproduction) and to chart its course (uphill, downhill, round corners, over obstacles). For a state or regime of minimal ambition may survive and reproduce itself over time, where an aggressive state/regime may incur opposition, conflict and collapse. Such an analysis-in-the-round merits a book rather than a chapter. For the sake of concision, I will advance a typology of state action, noting how it may shed light on the Mexican experience in the post-revolutionary period.[127]

First, I would distinguish between state actions which are (a) reflexive and (b) autonomous. For example, if we believe *either* that the Mexican state is a neutral area within which pluralist interests freely compete, *or* that it is a simple agent of dominant class, then we deny the state autonomy and see it as a reflex of society, albeit from contrasting liberal and 'classic Marxist' perspectives. However, if we think that such a perspective is the whole truth, we would be sadly mistaken; the Mexican state certainly possesses a measure of genuine autonomy; it is not simply a reflex of dominant class interests; still less is it a neutral arena.[128] At least some of its muscle (resources, payroll, logistical power or symbolic authority) is dedicated to goals formulated, or at least significantly

---

[126] 'Government', 'regime' and 'state' demand some disaggregation. In descriptive terms, 'government' denotes the incumbent party, faction or leader (hence the last Mexican government to be violently overthrown was Carranza's in 1920). 'Regime' refers to the system whereby governments are chosen and exercise power (democratic, authoritarian, one-party, pluralist, etc.). The Mexican regime changed — violently — between the 1900s and the 1920s and has experienced a progressive but incomplete transformation since the 1980s. The 'state' denotes the broad and enduring apparatus of power: the branches of government, the police and military, the bureaucracy and their related agencies (public enterprises, state schools, official mass organisations). The 1910 Revolution substantially changed 'the state', in terms of personnel, organisation and ethos; however, there is always likely to be some continuity at the level of the state, even when regimes and (of course) governments change. Political stability can be calibrated in respect of each entity; it is clear, however, that since the 1920s Mexico has been unusually stable at all three levels, compared to most of Latin America.

[127] This briefly recapitulates some of: Alan Knight, 'The Modern Mexican State: Theory and Practice', in Centeno and López-Alves (eds.), *The Other Mirror*.

[128] In which respect the Mexican state is, I would argue, like most states. It is the degree and character of 'relative autonomy' which need to be addressed.

determined, by the state rather than by 'societal' forces; goals which go far beyond the maintenance of a free, open, pluralist arena. (In fact, I would go further and suggest that through most of this period no such arena existed and that the state even actively discouraged its emergence). Some degree of state autonomy therefore seems to be an incontrovertible historical fact. But autonomy comes in varied forms. I would distinguish four versions:

[1] State autonomy exerted in defence of national sovereignty within the international state system (let us call this 'Prussian' autonomy).

[2] State autonomy exerted in the pursuit of economic growth, in this case within a capitalist framework, according to the logic of accumulation ('economic' autonomy).

[3] State autonomy exerted in order to promote the legitimacy of the social order (including the state itself); in other words, legitimation ('political' autonomy).

[4] State autonomy which obeys none of these ulterior purposes but which looks to the particularist interests of state incumbents and their cronies: hence, graft, nepotism, rent-seeking (this I shall tendentiously call 'Mafioso' autonomy).[129]

I am not suggesting that any one version captures the totality of the Mexican state which, as I have stressed, is a large, complex and shifting entity, the engagement of which with civil society may take contrasting forms over time and space. Rather, following Haber's injunctions that we should be precise in our terms, I hope to clarify what state action really entails: what higher goals and rationales it pursues; how, in turn, it impacts upon civil society; and what this might mean for state efficacy and longevity.

[1] *Prussian* autonomy is not a key feature of Mexican state action. Wedged between a world superpower (now the sole world superpower) and a string of minor Central American republics, Mexico has no great tradition of regional rivalry or warfare (compare Chile and Argentina). True, Mexico has had to withstand the threat of the United States and there can be no doubt that this inexorable geopolitical logic has influenced Mexican state-building and politics. External pressure did not, however, produce the classic response of military build-up and preparedness: given the imbalance between Mexico and the United States, that would have been futile and probably counterproductive. Rather than adopt, let us say, a stance of 'Polish' defiance vis-à-vis its giant neighbour, Mexico opted for 'Finlandisation'. Even Mexico's forays into Central American politics have been relatively peaceful and modest. Domestically, too, the Mexican military has eschewed a 'Prussian' role: military spending was pro-

---

[129] Tilly (see fn. 17) offers an interesting discussion of the state-as-Mafia. The application of the concept to Mexico is not new: Hansen, *Politics of Mexican Development*, ch. 5 ('cosa nuestra') drew the analogy.

gressively cut back after the Revolution; and popular antipathy to military service — heightened by the Huertista *leva* — prevented the barracks from playing the nation-building role which it has elsewhere performed.[130]

The Mexican state has, however, deployed civilian defences, peaceful manifestations of 'Prussian' autonomy: the active colonisation of the north; the development and integration of the border zone; the promotion of irrigation projects as a means to these ends.[131] Here, it is interesting to note, railroad- and road-building were ambiguous projects; they might respond to certain state objectives (internal policing and economic integration), but they also risked opening Mexico to the predatory power of the USA — a power both military, commercial and cultural. Policy-makers both Porfirian and revolutionary were aware of these risks.[132] But the attractions of building a (northern) transport system outweighed fears that the system would serve as a gringo bridgehead. By the 1930s, as road-building superseded rail-laying, US–Mexican relations had mellowed, and there were few fears that the Panamerican Highway would eventually echo to the rumble of gringo tanks heading south.[133]

A second set of state initiatives were diplomatic: resistance to US pressure; overt protests and discreet lobbying (which long antedated NAFTA); support for principles of non-intervention, such as the Calvo clause and the Carranza doctrine.[134] In this, Mexican governments were both skilful and successful. From Carranza to Salinas Mexican governments deployed their autonomous power (including their considerable discretionary funds) in order to deflect US threats and bend US policy to Mexico's perceived interests. While defence of national sovereignty afforded a justification for the state and, perhaps, contributed to the self-image of the ruling party, (so-called 'patriotic [electoral]

---

[130] Knight, *Mexican Revolution*, vol. I, pp. 18–19, 457–7, vol. II, pp. 78–9, on the leva; Lewis, *Life in a Mexican Village*, pp. 37, 42–3, and Blanca Torres Ramírez, *Historia de la Revolución Mexicana. Periodo 1940–46. México en la segunda guerra mundial* (Mexico City, 1979), pp. 135–6, on popular resistance to wartime conscription. An obvious contrast would be with France: Eugen Weber, *Peasants into Frenchmen. The Modernization of Rural France, 1870–1914* (Stanford, 1976), ch. 17.

[131] Aboites, *Norte precario*, pp. 248–9.

[132] Kuntz and Rigutti, *Ferrocarriles*, pp. 39, 73; Justo Sierra, *The Political Evolution of the Mexican People* (Austin, 1969, transl. Charles Ramsdell), p. 361.

[133] Alan Knight, *US–Mexican Relations, 1910–40: an Interpretation* (La Jolla, 1987), pp. 137–41. This period also saw a significant rise in US tourism to Mexico (evident in US consular reports) and, in the 1940s, a renewed flow of Mexican labour to the USA. The roads made possible this enhanced movement of people (and, in the 1940s, goods); they also encouraged greater economic interdependence and, perhaps, mutual comprehension, thus allaying fears of gringo aggression.

[134] Riguzzi, 'Los caminos del atraso', p. 73; Robert Freeman Smith, *The United States and Revolutionary Nationalism in Mexico, 1916–32* (Chicago, 1972), pp. 82–3.

fraud' was an extreme example of this syndrome), it is difficult to assess how far such defence — conducted by a politico-diplomatic elite, often behind closed doors — played a key role in bolstering or defining the state domestically.[135]

However, the defence of sovereignty also involved a (third) domestic, ideological effort. The Mexican state has a long history of seeking to inculcate national[ist] sentiments among its population. *Forjando patria* responded in part to fears of foreign intervention.[136] The upheaval and associated interventions of the revolutionary period exacerbated these fears and spurred further efforts at state- and nation-building: by means of education, propaganda and political mobilisation (for example, the grand rallies of March 1938, spurred by Cárdenas' expropriation of the Anglo-American oil companies). On the face of it, these efforts seem to have been successful: certainly, notions of Mexican nationhood appear to be fairly well rooted, even though it would be difficult to establish the causality at work.[137] For example, did the oil expropriation *engender* a new nationalism or merely *reflect* existing sentiments? Were the mass rallies of that month triumphs of organisation — and even compulsion — or signs of a new *prise de conscience collective*?[138]

Whatever the causality at work, it is crucial to note that state- and nation-building, though related, are not the same thing. Strictly 'Prussian' state-building implies the strengthening of the state — and of the state's enduring agencies, such as army and bureaucracy — through the pursuance of foreign policy goals. It need not engender broadly-based nationalism (note Bismarck's dislike of Pan-Germanism and preference for a *kleindeutschland*).[139] Nationalism, of

---

[135] Rodolfo A. de la Garza and Jesús Velasco, *Bridging the Border. Transforming Mexico–US Relations* (Lanham, MD, 1997), offers several perspectives on recent Mexican lobbying and politicking in the USA; however the tradition is quite old (Carranza's defence of Mexican sovereignty during the Revolution would be a classic — and successful — example: Knight, *US–Mexican Relations*, pp. 34, 75, 111–14). Sometimes, the defence of Mexican sovereignty responded to domestic motives — playing to the patriotic gallery. But that gallery was less packed and raucous than often imagined (Mexicans were not gullibly anti-American); and it is not clear that short-term political advantage necessarily translated into long-term state-building.

[136] 'The problem of cultural integration ... in Mexico, because of the urgency of its solution and because of the nature of the social forces we must integrate, presents certain special aspects. We are trying to accomplish in one generation what other nations have taken centuries to achieve ... The time is short and our culture is menaced by outside forces': Moisés Sáenz (one of the leading político-educationalists of his day, 1928), quoted in Simpson, *The Ejido*, p. 279.

[137] Mallon, *Peasant and Nation*, ch. 10.

[138] I would tend to stress organisation over revelation: Alan Knight, 'The Politics of the Expropriation', in Jonathan C. Brown and Alan Knight (eds.), *The Mexican Petroleum Industry in the Twentieth Century* (Austin, 1992), ch. 4.

[139] A.J.P. Taylor, *Bismarck. The Man and the Statesman* (London, 1965), p. 108.

course, is Protean and need not assume 'Prussian' forms either. The more pacific Mexican version of 'Prussian' state-building which I am describing also embodies an ambiguous relationship with nationalism. Juárez, Díaz and their revolutionary successors may well have sought to build a state that was strong and centralised in the face of foreign threats. But that did not necessarily convince provincial and popular patriots, whose notion of the patria was different.[140] Among the Chihuahua peasantry, for example, a 'nationalist' or patriotic commitment to Mexico was quite compatible with a 'localist' attachment to community and repudiation of the overweening central government.[141]

Still less did revolutionary state- and nation-building convince militant Catholics, who also conceived of state and nation in different terms. Catholic militants wanted a clerical corporatist state (à la Dollfuss), governing a God-fearing, Guadalupan nation.[142] Even middle-of-the-road Catholics combined their own brand of patriotism with a healthy suspicion of the state: at San José, de Gracia, 'they were in the habit of expecting only trouble from the authorities . . . everybody agreed that the government was bad — an opinion encouraged by their spiritual advisers'.[143] In Catholic eyes, therefore, the revolutionary nationalist project — especially the socialist variant of the 1930s — was an anathema, and could hardly serve as a force for genuine national cohesion or state legitimation. Catholic militants were, of course, a minority; but so, too, were their revolutionary counterparts. Most Mexicans were probably objects rather than agents in this particular battle for hearts and minds.

The point is not worth labouring: there are different conceptions of state and nation in Mexico as elsewhere. Forging a nation, as Renan pointed out, is as much about forgetting old rancours as fostering new reciprocities. States — that is, 'modern' nation-states — habitually try to appropriate and even monopolise nationalism. The PRI — a party, or perhaps a regime, which has enjoyed an unusually long tenure of state power — does this in particularly egregious fashion, by using the national colours and, more blatantly, by justifying electoral shenanigans on the grounds of national security. Such a strategy is, however, risky and, in my view, of limited success. Nationalism may have bolstered the revolutionary state on occasions, such as March 1938; but nationalism has also been turned against that state — by militant Catholics, insurgent liberals and nation-

---

[140] Mallon, *Peasant and Nation*, pp. 103–33.

[141] Vanderwood, *The Power of God*, and Daniel Nugent, *Spent Cartridges of Revolution. An Anthropological Study of Namiquipa, Chihuahua* (Chicago, 1993) deal with Chihuahuan communities which, while thoroughly Mexican in terms of their make-up and outlook, with a history of patriotic mobilisation, were also deeply hostile to the pretensions of the central state.

[142] Knight, *US–Mexican Relations*, pp. 39–46.

[143] González, *Pueblo en vilo*, p. 139.

alist leftists (Cristeros and Sinarquistas; Vasconcelistas; Lombardistas). The EZLN is nothing if not nationalist. Nationalism, in other words, is fungible and, almost by definition, any party/regime/state which seeks to monopolise nationalism risks the accusation of partiality, hypocrisy and cynicism; it then finds its own nationalist rhetoric turned against itself. States can derive benefits — allegiance, compliance, legitimation — from nationalism, but only to a degree and only so long as their nationalism remains inclusive and relatively bipartisan.

Partisan nationalisms are a different matter. Nationalists who, for example, honour Juárez thereby offend some Catholics; those who revere Cárdenas alienate the right; those who exalt Iturbide antagonise the left.[144] At the same time, official *indigenismo* disgusts Hispanophiles (who may be more numerous in Mexico than sometimes supposed); while foundation myths which hark back to Aztec Tenochtitlán are unlikely to inspire Maya or Yaqui Indians.[145] Nationalisms of this sort tend to be divisive and even counter-productive. (They may be very good for rallying one's own partisan supporters, but that is not the same as forging a united *patria*). In other words, the analytical (etic) distinction between state and nation has a concrete, historical (emic) reality. Nation- and state-building are related but distinct operations. The Mexican Revolution may have helped build a nation, in part by design, in part unwittingly. It also generated a variant of Mexican nationalism — actually, several subvariants: Zapatista and neo-Zapatista; Callista and Cardenista; Vasconcelista and Echeverrista. But the state never enjoyed a monopoly of nationalism; official nationalism changed over time; and the marriage of state and nation was, as in most countries, a strained matrimony. Thus I would not see 'Prussian' state-building as playing a central role in the modern Mexican experience.

[2] In contrast, the exercise of state autonomy in pursuit of economic development has clearly played a role in Mexican state-building. Gerschenkronian state intervention — designed to unlock the 'advantages of backwardness' — characterised Porfirian policy, especially with regard to infrastructure.[146] Railways, as I have argued, did not unequivocally strengthen the state vis-à-vis society, nor did they obey a 'Prussian' rationale, but they did decisively spur economic growth and make possible a dramatic increase in market production and exports. The state thereby promoted positive externalities which the private sector — especially the Mexican private sector — could not have accomplished.[147]

---

[144] For example: Vaughan, *Cultural Politics*, pp. 57, 78; Loyo, *Los maestros*, p. 75.

[145] Natividad Gutiérrez, 'The Culture of the Nation: The Ethnic Past and Official Nationalism in Twentieth-Century Mexico', unpubl. PhD thesis, LSE, 1995.

[146] Alexander Gerschenkron, *Economic Backwardness in Historical Perspective* (Cambridge, 1962); see also Paul Gootenberg's analysis in Centeno and López-Alves (eds.), *The Other Mirror*.

[147] Kunz and Riguzzi, *Los ferrocarriles*, pp. 54–64.

The revolutionary state followed Porfirian precedent. Railway-building gave way to road-building; irrigation projects favoured large northern producers; Calles established a central bank which, by the 1930s, proved capable of roughly Keynesian demand management; and a series of related banks (BNA; BNCE; NAFINSA) channelled funds to agriculture and industry. Agrarian reform, trumpeted as a contribution to social justice, also favoured accumulation in certain respects: it shifted resources out of latifundia and into more productive sectors; it encouraged agrarian mechanisation; and it helped deepen the domestic market.[148] For some policy-makers, these were conscious goals, for others, they were secondary by-products of the struggle for social justice or of the political need to appease the peasantry. In two areas — railways and oil — the Cardenista state resorted to outright nationalisation, culminating a trend toward increased state regulation which antedated the Revolution. Bereft of capital and out-competed by road transport, the state railways languished (despite some US chivvying during the Second World War); but PEMEX became an important buttress not only of government finances but also of private sector growth in the post-war period.[149]

The degree of state intervention in the Mexican economy, prior to the 1970s, was in fact quite limited. Regulation increased, but the impact of regulation varied from place to place, period to period and sector to sector (therefore, it must be evaluated in light of particular cases: the 'weight' and 'impact' of regulation *in toto* are, I think, impossible to measure). As we have seen, government spending as a percentage of GDP rose only gradually to 1970, but dramatically thereafter. After 1940 the ejidal sector accounted for a small and declining share of government spending; credit and infrastructural investment favoured big commercial farmers.[150] PEMEX served as a milch cow for both the state and the private sector, but it was an unusual case. Prior to 1970 the state's role in the burgeoning manufacturing sector was small and greatly outstripped by private capital, domestic and foreign.[151] The Mexican government protected industry and engaged in extensive regulation; but state ownership was limited and corporate taxation was low. The 'bankers' alliance' ensured that fiscal policy remained generally conservative, restraining inflation.[152] This, coupled with political stability, created a generally

---

[148] Knight, 'The Mexican Revolution'; Whetten, *Rural Mexico*, pp. 238–9, 568.

[149] Isidro Morales, 'The Consolidation and Expansion of Pemex, 1947–1958', in Brown and Knight, *The Mexican Petroleum Industry*, pp. 209, 216.

[150] Merilee S. Grindle, *State and Countryside. Development Policy and Agrarian Politics in Latin America* (Baltimore, 1986), pp. 62–4.

[151] Particularly domestic: Dale Storey, *Industry, The State, and Public Policy in Mexico* (Austin, 1986), pp. 67–9, 75.

[152] Sylvia Maxfield, *Governing Capital: International Finance and Mexican Politics* (Ithaca, NY, 1990).

favourable climate for capital accumulation from the 1950s through the 1960s. Of course, this coincided with a phase of sustained growth in the world economy; and Mexico's performance, impressive when placed within a Latin American context, looks less rosy when viewed globally and in per capita terms.[153]

It is not easy to evaluate the contribution of state policy to the so-called Mexican economic miracle. Mexico's was far from being a command economy, and the essential dynamics were those of the market. The state, refraining from extensive ownership or heavy corporate taxation, allowed the private sector to flourish, albeit in a supportive environment of protection and regulation. Was the state's role optimal? Would less intervention have resulted in faster growth? The question is particularly difficult, since it begs the question of time frame: the expert consensus would seem to be that policy was reasonably successful in the short to medium term (c. 1950–c.1970), but — to use the old cliché — it contained the seeds of its own downfall, by perpetuating policies of protection and intervention beyond the point of diminishing returns, while failing to undertake necessary fiscal reforms.[154]

However, this argument must take into account three additional considerations: the state expansion of the 1970s; and the two alternative rationales of state agency which remain to be discussed — the political and the mafioso. As regards the first point, we have seen that state intervention in the economy rapidly expanded in the 1970s. Apart from the political — and mafioso — motives which were at work, there was also an underlying economic rationale: the state sought to promote growth (accumulation) beyond the perceived limits of the ISI model, drawing on foreign capital and the providential flow of oil (while avoiding tax reform or trade liberalisation). Compared to the preceding phase/project of *desarrollo estabilizador*, this was an egregious failure. The bloated state — and the so-called 'economic populism' — which became the bugbears of neoliberal critics in the 1980s and 1990s were, in Mexico's case, largely creations of the 1970s, not the 1950s, still less the 1930s.[155] Mechanisms of protection and regulation were old and entrenched, but the proliferation of state enterprises and payrolls, and the associated fiscal crisis of the state, which drove

---

[153] Victor Bulmer-Thomas, *The Economic History of Latin America since Independence* (Cambridge, 1994), pp. 287–8.

[154] I have imaginatively cobbled this consensus together from various sources, including Bulmer-Thomas, *Economic History of Latin America*, p. 288; Storey, *Industry, the State and Public Policy*, p. 75; and Rosemary Thorp, *Progress, Poverty and Exclusion. An Economic History of Latin America in the 20th Century* (Washington, 1998), pp. 184–5, 197–9 (the first of which is more critical of the model than the other two).

[155] Public sector expenditure rose from 21 per cent of GNP in 1970 to 48 per cent in 1987: James M. Cypher, *State and Capital in Mexico* (Boulder, 1990), p. 174. In 1970 there were 616,000 'public servants', in 1983 3.3 million: Centeno, *Democracy Within Reason*, p. 82.

up the public debt, were of more recent creation.[156] In the economic realm, therefore, the weight of the state grew incrementally, but in two distinct phases and forms: a progressive (in both senses of the word) accumulation of regulatory responsibilities, coupled with limited state ownership and fairly cautious fiscal policy between 1920 and 1970; a rapid and, many now say, irresponsible extension of state activity, associated with debt and inflation, in the 1970s. Pursuing my crude corporeal metaphor, one could say that the state put on muscle in the first period, but accumulated flab in the second.

[3] The supposed autonomous role of the state in achieving political legitimation is perhaps the best-known example of the rationale of relative autonomy. If, in the economic realm, the state serves the higher goals of accumulation which uncoordinated and short-sighted business interests cannot address, in the political realm the state has to convince citizens — subordinate groups in particular — that the sociopolitical order is in some measure just, reasonable and tolerable. Rhetoric alone will not do the job,[157] so the state must undertake some (limited, controlled, cosmetic) reforms and must, on occasions, prejudice business interests (in the short term), in order to serve the higher goals of stability and further accumulation (in the long term). Thus, government involves a constant trade-off between legitimation and accumulation.

Like any functional argument, however, this presents major problems. Any reform — short of a socialist revolution — can be designated as limited, controlled, cosmetic and, in the last analysis, system-maintaining. Radical critiques of *cardenismo* take this stance. Cárdenas' reforms were designed to bamboozle the plebs, avert radical protest and shore up the capitalist status quo.[158] Or, at the very least, they had this effect. Of course, these two propositions — one dealing with motive, the other with outcome — are different. In appraising the argument, which has some merit, we must (a) take care to separate out imputations of indi-

---

[156] The public sector deficit rose from 1.8 per cent of GNP in 1970 to 17.9 per cent in 1982; after three years of retrenchment, it again climbed to 16.3 per cent in 1986: Cypher, *State and Capital*, p. 174.

[157] There is a marked tendency in Mexican historiography to assert — but rarely to explore or to demonstrate — the power of 'the ideology of the Revolution' (or some such reification). One example among many would be Ilene V. O'Malley, *The Myth of the Revolution. Hero Cults and the Institutionalization of the Mexican State, 1920–40* (New York, 1986), especially ch. 6, which, while presenting a vigorous critique of the official myth, too readily assumes that the Mexican people — mired in 'ideological ignorance' (p. 117) and constrained by both a 'limited collective understanding of what would actually improve their welfare' and an 'inchoate comprehension of their experience' (p. 131) — buy this ideology wholesale.

[158] Examples would include Arturo Anguiano, *El estado y la política obrera del cardenismo* (Mexico City, 1984); Ariel José Contreras, *México, 1940: industrialización y crisis política* (Mexico City, 1977).

vidual motive (these are notoriously difficult to resolve and, to the extent that resolution can be achieved, I think it inconceivable that Cárdenas thought in these terms); and (b) try to take the long view. Over time, the *cardenista* reforms did contribute to these consequences; more precisely, the organisations set up in the 1930s (the corporate party, the CTM and CNC, the labour arbitration system, the ejidal programme and its institutional agencies, such as the BNCE) increasingly became instruments of control rather than representation and were yoked to a project of accumulation rather than social justice. However, this was not their initial purpose; nor was it their immediate consequence during the years of the Cárdenas presidency. Above all, the supposed bourgeois beneficiaries of these reforms (according to the functionalist argument) were vocal in their criticism of Cárdenas and his policies, hence they were, at best, naively blind to their own best interests, while the project's supporters — trade unionists, *agraristas*, *ejidatarios*, schoolmasters and leftists — did not see themselves as salvaging capitalism; some in fact thought they were building socialism (though what they meant by 'socialism' varied) and most believed that they were developing Mexico's human resources, promoting health, literacy and material well-being, along with a measure of social justice. The Cardenista project — radical, in its day, by Mexican and Latin American standards — went far beyond system-maintenance; and it would be counter-factual dogma to say that it averted a socialist revolution.

Given that the project was genuinely popular and radical, it exerted a legitimising appeal at least in many quarters. It also excited fierce hostility in others.[159] Contact between state and society increased and with it the two-way process of cognitive exchange. People encountered Cárdenas, and Cárdenas listened to the people. Practical benefits flowed from these encounters: ejidos, schools, roads, trucks, tractors, drains, water tanks. The presidential visit was engraven on stone tablets and in collective memory; it nurtured the notion that the state, apart from demanding taxes, conscripts and dull compliance, could also provide benefits; thus communities like San José, de Gracia, 'reluctant to blend in with Mexico, dismissive of the national authorities, abandon(ed) their traditional suspicion of the nation and its leaders thanks to the visit of Don Lázaro Cárdenas'.[160] Above all, the *agraristas* felt a 'sense of indebtedness' to the federal government — and to Cárdenas personally — for their *ejidos* and the sense of empowerment which they conferred.[161] This shifting perception of the state informed not only 'bottom-up' popular action (mobilisations, petitions, demonstrations) but also 'top-down' political campaigning (*giras*, rallies, populist walkabouts), thus establishing a set of enduring and distinctive political practices.

---

[159] Raquel Sosa Elizaga, *Los códigos ocultos del cardenismo* (Mexico City, 1996), chs. 3, 4, 7, 8, offers a good resumé.

[160] González, *Pueblo en vilo*, pp. 191–2.

[161] Ann L. Craig, *The First Agraristas. An Oral History of a Mexican Agrarian Reform Movement* (Berkeley, 1983), pp. 136–7.

Although the impact dulled with time, as raw populism was routinised and institutionalised, it was also sporadically repeated and refurbished, albeit never on the scale of the 1930s.[162] Bursts of agrarian reform, programmes of public works, recurrent educational and antipoverty initiatives, gave a lingering legitimacy to the Mexican state, which contrasted with the palpable illegitimacy of many Latin American states, especially during the 1960s and 1970s. Post-*cardenista* reforms were certainly more moderate and contrived than those of the 1930s. But bourgeois opposition — to Echeverría, for example — suggested that this was not all populist smoke-and-mirrors, designed to further the higher goals of political stability and capitalist accumulation.[163] Political stability was not necessarily served; nor was capitalist accumulation necessarily advanced (consider the consequences of the 1976 *reparto* in Sonora).[164] The problem with the 'late populism' of Echeverría was not that it functionally served capitalist interests, but rather that it incurred capitalist wrath, which in turn forced Echeverría (and his successor) to beat a chastened retreat.[165]

Indeed, the 1970s — the decade when the Mexican miracle came to a definitive end — revealed a basic paradox. On the one hand, state intervention grew apace, fuelled by rising debt and increased oil production. State agencies dramatically expanded their payrolls and purviews. Outlying regions, like Chiapas and Yucatán, received the imprint of the central government as never before.[166] With the bank nationalisation of 1982 — the last fling of the interventionist project — state control of the commanding heights of the economy (railways, oil, banks, electricity) reached its peak. In formal terms, Mexico had never been so statist. Yet the legitimacy of the PRI seemed shakier than ever, certainly shakier than it had been during its golden age, c. 1954–68.[167] The weight of the state had grown

---

[162] Jorge Basurto, 'Populism in Mexico. From Cárdenas to Cuauhtémoc,' in Michael L. Conniff (ed.), *Populism in Latin America* (Tuscaloosa, 1999), ch. 5.

[163] Samuel Schmidt, *The Deterioration of the Mexican Presidency: The Years of Luis Echeverría* (Tucson, 1991), ch. 4.

[164] Steven E. Sanderson, *Agrarian Populism and the Mexican State: The Struggle for Land in Sonora* (Berkeley, 1981).

[165] Basurto, 'Populism in Mexico', p. 81; Centeno, *Democracy Within Reason*, p. 184 ff.

[166] Cancian, *Decline of Community*, pp. 29–48; Jeffery Brannon and Eric N. Baklanoff, *Agrarian Reform and Public Enterprise in Mexico. The Political Economy of Yucatán's Henequen Industry* (Tuscaloosa, 1987), pp. 13–15, 123–49; Schryer, *Ethnicity and Class Conflict*, pp. 194–5 ff.

[167] Molinar, *El tiempo de la legitimidad*, ch. 3. Schryer, *Ethnicity and Class Conflict*, p. 193, notes how, despite the build-up of central government power in the Huasteca, federal political interventions 'only made things worse, to the point where the state lost legitimacy in the eyes of most of the population of Huejutla': a judgement which, by virtue of its basis in 'local knowledge', carries more weight than blanket attributions of delegitimisation at the national level.

prodigiously, but the state was less legitimate, and more erratic, than before; its very capacity to guarantee stability and to reproduce itself seemed threatened.

[4] The paradox of a state which, by extending its powers in an effort to secure legitimation, contrives to delegitimise itself, is not in itself unusual. The collapse of the classical Maya cities was preceded by a flurry of monumental construction. Closer to home, the 'economic populism' thesis embodies a similar argument: governments irresponsibly boost spending in a counter-productive effort to court popularity. However, the 'economic populism' thesis is dangerously one-sided: it generalises the phenomenon excessively and reads like a hellfire sermon against government spending.[168] In the Mexican case, explanation of the paradox requires some consideration of politics, which is where the Mafia comes in.[169] I have conceded that some state initiatives clearly build legitimacy, both by design and accident: the Agrarian Reform generated reservoirs of support for the revolutionary regime which proved valuable in moments of crisis (e.g., 1923–24, 1938–39) and which — in regions like the Laguna — still lingered in 1988. At the same time, I have pointed out that such initiatives are often double-edged: they offend as well as reward, they engender enemies as well as friends. Such divisiveness is not always a regrettable by-product of policy; it can be a valuable weapon for Machiavellian rulers, who may choose to govern by means of threat and exclusion, rather than by reward and inclusion. Thus, the 'colonial' mode of governance comes to compete with the 'consensual', giving rise to a complex, 'schizoid' political culture.[170] In addition, increased state initiatives offer scope for political patronage, graft and rent-seeking. Political leaders and their *camarillas* batten on to such initiatives, distorting not only their manifest ('public transcript') purposes (e.g., social justice, redistribution), but also their latent functions, as just described. Social justice is not served; neither is 'Prussian' autonomy, rational accumulation or political legitimation. On the contrary, the Mafia state is likely to compromise national sovereignty, obstruct rational accumulation and undermine political legitimation.

---

[168] Luiz Carlos Bresser Pereira, 'Economic Reforms and Economic Growth: Efficiency and Politics in Latin America', in Bresser Pereira, José María Maravall and Adam Przeworksi, *Economic Reforms in New Democracies. A Social-Democratic Approach* (Cambridge, 1993), pp. 53–5.

[169] The theoretical formulation derives from Tilly (see fn. 17), although models of rent-seeking are also germane. In terms of Mexican studies, the Mafia analogy is hardly new (see fn. 129); foreign observers, fastening upon one aspect of Mexican revolutionary politics (at the expense of others), also deployed the concept — or something very close; thus, as W.W. Cumberland put it ('Latin America': see fn. 32), 'in Mexico as in Russia, the "revolution" is a business enterprise on the part of a small minority of the population and has never represented ... such inchoate and amorphous public opinion as might be said to exist'.

[170] Knight, 'México bronco'.

This is an old story. The gap between formal precepts of government —
colonial and republican — and actual political practice has always yawned (and
not just in Mexico, of course). Calibrating the 'gap' is not easy. But it is a safe
assumption that, to the extent that state activities expand so the potential for
graft and rent-seeking expands as well.[171] The armed revolution, for example,
thrust into the hands of parvenu military leaders a range of assets: haciendas,
railways, urban real estate. It also pushed the state to impose new forms of taxation (e.g., of oil) and, by virtue of extensive popular mobilisation, it created
new mass organisations which could further political careers. As a critical insid-
er put it, writing in 1944: 'politics alters and corrupts everything. With an
unfortunate frequency everything is subordinated or is tried to be made subordinate to politics: governmental action, economic convenience in matters of
credit, technical experience, etc. There are big, medium and small politicians,
giants and dwarfs, and they are found everywhere: in the offices and reception
rooms of officials, in the schools, in the labor unions, in ... the eijdos.'[172] Vox
populi concurred.[173] This is not to say that the Revolution was solely about
graft and rent-seeking (as some revisionists seem to say); rather, graft and rent-
seeking were integral parts of a much bigger and more complex process.
Idealism and self-interest combined in odd constellations; 'colonial' and 'consensual' forms of government intertwined.

Here I can only mention a few salient features. Straightforward peculation
— presidents and state governors taking bribes from foreign companies, for
example — was common, and made more feasible by the increased regulation
of the post-revolutionary period. It no doubt subverted the higher functions of
the state in significant respects: it created a gratuitous dependence on foreign
capital, distorted the optimal allocation of resources and — especially if it
became common knowledge — undermined state legitimacy. However, such a
relationship — what I have elsewhere termed 'government at the service of
graft' (i.e. the use of government office to extract personal benefits) —[174] is less
important than an alternative practice, 'graft at the service of government', that
is, the use of improper (non-Weberian) practices to advance the interests of
political incumbents and to perpetuate the entire Mafioso order. Though such
practices are no doubt global, Mexico has an old and rich tradition of patrimo-

---

171 Knight, *Mexican Revolution*, vol. II, p. 459 ff.

172 Jesús Silva Herzog, quoted in Whetten, *Rural Mexico*, p. 544.

173 Politics, according to respondents in Tepalcingo, Morelos (c. 1972), 'is the dirtiest
game there is', 'is just about making money', 'is a game where anything goes': Azaola
Garrido y Krotz, *Los campesinos*, p. 126; see also Lewis, *Pedro Martinez*, p. 209.

174 Alan Knight, 'Corruption in Twentieth-Century Mexico', in Walter Little and
Eduardo Posada-Carbó (eds.), *Political Corruption in Europe and Latin America*
(Basingstoke, 1996), pp. 226–7.

nial politics, characterised by ample discretionary power, lack of accountability, nepotism and clientelism. Ostensibly fair, impartial and impersonal mechanisms — elections, budgets, laws and legal codes, systems of bureaucratic recruitment and conduct — have regularly been 'captured' by particular interests. Formal rules of government have been cannibalised by informal camarillas, which are often captained by that ubiquitous and durable figure, the cacique.[175] Indeed, it would not be a wild exaggeration to depict modern Mexican politics as a constant three-way battle between democratic, bureaucratic and patrimonial principles; a battle conducted at all levels of the political hierarchy, from Los Pinos down to the humblest *presidencia municipal*. And patrimonialism is sufficiently entrenched to become 'naturalised'; it is seen as inevitable; its very durability deters would-be reformers.[176]

Conclusions

My conclusions are two-fold: methodological and substantive. Having set out with the best positivistic will in the world, I concluded that careful calibration, however desirable, especially for comparative purposes, is difficult and often impossible. There is the simple problem that data series are either unavailable or downright misleading. So, we run the risk of fashioning conceptual giants with feet of statistical clay. One push and they fall over. But there is also the more complex problem of defining what — in an ideal statistical world — we wish to measure, and for what purposes. It is clearly useful to estimate the state's consumption of resources, although the effects of that consumption will vary greatly depending on circumstances: the outcome may be, in Salinas' words, an *estado obeso* rather than an effective, muscled executive. Several of the supposed indices of state power — those relating to expenditure, payroll, communications, military resources — prove, on closer inspection, to be ambivalent in their effects. They may bolster the state; but they may also bolster societal dissent or even praetorian challenges. Evaluating state power *in vacuo* proves something of an analytical dead end; but if we turn to civil society and attempt a more ambitious 'dialectical' analysis, we confront even greater problems of definition, data collection and measurement. Who, in seeking to grasp 'civil society', has managed to go beyond trite generalisations?

This is not to say that the entire task is hopeless. We can try to measure what is measurable and, in addressing the great universe of the non-measurable, try to present clear arguments, backed up by sound data, however 'impressionistic' or 'anecdotal'. Some tentative (substantive) conclusions do then emerge. The

---

[175] Knight, 'Caciquismo and Political Culture' develops this analysis.

[176] 'The most serious of all aspects [of corruption] is that the public in general admits that this is so and considers it the most natural thing in the world': Whetten, *Rural Mexico*, p. 549, citing 'The Fight against the Mordida', *El Universal*, 25 Nov. 1942.

Mexican state is more notable for its endurance and longevity than for its effective control over society — a society which is much more varied and recalcitrant than often imagined and which, furthermore, has itself often been 'strengthened' by 'modernisation', along with the state. State-civil society relations have been subject to changing patterns over time and place; a 'zero-sum' relationship in some cases contrasts with state-society 'synergy' in others. Historians have begun to grapple with this complexity by means of local and regional case studies. In particular, we might differentiate between what I have called 'colonial' and 'consensual' modes of governance: the first depending on Machiavellian manipulation and factionalism; the second corresponding to the liberal-pluralist norm of positive state-society relations. It follows that Mexico cannot be said to possess a seamless political culture.

These contrasting patterns can be seen running throughout the two main phases of state expansion which the quantitative data reveal: first, a period of 'progressive' statism, characterised by extensive regulation but limited state expenditure, roughly 1920–70; and, second, a rapid increase of state expenditure, payroll and interventionism after c. 1970 (which did not, however, translate into greater state efficacy or legitimacy). At no time during this long twentieth-century odyssey did the state conform to the liberal model of the disinterested night-watchman; nor did it act as a simple agent of dominant class interests. Several competing functions or rationales were apparent — again depending on time and place.

Geopolitical logic prevented the Mexican state from adopting a 'Prussian' rationale; and, domestically, the state's efforts to harness nationalism were less successful than often supposed, given the partial character of most Mexican nationalisms and the cultural diversity of the country. State and nation appear to be not only analytically (etically) separable, but also historically (emically) distinct.

The state did assume a more autonomous role in respect of the economy: although it seems that it had greater success when it (the state) was smaller and confined its activities to indirect regulation of the market (tariffs, subsidies, labour laws) rather than direct ownership of the means of production. The high point of economic statism coincided with economic crisis and declining legitimacy. Finally, the political rationale of the state — its engagement with civil society in general — displays a schizoid character. In its consensual mode, the Mexican state has pursued policies of social reform, inclusion and, as a result, legitimation — most notably in the 1930s. These helped underpin the stability of later years. At the same time, however, we find constant evidence of a form of Mafioso politics which served the interests of state incumbents and their camarillas. The latter were therefore capable of capitalising on state projects and resources which, far from enhancing national sovereignty, economic performance or political legitimacy, came to serve particular, patrimonial interests. *Caciquismo* was a key element in this Mafioso syndrome. Neither development, nor modernisation, nor urbanisation, nor state-expansion, nor state-shrinking have put an end to this syndrome, and to the schizoid politics which it perpetuates.

Both my substantive and my methodological conclusions are, therefore, somewhat negative, even pessimistic. The Mexican state and its incumbents do not emerge trailing clouds of glory. And we, who try to read the entrails of the beast, are sadly fallible. If we try to be rigorous and positivistic we often fool ourselves. If we rest content with limited bits of 'thick description', we run the risk of myopia. Historians, it is sometimes said, tend to know more and more about less and less. Comparative political scientists, on the other hand, maybe know less and less about more and more. Perhaps the collective endeavour which produced this book will help us better grasp these grand notions — state, nation, civil society — which we constantly encounter, cannot avoid, but still poorly understand.

CHAPTER 10

Seeing a State in Peru:
From Nationalism of Commerce to the Nation Imagined, 1820–80*

Paul Gootenberg

Peruvian States

This chapter is a modest attempt to review a body of research by myself and others about nineteenth-century Peru that tried to deploy both state and nation-building as basic constructs. I adopted these concerns myself in the 1980s simply because 'state-building' seemed an apt device for making sense of a deeply chaotic and misunderstood period in Peruvian political history. Research on nineteenth-century economics and economic policy initially prompted this national-statist interpretation, which later expanded into a larger state and society approach for Peru.

On the whole, during Latin America's post-colonial era — precisely when its current array of national states first coalesced — this research underscores how the national state as institution preceded 'nationalism' as a full-blown ideology, movement or 'discursive regime'. But the state then did proceed to spawn a peopled nation (in the Peruvian case a relatively imaginary one) under its wings. Of course, this is a modernist autonomy model that pertains as much to Europe (as in Eric Hobsbawm's portrayal of mounting official nineteenth-century nationalisms) as to Latin America.[1] As simple as such a 'state-first' distinction seems, it may help correct the tendency of scholars of Peru to view the country solely from the vantage of its historical shortcomings or aberrations.

Over the past decades, those who studied the state in Latin America were by and large Marxists or dependency thinkers looking at its structural bases for transformation into something else. In the simplest terms, these thinkers were

* I thank Jeremy Adelman for comments on an earlier draft, Miguel Centeno and Fernando López-Alves for intellectual comradeship during the 1999 London–Oxford marathon and the Woodrow Wilson Center (in Washington) for some peace and quiet during the revisionist stage.

[1] E.J. Hobsbawm, *Nations and Nationalism since 1780: Programme, Myth, Reality* (Cambridge, 1990); 'official' nationalism is also the term used by Benedict Anderson for European movements in *Imagined Communities: Reflection on the Origin and Spread of Nationalism* (Verso, 1983); see Craig Calhoun, *Nationalism* (Minnesota, 1997), for 'discursive' nationalism and the general split between 'constructivist' (state-led, instrumentalist) and 'primordialists' (ethnicity, community, identity) in the study of the nation-state (pp. 8–9, 30–4) .

seeking (even historically) more 'autonomous' or powerful states, endowed with their own national agency, states that could do the hard work of economic development, national integration or even social justice. This chapter builds from research conducted during that period and under its structuralist influences. Yet at the start of the twenty-first century most of these recovering, retreating or recalcitrant materialists have either abandoned the state altogether as a concern or have joined today's policy-dominant neoliberals in demonising it from a new cultural or so-called 'subaltern' perspective.[2] To be sure, today's retreat from the state is not simply a product of the post-'89 identity crisis of academic Marxism or of the deep fiscal and political breakdowns of the Latin American state itself in the 1980s. It was also a reaction against the repressive 'bureaucratic authoritarian' regimes of that era, which while supremely autonomous, were hardly effective, productive or liberating ones — and which bequeathed horrific legacies for civil society in their wake.[3]

Latin Americanists, rather than continue this reactive retreat from the state, could seize the intellectual opportunities opening up with today's global ideological thaw. There are emerging perspectives that allow us to view the state in fresher terms, such as the 'patterned (giant) mess' of Michael Mann. Weber (Durkheim, Elias and Mauss) are now gaining ground in social thought, not only due to the vacuum left by Marxism but because they long appreciated a crucially *cultural* element to the state ('bureaucracy') and to its historical forms of governmentality (in diverse readings of 'rationality'). This intellectual shift also assumes a more natural agency or autonomy of the state in developmental, military and political spheres. There is a detectable turn from classical pessimism about the state's caging or repressive instincts, now mainly associated with the autonomy of state pow-

---

[2]   See Alfred Stepan, *The State and Society: Peru in Comparative Perspective* (Princeton, 1978) for statist concerns. For a newer Latin American 'subaltern state', Fernando Coronil, *The Magical State: Nature, Money and Modernity in Venezuela* (Chicago, 1997); a hybrid of Marxian and cultural lenses, it revives 1970s dependency (Roseberry, *AHA*, 1998) and, unwittingly, slogans of the 1920s (Mussolini, who termed marginal nations such as Italy not subaltern but 'proletarian states').

[3]   Albert O. Hirschman, 'The Rise and Fall of Developmental Economics', in A.O. Hirschman, *Essays in Trespassing: Economics to Politics and Beyond* (Cambridge, 1981), pp. 1–24. A larger sociological literature ponders the ambiguities of state autonomy: John A. Hall, 'States and Economic Development: Reflections on Adam Smith', in J.A. Hall (ed.), *States in History* (Oxford, 1986), pp. 154–76, and Michael Mann, 'The Autonomous Powers of the State: Its Origins, Mechanisms and Results', *ibid.*, pp. 109–36. Such writers stress excess autonomy (of that kind *not* socially embedded) as a structural difficulty as perilous as the classic (Marxist) one of the state as strictly Chairman-of-Board of the bourgeoisie (landed nobility; neo-colonial elite whatnot). See Maurice Zeitlin, *The Civil Wars in Chile (or the bourgeois revolutions that never were)* (Princeton, 1984) for some historical state autonomy.

ers.[4] Newer views also resist the stubborn dichotomy between students of the state (mainly structuralists) and students of the 'nation' (mainly culturalists).

Instead, more socially and culturally 'embedded' states (rooted, regulated, socialised, regionalised, communicative, diverse) and public spheres are projected — in part as a political foil to the contemporary neoliberal world-view and its methodological individualism and reductionism. Such 'embeddedness' is best located in the interstices of states and nations, reflecting the qualitative relationships between people(s) and emerging power institutions. Sociological fascination with comparison-ready ideal types does not lead, as Mahmood Mamdani warns for Africa, to mere 'history by analogy', but it can help to decipher a genuine and unique history for Latin American states.[5]

In Peru itself independence from Spain (1821–24) was not prompted by political mobilisation (in the name of the Peruvian 'nation', 'the people' or abstractions like 'liberty') but effectively happened by default and through the moves of a small socially conservative urban elite. On paper this new Peru stretched over a notoriously challenging Andean geographic space, and it was a deeply divided and regionalised landscape in terms of ethnicity or caste, with 60 per cent or so of its population initially classed as colonial-style 'Indians'. As in other parts of Spanish America, the first three decades of politics after Independence were largely consumed by the localised internecine warfare known as *caudillismo*, rather than in concerted processes of state- or nation-building. The state had no monopoly of violence or of legitimate authority. But when that central state did swiftly coalesce in the 1850s, at least in its 'despotic'

---

[4]   Michael A. Mann, *The Sources of Social Power* (Cambridge, 1986) and subsequent volumes (1993, vol. 2, for 'patterned mess'); Philip Corrigan and Derek Sayer, *The Great Arch: English State Formation as Cultural Revolution* (Oxford, 1985) with its explicit mix of Marx, Durkheim and Weber in a cultural history of the state, translated powerfully to Latin American contexts in Daniel Nugent and Gilbert Joseph (eds.), *Everyday Forms of State Formation: Revolution and the Negotiation of Rule in Mexico* (Durham, NC, 1995). For another view of Weberianism and power, see Eric R. Wolf, *Envisioning Power: Ideologies of Dominance and Crisis* (Berkeley, 1999), ch. 1. For Latin America, Peter Evans, *Embedded Development: States and Industrial Transformation* (Princeton, 1995) exemplifies shifts from Marxian dependency to Weberian possibilities, as do presumably pragmatics such as Fernando H. Cardoso (president of Brazil at the time of writing, erstwhile dependency theorist). For a closer look at these trends in Latin American 'political economy' see my '*Hijos* of Dr. Gerschenkron: "Latecomer" Conceptions in Latin American Economic History', in Miguel Centeno and Fernando López-Alves (eds.), *The Other Mirror: Grand Theory Through the Lens of Latin America* (Princeton, 2000), pp. 55–80.

[5]   Mahmood Mamdani, *Citizen and Subject: Contemporary Africa and the Legacy of Late Colonialism* (Princeton, 1996); also Crawford Young, *The African Colonial State in Comparative Perspective* (Yale, 1994), ch. 2, 'On the State'. See George Steinmetz (ed.), *State/Culture: State Formation after the Cultural Turn* (Cornell, NY, 1999) for attempted bridging of structuralist/cultural concerns, across lines of states and nations, especially discussion (ch. 11) by Berezin for Fascist Italy.

peacekeeping powers, it was dramatically tied to the coastal export economy of *guano* (bird-dung fertiliser sold to Europe), as was most of Peru's nascent commercial society. In other words, modern governance was mainly confined to Lima and did not greatly expand its softer 'infrastructural' powers (to use Mann's distinction) over the next decades.[6] Even those incipient capitalist institutions, however, were utterly destroyed during the disastrous period 1875–83 (the guano collapse and then military defeat by Chile), leaving a puzzling discontinuity in the history of the modern Peruvian state. It was rebuilt again in the late 1890s, finally approaching a national scale, following new roads and markets, sometime during the 1920s.[7] Nevertheless, for the rest of the twentieth century, the Peruvian state is fairly characterised as thinly-based, unstable and extra-constitutional and 'weak' in its size, capacities and national integrative powers — even by Latin American standards. Moreover, even today a broad sector of the Peruvian population (including a few national historians) regard their state if not as illegitimate then as a distinctly indifferent one, dogged by a chronic history of 'failures': failures to properly develop the country's wealth, failures to secure sound citizenry rights for its people, even failures to instil a proper national consciousness. So it is unclear what lasting legacies to read from 'republican' Peru's formative process of the nineteenth century. Given such extremes (of scant mobilisation from below and of fragile centralism from above) Peru is an outlier case, though this does not make it fully exceptional or a failure writ large. Rather, Peru exemplifies one kind of Latin American state.

With these contexts clear, this chapter will review a few of Peru's overlooked political achievements in the previous century. The first section, following the 'structural' concerns of my book *Between Silver and Guano* (1989), considers how early Peruvian commercial and regional struggles may be read as a *relatively successful* process of establishing territorial statehood and sovereignty. A concentrated and autonomous Lima elite ended up 'inventing' and adopting a sovereign state, largely out of efforts to shield their localised material interests. Their state became paradoxically more liberal as it took hold by the 1840s. The second section, which flows from the more ideational concerns of a later book, *Imagining Development* (1993), follows the liberal conceptions of the Peruvian elite as they expanded over mid-century into more inclusive, spacious or national perspectives.[8] Again, it was a restricted and state-centred elite that imagined this discursive and more social-

6   Mann, 'Autonomous Powers of the State'.

7   A fine description of this process (focused on 'modes of production') is Florencia Mallon, *The Defense of Community in Peru's Central Highlands* (Princeton, 1983), part II.

8   Paul Gootenberg, *Between Silver and Guano: Commercial Policy and the State in Postindependence Peru* (Princeton, 1989); and *Imagining Development: Economic Ideas in Peru's 'Fictitious Prosperity' of Guano, 1840–1880* (California, 1993). See Peter Taylor, *Modernities: A Geohistorical Interpretation* (Minnesota, 1998), ch. 4, 'The Modern State', on confluence of 'modern' states and nations, enabled by bounded territoriality of the eighteenth century.

ly-diverse nation, in part to rescue their tottering state from an impending collapse, in part because liberalism alone could not seemingly build a durable state.[9] All in all, we glimpse an active process of state formation, followed by attempts (however clouded) to forge a more embedded nation in its wake.

To See a State in the Making

I would argue that while Peruvians apparently were lacking in lucid 'national consciousness' before 1821, as is often enough said, sufficient nationality surfaced (mainly from a conservative economic nationalism) to guarantee the survival of Peru's post-Independence state. As that Peruvian regime stabilised after 1845 — the result of a shifting maze of regional, social and fiscal struggles — it would acquire a more 'liberal' hue, well integrated with worldly commerce and with more cosmopolitan political currents.

These themes respond to terms of discourse popularised in the 1970s by the local branch of the Latin American 'dependency school'. That was the notion that Peru and many other structurally-dependent nations were initially founded by '*comprador*' elites, leaders who at base lacked a viable political project (a *proyecto nacional*) — beyond the one of subjecting their people and resources to the dictates of British free-trade commerce. Simply put, the very nature of the Peruvian state was determined by its form of integration into the world division of labour of the nineteenth century. A corollary was that the chaotic caudillo conflicts of the early nineteenth century were politically meaningless — anarchic struggles for spoils in the absence of a serious founding vision and an integral national ruling class. These strange notions actually made good clues for study of the state in Peru. But after much archival digging into the origins of (state-centred) trade policies, and their related political and regional struggles, such conceptions were turned on their head. (The new state-building view also benefited from exposure to writings of outside academic agitators: Tilly, Skocpol, Anderson, Gerschenkron and the 'statist' or corporatist school of Latin American studies.)[10]

---

[9]   Works on 'state/nation-building' in Peru include: Julio Cotler, *Clases, estado y nación en el Perú* (Lima, 1978); Stephan M. Gorman, 'The State, Elite, and Export in Nineteenth-Century Peru: Toward an Alternative Reinterpretation of Political Change', *Journal of Interamerican Studies and World Affairs*, vol. 21, no. 3 (1979), pp. 395–418; Ronald Berg and Frederick S. Weaver, 'Toward a Reinterpretation of Political Change in Peru during the First Century of Independence', *ibid.*, vol. 20, no. 1 (1978), pp. 69–84; Javier Tantaleán A., *Política económica-financiera y la formación del estado: siglo XIX* (Lima, 1983); Douglass Friedman, *The State and Underdevelopment in Spanish America: The Political Roots of Dependency in Peru and Argentina* (Boulder, 1984).

[10] On one of these grand schemers, see Gootenberg, '*Hijos* of Dr. Gerschenkron'; Charles Tilly (ed.), *The Formation of National States in Western Europe* (Princeton, 1975). On dependency and Peru's regime, Heraclio Bonilla, 'Continuidad y cambio en la organización política del Estado en el Perú independiente', in I. Buisson et al. (eds.), *Problemas de la formación del estado y nación en Hispanoamérica* (Vienna, 1984), pp. 481–98.

Taking a resolutely sociological perspective, we can see how early Peruvian state formation passed through three discernible phases: a breakdown phase (1824–45), a consolidation phase (1845–50) and the age of the liberal high guano-age state (1850–1870s). These formative processes can be viewed in several dimensions in addition to the focus on overseas commerce in relation to the 'state' adopted here: evolving regional conflict (*caudillismo* or national integration); intersections with foreign power (international diplomacy or imperialism); social bases (class character and social constraints); and classical fiscality (who paid what to keep it afloat). The fundamental challenge is in trying to make some patterned sense of Peru's messy and prolonged transitional era of *caudillismo*, some 40 years between the breakdown of a conservative Spanish viceroyal regime (based on a politics of silver) and the mid-century liberal export order of 'guano'.

In terms of regionalism or *caudillismo*, Peru's post-1821 sectional conflict erupted between a matrix of colonial interests concentrated around the capital Lima and a related national axis along the protectionist 'nationalist' *north* coast versus the free-trade 'liberal' *south*. Motley Andean regions, led by a new brand of rustic caudillos, shifted between these two coastal national poles, moving from an initial autarkic, almost xenophobic reaction to Independence, until by the 1840s the Andes became partisans of the decentralist, commercial impulses of the south. An heroic and then novel assumption here — supported by new evidence — was that Peru's armed caudillo bands were not so 'apolitical' or senseless after all, but often divided into discernible 'parties' that identified messily with trade issues and that often mobilised (politically, militarily or in terms of levies and funds) with these zones in tow. The meandering course and outcome of these polarising conflicts over the next two decades 1825–45 could be interpreted in a larger sense as struggles over the shape of the Peruvian state.[11]

Northern caudillos (Salaverry, La Fuente, the *gamarristas*) and their movements articulated a number of vocal economic interests, espousingwhat I call a 'merchant nationalist' cause. By 1830 these interests included northern slaveholding sugar planters (seeking to uphold their colonial-era protected trade corridor with Chile); Lima's millers (reliant on Chilean wheats and urban slavery); guild-organised artisans (largely in colonial-style luxury crafts); surviving rustic Sierran cloth makers and traders; defensive small-scale Cerro de Pasco sil-

---

[11] Summed up in Paul Gootenberg, 'North–South: Trade Policy, Regionalism, and *Caudillismo* in Post-Independence Peru', *Journal of Latin American Studies*, vol. 23, no. 2 (1991), pp. 1–36. French (southern) consular reports of the 1830s (Paris: Correspondance Consulaire, Arequipa/Arica, Consul-General Barrére) are rich on this issue; 'Tratado de Comercio entre Chile y el Perú', *El Redactor Peruano* (Lima), May 1836. See Charles F. Walker, *Smoldering Ashes: Cuzco and the Creation of Republican Peru, 1780–1840* (Durham, NC, 1998) and Sarah C. Chambers, *From Subjects to Citizens: Honor, Gender and Politics in Arequipa, Peru, 1780–1854* (University Park, PA, 1999) for recent elaborations of regional coalitions and identities.

ver miners; and food suppliers (*chacareros*) from the coastal valleys of greater Lima. The most strategic members of this alliance were, however, Lima officials, reluctant heirs of the viceregal bureaucracy, and the core Lima merchant class, organised in Lima's still privileged colonial-corporate *Consulado de Comercio*. What all these groups held in common, besides their 'statist' colonial compass, was stiff opposition to the free-trade that entered Lima after 1821, and particularly against the free-wheeling North American shippers who plied the simple goods that competed with those of Peru's would-be ruling groups.[12] What they articulated, often in blunt reaction to meddling (Bolivarian) liberals and foreign consuls, was a primitive but pointed form of Peruvian 'nationalism.' National groups, 'Los Hijos del País' as they were called, seized the new state and sought to protect the new-found and vulnerable sovereignty of Peru's national wealth.

Southern caudillos (Vivanco, Obregoso and others) were a far weaker and more regionally restricted force; lacking an authentic state, they swiftly became a 'separatist' movement. Arequipa, their *patria chica*, was linked to nascent British commercial interests along the southern coast and to the persistent idea of liberal export and political alliance with upland Bolivia (briefly embodied in Andrés Santa Cruz's Peru–Bolivia Confederation of the mid-1830s). Portalian Chile, the ideal trade partner of the north, was their commercial and political nemesis. The movement also drew on Arequipan liberal and anti-centralist social characteristics and racialist identities, and besides some of the converting southern Andean regions, found spiritual alliances with a handful of vocal intellectual functionaries in Lima (heirs to Bolivarian liberalism like José María Pando, Peru's only 'internationalist' philosophers).

The significant issue here — besides the fairly transparent trade-zone influences and their overlooked early 'projects' for the Peruvian state — is that such regional dynamics might explain the meandering course of Peruvian caudillo strife until 1850.[13] Just as vital, such regionalisms seemed to gel into two embryonic versions of Peruvian 'nationalism', with some roots extending back into both colonial Habsburg and Bourbon mentalities and models of the state. Northern nationalism, reacting against liberal integration with the Atlantic world (and especially against the new foreign merchants in their midst)

---

[12] Paul Gootenberg, *Tejidos y harinas, corazones y mentes: el imperialismo norteamericano del libre comercio en el Perú* (Lima, 1989). Based on research in US, British and French consular despatches, esp. RG 59 (Dept. Of State) M154, US Consuls in Lima, vols. 1–6. For northern interests and grievances, see *Los Clamores del Perú* (Lima), May 1827, or *Reflexiones sobre la ley de prohibiciones reimpresadas y aumentadas con notas* (Lima, 1831).

[13] *Between Silver and Guano*, chs. 3–4: these trade-zones are analogous to geographies of liberal/conservative influence traced in Mexico (in R. Sinkin, or bottom-up, P. Guardino) or Argentina (Burgin), but are not fully concurrent with Peruvian liberal-conservative dynamics of 'traditional' historiography — Jorge Basadre, *La multitud, la ciudad, y el campo en la historia del Perú* (Lima, 1929) is a fine example of social mapping.

revolved mainly around a militarist (caudillo) compact with Lima's 'merchant nationalists'. The southern nationalists vaunted a federalist commercialism. The northern centralists would dominate the unstable polity through the late 1840s and were able to establish the principle of Peruvian sovereignty (at first against the Colombian invader liberals, then intrusive North Americans and Europeans), at least in their nationalist regime and protectionist programme. Yet, by 1830 Peru's north-south conflict transmuted into chronic *caudillismo*, which was to preclude the early consolidation of a prospering national state.

The external bases of state-building — all modern states emerge into a world of interlocking foreign states — cannot be ignored. 'Internal' Peruvian political dynamics explain much, but these domestic factions and projects also articulated with overseas influences and states, which were certainly hard at work. There were important Chilean and Bolivian market influences, related to larger Peruvian regional spaces and the fragmentation of former viceregal administrative 'borders'. The interests, postures and activities of three new foreign commercial powers in Peru — the British, North American and French — and their respective wholesale merchant houses, show that nineteenth-century 'free-trade imperialism' is no myth, but also that it failed: for the sheer 'weakness' of the initial Peruvian state, for lack of credible local intermediaries and because it sparked highly nationalist and passionate Peruvian responses.

The British, often presumed to be the predominant early power over republican Peru, certainly harboured neo-'imperial' projects for the area, grand free-trade treaty schemes that would tie Lima into their expansive South American trading sphere. They even supported political surrogates (like Santa Cruz) in these ambitions. However, each of their large interventions in Peruvian politics collapsed, exciting waves of anti-English sentiments across Peru. In the wake of these failures (for example from 1838–44), the British would simply withdraw their official and working presence in the zone, and they could barely defend their merchants against attack. The notion of London 'finance' capturing the Peruvian state was untenable: an erratic Peru went into default on its it earliest loans by the mid-1820s and the general mayhem worked to keep private merchant influence at bay. The French, on the other hand, were persistent in aggressively defending their small-scale luxury trades in Peru and made no friends in the process. The surprisingly early role of the USA in Peru was sparked by conflicting commercial trade interests (simple flours, cheap textiles and the like ran against the hopes of the northern pro-Chilean nationalists) and because of the liberal interventionist campaigning of Mr Samuel Larned, their energetic consul-general of the late 1820s. Yet, his meddling helped Peruvian factions, especially protectionist officials and warlords, to defend and focus themselves in ever-more nationalist terms. In this way, free-trade imperialism was the external 'other' in the definition of early Peruvian sovereignty — so a lot would have to change in the 1840s for Peru to transform into a stable free-trader state, peacefully integrated into the hegemonic liberal world order.

All states, especially at their birth, relate to some visible social and institutional base, but much written history about Peru treats politics as if it were freely autonomous of society or vested mainly in the actions of exceptionally corrupt and/or virtuous individuals.[14] For early republican Peru, one can discern a number of creole urban groups (close to the state), such as artisan guilds, millers and Lima merchants, who exerted a large, often overshadowing, influence over their relatively weak and disorganised polity. Local artisans and shopkeepers constituted a new 'middle sector' group, who raised a stirring 'hijos del país' rhetoric, as well as specific political services and mobilisations for their causes. Some regional actors — long-distance traders, for example — could affect policies, but these had to be filtered through the *consulado* (Lima merchant guild) or by regional caudillos or via surprisingly active provincial councils (*juntas departamentales*) or even in Peru's intermittent national congresses. The 'state' administration itself — especially officials of the finance ministry or full-time or professional strongmen — often displayed a rudimentary kind of political autonomy, but not much direct sway and administration outside the environs of Lima. However, the key social relationship in the early state was between institutionalised Lima merchants (no more than a hundred in the upper echelon) and caudillo armies — a symbiotic relationship that for fiscal and ideological affinities can be seen as a form of colonial 'corporatism'. External forces, as just seen, were few, but would take root as a grounded interest when the state stabilised and then liberalised after 1850. Although some institutions stood out, the leadership of the treasury and Junta Departamental de Lima, for instance, was for the most part 'charismatic' or autonomous rather than administrative and impersonal, in this transitional era between state forms. Such social groups related to public institutions in directly personalistic ways; embedded social networks — much less a wider imagined political community — were still little developed.

States are, in the last analysis, fiscal mechanisms of one kind or another (for self-survival, landed piracy, rent-seeking and distributive aims) — a function recognised throughout classical works of historical sociology.[15] Peru's republican state was born in a peculiar period of deep economic depression (1821–45) and was incubated through decades of chronic political instability, high militarism and state protectionism. Its fiscal character therefore acquired peculiar characteristics relating to its penurious survival as a caudillo regime. By 1825, the core Spanish colonial fiscal regime — based on extracted indigenous tribute or taxed and protected silver trades — had largely collapsed. The prescribed 'liberal' alternative of the era — external loans, trade-treaty guarantees, swelling

---

[14] See, for example, Frederick Pike, *The Modern History of Peru* (Westport, CT, 1967), ch. 4.

[15] John Hicks, *A Theory of Economic History* (Oxford, 1969); for Latin America, see recent comparative work of Marcelo Carmagnani (ed.), *Federalismos latinoamericanos: Mexico, Brazil, Argentina* (Mexico City, 1993).

liberal commercial revenues or profit taxes — was also precluded, due to warfare, defaults and high tariffs.[16] Thus, the chronically unstable Lima state quickly propagated its own form of fiscal policy, based on a set of elaborately developed institutionalised emergency 'loans' (forced or otherwise) from the national merchant class, setting into motion millions of pesos. By 1830, there emerged a formal *consulado* institution for caudillo lending — the 'Ramo de Arbitrios', backed by the intricacies of various customs bonds — which was linked to the national projects and privileges of the *limeño* merchants. The byzantine underground history of this body in the 1830s goes a long way toward explaining the persistence in Peru of both freewheeling 'nationalist' caudillos and their deepening political compact with national traders in Lima.

These hidden fiscal mechanisms, and their dynamic of nationalist politics, are helpful in explaining the eventual transition to the stable (non-caudillo) and liberal state of the guano age. The reversal of all these processes and constellations tied up with caudillo instability constituted the process of forming a more viable national state. This was finally to occur in the late 1840s, around the time of the rising guano trade, under the stewardship of General Ramón Castilla.

Consolidation ran deeper than the assumed *deus ex machina* of the guano trade. In regional terms, the 1840s saw the definitive military and political defeat of the Arequipan south, though after 1844 Peru saw the rise of Lima-based southerners (such as the ex-*gamarrista* Castilla himself), as well as of spokesmen eager to accommodate and integrate the south on more liberal and less centralist terms. Other regional pressures on caudillo nationalism, such as now dying sierran manufactories (*obrajes*), disappeared or transformed into liberal ones. Social changes were at work; for example, native artisans and shopkeepers of Lima had decayed under trade pressures into a weakened and expendable force. In fiscal terms, the turning point was the highly destructive round of caudillo warfare in 1841–44 that destroyed the 'arbitrios' loan system, bankrupting the national merchant clique and, most importantly, converting them into sharp sceptics of militarist-style nationalism.

Peru's statesmen would have to look elsewhere for funds, and thus immediately made guano exports into another of their personal-style statist monopolies. Once a semblance of order took hold by 1845–47 (in part due to Castilla's centralisation of armed forces), foreign powers were able to relate to Peru as a predictable power; treaties, freer commerce and even substantial European loans began to take hold by 1850. Peruvian merchants began to support this state-centred 'free-trade' alliance by the late 1840s because their recovery was tied

---

[16] P. Gootenberg, 'Paying for *Caudillos*: The Politics of Emergency Finance in Peru, 1825–1845', in V. Peloso and B. Tenenbaum (eds.), *Liberals, Politics and Power: State Formation in Nineteenth-Century Latin America* (Georgia, 1996), pp. 134–64, much of this based on the 'Consulado' and 'Arbitrios' loan documents in Archivo Nacional del Perú, sections H-4 or H-1. For Mexican comparison, see Barbara A. Tenenbaum, *The Politics of Penury: Debts and Taxes in Mexico, 1821–1856* (New Mexico, 1986).

into a number of fiscal instruments embedded in both guano expansion and in Castilla's pact of stability, notably the 'consolidation' of dated public debts.[17] These developments made for an institutionalising liberal-style authoritative state by 1850, albeit one that by its dominating and sovereign guano *estanco* retained vestiges and mentalities of the state's earlier nationalist origins.

In sum, between silver and guano, and even out of the murkiest of caudillo frays, one discerns the outlines of a process of state formation in early nineteenth-century Peru. It becomes visible through a kaleidoscope of regional conflicts, shifting social and institutional bases, external interactions and new forms of politics and fiscal struggles that erupted in the wake of the imploded Spanish mercantilist state. But those pieces took fully two decades to resolve into a stable 'republican' state tied into rising world political and commercial currents. Evidence from that 'patterned mess' draws a picture of a rudimentary but durable state following the European administrative and territorial model, but without an embedded people or popular 'nation' inside nor much incubation under elite literate or literary 'proto-nationalism'.[18] It established borders and institutions, but with limited nationalist content or links to a civil society. Instead, the state's genesis was defined by autonomies and *dis*connectedness: from active citizenries, from external domination, from ethically-distinct and spatially remote regional societies or from a defined ruling class or master plan.

To See a Nation of Citizens

This depiction of social forces demonstrates the difficulty of detecting a tangible 'citizenry' or ideals of civic integration during initial Peruvian state formation, beyond these rival corporatist and liberal cliques. *Imagining Development* did look (squinting through the lens of economic ideas) for broadening conceptions of Peruvian nationality during the era of the quite prosperous guano-age state (1845–80). These ideals were produced and preached by a notable set of liberal *pensadores,* men deeply implicated with Peru's now stabilised and expanding government. The ideas themselves are quite remarkable, since Latin American liberalism, especially regional economic liberalism, is usually depicted as particularly impoverished or imitative.[19] In part, this was because laissez-faire revealed itself as inadequate for widening the social base for the regime, but these developmental aspirations also reflected slowly changing social realities, as more people participated in the urban economy and culture of Lima's modernising state. There

---

[17] *Between Silver and Guano*, pp. 93–9, 128–37, for key facets of these changes; the 1850–53 'consolidación' analysed by Alfonso Quiroz in *La deuda defraudada: Consolidación de 1850 y dominio económica en el Perú* (Lima, 1987).

[18] Michael Mann, *The Sources of Social Power*, vol. II, chs. 1–3; Hobsbawm, *Nations and Nationalism*, ch. 2; Anderson, *Imagined Communities*.

[19] See Burns, *Poverty of Progress* or Joseph Love, 'Structural Change and Conceptual Response in Latin America and Romania', in Love and Jacobsen, *Guiding the Invisible Hand*, pp. 1–34.

was in short, a movement from a Lima state to a Peruvian nation, at least when we shift the lens from historical sociology to a social history of ideas.

These nationalist ideas were anything but generated from 'below' or from some autonomous 'private' sector (which barely existed in Peru), but rather from individuals close to or inscribed within the liberal state. This was the 'governmental perspective', to borrow again from Hobsbawm's European lexicon. The ideas reveal a continuing current of Peruvian 'statism' (in proposed new roles for the public sector) even during the ideological height of international laissez faire.[20] Second, as the perceived gap between Peru's over-extended state and the state of the country's lagging development widened, these thinkers called out louder for the nurturing of a citizenry base for the republic. By the 1860s 'productive' citizens — or active political alliances with real-life middle or popular-class groups — were seen as crucial to Peru's future, especially as the guano commerce (by then branded 'fictitious' by liberal critics) tumbled into crisis. By the 1870s such ideals were being developed by President Manuel Pardo's national campaign of civil society and party-building, *Civilismo* — a political movement cut short by the war of 1879 and Peru's subsequent national collapse. Such a nationalist-liberalism was an elitist effort to bolster a shaky state, uphold social stability and prevent a regression to the militarist 'barbarism' of Peru's early decades.

This is not to say that the Peruvian state was evolving a 'democratic' or representative character over time. In some senses, the opposite trend was occurring. Mark Thurner argues in his insightful study of Indian 'republicanism' in Ancash that Peru was also developing a coeval '*un*-imagined' national community, as race assumed more exclusive or dualistic meanings, markers and boundaries over the nineteenth century. We know practically nothing about how the Peruvian 'nation' was perceived and received by era's 'subaltern' or *sierran* folk, but this should not lead us into ignoring how the state saw things — especially in the study of states — in favour of imaginary or ahistorical nationalist movements.[21]

---

[20] Hobsbawm, *Nations and Nationalism*, ch. 3; this is common in the history of economic thought, which emerged alongside European statecraft, see Phyllis Dean, *The State and the Economic System: An Introduction to the History of Political Economy* (Oxford, 1989). In other words, no sharp dichotomy exists here between 'statist' and 'liberal' ideas, much less 'national' versus 'European' thinking of dependency works, or even Nicolas Shumway, *The Invention of Argentina* (California, 1991).

[21] An institutional 'democratisation' thesis is being honed by sociologist Carlos Forment in a long-awaited comparative tome on nineteenth-century Latin America; see Forment, 'La sociedad civil en el Perú del siglo XIX: democrático o disciplinario?' in Hilda Sabato (ed.), *Ciudadanía política y formación de las naciones: perpectivas históricas de América Latina* (Mexico City, 1999), pp. 202–30. Mark Thurner, *From Two Republics to One Divided: Contradictions of Post-Colonial Nation-making in Andean Peru* (Durham, NC, 1997); Florencia Mallon, *Peasant and Nation: The Making of Post-Colonial Mexico and Peru* (California, 1994); David Nugent, *Modernity at the Edge of Empire: State, Individual and Nation in the Northern Peruvian Andes, 1885–1995* (Stanford, 1997) — which reminds us that 'resistance' was not the only conceivable response to state expansion.

The idea of progress tied to the growing state grew from the cracks of the post-Independence 'nationalist' dynamics just explored. In the late 1840s, as guano revenues soared, a brief public movement arose for purposely diverting state export revenues into diversifying the larger economy, much against the teachings of free trade. The first articulation, soon lost from history, erupted during the 1845 Congress in Lima from motley provincial delegates who passionately demanded the financing of modern factories in the forgotten outbacks of the Andes. Their argument was that industrial employment would help to forestall the kind of social misery that had fed into the spiral of *caudillismo*.[22] Theirs was a social grasp of instability which found its source in the misery, dislocation and desperation of the popular masses, an argument that would reappear under different guises over the next three decades.

The actual response, however, was concentrated in Lima, where by the late 1840s a clutch of the capital's innovative merchants began to invest heavily in modern imported factory equipment. They dreamed of winning government backing for their precocious industrialising drive, and Castilla together with some liberal notables (among them Domingo Elías, Peru's first civilist) did lend their concerted support. The group's spokesman was Juan Norberto Casanova, who published an extended pamphlet of more than a hundred pages publicising the drive as well as his own *Tres Amigos* textile factory. State-assistance was justified, Casanova averred, because prospering 'mercantalist' states (in his eyes eighteenth-century Britain or France) had always acted so, and because Peru itself had the good fortune of a great 'national bank' in guano. Such subsidies and tariffs would also help in disciplining the unruly idled workers of Lima (and tame caudillo-fodder) and furthermore create useful national capitalists — a new breed of industrialising *hijos del país* — to buttress and fund a national state. However, this incipient industrial movement was turned back by the dramatic free-trade offensives of 1850–51 in Lima, demolished by purist liberal ideologues and by urban elite panic around the city's now politically-desperate artisan guilds. The factory experiments, abandoned by the government, folded by 1852.[23]

Throughout the 1850s, official Peru faced a major paradox: the size of its state and state budgets expanded dramatically (as did the complexity of many civil institutions in Lima) due to galloping guano export revenues and a prospering commercial economy. Public expenditures multiplied over fivefold in real terms between 1847 and 1872, half of that during the 1850s. But the same economic and political liberals supporting this expansive policy did not find much of a citizenry or national base to staff or support their state-building proj-

---

[22] These debates are in *El Comercio* (Lima), July–Sept. 1845, reprinted in *Extracto de las sesiones de la Cámara de Diputados publicados en 'El Comercio' de Lima* (Lima, 1845).

[23] P. Gootenberg, 'The Social Origins of Protectionism and Free Trade in Nineteenth-Century Peru', *Journal of Latin American Studies*, vol. 14, no. 2 (1982), pp. 329–58, for industrial movement and political context. Juan Norberto Casanova, *Ensayo económico-político sobre el porvenir de la industria algodonera fabril del Perú* (Lima, 1849).

ect.[24] Liberals were in part hobbled by their attitudes towards the country's 'real and existing' popular or middle classes, viewed as congenitally backward Indians in the *sierra* or in the city as low-quality racially-mixed artisans and wrong-thinking shopkeepers. To be sure, some Jacobin and liberal thinkers, drawing on new European democratic categories and discourse, made much of Peru's fictive 'middle-class' for expanding liberties and enlightened government, while ignoring or actively denigrating the ones in their midst. These attitudes only began to change in the early 1860s, when some radical liberals embraced real-life struggling *limeño* artisans against Castilla's now markedly conservative authority. The most dramatic opportunity occurred in late 1858 when artisans and urban unemployed violently revolted against free manufactured imports and then Castilla's cavalry, and gained the support of maverick liberal writers in the sardonic and subversive paper *La Zamacueca Política*. By the mid-1860s, novel clubs, inspired by electoral reforms and the patriotic zeal of artisans in the 1864 struggle against the invading Spanish fleet, addressed these popular groups as respectable voters and citizens.[25] The telling social milieu of Lima, with its combustible mix of riches and neglect, was made visible by new *costumbrista* writers and *statisticians* (in the literal and French 'state' sense of the time), exemplified by M.A. Fuentes, who helped to shift liberals away from a triumphant laissez-faire dogma during the height of the guano age.

The watershed in liberal-statist thinking during the 1860s was marked by two eminently elitist 'projects' for the overhaul of the Peruvian state: Manuel Pardo's 1860 *Estudios sobre la provincia de Jauja* and the related writings of Luis Benjamín Cisneros, notably his 1866 *Ensayo sobre varias cuestiones económicas del Perú*. Both of these texts, paradoxically, have been viewed by historians as emblematic of the Peruvian elite's incapacity to think in national terms during the nineteenth century, whereas a closer reading reveals something quite different.[26] Under the spell

---

[24] 5.25 times to be precise: in nominal terms, all expenditures went from 4.5 to 48.8 million pesos from 1847–72, deflated here by 1.8 for inflation and excluding debt service; real revenues expanded 4.7 times. Roughly half this growth occurred before 1860, half after. P. Gootenberg, '*Carneros y Chuño*: Price Levels in Nineteenth-Century Peru', *Hispanic American Historical Review*, vol. 70, no. 1 (Feb. 1990), pp. 42–4. The best analysis of this expansion remains Shane Hunt's 'Growth and Guano in Nineteenth-Century Peru', discussion paper 34, RPED (Princeton, 1973), esp. Tables 8–9; Hunt came to the conclusion — which discursive analysis here supports — that expenses for social 'development' actually rose dramatically, in contrast to the 'oligarchic orgy' image of the guano-age state left by critics like Fernando Casós in *Los hombres de bien*.

[25] See analysis in *Imagining Development*, pp. 64–70, 133–50; or Juan Espinoza, *Diccionario para el Pueblo* (Lima, 1855) or Francisco Bilboa, *El Gobierno de la Libertad* (Lima, 1855), for liberal denigration; Manuel A. Fuentes, *Estadística general de Lima* (Lima, 1858); radical voices in *La Zamacueca Política* (short-lived broadside of Dec. 1858–June 1859).

[26] See Heraclio Bonilla, *Guano y burguesía en el Perú* (Lima, 1974), pp. 54–63; Ernesto Yepes del Castillo, *Perú 1820–1920: un siglo de desarrollo capitalista* (Lima, 1972), pp. 80–96; Tantaleán, *Formación del estado*, pp. 228–9.

of the fiscal crisis of the undisciplined Peruvian treasury, both men called for strong and illiberal measures to safeguard the state, develop the economy and nurture the nation. Pardo and Cisneros hoped to prevent a regress to the 'barbarities' of the chaotic post-Independence caudillo period. For Peru's state to become stronger and stable, it had to invest in the nation.

Pardo, as is well-known, wrote about railroads. The 1860 project was built around an imaginary case-study of the central Andean Jauja region. How would a modern transportation revolution transform a smallholder mestizo zone like Jauja? To Pardo the strategic imperative was to bring politically unintegrated provinces into the guano-age state. This would extinguish smouldering provincial caudillo activity, but he was also explicitly concerned that 'regional development' (as we might dub it today) spawn a broader and more stable base for the state, turning Peru's peasant 'helots' (as he saw them) into productive and peaceful citizens.[27] Pardo's idea of shifting public resources into steam-age technology and regional production even specified varied forms of import substitution, including mass-production woollen textile factories in the high Jauja valley. All these efforts would help to reduce Peru's projected fiscal and commercial deficits, strengthening a state that continued to throw away valuable revenues in current expenditures, unproductive imports, frivolous consumption or grandiose construction in its modern capital. Legitimation of the state was redefined here from buying out *limeño* aristocrats (a pressing theme of the 1850s) towards more lasting productivity and a more national scope and cast of citizen-subjects.

Pardo was not alone: his regionalist argument for railroads — aimed at political and social integration of Andean Peru (rather than mere export extraction) — was soon echoed in dozens of dizzy regional proposals written for railroads throughout the 1860s. This campaign may indeed have contributed to Peru's infamously generous spending on 'railways to nowhere' — expenditures which would, during Pardo's ill-fated presidency in the 1870s, bankrupt the treasury.[28] Peru's guano-age railways are perhaps best read for their national and re-distributive aims, rather than for their inherent economic sense.

Luis Benjamín Cisneros, writing deep into the much-predicted fiscal crisis of the late 1860s, was less generous than Pardo to Peru's people, but equally nationalist and statist in his reformist zeal. His objective was the drastic overhaul of the fiscal system, laid out in detail in his 1866 *Ensayos sobre cuestiones económicas*. Yet as others have suggested, Cisneros's reform of the guano-consignment lending

---

[27]   Manuel Pardo, *Estudios sobre la Provincia de Jauja* (Lima, 1862), orig. in 1860 *Revista de Lima* (read above as mouthpiece of Peru's 'comprador' bourgeoisie). See Juan Maiguashca, 'A Reinterpretation of the Guano Age' (DPhil thesis, Oxford, 1967), chs. 3–4, for insight as developmental group; Carmen McEvoy, *Un proyecto nacional del siglo XIX: Manuel Pardo y su visión del Perú* (Lima, 1994) is a concerted revisionism about Pardo, emphasising (like myself) his citizen-making ideals; *La utopía republicana: ideales y realidades en la formación de la cultura política peruana (1871–1919)* (Lima, 1997), mines this vein further.

[28]   *Imagining Development*, pp. 89–111, for regional rail literature.

system was actually rooted in a strong personal reaction against perceived threats of growing political instability.[29] Political factionalism dominated Peru because, lacking respectable and productive middle-class employment, the state had became a redistributive or rentier prize, the public sector overly politicised. Besides its harsh dose of fiscal austerity, Cisneros's plan had two major planks. First were steps to augment the fiscal and political autonomy of the Peruvian state, by depoliticising its revenue and expenditure bases, and the famous plan to farm Peru's guano contracts out to European contractors, away from a predatory circle of national merchants. The French house of Dreyfus would play this controversial role in 1869. The second feature was the effort to conserve and then invest revenues for specific developmental projects. Cisneros not only reiterated Pardo's vision of integrating railways, but articulated a host of other more statist ideas, including tariff-promoted industries and a national shipping line to Europe. Yet Cisneros had an instinctive distrust of direct popular participation in such projects; we might see this perspective as 'technology from above'. Citizen-making appears as a by-product of productive enterprise.[30]

It is not until the 1870s that we encounter an elite developmental discourse (now in a full crisis mode as guano supplies were truly running out) in combination with a more active and even inclusive politics from below. By the early 1870s, Lima had become home to a novel range of 'micro-industries' (founded by a new breed of middle-class European immigrant), a proto-worker's movement (with a self-styled 'obrero' consciousness) and a vibrant local revival of 'the arts' and artisan political culture. The latter had incubated at the city's expansive Escuela de Artes y Oficios, which was founded in the 1860s as a welfare overture to moribund craft guilds. In this milieu, a new cult of worker and artisan education becomes discernible, stirred by the workers' press as well as anti-aristocratic mavericks such as educational reformer Mariano Amézaga. In the hands of prominent *civilista* writers, like José Arnaldo Márquez, humble and underappreciated workers were reworked into the productive solution to Peru's commercial crisis, extending on the populist-productive tropes developed by Amézaga. Márquez's *El Trabajo* was designed to bring artisans, shopkeepers and their ilk into the new Civilista Party, organised by Pardo in 1870. As recent studies show, they came in droves, helping Pardo to become Peru's first civilian president in 1872.[31] Pardo

---

[29] Maiguashca, 'Guano Age'; Luis Benjamín Cisneros, *Ensayo sobre varias cuestiones económicas del Perú* (Le Havre, 1866), analysed in *Imagining Development*, pp. 111–29.

[30] Nationalist technology and determinism are exemplified by *La Asociación de Ingenieros del Perú* (Lima, 1871). See also a work of regional (strategic) developmentalism (for the south) by Cisneros's brother, Luciano B. Cisneros, *Apuntes sobre la comisión del sur por el ex- ministerio de beneficencia* (Lima, 1868).

[31] See Mariano Amézaga (A. Tauro, comp), *Problemas de la educación nacional* (Lima, 1952), articles of the early 1870s; *El Trabajo* (Lima, 1874); Jorge Basadre, 'Prólogo', in Copello y Petriconi, *Estudio sobre la independencia económica*, pp. vii–viii, on micro-industrialism. McEvoy, *Un proyecto nacional*, esp. ch. 4 and appendices.

and some of his closest advisers, notably Andrés Avelino Aramburú, hoped that their 'Practical Republic' would expand the boundaries of citizenship and economic participation to urban popular groups and beyond. This was something more than a narrow oligarchic vision.

A highpoint of these trends was Juan Copello and Luis Petriconi's *Estudios sobre la independencia ecónomica del Perú* (1876) — often celebrated as a kind of nineteenth-century dependency tract *avant la lettre*.[32] Copello and Petriconi's manifesto, first published in the Civilist mouthpiece *El Nacional*, is more aptly read as a call for a participatory economic and social policy, combining these new elements of middle-class, civil, immigrant and artisan nationalism. Built rhetorically around a series of progressive 'what ifs' (shameful lost opportunities) of the clearly passing age of guano prosperity, the 111-page book focuses on the public sector and a diverse array of mobilised small property owners and producers as the salvation of a crisis-ridden country. They harshly criticise the liberal model of the guano age for its damaging impact on the country's prior social diversity and for its penchant for macro-integration projects such as the Andean railways and coastal export plantations, now in moral as well as financial bankruptcy.

Copello and Petriconi were openly statist in proclaiming national 'economic independence' the elusive goal of Peruvian nationalism since 1821. The state as the social organiser and protector of national productive forces was a familiar theme, but the plan was also inspired by newer European theories of smallholder corporatism, such as that of Sismondi. The reform agenda in Copello and Petriconi did not adhere to a single school; rather, there is an array of proposals on the 'perfection' of domestic civic institutions, small-scale initiatives, popular and technical education ('saber es poder') and liberal associationism, combined with staunch protectionism in external affairs. A thriving petty industrialism would contribute to the country's 'bienestar moral', not only to state coffers and a durable economy. There is a common good, a 'social pact' and an unacknowledged political affinity with the beleaguered Civilist regime of Pardo. Centralised 'Councils of Promotion', staffed by enlightened notables, were to lead the way to this new diversity, but the ideological aim was articulated as a 'programme of *trabajo humano* ... a real and progressive prosperity ... with the open, faithful and energetic cooperation of the *pueblo*, who organise work and of the public authorities called forth to protect and foster it'.[33] This marks an emerging conception of popular agency and citizenship, combined here with the state's responsibility for guiding their social development and national social stability. Hardly the isolated utopians that they were usually portrayed as, Copello and

---

[32] Copello and Petriconi, *Estudio sobre la independencia económica del Perú* (Lima, 1876, repr. 1971), placed in genealogical context in *Imagining Development*, pp. 163–81; in Yepes, *Peru: Siglo*, pp. 103–5, as a dependency work.

[33] Copello and Petriconi, *Estudios sobre la independencia económica*, pp. 101–3 and *passim*, especially chapters 29–34.

Petriconi's nation would collapse — like the rest of the Peruvian state and coastal society built on guano — in the multiple convulsions of the late 1870s.

Such a genealogy of nationalist ideals fades away after defeat in the War of the Pacific with Chile (1879–83) and the devastation of the state and elites of the nineteenth century. After 1880 we hear more retrospective voices — the flaws of post-Independence era were now tragically-clear history to literate Peruvians — but these reflections also point to the more 'modernist' radical social critiques of the early twentieth century, in which Peru would excel (Haya de la Torre and Mariátegui being exemplars). At this moment, Peru's regions suddenly take precedence over a demolished and centralist Lima, and even the invisible majority — Peruvian Indians — are transformed into the future stock of Peru's national development. A forgotten strand of economic *indigenismo* marks the 1880s. Civilist journalist, medical-man and geographer Luis Carranza, who criss-crossed the Andes with Cáceres's *montoneros* during the anti-Chilean resistance struggles of 1880–81, condemned the oppression of the Indians beyond the usual liberal suspects (priests and caudillos) including the excessive centralism of the guano-age state and its free-trade policies, which had drained and wasted the interior's (especially his native Huamanga's) sources of livelihood and social diversity.[34] Another forgotten voice was that of Luis Esteves, an ex-Civilist deputy who sat out the war writing the country's first full-length economic history, *Apuntes sobre la historia económica del Perú* (1882). Aided by a republican geographic national 'discovery' literature (Raimundi and company) and the few operating Andean railways of the 1870s, the book covered the whole expanse of Peru. Critical of failed Lima-centric policies, Esteves advocated from a positivist stance three 'I's' for Peru's economic and national future: industrialism (in the Andean provinces, near to raw materials and good labour); *indigenismo* (previously-ignored and oppressed Indians were to be liberated as 'industrial beings'); and anti-imperialism (in the book's bitter attacks on the global technological monopoly left by the century's European imperium of free trade).[35] The object was psychologically to 'awaken' Peruvians from their national despair and to bring a now awakening interior and peasant (as potential proletarian and mestizo) into a now flagrantly dis-integrated and dis-united nation. This was a fitting reflection on Peru's nineteenth century, now passing into history.

---

[34] Luis Carranza, 'Consideraciones generales sobre los departamentos del centro', (1883) in Carranza, *Colección de artículos publicados por Luis Carranza, médico* (Lima, 1885–88).

[35] Luis Esteves, *Apuntes sobre la historia económica del Perú* (Lima, 1882), rept., 1971; Esteves has been overlooked by even recent chroniclers of *indigenismo*, e.g., Efraín Kristal, *The Andes Viewed from the City: Literary and Political Discourse on the Indian in Peru* (New York, 1987).

Conclusion: Can We See Clearly Now?

It is clear, even through the discursive political-economy lens here, that a two-stage process of state formation works quite well for the experience of nineteenth-century Peru.[36] First, there was a perceptibly active process of 'state-formation' in Peru between 1820 and 1850, which at the very least consolidated the territorial, fiscal and despotic powers of the Lima state — no small feat given its many obstacles and historically missing precursors or prerequisites. Contrary to nationalist mythologies, Peru's state did not draw on a long conception before 1821 nor did 'Peru' as a state-entity have to survive long into the century. Secondly, this consolidation was followed between 1850 and 1880 by active expansion of the softer infrastructural powers of the state, which brought to the fore discourses of 'national progress' that envisaged a greater cast of citizen-subjects. That is to say, Peru's maturing but crisis-prone state helped to establish (at least representationally) a prospective 'nation' within its territorial bounds. That state did display the features of modern administration, but it was not the ordered, reductionist, top-down and Manichean nation James Scott might have us see.[37] In a sense Peru required this working central state before a 'nation' or more embedded forms of national life and politics became thinkable and practicable. Yet liberalism, as utilitarianism or economic laissez-faire, even in the nineteenth century, proved quite inadequate to the complex tasks of forging the Latin American nation-state and so it was purposefully and quickly amended by Peruvian statesmen.[38] Again, Peru's statist sequence and agency are not intellectually shocking, given the parallels with contemporary Europe, and also given our own disciplinary scepticism about the role of 'primordial' national

---

[36] Since the 1980s Peru has inspired and produced many new historical works that continue to develop state/society/nation perspectives or that view civil society or Peruvian political history through novel social or cultural lenses. Yet this outpouring has not led towards a re-synthesis of the Peruvian state, either as national process or national imaginary, comparable to the synthetic narrative supplied by traditional political periodisation or historiography (Basadre and facsimiles) or for that matter, by the well-defined dependency/Marxist/social history schools of the 1970s and 1980s, which many of today's younger scholars are reacting against. This fragmentation is partly deliberate, given the stress on regionalism, local cultures or diversified (ethnic or gendered) experiences of power and domination in Peru. Given this range of new material, I still wonder whether Peruvian historiography might profit from a new research agenda that could bring it together.

[37] Due time to mention Scott's book, *Seeing Like A State: How Certain Schemes to Improve the Human Condition Have Failed* (New Haven, CT, 1997), which (unlike much Latin American literature) seems to award states unlimited powers and autonomy to define and mould their social and discursive realities (rather than being messily negotiated affairs of state).

[38] There were no stateswomen in the group, save around later educational issues.

feelings in nation-building at large.[39] Statism achieved something here, though a 'Modest Arch' seems the most apt cultural metaphor for the nascent Peruvian state, to play on the one tossed from E.P. Thompson to Corrigan and Sayer and lately onto Nugent and Joseph.

'Autonomies' of the state (and of its elite public sphere) were visible behind both modest arches, though I have tried to suggest also a deeper play of social relations and actors during both phases. The new-born Lima state was soon 'freed' of foreign states and most local constraints save for the links between national merchant-finance, northern caudillos and a handful of loyal administrator-ideologues. That peculiar Lima nexus probably kept Peruvian *caudillismo* kicking beyond its time. After 1850 the ensuing guano-age state became even more autonomous because of its special fiscal character (an unlimited three-decade supply of easy public guano-revenues) and, as expected, behaved erratically, without sinking deep and stabilising roots into Peruvian society. Moreover, the ideational groups that gathered around the state — the financiers, lawyers, officials, engineers, journalists, plutocrats and reformers — were themselves an extraordinarily independent lot, at least as regards the usually depicted (class or cultural) constraints or blinkers of an export-dependent society.[40] That gave them the liberty to project a different state with a distinct future, though the Peruvian 'cultural revolution' that they made was a modest one. It was both limited and utopian, I speculate, precisely because of these autonomies, or as glimpsed from the other side, because of the state's remoteness from other social forces.

At the start of the chapter I urged Latin Americanist scholars to defy ephemeral trends and return to their traditional concerns with the state, whatever their present methodological mood. Some historians, to be sure, have started to venture more seriously back into political (and to lesser extent legal and institutional) history. In countries such as Peru this movement was born from the shocks to political 'civility' and fundamental human rights felt from the 1980s until today (the age of 'Gonzalo' and Fujimori), which has left a kind of deep anxiety about the past and future soundness of the public domain. Others, more pessimistically, are plumbing beyond public and political spaces for societal or discursive questions of governmentality or 'technologies of rule', inspired by Foucault, with 'race' an obvious marker in the ordering of Andean societies.[41] Such approaches may help

---

[39] Arjun Appadurai, *Modernity at Large: Cultural Dimensions of Globalization* (Minnesota, 1998), esp. ch. 7, 'Life after Primordialism'; Calhoun, *Nationalism*, which warns too of excessive 'state-building' concerns. Corrigan and Sayer, *The Great Arch: English State Formation as Cultural Revolution*.

[40] E. Bradford Burns, *The Poverty of Progress: Latin America in the Nineteenth Century* (Berkeley, 1983), for a standard view. *Between Silver and Guano*, pp. 132–7, and *Imagining Development*, pp. 205–8, for axes of autonomy/embeddedness.

[41] For this kind of 'new' political history see especially McEvoy, *Un proyecto nacional* and *La utopía republicana*; Fernando de Trazegnies, *La idea del derecho en el Perú republicano de siglo XIX* (Lima, 1980) both legalistic and Foucaudian; for an earlier era, Cristóbal Aljovín

weave threads of culture and power into study of the state in newly sophisticated ways — in ways that avoid the pitfalls of the past (facile and timeless essentialisms like 'patrimonialism') and present (vague and loaded concepts like 'hegemony'). Recent work on Mexico marks progress in this direction, notably by visualising state formation as an ongoing process negotiated from above and below, in both its long and short *durées*.[42]

The historical Peruvian state, with its structural instabilities, institutional infirmities and long-run political legacies has not been an easy one to envisage, and easily pales against something as obvious and obtrusive as Mexico's or Brazil's modern Leviathan. Save for some middle years of the nineteenth century, when bloated by its guano monies, Peru has always been a smaller entity. Such a small arch hardly needs to be 'de-centred' to spot its failures and frailties. Modern Peru, however future research fares, will likely remain an outlier case, one looked at mainly for its glaring failures and lacunae rather than for any of its fitful early stages or modest architrave. But mindful of Albert O. Hirschman's long call to transcend our chronic intellectual 'fracasomanía', I'll end on the hope that past and present Peru (which greatly deserves a far better state) can be seen in a new and different light — from *las luces* of *problema y posibilidad*.[43]

---

de Losada, 'Representational Government in Peru: Fiction and Reality, 1821–1845' (PhD diss., University of Chicago, 1996) or Walker, *Smoldering Ashes*; for examples of race, Thurner, *Two Republics to One Divided* or Cecilia Méndez, *Incas sí, indios no: apuntes para el estudio del nacionalismo criollo en el Perú* (Lima, 1993). These civility and race concerns were voiced by Albert Flores Galindo in the early 1980s. For Latin America at large, consult Sabato, *Ciudadanía política y formación de naciones*.

[42] Implicit in Alan Knight's corpus, and more programmatically in Nugent and Joseph, *Everyday Forms of State Formation*.

[43] Albert O. Hirschman, 'Fracasamania' (versus possibilism) in *Journeys Towards Progress* (New York, 1973); Jorge Basadre, *Perú: problema y posibilidad* (Lima, 1931–78) — a classical ambiguity. Jeremy Adelman, 'Spanish-American Leviathan? State Formation in Nineteenth-Century Spanish America', *Comparative Studies in Society and History*, vol. 40, no. 2 (April 1998), pp. 391–408, laments a wider deep-seated 'etiology of failure' around nineteenth-century states.

CHAPTER 11

Nationalism, Internal Colonialism and the Spatial Imagination: The Geographic Society of La Paz in Turn-of-the-Century Bolivia*

Seemin Qayum

In 1942 the North American human geographer Carl Sauer visited Bolivia while on a tour of the Andean countries. At the time of his visit, although formal independence had been achieved more than a century before, Bolivia was still a decade away from the national revolution and agrarian reform that would initiate far-reaching social and economic change.[1] Sauer's characteristically matter-of-fact remarks — made in passing about the cultural landscape of the city of La Paz and surrounding *altiplano* — resonate with secular representations of highland Bolivia:

> The country is up to its reputation as an Indian land with a thin, white, upper crust. It is primarily Aymara in speech, physiognomy, dress and custom, even down to the central plaza of the capital.

> A strange place, La Paz — the highest and perhaps the most remote big city of the world, a city in which the Indian, unabashed in native costume and speech, far outnumbers the 'people of reason.'[2] ... The Indian theme is the first problem in Bolivia. Four-fifths of the population is pure Indian, and the Indian culture has great vitality and lack of self-consciousness, in spite of the fact that there is no Indianismo policy as in Mexico. The Indian is just the dominant element of the fauna, but the government is for the rest of the population. The Indians are mostly very poor, they have no privileges and not many rights, but they don't give the impression of being degraded or ashamed as they do somewhat in Peru ... There is meaning in the persistence

---

* I would like to give particular thanks to James Dunkerley, Olivia Harris, Florencia Mallon, Gustavo Rodríguez and Sinclair Thomson for their comments on earlier versions of this essay.

[1] For broad overviews of the processes of 1952–53 and their consequences, see James Malloy, *Bolivia, the Uncompleted Revolution* (Pittsburgh, 1970); James Dunkerley, *Rebellion in the Veins: Political Struggle in Bolivia, 1952–1982* (London, 1984); Manuel Frontaura Argandoña, *La Revolución Boliviana* (La Paz, 1974); Guillermo Lora, *El proletariado en el proceso político, 1952–1980* (La Paz, 1980); Rene Zavaleta, *El poder dual en América Latina* (Mexico City, 1974); William Carter, 'Revolution and the Agrarian Sector', in James Malloy and Richard Thorn (eds.), *Beyond the Revolution: Bolivia Since 1952* (Pittsburgh, 1971).

[2] Here Sauer alluded to the colonial epithet 'gente de razón' which referred to 'civilised' and 'cultivated' people as opposed to 'barbarous' commoners or, more specifically, the white, Spanish or creole elite as contrasted to the indigenous plebe.

of the beautifully woven costumes; the people will not hide themselves in the white man's shoddy or cast-off clothing.

The literate Bolivians are becoming somewhat aware of the peculiar quality of their land, of its indigenousness. I have gathered what I could of late Bolivian literature, and the emergence of the native is slight as compared to Mexico. The intellectuals don't snoot the Indian as they do at present in Peru, nor do they fear him; they haven't quite discovered him. I get the feeling of inarticulateness out of the literate Bolivian with regard to his homeland; it hasn't really been discovered by him, or for him.[3]

La Paz was indeed a singular place. Founded in the sixteenth century upon an older Aymara settlement, the city retained its indigenous demographic and cultural predominance through the colonial and republican periods.[4] Alcide D'Orbigny, the nineteenth-century French scientific traveller who arrived in La Paz in 1830, was similarly struck by the qualities that set it apart from other major cities in South America:

La Paz does not resemble in the slightest way any of the other American cities. All of the ones I had seen so far are more or less similar to our cities in Europe. In La Paz ... not only is the mass of the population indigenous and speaks nothing but its primitive language, but national dress also dominates ... if not the most picturesque, at least the most original.[5]

Although a century and more separated D'Orbigny's and Sauer's sojourns in the region, both were impressed by the unusual nature of race relations and cultural identity in Bolivia. For foreign travellers, be they explorers, diplomats, scouts for capital or scientists and scholars, the fascination of republican Bolivia in the nineteenth century and beyond has been, above all, the Indian question. While they may have pursued their strictly practical and scientific investigations involving natural resources and production, mining and agriculture or navigation and commercial routes, nearly all were intrigued and perplexed by the varied manifestations of indigenous peoples and their counterparts in national society. Undoubtedly most brought with them preconceptions and half-formed ideas regarding what they would find: civilised heirs of the Incas or uncouth savages,

---

[3]   The three quotations are from Robert West, *Andean Reflections: Letters from Carl O. Sauer While on a South American Trip Under a Grant from the Rockefeller Foundation, 1942*. (Boulder, 1982), pp. 66, 71–2.

[4]   Thierry Saignes, 'De los ayllus a las parroquias de indios: Chuquiago y La Paz', *Los andes orientales. Historia de un olvido* (Cochabamba, 1985); Rossana Barragán, *Espacio Urbano y Dinámica Etnica, La Paz en el Siglo XIX* (La Paz, 1990); and Herbert Klein, *Haciendas and Ayllus: Rural Society in the Bolivian Andes in the Eighteenth and Nineteenth Centuries* (Stanford, 1993), pp. 6, 9, 127.

[5]   Alcide d'Orbigny, *Viaje a la América meridional* (Buenos Aires, 1945), 4 vols., p. 982.

along with elegant, *creole* elites and crude, ill-bred mestizos.[6] They might have expected an equally exotic landscape palette: following Pratt's formulation, the Humboldtian triad of snow-capped mountains (Andean cordillera); vast interior plains (eastern lowlands and Chaco); and lush tropical forests (Amazon basin).[7]

The quest for geographical and anthropological knowledge, manifested in D'Orbigny and Sauer, was a quintessential component of the North Atlantic imperial project explicated by Edward Said in *Orientalism*, as texts in the studies of colonial discourse and postcolonial criticism. Extending Vico's observation — that people make their own history, and that what we can know is what we have made — beyond history to geography and culture, Said argues that geographical and cultural entities, such as the Orient, were also socially constructed. The colonial project, then, involved the 'coincidence of geography, knowledge and power'. In this sense Said cites the 23-volume *Description of Egypt (1809–1828)*, the formidable textual yield of Napoleon's military and scientific invasion of Egypt, as the 'great collective appropriation of one country by another'. Imperial appropriations were fuelled by *imaginative* geography and *imaginative* history as practised in European state and public spheres. The summoning up of speculations and projections about other places, peoples, traditions, customs, flora and fauna, helped to fill in the blank spaces on the map, as it were.[8]

The exercise of geography, whether as a scientific discipline or a popular pastime in the core countries of Europe, helped promote, justify and legitimate territorial conquest, economic accumulation, cultural subjugation and colonial administration. The 'tremendous efflorescence' that Said notes of geographical societies in Europe in the nineteenth century was central to the imperial and colonial enterprise.[9] The geographical societies sponsored explorations and celebrated explorers when they came back from unknown, dangerous and 'exotic' places. Originally engaged in the promotion and dissemination of 'scientific' research and discovery, the societies rapidly became instrumental to colonial expansion, and handmaidens to trade and commerce. The scope of geography as a field of study in the nineteenth century was vast, encompassing a multi-

---

[6] 'Creole' refers to persons of European descent born in the Americas. In Bolivia, since Independence in 1825, this has been a synonym for 'whites' (defined in terms of colour, culture and/or socioeconomic class). 'Mestizo' is a loosely-defined racial and cultural category referring to people perceived to be of mixed European and indigenous background.

[7] Mary Louise Pratt, *Imperial Eyes: Travel Writing and Transculturation* (London, 1992), p. 125.

[8] Edward Said, *Orientalism* (New York, 1978), especially pp. 1–28, 49–56, 83–5, 214–19.

[9] This was above all a French phenomenon. Of the 106 geographical societies in existence in 1896, 29 were in France or its colonies; the combined worldwide membership was 47,968, and the total French was 16,508 — 34%. See William Schneider, 'Geographical Reform and Municipal Imperialism in France, 1870–80', in John MacKenzie, *Imperialism and the Natural World* (Manchester and New York, 1990), pp. 90–117.

plicity of amateur and scientific pursuits, from astronomy to zoology. The membership was also multifarious, ranging from aristocratic and upper-class 'gentlemen of science' to academic scholars and scientists and, of course, the affiliated or sponsored adventurers-cum-explorers. An overarching objective for the French and British geographical societies in the nineteenth century was the exploration and intellectual appropriation of parts of Latin America, the Middle East, Asia and, above all, Africa.[10]

Recent work has begun to deepen our appreciation of the central place of geography and affiliated disciplines in the spatial, cultural, racial and gender construction of empire and colony.[11] Yet this work is particularly focused on the European expansion into Africa, Asia and the Pacific and the Middle East, and as such is largely confined to the colonial period beginning in the nineteenth century and drawing to a close with mid-twentieth-century independence movements. The American colonies, in contrast, had for the most part become independent nations by 1825. Latin America was thus on a different temporal cycle in terms of colonial/post-colonial experience — already inventing modern nationalism by the end of the eighteenth century, and in the throes of nation-building in the nineteenth century.[12] Not only does geography need to be studied in the early modern context of Spanish colonialism, but especially as a post-colonial field of knowledge. What I wish to emphasise here is that the links between geography and culture, between territory and identity, are as key to nation-building as they are to the construction of colonial and imperial spaces and subjects. Moreover, these two processes are not necessarily antithetical. In the present Andean case in question here, I would argue that the two were related through *internal colonialism*.

D'Orbigny and Sauer were unquestionably metropolitan geographers, but they did not make their observations in an imperial colony. Sauer's remarks

---

[10] For the history of geography in this period, see David Stoddart, *On Geography and its History* (Oxford and New York, 1986); and David Livingstone, *The Geographical Tradition: Episodes in the History of a Contested Enterprise* (Oxford, 1992).

[11] See, for example, Pratt, *Imperial Eyes*; Peter Raby, *Bright Paradise: Victorian Scientific Travellers* (London, 1996); Felix Driver, 'Geography's Empire: Histories of Geographical Knowledge,' *Environment and Planning: Society and Space*, vol. 10, (1992), pp. 23–40; Anne Godlewska and Neil Smith (eds.), *Geography and Empire* (Oxford, 1994); Edward Said, *Culture and Imperialism* (London, 1993); Simon Ryan, *The Cartographic Eye: How Explorers Saw Australia* (Cambridge, 1996); and Anne McClintock et al. (eds.), *Dangerous Liaisons: Gender, Nation, and Postcolonial Perspectives* (Minneapolis, 1997).

[12] Benedict Anderson, *Imagined Communities: Reflections on the Origin and Spread of Nationalism* (London, rev. ed., 1991), especially ch. 4, 'Creole Pioneers'. As Peter Hulme notes, the historical specificity of Latin America has not been adequately addressed by work on 'postcolonial' studies. See Peter Hulme, 'Including America', *ARIEL: A Review of International English Literature*, vol. 26, no. 1, pp. 117–23, Jan. 1995.

could only have been made in a *national* context — they referred directly to Bolivia's creole leaders and elite who seemed unable to comprehend either the country or its Indian inhabitants. Yet can the accuracy of Sauer's observation about the creoles' lack of consciousness of 'the peculiar quality of their land, of its indigenousness' be gauged? How, in fact, did those elites, who a century or more before had taken on the historical responsibility of constructing a nation, look upon the relations between creoles, mestizos and Indians?

The development of creole identities and ideologies during the first century of republican life, and how they helped to shape and were in turn affected by the forms and practice of nation-building in Bolivia, can only be understood in direct relation to Indian and mestizo identities. The relation of creoles to the rest of society may be profitably conceptualised in terms of internal colonialism. As La Paz Aymara intellectuals in the 1980s and 1990s have defined and employed the concept, internal colonialism refers at once to a fundamental set of social relations marked by significant ethnic and class divisions and an ideology of racial/ethnic discrimination; we should add that it also refers to a specific geographic-territorial configuration. Internal colonialism structured the relations among the descendants of colonising and colonised peoples in ways that shaped the nature of politics, economics and cultural and intellectual life in post-Independence Bolivia. In other words, internal colonial hierarchies reproduced colonial legacies of ethnic, economic and political domination and subordination.[13] While the complexity of racial thinking and practice in republican Bolivia should not be underestimated and bears deeper investigation, these hierarchies were manifested in persistent notions of European/white cultural superiority and indigenous (and sometimes mestizo) barbarism and backwardness. Just as colonialism formed a geographical nexus between metropolis and periphery, the internal colonial hierarchies were also present spatially in the distinction between the capital, La Paz, and its hinterland, the town (*'pueblo de*

---

[13]   The argument here differs from interpretations that downplay the colonial continuities in highland Peru and Bolivia by arguing for a 'refunctionalisation' or resignification of colonial categories after Independence that imbued them with new republican content and meanings. Such work exaggerates the power of liberal discourse and the hegemonic capacity of liberalism to absorb indigenous and popular expression and participation, and it also minimises the enduring structures of colonial class and racial domination and subordination. Nor can the conceptualisation of subaltern agency be limited to a process of conquering citizenship rights in the liberal public sphere. Indigenous appropriation of liberal discursive forms as a means of defending community and territory, for example, did not necessarily imply an assimilation of the rhetoric of democracy and citizenship, but rather the deployment of new weapons in ancient battles. See, for example, Marta Irurozqui, 'A Bala, Piedra y Palo': la construcción de la ciudadanía política en Bolivia, 1826–1952 (Seville, 2000) and Mark Thurner, *From Two Republics to One Divided: Contradictions of Postcolonial Nationmaking in Andean Peru* (Durham, NC, and London, 1997).

vecinos') and surrounding Indian countryside, and the nation and its frontiers — all of which had their specific colonial derivation.[14]

Bolivian internal colonialism posed key contradictions for the ideology and practice of liberalism, and the attendant discourses of civilisation, race and citizenship. In fact, the conundrum was posed by the mere *possibility* of citizenship. With Independence, this potentiality — the granting of equal civil rights and duties to all under an all-encompassing Constitution and set of laws — generated the Indian problem and, in turn, the national problem. This potentiality should be emphasised since by law as well as in practice, most indigenous people in Bolivia were excluded from citizenship until the 1952 National Revolution due to a shifting set of legal criteria which included literacy, employment status, income level and property ownership.[15] Nineteenth-century creole enthusiasts of the liberal ideals of nation-building saw in the moral mission of liberalism the redemptive triumph of civilisation over barbarism. The idea of civilisation was translated into discourses of citizenship, the heart of which was the 'improvement' of the Indian through education, and the transformation of the indigenous rural community and its constitutive property relations. The nature and challenge of these transformations have been a matter of contention for most of modern Bolivian history. Not only were there deep-rooted tensions within the creole elite with reference to the Indian question, but indigenous people themselves elaborated contestatory projects, some that were congruous with aspects of elite liberal ideology, such as citizenship claims and demands for education, and others that diverged from it, above all the communal struggles for territorial control and political autonomy throughout the nineteenth and early twentieth centuries.[16]

---

[14]   Aside from the classic formulation of Pablo González Casanova, 'Internal Colonialism and National Development,' *Studies in Comparative International Development*, vol. 1(4), 1965, for the Bolivian case see Víctor Hugo Cárdenas, 'El katarismo y otras formas de ideologías autóctonas,' *CEPROLAI, Serie Cuadernos de Documentación*, no. 6, 1989; and Silvia Rivera Cusicanqui, 'La raíz: colonizadores y colonizados,' in Xavier Albó and Raúl Barrios (eds.), *Violencias encubiertas en Bolivia* (La Paz, 1993).

[15]   Rossana Barragán, *Indios, mujeres y ciudadanos: legislación y ejercicio de la ciudadanía en Bolivia (siglo XIX)* (La Paz, 1999); Marcelo Galindo de Ugarte, *Constituciones bolivianas comparadas, 1826–1967* (La Paz, 1991).

[16]   The key indigenous projects in the period under question were the rebellions led by Zárate Willka and others during the Federal War of 1899, and the *cacique apoderado* movement of the first three decades of the twentieth century. See Ramiro Condarco Morales, *Zárate el 'temible' willka: historia de la rebelión indígena de 1899*, 2nd ed. (La Paz, 1983); Taller de Historia Oral Andina, *El indio Santos Marka T'ula: cacique principal de los ayllus de Qallapa y apoderado general de las comunidades originarias de la República* (La Paz, 1984); Leandro Condori and Esteban Ticona, *El escribano de los caciques apoderados* (La Paz, 1992); Carlos Mamani, *Taraqu, 1866–1935: masacre, guerra y 'renovación' en la biografía de Eduardo L. Nina Qhispi* (La Paz, 1991); Roberto Choque et al., *Educación indígena: ¿ciudadanía o colonización?* (La Paz, 1992).

The neocolonial and civilisational projects as formulated and applied by the liberal creole elite were heterogeneous, but they coalesced conceptually and practically in one institution that was at the cusp of state and civil society — the Geographic Society of La Paz and its sphere. Nineteenth-century geographical societies offered a key arena for nation-building as they brought together scientific, intellectual, military and professional sectors who were at the same time members of the political and economic elites. The societies provided a forum for elite research and reflection on national realities and visions, and they performed the crucial task of engaging with international researchers and ideas and receiving or assimilating them within the national context. The existence of geographical societies was by no means restricted to the metropolis. Of the more than 50 societies founded worldwide between 1821 and 1880, a handful were non-European, and of those, three were Latin American: Mexico (1833–39), Rio de Janeiro (1838) and Buenos Aires (1879).[17] The Geographic Society of La Paz was founded rather later, in 1889.

The Geographic Society came into being during a turn-of-the-century conjuncture of tremendous change. Bolivia had suffered its first serious territorial loss to Chile in the War of the Pacific in 1879–80, effectively rendering it a landlocked entity and eliminating sovereign access to Pacific Ocean ports. A momentous debacle that would only make its indelible and definitive mark on national consciousness much later in the twentieth century, the loss of the seaboard would be bitterly mourned and periodically resurrected by nationalist historians and the political class in sporadic low-intensity diplomatic warfare with Chile. In the aftermath of the defeat, with longstanding links to Chilean capital, transportation and communications networks severed, the jockeying for political and economic power and ascendancy among regional elites, principally those of La Paz and Chuquisaca, culminated in the Federal War of 1899. La Paz and the Liberal Party emerged victorious, winning from Sucre the primacy as capital city and inaugurating 20 years of liberal governments.[18]

A surge of economic dynamism equally marked the end of the nineteenth century. Tin mining greatly increased in importance, gradually replacing silver which had once been the source of the region's wealth. New commodities, such as rubber extracted from tropical forests in frontier territories, enjoyed a boom. Efforts were made to create a land market and foment capitalist agriculture in the countryside through the forced sale of Indian community lands. Projects to build railroads and highways that would drive the internal and external markets proliferated, and foreign investors arrived to finance mining, railroads and communications. The state promulgated a series of administrative and tax reforms, and the creole elite vigorously debated the merits of regionalism, federalism and nationalism, on the one

---

[17] Schneider, 'Geographical Reform', p. 92.

[18] Sucre remains the seat of the judicial branch while the executive and legislative powers are in La Paz.

hand, and protectionism and free trade, on the other. In sum, these political and economic measures undertaken by liberals in tandem with capitalists in the emerging tin mining sector seemed to herald a capitalist transition in Bolivia, similar to processes underway in other countries in Latin America.[19]

The promise of these initiatives was to remain unrealised during the first half of the twentieth century. The mining sector retained its enclave status and, in the absence of vertical or horizontal linkages, was unable to generate significant manufacturing industry. Agricultural production was still mired in the lack of development of the forces of production and the expansion of a servile labour force as haciendas appropriated the land and labour of erstwhile free communities. The internal market remained underdeveloped; and the economy as a whole was subject to the world market and, increasingly, to the direct will of foreign companies and governments.

However, the economic dynamism at the turn-of-the-century was accompanied by an intense burst of what may be termed nation-building activity. As Corrigan and Sayer remark, while social theory has recognised the link between nation-state formation and the transition to capitalism, it has not adequately addressed the 'profoundly cultural content of state institutions and activities nor the nature and extent of state regulation of cultural forms'.[20] A consideration of nation-state formation in nineteenth-century Bolivia necessarily involves the geography or space of the nation. Central here was the participation of geographers and ethnographers in the sphere of the state and what may be called the geographical apparatus (institutions, maps, censuses, expeditions) and geographical imagination in defining and shaping the nation.[21]

While the spatial and cultural dimensions of nation-state formation in nineteenth-century Latin America are scarcely understood, some new work on the region's geography and geographical societies places them at the juncture of culture, space and nature. Geographical societies served as vehicles for exploration and inventory of exploitable and extractable natural resources and, in similar fashion, the categorisation and attempted assimilation — or eradication — of indigenous human groups; territorial delimitation and consolidation;

---

[19] For an overview of these processes, see Herbert Klein, *Bolivia: The Evolution of a Multi-Ethnic Society* (New York, 1982) and *Parties and Political Change in Bolivia, 1880–1952* (Cambridge, 1969); Erick Langer, *Economic Change and Rural Resistance in Southern Bolivia, 1880–1930* (Stanford, 1989); Antonio Mitre, *Los patriarcas de la plata: estructura socio-económica de la minería boliviana en el siglo XIX* (Lima, 1981) and *Bajo un cielo de estaño: fulgor y ocaso del metal en Bolivia* (La Paz, 1993); Tristan Platt, *Estado boliviano y ayllu andino* (Lima, 1982); Condarco Morales, *Zárate el 'temible' willka.*

[20] Phillip Corrigan and Derek Sayer, *The Great Arch: English State Formation as Cultural Revolution* (Oxford, 1985), pp. 1–10.

[21] Anderson, *Imagined Communities.*

and, not least, national and patriotic self-definition and identity formation.[22] Returning to Said's formulation of the critical conjuncture of geography, knowledge and imperialism, the geographical societies in independent Latin America were the conjunctive site of geography, knowledge and nationalism.

The La Paz Geographic Society was the most important of the scientific societies in Bolivia at the turn of the century. Founded by a small group of 11 self-defined 'men of science' to promote the study and diffusion of knowledge about the geography of Bolivia and, especially, the Department of La Paz, it nevertheless aspired to incorporate all the arts and sciences. Invoking the example of geographical societies in the rest of what was called the 'civilised' world, its purpose was stated to be a 'new civilising mission'.[23] The membership was composed of both amateur and more professional geographers and ethnographers, most with a university education in law, letters or engineering. There were also local, regional and national politicians and government officials, including presidents (mostly liberals); and prominent figures from the La Paz regional elite, including bankers, industrialists, miners, *hacienda* landlords, coca leaf producers and businessmen — commerce historically being the lifeblood of the La Paz region.[24] Fifteen years after its founding, in 1904, the Geographic Society had some 50 members and a long list of corresponding members in the rest of Bolivia, the Americas and Europe. By 1918 it had 80 active members, remaining a rather restricted group of quite influential individuals.

The Geographic Society performed an important mediating function by articulating national ideologies with European and US thought and science, and by incorporating and translating foreign research for domestic consumption. It championed earlier travellers such as D'Orbigny whose works were studied and cited through the nineteenth century as they have been to the present. The Society maintained formal relationships with prominent contemporary travellers, geographers and anthropologists of its day such as Edwin Heath (whose explorations were written up in the Society's Bulletin), Elisée Reclus, Clements Markham and Adolph Bandelier. Markham's studies of the Incas and the Aymara language and Bandelier's monograph on Aymara communities on the Islands of the Sun and

---

[22] For Peru, see Leoncio López-Ocón Cabrera, 'El nacionalismo y los orígenes de la Sociedad Geográfica de Lima', in Marcos Cueto (ed.), *Saberes andinos: ciencia y tecnología en Bolivia, Ecuador y Perú* (Lima, 1995); on Bolivia, see Seemin Qayum, 'Espacio y poder: La élite paceña en el período geográfico', *Autodeterminación*, vol. 11 (La Paz, 1993); and on the Argentine Geographical Institute, Klaus-John Dodds, 'Geography, Identity and the Creation of the Argentine State', *Bulletin of Latin American Research*, vol. 12, no. 3 (1993), pp. 311–31.

[23] Luis Crespo, 'La "Sociedad Geográfica de La Paz"', *Boletín de la Sociedad Geográfica de La Paz*, año V, 2a semestre de 1904. This article was written for a US guide to learned societies and institutions ('Manual de sociedades e instituciones sabias' de Washington).

[24] On the composition and origins of the La Paz elite, see Roberto Laura, 'Constitución de la oligarquía en La Paz, 1870–1900', *Licenciatura* thesis in Sociology (La Paz, 1988).

Koati in Lake Titicaca, were all translated and published by the Geographic Society. This effort of translation and diffusion was both a sort of public service for the literate community, as well as a stimulus for the Society's own research.[25]

The Geographic Society could be considered the intelligentsia of the Liberal Party. The Society played a prominent part in shaping state policy and creole identity and discourse through its research and publications on Indian communities. Agustín Aspiazu, one of the founders of the Society, conducted the first systematic analysis of urban and rural property, taxes and regional political economy in republican Bolivia, and authored perhaps the only dictionary of civil law. Luis Crespo, historian and geographer, wrote classic texts on those subjects, and practised his craft as sub-director of the 1900 National Census and director of the 1909 Census of the city of La Paz. Rigoberto Paredes wrote exhaustively on the different regions of the Department of La Paz and on indigenous history, culture, myths and folklore. Bautista Saavedra, prominent criminologist, lawyer and future president (1921–25), composed a study of the *ayllu* — the indigenous social/territorial community formation — and collaborated intermittently with Aymara political leaders. Several members made studies of Aymara language, culture and civilisation, especially the question of 'national' origins and the ruins at Tiwanaku.[26]

The case of Manuel Vicente Ballivián, president of the Society from 1897 to 1921, is particularly instructive. Not only was he a member of various liberal governments in different strategic capacities, but he was also the scion of an established creole elite family, that could trace its political prestige and economic fortunes back to at least the end of the eighteenth century. The Balliviáns profited from the government policy of forcing the sale of Indian community lands in La Paz, their landed estates increasing tremendously in the first 20 years of the sales (1881–1900).[27] The portfolio of the family also encompassed interests in railroads, commerce and urban property. The position of many other Society members was not dissimilar.

---

[25] Edwin Heath, 'Exploración del Rio Beni en 1880–81', *Boletín de la Sociedad Geográfica de La Paz*, vol. 14–15 (1902); Clemente Markham, *Las posiciones geográficas de las tribus que formaban el imperio de los Incas con un 'apéndice' sobre el nombre aymar …una introducción por Manuel V. Ballivián* (La Paz, 1902); Adolfo Bandelier, *Las islas de Titicaca y Koati, versión española de Edmundo Sologuren colaborado por Manuel V. Ballivián y Belisario Díaz Romero* (La Paz, 1914).

[26] Agustín Aspiazu, *Diccionario razonado del derecho civil boliviano* (La Paz, 1885); and *Informe que presenta Agustín Aspiazu al señor ministro de Hacienda desde el departamento de La Paz* (La Paz, 1881); Luis Crespo, *Monografía de la ciudad de La Paz de Ayacucho* (La Paz, 1902); Bautista Saavedra, *El Ayllu* (La Paz, 1903); Arturo Posnansky, *Tihuanacu y la civilización prehistórica en el altiplano andino*, 2a edición, aumentada y corregida (La Paz, 1911).

[27] See Rossana Barragán, Ana María Lema and Seemin Qayum, 'Yo tengo, yo pienso, yo soy: economía, sociedad e ideología de las elites paceñas, 1880–1900,' paper presented in the 'Regional Economies and Societies, XIX and XX Centuries' Conference (Cochabamba, 1992).

The members of the Geographic Society were both key players in, and ideologues of, the political and economic dynamism of the turn of the century. They contributed, along with others in liberal creole elite circles, to the construction of new spatial conceptions that corresponded to that particular moment of economic transformation and nation-building. These spatial conceptions were by no means homogeneous, but together they did signal a change in the *mentalité* and ideology of certain sectors of the elite. The new geographic consciousness was most notably announced by José Manuel Pando, Society member and future president of the country (1899–1904), in 1897 when he was the leader of the Liberal Party: 'We have entered a period characterised by explorations and scientific studies, which may properly be termed the *geographic period*.'[28]

In an analysis of the spatiality and territoriality of the Bolivian nation for the period under question, Zavaleta poses a contrast between seigneurial space, which was dominant, and Andean space, or the space of the indigenous communities. Seigneurial space was the spatial nexus of the hacienda landowner, characterised as localist, regionalist, insular, stagnant, in fact, effectively feudal — always inward-looking, and neglectful of broader national duties and initiatives. For Zavaleta, Bolivian regionalism, the sort of regional factionalism that led to the Federal War in 1899, signified nothing more than the incapacity to imagine, to conceptualise and to construct *national* space. The absence of collective sentiment concerning the space of the nation, especially on the part of those of the landed classes who shaped seigneurial space, was strikingly demonstrated during the 1879–80 War of the Pacific. By contrast, Zavaleta distinguishes Andean space as having been integral, collective and all-encompassing. (In fact, Andean space was transnational in that it surpassed the boundaries established by colonial jurisdictions and those which replaced them after Independence.)[29]

There is a certain appeal in this contrast. It is undoubtedly true that the indigenous occupation of space was significantly different from the seigneurial. Although the relationship between indigenous communities and the land was often dramatically transformed in the colonial and the republican periods — witness the land sales of the end of the nineteenth century — and indigenous market and commercial networks diminished, the indigenous communities did survive and evinced remarkable tenacity in resisting colonial and republican incursions. Above all, what was conserved was a singular conception of territoriality, marked by the union of community space, productive space and sacred space in the landscape.

Building on Zavaleta, we can argue for the development of yet a third sort of geographical consciousness. There were elements of the La Paz elite, espe-

---

[28] José Manuel Pando, *Circular del Jefe del Partido Liberal a los Directorios Departamentales* (La Paz, 1897), p. 2.

[29] René Zavaleta Mercado, *Lo nacional-popular en Bolivia* (Mexico City, 1986), especially the prologue and section I. For a cartographic representation of these key constitutive moments, see Ramiro Condarco Morales, *Atlas histórico de Bolivia* (La Paz, 1985).

cially as constituted in the Geographic Society, that broke with the seigneurial conception of space. This new consciousness, both producer and product of the political and economic changes in the geographic period, was specifically creole and specifically national. The dialectic of creole national geographical consciousness found expression in the drive towards expansion, domination and consolidation of national space. The *nationalist* projection of this consciousness and class project set La Paz apart from the more regionalist designs of the Cochabamba and Santa Cruz elites of the time. Sucre's demotion and defeat in the Federal War would have also deflated any nationalist pretensions of the Chuquisaca silver-mining oligarchy as it was eclipsed by the emerging tin-mining sector and La Paz's consolidation as the seat of political power.[30]

The prime focus of the new geographical consciousness, then, was the administration and control of national territory, undertaken through a number of complex processes: first, the sale of Indian community lands and the concomitant expansion of the hacienda; second, the employment of instruments and mechanisms of state administration to regulate land, population and resources, e.g., land surveys (*catastros*), population censuses, statistics of all sorts and fiscal and tax measures; third, the financing and construction of railroads; and last, the expansion and consolidation of the real or imaginary frontiers of the nation through expeditions, mapping and cartography and colonisation and immigration. The work of Ballivián and his colleagues in the Geographic Society in numerous instances constituted the strategy, the legitimation and the execution of these processes which marked the geographic period.

Forced Sale of Community Lands

Indigenous communities suffered two separate but linked attempts by the state to wrest control of their territories in the latter part of the nineteenth century. The first, a frontal onslaught at the hands of notorious *cacique bárbaro* Mariano Melgarejo (1864–71) and his military and landed allies, was reversed through the concerted protest and uprisings of mobilised indigenous communities coupled with a tactical about-face on the part of the Bolivian government after Melgarejo's downfall.[31] A second and more strategic effort to liberalise the agrarian structure began in the 1881 with the execution of the 1874 Disentailment Law (*Ley de Exvinculación*) and related measures under the

---

[30] A fascinating comparison is offered in Gustavo Rodríguez, *Poder central y proyecto regional. Cochabamba y Santa Cruz en los siglos XIX y XX* (Cochabamba, 1993).

[31] The contemporary debate on Melgarejo and the violent usurpation of community lands is reproduced in the journal *Illimani*, vol. 8–9 (La Paz, 1976). See also, Marco Antonio Peñaloza, 'La expoliación de tierras comunales en el departamento de La Paz durante el gobierno de Melgarejo, 1864–1871', *Historia*, vol. 20 (1990); and Luis Antezana, *El feudalismo de Melgarejo y la reforma agraria* (La Paz, 1970).

direction of liberal elites who were more cautious than Melgarejo as far as means chosen but still ruthlessly effective. This legislation abolished colonial indigenous tribute (even though Indians continued to pay a head tax well into the twentieth century), undermined the indigenous community as a corporate legal entity with landholding rights and sought to spur the development of individualised, private property relations and a land market. It established a land survey commission (*mesa revisitadora*), which demarcated and registered landholdings, issued property titles, sold off uncultivated lands and paved the way for community division and sale.[32]

It would be difficult to overestimate the impact of the community land sales on agrarian structure during the 1880–1920 period. Ancient communities were fragmented as haciendas 'captured' the land and labour of entire communities through coercive and fraudulent transactions: in the 1880s alone, 30 per cent of communal lands passed into private, non-Indian hands. An explosion of land speculation fuelled hacienda expansion as well as yielded profits for investment in the railroads and other ventures; indeed, the construction of the railways caused land values to increase dramatically. Multi-faceted Indian resistance to private and public usurpation of community lands was unleashed, reaching its apex with the 1899 rebellion of Zárate Willka in the midst of the Federal War and persisting through to the 1930s under the leadership of *cacique apoderados* such as Santos Marka T'ula, Prudencio Kallisaya and Eduardo Nina Qhispi. Moreover, the land sales were pivotal for the realisation of the liberal project and for the construction of creole elite identity and power in opposition to the communities. It is noteworthy that many of the principal landowners to benefit from the sales held important posts within the state apparatus and also within the dominant ideological apparatus. Of any membership list of the Geographic Society, an easy majority would have belonged to landowning families.[33]

What is remarkable in the publications of the Society during this time, however, is the almost complete absence of writings on the forced land sales, hacienda expansion or community–state conflicts.[34] Of course, the fact that so many

---

[32] Silvia Rivera Cusicanqui, 'La expansión del latifundio en el altiplano boliviano: elementos para la caracterización de una oligarquía regional', *Avances*, vol. 2 (1978); Gustavo Rodriguez, *¿Expansión del latifundio o supervivencia de las comunidades indígenas? Cambios en la estructura agraria boliviana del siglo XIX* (Cochabamba, 1983); Erwin Greishaber, 'Survival of Indian Communities in Nineteenth-Century Bolivia: A Regional Comparison', *Journal of Latin American Studies*, vol. 12, no. 2 (1980).

[33] Erwin Grieshaber, 'Resistencia indígena a la venta de tierras comunales en el Departamento de La Paz, 1881-1920', *Data*, vol. 1 (1991), p. 114; Barragán, Lema and Qayum, 'Yo tengo, yo pienso, yo soy'.

[34] An interesting exception was Rigoberto Paredes, especially in *Provincia Inquisivi. Estudios geográficos, estadísticos y sociales* (La Paz, 1906), who criticised the dispossession of indigenous lands and the injustices and abuses committed against the communities,

of the leading members of the Society were not only implicated but prime instigators and beneficiaries of the forcible sales may be an obvious reason why they refrained from mentioning these matters.[35]

Another possible explanation, involving the arrangements these elites employed to manage their properties, emerges from a more intimate examination of the landowning class. It is immediately apparent that most of the landowners in question had others to administer the estates for them. However, recent oral historical research has revealed a previously unrecognised facet of life among the landed elite in La Paz around the turn of the century: a gender division of labour prevailed in which the women of these elite families would dedicate themselves to the land and the countryside, while their husbands pursued professional or political or business interests in the city. In this sense, the administration of the haciendas was seen as part of the sphere of domestic work, that is, an extension of the administration of the townhouse or mansion in the city. Of course, these women had estate agents just as they had housekeepers and servants in town. In this recent research, interviews were undertaken with several women who were the daughters or granddaughters of members of the Geographic Society during the period under consideration. One woman from a prominent ex-landed elite family gave the following account:

> The countryside of cattle and crops was in large part managed by women because naturally the men, in the first place, were too proud to be involved with things like sheep dung and wool, and they were also generally in the city wrapped up in commerce or politics.[36]

The violence associated with the period of the land sales pitted haciendas against communities; the local state, police and army troops against communities; and

---

and also warned of the probable consequences in the form of violence and rebellion. To be sure, Paredes was of provincial origin, and his class and cultural position was different from the powerful liberal landowning families. For an analysis of Paredes's perspective, and ambiguous, intermediary status, see Sinclair Thomson, 'La cuestión india en Bolivia a principios de siglo: el caso de Rigoberto Paredes', *Autodeterminación*, vol. 4 (1988), pp. 83–111.

[35] For a stimulating analysis of the involvement of Society member Ismael Montes, owner of vast expanses of *altiplano* and lacustrian lands and liberal president (1904–09, 1913–17), see Marcelo Fernández, 'El poder de la palabra: documento y memoria oral en la resistencia de Waqimarka contra la expansión latifundista (1874–1930)', *Licenciatura* thesis in Sociology, Universidad Mayor de San Andrés, La Paz (1996).

[36] Seemin Qayum, Rossana Barragán and María Luisa Soux, *De terratenientes a amas de casa: mujeres de la élite de La Paz en la primera mitad del siglo XX* (La Paz, 1997), p. 49. For example, Víctor Muñoz Reyes, distinguished member of the Geographic Society, lawyer, diplomat (Bolivia's first ambassador to Japan), politician, encyclopaedist, was neither born to a landholding family, nor took much interest in the properties he acquired upon marrying Carmen Ibargüen. In contrast, his wife not only bore and raised 12 children, but looked after the estates as well, moving the entire household — except for her husband — to the country when the seasons required it.

even communities against communities and families against families. Such violence and the routine abuses of Indian labourers on haciendas are amply reflected in archival documents and have been quite extensively treated in the secondary literature.[37] If the liberal landowners who belonged to the Geographic Society did not acknowledge such violence explicitly, this does not mean that their estate agents or hirelings, or even the state security apparatus, did not exert force in their interest. Most of the landowners personally involved in violence and conflict were local or provincial elites actually resident in the countryside, while those of the Geographic Society set had their permanent homes in La Paz. The propensity for absenteeism and delegation of administrative responsibilities to wives and women of the family and estate managers suggests a certain personal detachment from rural matters. Even if their fortunes were sustained materially by livestock, land and labour, such rural wealth was associated with the domestic/private sphere to which women, Indians and the relations of feudal/colonial domination and subordination also pertained. Landowners themselves apparently preferred to keep a physical and intellectual distance from this world, which they separated from the grander, more 'enlightened' sphere of urban politics and capital. So as the countryside was becoming increasingly polarised, the Geographic Society, with few exceptions, dealt with the 'Indian problem' in terms of demographics and descriptions of traditions, customs, habits — as well as how to change cultural patterns that were perceived to be refractory to progress and civilisation. Ultimately, the Society failed to acknowledge critical forms of violence and conflict within the rural sphere, which derived in fact from elite interests and the 'modernising' liberal programme.

The land sales were bound up with the structures of internal colonialism, understood as the acute political and economic violence and polarisation along 'racial' lines which was a prime colonial legacy. At the same time, the sales were an attempt to control the territory of unincorporated Indians through the forced transformation of the nature of that property, that is, from communal to private ownership. It was the means by which a relatively weak state appropriated territory that did not pertain to it. Since Independence there had been recurrent attempts to gain control of indigenous community lands through diverse stratagems, of which the land sales were the latest and most successful. This process, a sort of 'reconquest' or reprise of original sixteenth-century Spanish occupation, had contradictory and perverse consequences. In the words of one authority in La Paz who challenged the process underway, these consequences were: 'Reduction of state revenue, decline in public services, tumults and disturbances of social

---

[37] Condarco Morales, *Zárate*; Grieshaber, 'Resistencia indígena'; Silvia Rivera Cusicanqui, *Oprimidos pero no vencidos: luchas del campesinado aymara y qhechwa de Bolivia, 1900–1980* (La Paz, 1984); Tristan Platt, 'Liberalism and Ethnocide in the Southern Andes', *History Workshop Journal*, vol. 17 (1984), pp. 3–18. Roberto Choque, *La masacre de Jesús de Machaca* (La Paz, 1986); Roberto Choque and Esteban Ticona, *Jesús de Machaqa: la marka rebelde 2. Sublevación y masacre de 1921* (La Paz, 1996).

order, threats of uprising, on one hand; and on the other, none of the benefits proposed by the legislators in favour of the indigenous race.'[38]

The Instruments of State Administration

The imposed transformation of the relation between people and the land, and in the very meaning of property, was only one option among the range of state strategies to occupy and administer indigenous territory. The state also deployed an array of techniques for purposes of spatial and social control; among them were the rural/urban property surveys, censuses, maps, statistical compilations, geographical dictionaries and the fiscal reforms associated with the liberal project for the privatisation and commercialisation of community property. Many of these were undertaken by members of the Geographic Society, most notably Ballivián in his different incarnations as president of the Society, director of the National Office of Immigration, Statistics and Geographic Propaganda and minister of agriculture and colonisation.

Anderson has indicated the importance of the census, map and museum in nation-state formation, and these certainly constituted artefacts of power linked to spatial or territorial control in the case of turn-of-the-century Bolivia.[39] Murra also made this point in general for the Andes: 'An efficient census system is, among other things, an indication of the strength of the state.'[40] Knowledge at the service of power was the essence of the new scientism promoted by the ideologues and practitioners of the Geographic Society. Pando, who combined both aspects as liberal leader and inveterate explorer, understood what was required to achieve control of both population and territory and their incorporation into the nation: '... the imperious necessity to know our territory in its entire extension and to request of science the bases that may lead to just outcomes ... It is necessary that government ensure execution of detailed and complete topographic studies.'[41] In a recapitulation of its mission upon its twenty-fifth anniversary in 1914, the Geographic Society reviewed its contributions to the development of a patriotic science:

> ... establishing the foundations of national geographic science; contributing to the study of ethnic and sociological problems; disseminating knowledge about our international boundaries with neighbouring countries, thereby facilitating governmental action; promoting the spread of effective historical rights of a nationality that has yet to be constituted ...[42]

---

[38] Jenaro Sanjinés, *Informe de Prefecto del Departamento de La Paz al Ministerio de Hacienda* (La Paz, 1893).

[39] Anderson, *Imagined Communities*, pp. 163–86.

[40] Cited in Zavaleta, *Lo nacional-popular*, p. 29.

[41] Pando, *Circular*, pp. 1, 3.

[42] Sociedad Geográfica de La Paz, *Sesión pública realizada en celebración del XXV Aniversario de la Fundación de la Sociedad* (La Paz, 1914), p. 11.

In his introduction to a geographical dictionary of La Paz, compiled with a colleague from the Society, Ballivián remarked that the work would have a twin purpose: to serve the interests of travellers and foreigners who so frequently visited and the 'the practical objectives of public administration'. He went on to mention that it would correct the deficiencies and errors of official documents, most notably the recently completed land surveys.[43] Writing in the 1898 Bulletin of the Geographic Society, he maintained that geography, together with statistics, must answer the questions posed by the discipline of political economy — in the interests of the national political economy.

The censuses that were elaborated and applied at the end of the nineteenth century in Bolivia were shaped by the ideologies of the time and place. The 1900 national census devoted a section to the subject of race, identifying indigenous, white, mestizo and (minimal) black sectors.[44] In the demographic analysis, it differentiated the Andean peoples, namely the Quechua and Aymara, from the many other ethnic groups in Bolivia, most particularly those who inhabited the semitropical and tropical regions of national territory. The former were considered 'guardians of primitive civilisation and those who in America have been in the vanguard of progress', while the latter would have been considered 'savages'. The mestizo group was defined as originating in the union of the white and indigenous races, and 'while it was inferior to the Spanish race, it was much superior to the indigenous'.[45] The most remarkable aspect of this discussion in the 1900 census was the categorical assertion that the indigenous peoples of Bolivia were slowly but inevitably dying out:

---

[43] Manuel Vicente Ballivián and Eduardo Idiaquez, *Diccionario geográfico de la República de Bolivia. Tomo primero. Departamento de La Paz* (La Paz, 1890).

[44] Oficina Nacional de Inmigración, Estadística y Propaganda Geográfica, *Censo general de la población de la República de Bolivia según el empadronamiento de 1 de Septiembre de 1900, Tomo. 2* (Cochabamba, 1973), pp. 30–41. The census was carried out during the presidency of Pando by Ballivián and Crespo. This section was copied wholesale by Crespo in his official geography manual for secondary instruction: Luis Crespo [Secretario General de la Sociedad Geográfica de La Paz], *Geografía de la República de Bolivia* [Compilada en cumplimiento del Decreto Supremo de 27 de Febrero de 1905, para la asignatura de ramo en los colegios oficiales de instrucción secundaria de la República.], 2nd ed. (La Paz, 1910).

[45] This would probably have been a common though contested notion even within the Society. In this period the 'optimistic' view of ongoing civilisational and racial evolution was pitted against the 'pessimistic' predictions of racial degeneration through miscegenation. Geographic Society folklorist and ethnographer Rigoberto Paredes, for example, would have argued against the optimistic view of *mestizaje* and racial mixture: Even if Indians had culturally declined since the time of the Inka, they were preferable to unruly and unscrupulous mestizos. On Paredes, see Thomson, *op. cit.* A more famous example from the early twentieth century was Alcides Arguedas, *Pueblo Enfermo* (La Paz, 1975).

It is necessary to state that for a long time a noteworthy phenomenon has been underway in Bolivia: the slow and gradual disappearance of the indigenous race ... In little time, following the progressive laws of statistics, the indigenous race will be if not completely erased from the scene of life, at least reduced to a minimal expression. The reader will appreciate that this may be to the good, considering that if there has been a retarding cause in our civilisation, it is due to the indigenous race, essentially refractory to any innovation or to any progress, given that it has refused and refused tenaciously to accept any customs that have not been transmitted by tradition from its remote ancestors.[46]

The document cites Dalence, recognised as the first state demographer in the nineteenth century, as the most trustworthy source. Dalence's figures indicated that in 1846, that is, shortly after Independence, Indians constituted slightly more than half of the total population of nearly 1,400,000.[47] The size of the indigenous population at the turn of the twentieth century was much the same, yet the numbers of whites and mestizos had increased. The census speculates about probable causes for this relative decline in the importance of the indigenous population: 'natural' phenomena (drought, plagues, hunger), cultural and social habits such as alcoholism and miscegenation (though this last factor is left implicit).

A century later, Bolivia continues to be predominately indigenous; however, at the time, the predictions of the 1900 census fit perfectly within national creole logic. Anticipating the eradication of ethnic and spatial heterogeneity — that is, the ineluctable elimination of distinctive Amerindian races and cultures and non-capitalist property forms — was conceived of as an indicator of progress, thus perpetuating the logic of internal colonialism. In other words, the aim to regulate indigenous populations and control their territoriality recreated colonial situations.

The Railroad

The maximum expression of the national creole spatial conception was undoubtedly the profound faith in progress represented by the railroad — the axis structuring discourses of space and power. Ismael Montes, liberal president (1904–09, 1913–17) and supporter of the Geographic Society, declared in his presidential campaign platform that the goal of his administration would be to protect national sovereignty by fixed delimitation of frontiers and constant vigilance over national territory, based on the assumption that territorial integrity was an unmatched priority for nations and citizens. In the economic sphere, he would seek to promote nascent national industry and an internal market, but

---

[46] Oficina Nacional de Inmigración, Estadística y Propaganda Geográfica, *Censo general*, p. 36.

[47] José María Dalence, *Bosquejo estadístico de Bolivia* (La Paz, 1975). It must be emphasised that Dalence's figures were certainly underestimates as the census counted only known and accessible indigenous groups.

also mineral and rubber exports. Both of these objectives would be realised with development of the railway system.[48]

To be sure, his administrations would oversee the completion of the critical rail project that was initiated during the conservative presidency of the silver miner Aniceto Arce (1888–92), and which linked the mining centre of Huanchaca (subsequently the city of Oruro) with the Chilean port of Antofagasta, giving Bolivia its first rail connection to the Pacific Ocean. Arce had established the Huanchaca mining company with majority Chilean capital in 1873, and the construction of the railroad made it possible profitably to export mineral to Europe — thus making patent the concatenation of political power, national and foreign mining capital, and modernising spatial projects. Indeed, in signing the 1904 War of the Pacific peace treaty with Chile, the governing liberals ceded claims to captured territory and ocean ports in return for monetary compensation, loans for building domestic railroads and the Chilean construction of a railroad between La Paz and Arica on the Pacific coast.[49]

The modernising ambitions associated with the railroad, and the accompanying visions of progress and civilisation that would permit the occupation and integration of national territory, contradicted seigneurial and Andean spatial conceptions. An example of the national creole vision, as distinguished from the localism and insularity of the seigneurial, comes from Ignacio Calderón, corresponding member of the Geographic Society and Bolivian representative who justified the expansion of the railway system to the US government. Calderón evoked the dilemma of his country thus:

> Asphyxiated by the roughness of our mountains; almost cut off from the world; lacking internal commerce which cultivates and foments good relations and mutual interest among the departments of the Republic; the isolation in which we live has produced the fatal infirmity of localism and given rise to rivalries, not of labour and effort which uplift and stimulate, but rather to petty rancour and jealousy, typical of sick, egotistical or ignorant souls, and the only possible result is national ruin and dissolution.[50]

La Paz elites had for some years appealed to foreign capital to finance railroads that would simultaneously promote private and national interests and the internal market. In 1889, Federico Diez de Medina, president of the Association of Landowners of Yungas — the powerful coca leaf producers — and future member of the Geographic Society, had requested foreign investment for building the railroad between the city of La Paz and the Yungas valleys. Ballivián also had an early proposal for the building of the railway to Yungas.[51]

---

[48] Ismael Montes, *Carta-Programa del candidato a la Presidencia de la República y Jefe del Partido Liberal Doctor, Coronel Ismael Montes* (La Paz, 1903), pp. 11–20.

[49] Mitre, *Los patriarcas*, pp. 92–3; Klein, *Bolivia*, pp. 160–8.

[50] Ignacio Calderón, *Los ferrocarriles en Bolivia* (Washington, DC, 1906), p. 3.

[51] Federico Diez de Medina, *Breve informe que como Presidente de la Sociedad de*

A year later, Federico Zuazo, a member of the La Paz landowning elite with no previous business experience, insisted on the importance of the railroad between La Paz and the Peruvian border. He argued that nationalising and unifying the republic by means of the railroad was to think like a Bolivian and cease internal political struggles.[52] During this period regional discord was constant, he observed, and regionalism was to be criticised for undermining national integration and Bolivian identity and for promoting instead the divisive, regional identities of *paceño, cochabambino, chuquisaqueño*. Concluding that departmental and regional conflicts were aggravated by the lack of communications and transportation infrastructure, he argued that railways would be the answer.[53] Others also predicted that a rail network would revitalise the ties between La Paz and Cochabamba (the commercial and agricultural centre), between La Paz and Santa Cruz (the link to the eastern lowlands), and between La Paz and Lake Titicaca, conduit to the ports of the Pacific coast. At the same time, the desired consolidation of the internal market would support national production and reduce dependence upon imported goods.[54]

The tension, typical of the nineteenth century, between vaguely protectionist tendencies favouring the internal market and domestic production and the more free-trade policies intended to ensure the access of silver, tin and rubber to the world market was never fully resolved and, indeed, reverberated through to the National Revolution and much beyond. Yet there can be no doubt that the internal market restructuring that did occur with the advent of the railroad

---

Propietarios de Yungas y autorizado por el consejo de administración, dirije a los capitalistas extranjeros (La Paz, 1889). The Association of Landowners of Yungas brought together some of the most powerful landowners in La Paz — the producers of coca. Ballivián's proposal: *Proyecto que presentan a la Honorable Camara de Diputados los señores Manuel Vicente Ballivián y Eduardo de la Fuente pidiendo autorización para construir un ferrocarril de la frontera peruana a la ciudad de La Paz con facultad de prolongarlo a la provincia de Yungas* (La Paz, 1889).

[52] Federico Zuazo, *Propuesta para la construcción del ferrocarril de la frontera del Perú a la ciudad de La Paz* (La Paz, 1890). There were few voices within the elite who opposed the railroad plans; they were primarily wary of a direct link to Chile in the aftermath of the War of the Pacific. See, for example, Rodolfo Soria Galvarro, *¿Tinaje o nación? (cuestión ferrocarrilera)* (Cochabamba, 1885).

[53] Some early critics proposed instead connecting the principal cities via a network of highways. Narciso de la Riva, for example, advocated postponing railroad plans until internal and external commerce grew enough to require them: *Estudio sobre la hacienda pública de Bolivia por Narciso de la Riva, Año 1882* (Valparaiso), pp. 7–8.

[54] International Bureau of the American Republics, *Bolivia: Geographic Sketch, National Resources, Laws, Economic Conditions, Actual Development, Prospects of Future Growth* (Washington, DC, 1904), pp. 135, 165; and *Memoria que presenta al Congreso National de 1909 el Ministro de Colonización y Agricultura Dr. Isaac Araníbar* (La Paz, 1909), pp. liii, liv, lv, lvi.

especially impinged on altiplano indigenous communities. Community land sales had been spurred in part by the land speculation ignited in anticipation of profits to be made from railroad construction in tandem with hacienda expansion. Equally critically, the new commercial rail networks controlled by regional and national elites displaced longstanding indigenous mercantile arrangements. Indigenous communities had significantly participated in local and regional market circuits, and indeed driven them with their motor force of llamas, burros and mules. While liberal elites chafed at the slow pace of the llama and the burro, and hastened to supplant them with engines, the realisation of the railroad project came at a high cost to the highland and valley indigenous traders whose caravan routes had historically connected not only Bolivian regions but the interior republic with Pacific ports.[55]

Mitre vividly illustrates the imperatives that drove the Huanchaca company to replace animal transport with steam power, an act that would prolong the silver boom, usher in the tin era and stimulate a phenomenal growth in production and exports. As a result, the country was opened to foreign trade, with adverse consequences for regional economic space and national production as even the most basic necessities began to be imported.[56] Observers at the time did not fail to identify the pernicious effects on the internal market and national self-sufficiency:

> We meet all of our needs with imported products. Not long ago, Cochabamba was a good supplier of flour; Santa Cruz served the market in sugar; La Paz satisfied coffee consumption. Today flour from California is sent to Cochabamba, Peruvian sugar to Santa Cruz and Costa Rican coffee will probably come to La Paz. This phenomenon can only be explained by lack of initiative, that fatal laisser-faire, laisser-passer of the indifferent.[57]

Nevertheless, at the end of his tenure and probably the most intensive period of railroad construction, Montes proudly summed up the achievements of this spatial projection in occupying highland indigenous territory and linking it to the rest of the nation:

> What is the real significance of the efforts made over the past ten years? The country can observe the results ... The railroad has conquered the altiplano, bestowing new value upon its riches. Our principal cities are linked by the

---

[55] The threat to the regional indigenous economy and indigenous space was resisted by the communities who presented official complaints about the building of the railway and protested against abuses and labour exactions — Indians were obliged to work on the railroads. There were also constant attacks and sabotage against railway installations. See the numerous references in the 'Expedientes Prefecturales' of the Archivo Histórico de La Paz (AHLP) and Fernández, 'El poder de la palabra'.

[56] Mitre, *Los patriarcas*, pp. 156–79.

[57] *Memoria*.

railroad and under its civilising effect, and all of our sentiments have been refounded in a common ideal of nation and progress.[58]

Natural Frontiers

Ballivián shared one of the principal concerns of Bolivia's rulers: how to populate and thereby tame the immense national territory. The difficulties with defining national territory resulted from the absence of established and protected borders and from ignorance of the vast territorial expanses to the east of the core Andean highland region, above all in the tropical forests of the Amazon Basin and the Chaco. A key objective for state authorities, then, was to assure the mere presence of the Bolivian state in regions where 'savage', and hence dangerous, nature reigned and where hostile, untamed human groups were thought to live. As a means of confronting these problems, Ballivián was a vehement partisan of immigration and introduced policies for the colonisation of supposedly virgin areas in order to achieve what Zavaleta calls 'a territory or space socially incorporated into the logic of the nation'.[59] Based on his analysis of the North American experience that was considered a model to emulate in this matter, Ballivián was adamant in his preference for European immigrants, intrigued despite reservations by the potential of Japanese colonies and recommended forbidding entrance to the Chinese.[60] By encouraging culturally and racially-specific immigration, Ballivián anticipated that frontier regions would be domesticated as land was cleared for agriculture and pasture and civilised as colonisers established new settlements and missions that would subdue and convert native inhabitants.[61]

Like Pando, who had led a historic expedition through the territories in the north-west of the departments of La Paz and Beni and had produced a new map of this region bordering on Brazil,[62] Ballivián was an enthusiastic promoter of the rubber industry, which was then enjoying spectacular success. His ministerial preoccupations, stimulated by first-hand reports of exploration, recognised the

---

[58] Quoted in Fernández, 'El poder de la palabra', p. 36.

[59] Zavaleta, *Lo nacional-popular*, p. 38.

[60] See his comments on immigration in the *Revista económica y financiera* (La Paz, 1899).

[61] According to Fifer, immigration and colonisation schemes were in their majority doomed to failure given that they were 'astonishingly ambitious and disastrously impractical'. See J. Valerie Fifer, *Bolivia: Land, Location, and Politics since 1825* (Cambridge, 1972), pp. 30–1. The river navigation required to reach the frontier zones was completely inadequate, and the Bolivian government was unable to provide the infrastructure and security needed to settle these conflictive areas. The frontiers were subject to both external threats from neighbouring states such as Brazil and internal threats from Indian groups that remained beyond the reach of the Bolivian nation-state. The Chiriguanos in the Chaco, for example, successfully resisted state control until the very end of the nineteenth century.

[62] José Manuel Pando, 'Informe que el jefe de la exploración de los ríos del norte de Bolivia eleva al conocimiento del Supremo Gobierno en complimiento del contrato celebrado el 30 de mayo de 1892', AHLP, Fondo José Manuel Pando, 1891–97, documento no. 2.

urgent need to organise and administer this territory as a means of assuring the national development of the industry and, at the same time, furthering state interests. The regulation of rubber acquisition and exploitation, given the absence of legal land titles and the state's embarrassing inability to collect fiscal revenue in the midst of a boom, was paramount. (Some years later, the establishment of a customs house in Acre territory — then the richest rubber area in the world — to collect duties on rubber exported to neighbouring Brazil would result in a revolt by rubber-tappers and Brazil's annexation of this frontier region.) Regretting the lack of an 'inventory of our national wealth' that would have stimulated greater investment in the rubber and other extractive industries, Ballivián ultimately conceived of a 'titanic struggle against savage nature' in order to tame and civilise it.[63]

This same heroic and confident discourse of national creole spatial consciousness was expressed at the inauguration of the railroad from Guaqui on Lake Titicaca to La Paz in 1903. In the words of Pando, who had styled this the 'geographic period':

> There in Yungas and beyond in Beni are the fertile lands, the extensive forests and the swollen rivers awaiting the occasion to deliver up their inexhaustible treasures to us; there we have space for many millions of inhabitants who will earn their living with two hours of work a day; there we can produce rice, cocoa, sugar, cotton and coca, besides the livestock that we buy in foreign markets; there, close to the snowy peaks, we will find all that we lack, if we persevere in labouring and are worthy of conquering those treasures ... To the south, those extensive regions of the Andean plateau, which grudgingly produce with the primitive plow and the uncertain rains of summer, are tired of awaiting the railway lines and the locomotive; when they receive them, they will rejoice from the depths of their sediments, turning verdant again with artificial irrigation and yielding crops that do not fail.[64]

Conclusion

The chapter opened with reference to Said's appraisal of the role of the geography and the geographical imagination in the imperial project, and I have sought to bring out the related concern of geography's place in the national project. In the case of Bolivia these are not divergent concerns, for national building was

---

[63] Ministerio de Instrucción Pública y Colonización, *Apuntes sobre la industria de la goma elástica en los territorios dependientes de la delegación nacional en el Noroeste y el Departamento del Beni* (La Paz, 1896). Ballivián would have been both chastened and goaded by the comment from the 1894 *The Indian Rubber World*: 'There need be no reason for wonder at the lack of definitive information concerning the extent of the rubber production of Bolivia, when it is considered that even the extent in area of that Republic is in doubt'. See Fifer, *Bolivia*, p. 121.

[64] José Manuel Pando, *Discurso pronunciado por el Presidente de la República General José Manuel Pando en el acto de la inauguración del ferrocarril de Guaqui al Alto de La Paz, el 25 de octubre de 1903* (La Paz, 1903), pp. 4–5.

intimately bound up with *internal* colonial relations. Pando conjured up the image of a new conquest — of Indians, land, resources, frontiers — in his vision of national expansion. Just as the national project set out to push back external frontiers by incorporating peripheral regions, the internal colonial logic sought to overcome internal frontiers by domesticating unassimilated and ethnically alien indigenous populations and regions. This reproduction of coloniser-colonised relations within the republic and territorial reconquest was effected most strikingly in liberal land legislation, the buying up of community property and the expansion of the landed estate.

What were the effects of the research, policy, state geographical apparatus and the new geographical imagination, on the part of the Geographic Society? Colonial/imperial projects typically set 'strong' states of the core against less strong polities of the periphery. In turn-of-the-century Bolivia, however, the internal colonial project of the Geographic Society was frustrated by the weakness of the state. Militarily, Bolivia had suffered enormous setbacks in the War of the Pacific and subsequently in the dispute with Brazil over Acre territory. It was to suffer perhaps its most devastating and poignant defeat in the 1930s in the Chaco War with Paraguay. Internally, despite measures of sometimes extreme violence, it was unable fully to contend with indigenous communities in the highlands and still counted nearly 100,000 indigenous individuals as '*no sometidos*' — those who had not submitted — in the census of 1900. Beginning in the 1910s and 1920s, indigenous political projects would once again take on greater life and movement after the summary repression of Zárate Willka in 1899.

Clearly, the project that was expressed through the Geographic Society did not succeed in overcoming the country's internal contradictions and consolidating the Bolivian nation-state. There were a number of reasons for this — above all indigenous resistance and structural economic factors relating to Bolivia's position in the world market. Almost from the outset a widening gap appeared between the projections of the new geographical imagination and actual material conditions. At the same time, Bolivian elites continued to operate within an internal colonial logic which reproduced national contradictions of colonial derivation. So, as remembered on its fiftieth anniversary celebration, the founding mission of the Geographic Society, that 'Bolivia know itself',[65] was truncated and remained in the realm of the imagined nation — or the illusory nation, as the case may be.

---

[65] 'Discurso pronunciado por el Ministro de Educación don Gustavo Adolfo Otero al celebrarse la Sesión de Honor de la Sociedad Geográfica de La Paz con motivo de su cincuentenario', *Boletín de la Sociedad Geográfica de La Paz*, no. 63, Jan. 1941.